The *Spectacular* Rise, Fall & Rebirth *of* HAIR METAL

The *Spectacular* Rise, Fall & Rebirth *of* HAIR METAL

An Era Not To Be Forgotten

Christopher P. Hilton

2020

The Spectacular Rise, Fall and Rebirth of Hair Metal

First printing edition 2020
Author: Christopher P. Hilton
Publisher: Independently Self-Published

www.HairMetalForever.com
info@HairMetalForever.com

ISBN 978-0-578-65403-4 (paperback)
ISBN 978-0-578-65404-1 (eBook)

"When I Die, Sprinkle My Ashes Over The '80s."

David Lee Roth

2004

Dedicated

To Kimberly

my hair metal concert partner-in-crime

Hair Metal Song Dedication:

"Wild Angels" by Pretty Boy Floyd

To Christina

so glad you were there to share the enthusiasm for this music

Hair Metal Song Dedication:

"Something to Believe In" by Poison

To Amy

for pretending to like this kind of music when we first met

Hair Metal Song Dedication:

"Thank You for Loving Me" by Bon Jovi

To My Parents

who tolerated my hair metal infatuation growing up

Hair Metal Song Dedication:

"Youth Gone Wild" by Skid Row

For: All Hair Metal Fans

we share a special bond, and we are a special breed

Hair Metal Song Dedication:

"Nothin' But a Good Time" by Poison

Contents

Prologue

Moscow Music Peace Festival
August 13, 1989

Drenched in sweat, the makeup slowly bled down his face as the larger-than-life rock star boldly stood on stage and gazed out at the swarm of over one hundred thousand heavy metal rock 'n' roll fanatics chanting his band's name in ear-piercing unison, literally begging the group to continue its musical assault.

Dressed to kill in leather pants and a brazen studded belt, Nikki Sixx brushed the high-teased hair out of his face and briefly paused, futilely attempting to take in the immense grandeur of the moment.

Nearly nine years prior, he had arisen from a broken family and a homeless life on the streets of Los Angeles to form Mötley Crüe, a group of misfits that would look, sound, and act unlike any band that came before them. For his part, Sixx would become perhaps the founding architect of the absolutely massive "hair metal" movement that was about to be birthed on Hollywood's Sunset Boulevard and surge to worldwide dominance during the following decade.

Over the course of the outrageously wild ride, there would be enormous highs and equally extensive lows, including every form of excess imaginable—sex, partying, rock 'n' roll, alcohol, drugs, and even deaths, not the least of which was his own (at least for a few minutes anyway).

But standing on stage at that moment, as one of a select number of high-profile bands privileged with performing the first-ever rock show in the Soviet Union, Sixx and his bandmates had finally ascended to the proverbial top of the mountain.

Indeed, in just eighteen days, Mötley Crüe's new album, *Dr. Feelgood*, would unleash itself upon the world and soar all the way to the No. 1 position on the Billboard Albums chart, eventually selling over six million copies. The band would successfully launch a colossal world tour in support of the record, playing to throngs of worshipping fans in sold-out arenas across North America, Europe, Australia, and Asia. In the coming year they would place no fewer than five hit singles on the radio and receive practically endless airplay on MTV.

Mötley Crüe, along with many of their contemporary hair band goliaths of the time, were kings of the music world living a real-life dream that was often more remarkable than fiction. The hair metal genre they represented had spiraled out of control to become so immensely successful and culturally relevant that it literally changed millions of people's lives.

But little did they realize it was all about to suddenly and violently implode in a spectacularly mind-blowing fall from grace. And not just for Mötley Crüe, but for nearly every single hair metal band on the planet. Almost overnight between late 1991 and early 1992, their style of music would abruptly and fiercely go so far out of fashion as to render anything and everyone even remotely associated with it an obsolete, outdated, laughing stock.

Countless hair bands would collapse, disintegrate, or splinter under the weight of suddenly non-existent sales. Many of those who attempted to struggle on were promptly and caustically dropped from their record labels and reduced from playing sold-out arenas to half-full woodsheds at best. Radio and MTV instantly and entirely cast the genre aside like the plague, with a reckless abandonment never previously thrust upon a musical style that just years before was churning out multitudes of Platinum-selling albums.

The dark times would last almost a full decade during the '90s as other musical styles such as grunge and alternative served as new Gods to worship, presenting themselves as the complete 180-degree antithesis of everything that '80s rock had stood for and symbolized.

But then, seemingly against all the odds, a peculiar sentiment began to arise near the turn of the century. People suddenly appeared poised to welcome back a musical culture of optimism and merriment, and a deep, heightened sense of nostalgia developed for the '80s rock of the past. Grunge music had mostly come and gone, and hair metal was at long last ready to emerge from its lengthy slumber and wake back to life.

Hair bands were quick to respond to this phenomenon, with many artists swiftly reforming and successfully getting back out on the touring circuit where they were met with flocks of fans thrilled to again experience "Nothing But a Good Time." New albums were issued that gloriously returned to the uplifting, feel-good party style of the past after the dark and more serious detour than was the '90s. To an extent, even radio and television jumped back on the hair metal bandwagon.

As for Nikki Sixx and Mötley Crüe, they had somehow defied the odds to survive, and the reunited former titans were not only a part of the resurrection but were naturally among those bands on the front line leading the charge. They issued a fresh new album designed to get back to their hair metal roots, and over the course of the two decades that followed, launched some of the biggest and most successful tours the industry had ever witnessed. The band even put out a New York Times bestselling autobiography and an immensely popular movie adaptation to match. Indeed, hair metal ostensibly achieved one of the most surprising and greatest comebacks ever witnessed.

But exultantly standing on stage in Moscow that historic day in 1989, Sixx and many of the bands that shared the bill could barely comprehend the meteoric rise they had just witnessed, let alone begin to possibly imagine the remarkable and sensational events that were still yet to occur.

Hair metal's fable was truly an incredible journey, unlike any tale ever told. The rise, fall, and rebirth of hair metal: it's a fascinating story—let's tell it.

I

Foundations

Chapter 1
The Hair Metal Lexicon

I have a confession to make . . . I hate the term hair metal. Don't get me wrong; I love hair metal *music*; I just hate the *term*. Why on earth then would I lavishly employ the idiom throughout this text, let alone bestow it the distinguished honor of the book's title?

As it turns out, the answer requires a quick trip back in time and perhaps a small history lesson. You may be surprised that the maxim "hair metal" wasn't even invented until several years after the period when the music it commonly refers to was most popular, generally considered to be 1986 through 1991. But to adequately address my seemingly disjointed dichotomy, we will have to first travel back a little further—way back, in fact.

Although the phrase "rock 'n' roll" (or simply "rock") made its first scant appearances in the US around 1930, music categorization prior to the 1950s was often limited to classifications such as jazz, blues, gospel, swing, folk, or even country. All that changed, however, when Elvis Presley rose to fame in the mid-'50s, helping to launch a new generation of music based on hip-swiveling rockabilly, and in the process, making the expression "rock 'n' roll" a worldwide phenomenon in both music and culture alike.

The rock 'n' roll axiom held steady through the '60s and '70s, while at the same time a distinct subgenre began to emerge, bands that were emulating a bigger, "heavier," sound characterized by prominent electric guitar solos, thunderous drums, and a focus on loud, aggressive lyrics. The term assigned to this new style was "heavy metal," with some of the most famous pioneers including Black Sabbath, Led Zeppelin, and Deep Purple.

The heavy metal genus then proceeded to spur off its own partitions and subcategories as the '70s rolled on, specifically to include "glam metal," appointed to flashy artists such as Kiss, Alice Cooper, and David Bowie. Simultaneously, overly generalized trademarks such as "hard rock" and "metal" were assigned to countless other rock 'n' roll acts, as axioms and lines continued to blur.

On the whole it was these assorted labels that were most commonly employed as rock music ran its course during the famed 1980s. To be fair, a particular segment of further delineation did emerge toward the middle of the decade that attempted to parse out glam metal separate from heavy metal. In these instances, the latter term was reserved for only the heaviest thrash music, bands such as Megadeth, Metallica, Anthrax, and Slayer.

But for the emerging segment of rock that was becoming increasingly adept at merging the more accessible and commercial elements of pop music (melodies, hooks, catchy choruses) with the rougher aspects of heavy metal, the glam metal (or synonymous "pop-metal") label plainly became more appropriate, as evidenced with popular bands like Bon Jovi.

Glam metal during the '80s was markedly notable not only for its broad commercial appeal, but also for its ability to practically double the audience heavy metal had garnered by attracting not just the traditional testosterone-filled males, but now the swooning females as well.

Style changes notwithstanding, however, strategic application of the more granular glam metal or pop-metal labels was mostly limited to genre aficionados. Most people (musicians included) generically lumped the overwhelming majority of '80s rock 'n' roll under the broader umbrellas of heavy metal or hard rock throughout the course of the decade. Hard as it may be to believe, during the late '80s, bands like Def Leppard and Poison were most commonly referred to as heavy metal. The term "hair metal" (for the most part) was still waiting to be formulated.

Then "grunge" happened. Grunge music is a topic that will be covered in great detail later on, but for now, suffice it to say the grunge/alternative music style that rose to prominence in the early '90s was virtually the complete antithesis of '80s hard rock and heavy metal. The presence of grunge instantly forged a landscape where glam and pop-metal were suddenly derided as appalling and embarrassing, and as a result, a revised tagline for the now-discredited musical style was seemingly mandatory. And thus, the expression "hair metal" was precipitously born into existence.

Historical detractors of '80s glam metal were particularly drawn to new hair metal classification as, at its root, the phrase was intended to be disparaging, dismissive, and reflective of the perceived gross illegitimacy of the genre in general. Specifically, the hair metal stamp insinuated that glam metal was supposedly more about fashion (i.e., a band's hair) than it was about the actual music itself. And this brings us back to my expression of disdain for the hair metal tagline, because, in reality, the broader implication that '80s metal was more about style than substance just simply isn't true.

Admittedly, fashion and appearances were a big part of glam metal's overall package, but the intent was to maximize entertainment value, not to minimize the musical offering. And certainly, there undeniably *was* a small segment of bands that were likely guilty as charged, but frankly, those circumstances represented more the exception rather than the rule. To imply that '80s rock musicians were nothing more than their high-coiffed hair did the genre a great injustice. At the end of the day, it was merely the old adage of judging a book by its cover, followed by a convenient, generalized, wide-sweeping application.

Take an alleged hair band such as Winger, for example. Thanks to their image (among other things), Winger was widely ridiculed in some circles as an MTV-creation of good looks and hair spray that lacked any real musical credibility. And while the band's over-the-top guise could undoubtedly be considered "silly" in retrospect, it is essential to note that, for the time, the persona was a perfect fit. Honestly, what past fashion trend from *any* time period doesn't look a little ridiculous in hindsight?

But back to the question of musical ability, the undeniable truth was that Winger possessed mountains of credentials to spare. Lead singer and bassist Kip Winger had formally studied classical music and composition since the age of sixteen and had already performed on two Alice Cooper albums prior to forming Winger. Guitarist Reb Beach, meanwhile, was a genuine virtuoso prodigy who graduated with honors from the Berkley College of Music. Keyboardist Paul Taylor and fusion drummer Rod Morgenstein were also well-respected masters of their crafts.

Hair metal critics may be quick to point out that any recognition of Winger's innate abilities notwithstanding, their actual '80s output, including songs like "Seventeen," was still preposterously lacking any musical legitimacy. But go back and take a closer listen. Putting aside its admittedly juvenile lyrics, "Seventeen" was actually a relatively intricate composition featuring killer technical guitar riffs, an amazing solo, complicated breakdowns, sophisticated structures, strong melody, and an insanely catchy chorus.

Setting "Seventeen" aside, however, I have never really understood the overarching widespread assertion that a song couldn't possibly be "legitimate" unless it was overly serious, dark, or complicated; does that correspondingly signify that simple, cheery songs like the Beatles' "Ob-La-Di, Ob-La-Da" weren't worthy of our admiration and enjoyment?

What about perhaps the most "hair band" of them all, the infamous Poison? In fact, seemingly goofball-guitarist C.C. DeVille was an accomplished, classically trained musician who studied under the revered Itzhak Perlman. Granted, it was understandably difficult for some to see past the excessive fashion emphasis conveyed on the cover of Poison's debut album, *Look What the Cat Dragged In*, but the truth was, in a non-internet age, MTV was the primary vehicle for exposure, and if you wanted to be on MTV you had to be "pretty."

In reality the overall appearance and entertainment package these bands were trying to deliver was not entirely dissimilar from the widespread theatrical antics of acts that came before them, including David Bowie and Alice Cooper, artists who would never be derided in the same manner '80s hard rock came to be. And yes, many hair metal bands were indeed *very* immersed in the sex, drugs and partying that accompanied the rock 'n' roll lifestyle (by the way, how was that also any different from the rock artists of the '70s?), but to assert that they lacked legitimate talent, and even innovation in many areas, was simply misguided.

So, back to the original question: why I would profusely adopt the usage of a belittling, misrepresentative term like hair metal given I feel it does such a disservice to the genre? For starters, the negative connotations associated with the hair metal idiom have somewhat softened over the past thirty years, as, for many people, the vernacular has evolved to more of a positive, nostalgic reference rather than a critical, depreciatory assessment. And while the era's most hardened antagonists still employ the term critically, hair metal has unquestionably grown to be the most recognizable and clearly identifiable phrase to characterize '80s hard rock and glam metal. Like it or not, "hair metal" is indisputably *the* universal identifier of the '80s rock music, style and culture fans grew to know and love.

This being the circumstance, I willingly concede to it; objections noted. For this book I unequivocally choose to view hair metal as more of a celebratory term versus any negative connotations others would aim to attach to it. It should be acknowledged, however, that the overwhelming majority of hair bands themselves have not acquiesced to anywhere near the same level of acceptance, understandably feeling the term unfairly reduces them to nothing more than their choice of hairstyle nearly thirty-five years ago. Def Leppard singer Joe Elliot has gone as far as to ineloquently refer to the label as "a bad case of herpes" he just can't seem to shake. Ask the average hair band, and they would likely suggest their music is simply "rock 'n' roll," no more, no less.

All said, however, in 2019, the labels hair metal, glam metal, pop-metal, and '80s rock are all basically interchangeable to the average consumer, but the former is clearly the most recognized and illustrative. And so I humbly bid forgiveness and understanding from the heroes of this text; for this book, for better or worse, "hair metal" it will be.

With the terminology now established, we can begin to take a closer look at precisely what hair metal was all about.

From a musical vantage, hair metal, in its early stages, took the heavy, rebellious aggression of traditional heavy metal and amalgamated it with the commercial foundations of pop music, specifically melodies, catchy hooks, and big choruses. Hair metal was basically upbeat, polished, heavy metal-lite.

Lead guitar and vocals were prominent features, with the former often focused on flamboyant, flashy wizardry (including the shredding guitar solo staple), and the latter concentrated on dramatic, often high-pitched screams and shouts that still managed to emphasize harmonies. The bass and drums were thunderous and driving, providing a powerful backbone from which the songs would operate. Lyrics were mostly celebratory and generally revolved around partying and sex, and in the case of the popular "power ballad," love and relationships.

The extravagant and sensational nature of the music was typically accompanied by a glitzy (some would say gaudy), glamorous, and often androgynous fashion that was a natural offshoot from what Bowie, Kiss, and The New York Dolls were doing in the '70s. Make-up was standard and customary, often including lipstick, eyeliner, mascara, blush, eye shadow, and to a lesser extent, even nail polish. Outfits focused on bright colors, spandex, tight leather, denim jackets, vests, and gigantic, ornate belts. Obviously, these attires needed to be draped in accessories as well, consisting of headbands, necklaces, chains, sunglasses, gloves, bracelets, hats, earrings, and anything else you could find to pile on top and call attention to yourself. The overindulgence of the look naturally aligned with the excess of the music.

As Poison's lead singer Bret Michaels stated, "It's showbiz. We want people to remember us. They remember guys in makeup. In the beginning, when we spent three years in sleeping bags behind a dry cleaner in L.A., I said, 'We've got to figure out a way to stand out from the crowd.'"

And of course, there was the infamous "hair." Simply put, it was a matter of "the more, the higher, the better." There was no getting around it—if you aspired to be a rock star in the mid-to-late '80s, long, high-teased hair was an unconditional requirement. Bands would literally go out on tour with dozens of hair spray cases in tow. As another Poison member, drummer Rikki Rockett, put it, "The higher the hair, the closer to stardom, don't you know that?"

The wild look and sound translated directly to the hair metal lifestyle, which was unquestionably centered on one overarching concept: excess, in all its forms. Or maybe it would be better to characterize it closer to flat-out hedonism. Whichever word you wanted to choose—"more," "bigger," "crazier," "faster," "showier"—they all applied. As Aerosmith's Steven Tyler stated, "we believed that anything worth doing was worth overdoing."

The modus operandi of excess was applied to everything from music to fashion, sex, partying, drugs, alcohol, money, marriages, attitudes, and anything else of which you could think. It was one gigantic, debauched, outrageous celebration. And it was glorious indeed.

Lifestyle aside, it should be noted, however, that as the '80s transitioned to the '90s, hair metal naturally evolved to ease off a lot of the fashion, glitz, and party-pop and began to incorporate darker, heavier and more serious elements into its music, lyrics and appearance. Many of the genre's core elements from the early '80s remained but evolved to mix with fresh ingredients and influences. The resulting new styles and concoctions would then continuously evolve up until the early '00s, at which point the genre mostly came back full circle, at least musically.

Characterizing the more notable aspects and attributes of hair metal is one thing, but trying to compartmentalize each and every band into a nice, tight little box is entirely another. For example, how should we label a band that incorporates more than just one sound or style into their overall complement? What if the blend within isn't wholly black or white, but rather a mixture of gray areas somewhere in between? Society has an innate need and a natural tendency to draw clear lines around entities and objects, but, unfortunately, it's often not that simple.

Along these lines, there exists an endless, polarizing debate centered on exactly which bands *were* and *weren't* "hair metal." The topic has historically generated a significant amount of discussion and controversy among enthusiasts of the era. Fans tend to have strong, definitive feelings around this categorization and often take great offense when "their" band is labeled differently versus how they choose to view the situation through their own prism.

It's an argument with no easy or real right or wrong answers, but one that's always guaranteed to spark a spirited deliberation. At the end of the day, people's view tends to fall into one of four factions:

Category 1

This segment typically reflects the perspective of most outside observers and even a large swath of more "casual" hair metal fans. In their revisionist-history view, practically every single '80s rock band who had long hair falls under the hair metal classification, regardless of any differentiation in musical style. Sadly, this homogenized outlook is overwhelmingly representative of the general population, although I suspect a very small percentage of those reading this.

Category 2

Individuals in this category tend to view things mostly similar to Category 1, with the notable exception of excluding the distinctly "heavier" metal, or so-called thrash metal bands from the hair metal moniker. These dismissals from the genre typically include artists such as Metallica, Megadeth, Slayer, etc.

Category 3

Fans in this group lean toward an even more restricted hair metal taxonomy, regularly edging out bands such as Van Halen, Aerosmith, Guns N' Roses, and often even Def Leppard. Van Halen, they would argue, was a "'70s rock band," or "too legitimate" to be hair metal, and they wouldn't necessarily be wrong perhaps, but are they aware that Van Halen epitomized almost all of the classic hair band characteristics long before the '80s even started? Or have they ever seen a picture of the band circa 1986-1988?

These folks may also present a similar rationalization for excluding Aerosmith, but the distinctly hair metal approach of merging hard rock with commercial pop-rock melodies was the precise strategy the band employed in 1987 to resurrect their career back out of the dumps (with the help of outside writers no less).

Many would claim Guns N' Roses were "too real," or "too edgy" to be classified as hair metal, and they certainly have a valid point, but did they by chance notice Axl Rose's teased-out, Aqua Net-bursting hairdo in the video for "Welcome to the Jungle"? Did they happen to catch his white leather jacket and matching pants in the clip for "Paradise City," à la Warrant in their video for "Heaven"?

Or how about Def Leppard, who they would credibly indicate got their start as a legitimate member of Great Britain's New Wave of British Heavy Metal movement in the early '80s, and later on, were too busy off in Holland piecing together the *Hysteria* album to be bothered with hair metal's explosion back in Los Angeles? Fair enough, but it's hard to listen to "Pour Some Sugar on Me" and not think, "hair metal."

As stated, there are no clear answers to these ruminations, and very little is black-and-white.

Category 4

These hair metal fanatics are disposed to limiting the term to a very isolated and narrow segment of the genre, often conjuring exceptionally distinct defense strategies as to why most bands surely deserve to be absolved from such a perceived pejorative label.

Arguments you might hear in this category as to why a specific artist was "definitely not" hair metal include: Skid Row was too "heavy," Whitesnake was really a late '70s and early '80s blues-rock band, Winger was surely a "prog-rock" group in disguise, Faster Pussycat and L.A. Guns were more "sleaze metal," White Lion, with songs like "When the Children Cry" and "Cry For Freedom," was too "political," Warrant was only hair metal on their first two albums, Bang Tango was just too "funky," Mr. Big was simply "too talented," Tesla was truly "'70s rock," Cinderella was actually just a blues-rock band that took a bad picture on their debut album cover, and Mötley Crüe . . . well, "they were their own animal entirely," it could be said.

And while it would be hard for the average person to categorize any of these bands as anything *but* hair metal, the contrarian points made by fans in this category undoubtedly have a certain degree of merit.

All differences of opinion aside, however, there are certain bands that almost all fans, rightly or wrongly, consider 100 percent pure hair metal. Among these artists are Poison, Quiet Riot, Ratt, Kix, Steelheart, FireHouse, Trixter, Danger Danger, Britny Fox, Slaughter, and Bon Jovi. (Although there are compelling arguments as to why the latter should be excluded as well, mostly centered on partitioning the band into two distinct segments, *during* and *after* the '80s.)

At the end of the day, though, there are no definitive truths on the matter, and in many cases, it really just comes down to the eye of the beholder. And truthfully, I'm not sure it even matters; the one thing fans generally tend to agree on is that the music is of relevance first and foremost, not necessarily the label applied to it.

For the purposes of this book, however, the scope will mostly subscribe to the outlines depicted in Category 2. Not necessarily because that is where my personal opinion falls, but because the overarching story this text aims to tell definitively applies to almost all bands in that segment, and a reasonable case could legitimately be made for tagging each of them under the broader hair metal umbrella (all negative connotations strictly cast aside).

Noted apologies then to the many great artists who fall just outside this scope but are acknowledged as talented and impactful members of the hard rock and heavy metal community, including Metallica, Megadeth, Scorpions, Testament, Ozzy Osbourne, Pantera, Judas Priest, Iron Maiden, White Zombie, Wednesday 13, Pretty Maids, Jeff Scott Soto, Primal Fear, Queensrÿche, and many others.

Chapter 2

A Method to the Madness

Now that we've established a bit of background and definition surrounding hair metal's etymology, attributes, and the bands it symbolized, our focus turns to how we should go about telling its astonishing tale.

For starters, a chronological account likely serves best seeing as hair metal's history is a fairly defined arc with five distinct stages: birth and development, a sensational rise to global dominance, a mind-blowingly spectacular fall from grace, resurrection back to life, and a generally steady state thereafter.

The focus will primarily be on the music itself, including the incredible journeys bands underwent along the way and exactly what transpired behind the scenes as these famous (and often infamous) albums were forged.

Perhaps the biggest challenge putting this book together was the need to consider a reasonable size versus the sheer amount of fascinating and noteworthy hair metal stories there are to tell. The goal was to keep the text under 125,000 words, but my original outline was dauntingly more than double that figure.

To trim the fat, emphasis was placed on the most prominent bands and interesting anecdotes, while still shedding a significant amount of light on some of the lesser-known artists and music that likewise offered an equal amount of remarkable appeal and importance. These so-called "middle tier" bands were unquestionably integral to the era, even if not all of them managed to achieve multi-Platinum sales status.

Lastly, space is devoted to touch on the somewhat lesser-known existence and thriving state of hair metal in the new millennium. Contrary to the average person's popular belief, hair metal did *not* die off after the mid-'90s, although admittedly, those dark days could legitimately be classified as a near-extinction level event.

It is also important that the genre's narrative and impact are represented as an interconnected, conceptual whole. Individual biographies exclusive to the most preeminent artists from the era (Mötley Crüe, Guns N' Roses, Bon Jovi, Def Leppard, etc.) have already been written; however, the overarching view of the genre as an entity, and how it came to reach dizzying heights of success only to spectacularly implode and then find relevant life again at a later point—that story simply can't be adequately conveyed by focusing on only a small subset of the bands within.

Additionally, to achieve a more comprehensive framework without violating size constraints, a brief section of "other noteworthy music" is included at the end of several chapters. Please note, however, that even the addition of these supplementary bands and records still falls intentionally short of a complete, exhaustive hair metal library (a listing that would require an entirely different format to do it justice). These ancillary albums may not have had the biggest commercial impact, but each of them doubtlessly features *something* that should be of significant interest or enjoyment for fans of hair metal.

I fully acknowledge some readers may be offended this book doesn't focus more on their favorite band or be skeptical of content completeness because I seemingly missed that "rare" hair band they know about but I presumably do not. Apologies in advance for any brevity or omissions, but please understand I was fairly confident not even the most hardcore hair metal enthusiasts would be up for reading an eight-hundred-page dissertation (not that I wouldn't have enjoyed writing such a thing).

Finally, a relatively concise "best of" list is appended to each time frame highlighting some of the most outstanding music produced during those periods. For most hair metal fans, you really can't go wrong with any of these records. All are marvelous offerings and represent some of the finest music the genre had to offer.

Speaking of spotlighted albums, one thing to make abundantly clear is that many of the musical evaluations made throughout this text are unquestionably subjective. This idiosyncratic element may seem like a detraction point, but I firmly believe it is rather one of the book's strengths. If all the reader is looking for are chart positions, album sales, and a historical, tactical play-by-play, that information could easily be attained via a simple internet search.

The somewhat unconventional inclusion of personal opinion and perspective in this manuscript is hopefully part of its allure. Of course, the book will also illuminate the more common, predominant views shared by others, even if they don't necessarily align with my own take on the matter. This will hopefully allow readers to speculate their own informed conclusions. And naturally, all official sales and chart rankings will still be referenced as needed, as one of my goals is to clearly outline the impact hair metal had (or didn't have in some instances) on the broader industry and cultural landscape.

There are acknowledged schools of thought that maintain opinions are the scourge of fact-based biographies, and some may understandably disregard this book because they don't agree with some of my viewpoints. But, honestly, what would music be without subjective interpretation anyway? A great deal of the fun associated with being a music fan is discussing and debating likes and dislikes with other fans. Personally, I think it can be wonderful when opinions differ. It's always fascinating to me when someone's favorite album by a band happens to be the one I like the least. It encourages me to go back and re-listen, seeking out what I may have missed or overlooked. Many times, my opinion won't change, but there are also welcomed occasions where I stumble upon something I hadn't picked up on before that I then have the opportunity to enjoy.

Frankly, I'm not sure what a purely objective measure of music would look like anyway. Sales seem to be a popular barometer to evaluate success (if not necessarily quality), but commercial viability isn't necessarily a measure of empirical truth as much as it is merely a larger cluster of opinions strung together. Some may suggest using complexity or technical prowess to judge quality, but, again, does that condemn songs like the Beatles' "Love Me Do"? Heck, Nirvana proved you don't even have to sing *in key* to make popular music. It would seem that "quality," then, is somewhat opinion-based in the eye of the beholder.

And as far as opinions on hair metal go, I humbly like to think I am qualified to have one. I am admittedly a hair metal *fanatic*. There are over one thousand hair metal compact discs meticulously organized up in my den; there are more than a thousand others on the hard drive of my computer. I have intently listened to them all, many countless times over.

Most people wake each morning and immediately check in on the world news or perhaps the previous night's sports scores. Not me. My day starts with logging on to eight or nine different hair metal websites, eagerly seeking to catch up on the latest events and happenings. I've been doing this every day, religiously, for over twenty years now. Call me crazy if you must; I will understand. And before that, as a teenager (pre-internet), I would excitedly run to the local drug stores each week, hoping to find a new issue of the many music magazines that specialized in covering the hair metal genre. For those old enough to remember, these periodicals included publications like *Metal Edge*, *Hit Parader*, *Circus*, *Kerrang!*, and *RIP*, among others. Stacks upon stacks of these precious treasures remain stored away in my closet.

On a more up close and personal level, I have been fortunate to attend literally *hundreds* of hair metal concerts over the years while also having the pleasure of not only meeting many bands but even interviewing some. Simply put, I have lived and breathed hair metal for more than thirty-five years now. And I have loved every minute of it.

I share none of this to boast or brag about so-called "credentials," though; I am sure if you searched hard enough, you could find people more knowledgeable about hair metal than me. And I certainly don't feel that any of my background necessarily makes any musical opinions I might have any more "correct" than anyone else's, as I don't believe there is such a thing. But if you are bothering to read this, I thought it might be of some comfort to know that I'm not just some guy who owns *Slippery When Wet* and *Pyromania* and suddenly decided to write a book.

At the heart of the matter, and this is perhaps the key—I am simply *a fan*. If you just wanted the raw facts and individual historical recounts of which most hair metal enthusiasts are already aware, this book could have been written by any "researcher." I aspire to offer you much more than that.

All subjectivity aside, though, hair metal's story is an objectively remarkable tale that both deserves and simply begs to be told. The music was so enormous and culturally relevant that it literally changed millions of people's lives. For those of us for whom the music has meant so much, this book hopefully serves to not only offer a nostalgically pleasant stroll down memory lane and a chance to revisit some fantastic moments, but also a big-picture connectivity of the genre's spectacular roller coaster ride. Also on the menu is an opportunity to discover previously unknown anecdotes and behind-the-scenes tidbits that feasibly allow the music and bands to be understood in a better light and context.

Lastly, I would fancy readers will be able to uncover and enjoy a good bit of music that had previously snuck past their radar. For example, did you know that many of the bands people loved back in the '80s are not only still around, but actually putting out some of their best material? Or what about some of the "lost" hair metal music that struggled to see the light during the dark days of the mid-'90s? Or the countless *new* hair metal bands emerging after the year 2000 that have proudly taken up the mantle and are carrying the hair metal torch forward? There is simply so much music to enjoy if you know where to look.

Mark Twain famously implored "write what you know"; to that, I would add "write what you love." Well, I know more about hair metal than almost anything else (for better or worse), and my love for the genre is irrefutable. Check and check. Let's rock 'n' roll then, shall we?

II

Sowing the Seeds

1981-1985

Chapter 3
In the Beginning
(1980-1982)

So, when exactly did hair metal begin? While there are no definitive answers to this question, the popular sentiment would seem to have us believe it was in the early '80s. That said, some would allege the origins of the genre trace back far earlier, to acts like David Bowie, Kiss, Alice Cooper, Aerosmith, The New York Dolls, Hanoi Rocks, Cheap Trick, early Van Halen, or even Led Zeppelin, to an extent. And it would be hard to argue they are wrong. Indeed, if you ask any of the '80s hair band legends we would come to know and love to name their heroes and influences, it's very likely these earlier artists will consistently be listed among their replies. Still, there is a difference between influences and origins. For this writing, we will advocate the widely held (and generally correct) view that hair metal began in the very early '80s.

Looking back to that time, the first pertinent band that really stands out is the legendary **Van Halen**. The classification of Van Halen as hair metal is a widely disputed topic, but it is hard to ignore the unique (at-the-time) blueprint they laid down that would come to represent many of the signature hair metal sounds and styles. If the primordial origins of hair metal were indeed rooted in '70s classic and glam rock, Van Halen managed to transcend those foundations on their first two albums in 1978 and 1979, creating a spectacular spark almost entirely of their own making.

Van Halen clearly possessed many of the attributes that would come to emerge as pillars of the genre. First, there was lead singer "Diamond"

David Lee Roth himself. The embodiment of the "entertainer" aspect of any good rock 'n' roll frontman, Roth's screechy vocals combined with his glam metal appearance and high aptitude for showmanship and over-the-top behavior cemented him as the definitive ringleader for all things party-rock.

And then there was Eddie Van Halen, objectively one of the most creative, talented, and influential guitar players in history—a legitimate "guitar god" who was famously married to popular television actress and America's sweetheart, Valerie Bertinelli. Eddie invented guitar techniques and a playing style that was literally unheard prior to his arrival on the scene. Devising a fascinating two-hand tapping approach, his blazing solos were genuinely mesmerizing. It wasn't long thereafter it seemed every rock 'n' roll fan on the planet suddenly yearned to play guitar. On stage, Van Halen's live performances became legendary tales of high-energy, ultimate-party festivals.

By the time Van Halen released their third album, *Women and Children First*, in 1980, they had practically perfected the art of merging hard rock with melodic pop hooks, layered alongside massive guitar riffs, blistering solos and the emotive howling of Roth's vocals. The album featured the infectious rockers "And the Cradle Will Rock" and "Everybody Wants Some!" alongside the scorchers "Romeo Delight" and "Loss Of Control," while also offering a little diversity with the hard rock, southern-blues stylings of "Take Your Whiskey Home" and the ultra-catchy, more pop-oriented "In a Simple Rhyme." *Women and Children First* went triple-Platinum in the US alone, selling over three million copies.

Van Halen continued to evolve, however, and wound up taking a couple of interesting turns on their next two albums. *Fair Warning*, issued in 1981, was somewhat of a departure in style while still holding true to many of the elements that comprised the band's earlier work. Eddie was determined to push his guitar playing to new limits and creative spaces while tensions had begun to build between Roth and himself that drove the music to darker places. For the most part the more pop-oriented, radio-friendly sounds were missing, but that's not to say the melodies were wholly abandoned. Indeed, the harmonies remained, and many of the choruses were as catchy as ever, but the structures surrounding them were harder-edged and heavier, and not for the worse in my view.

Eddie's guitar work on *Fair Warning* delivered as promised and proved nothing short of amazing throughout. Right from the start, he ensured the album had your full attention as the guitar intro comprising the first thirty seconds of the dark, chugging rocker "Mean Street" would manage to keep future guitarists fascinated for years after. Other highlights included the innovative "Dirty Movies," hard rocking and driving "Unchained," upbeat "Sinner's Swing," and the melodic "Hear About It Later." I am almost certainly in the minority, but *Fair Warning* is (on most days) my favorite Van Halen album. It may have lacked the radio "singles," but cohesively, from top to bottom, it was an unquestioned masterpiece.

Despite the strength of the album, the lack of commercial catering had a decidedly negative impact on sales as *Fair Warning* "only" went double-Platinum. This inevitably heightened tensions within the Van Halen camp as Roth sided with the band's management, believing the group needed to focus more on radio hits while Eddie was still bent on experimentation and new techniques.

In the end, Van Halen mostly settled toward the former on 1982's *Diver Down*, which clocked in at a tight thirty-one minutes featuring mostly cover songs, a few instrumentals, and a couple of lighter tongue-in-cheek numbers alongside only a couple of true original rockers. Eddie did manage to sneak in a few twists and turns, however, as more than one of the cover tunes featured his own unique take on the instrumentation and melody surrounding the basic song structures, and some of the album's instrumentals were pure guitar genius.

If Van Halen were intent on dominating the radio again, though, they succeeded with their spirited cover of the Roy Orbison classic "(Oh) Pretty Woman." The song was also Roth's first foray into directing music videos, entertainment staples for which Van Halen would later become well known with Roth displaying a high aptitude for producing engaging clips consistent with his flamboyant stage presence: over-the-top, full-steam-ahead showbiz. The beguiling video Roth constructed for "(Oh) Pretty Woman," however, was actually too long for the tune's run-time, so he composed the synthesizer track "Intruder" as an intro, which successfully served to dramatically build and launch the song. "(Oh) Pretty Woman" would climb all the way to No. 1 on the Billboard Mainstream Rock chart.

Outside of the additional cover songs and instrumental tracks, album-original "Hang 'Em High" was unearthed from the bands '70s-demos and worked well as a hard rocker, while "Little Guitars" (and the intro that preceded it) was the true gem of *Diver Down* for me, a sparkling pop-rock combination of Spanish flamenco guitar, strong harmonies and classic riffing by Eddie. The album was perhaps appropriately concluded with a joking, a-cappella version of the 1940's *Roy Rogers Show* theme song, "Happy Trails."

Diver Down was a polarizing release among fans as it was undoubtedly less than the full magic of which the band was capable (particularly when viewed as a follow-up to the magnificent *Fair Warning*), but at the same time, there was a sentiment that I too acknowledged—*Diver Down* was a flat-out *fun* album! It was an intentional return to the party-rock sounds that launched Van Halen in the first place, and in that regard, it was a success even if many would come to rank it near the bottom of the Van Halen cannon over the years to come.

If Van Halen were instrumental in providing some of the key blueprints and setting the general stage for what would fully become hair metal by the mid-'80s, then it was undoubtedly the infamous **Mötley Crüe** who truly took the bull by the horns and ran with it (right into the wall on many occasions, as we will see). The legendary members of Mötley Crüe are in many ways the true forefathers of hair metal, as the unique foundation they laid down and the trends they set saw them evolve to represent perhaps the one band that most personified everything upon which the genre was built and more: huge hard rock anthems, sleazy pop-metal, elaborate power ballads, outrageous concerts, Platinum-selling albums, excess, extremes, drugs, alcohol, celebrities, strippers, lawsuits, arrests, infighting, drama—just MORE of *everything*! And in most cases, the Crüe did it BETTER as well. Mötley Crüe would wind up possibly the most famous and notorious hair band of them all.

The band's story began in 1981 on the Sunset Strip in Los Angeles, the two-mile stretch of Sunset Boulevard that passes through the city of West Hollywood. The now-famous location would become the undisputed birthplace and eventual mecca of all things hair metal in the '80s. Convening and emerging onto the scene as a ragtag gang of misfits, Mötley Crüe independently released their debut album, *Too Fast for Love*, on November 10, 1981. The record presented a raw, gritty, heavy metal sleaze factor notably different from the party-rock offered up by Van Halen. Singer Vince Neil was far from the most technically proficient vocalist, but his enthralling high-pitched screams and almost feminine delivery would come to inspire a legion of followers and copycats. Guitarist Mick Mars, meanwhile, conjured a menacing, distorted, metal guitar tone and a series of riffs that were markedly unlike anything heard before, while bassist/songwriter Nikki Sixx and drummer Tommy Lee held down a thunderous bottom-end.

By the time listeners survived the ferocious assault that was album opener "Live Wire," they were fully aware they had just experienced something *new*, something that would categorically change the course of music over the next decade.

Too Fast for Love was primitive, inconsistent, unpolished, and even a little sloppy, but at the same time, it was patently genius just the same. Anything Mötley Crüe lacked in musical proficiency was more than offset by sheer attitude. Tracks like "Come on and Dance," "Piece of Your Action," and "Take Me to the Top" possessed harsh, ominous, metal guitar riffs, while conversely, it was hard to categorize the catchy, melodic "Starry Eyes" as anything much more than straight-ahead power-pop. The album also included a couple of more measured, slower tracks that could perhaps be considered proto-ballads, years in advance of the famous "power ballad" format that would come to occupy a distinct and vital place in the genre by the late '80s.

Record labels couldn't help but take notice of the band's uniquely aggressive image, penchant for insane concerts, and the vast following they quickly built up on the L.A. club scene. Mötley Crüe eventually signed with major label Elektra Records, who arranged for *Too Fast for Love* to be remixed and re-released in 1982. The album can legitimately be considered as the singular jumping-off point for the entire hair metal genre that was soon about to unfold. Indisputably, hundreds of bands to follow would use Mötley Crüe's musical template and extravagant image as the "how-to" book for making hard rock music in the '80s.

Also first appearing in the early '80s was a small band from Sheffield, England, going by the name of **Def Leppard**. At the time, Def Leppard was classified as part of the New Wave of British Heavy Metal (commonly abbreviated as NWOBHM), a national music movement in the UK coined to reflect the emergence of heavy metal bands that were quickly replacing the popular punk rock with a heavier, faster, and more aggressive sound.

Def Leppard released their debut album, *On Through the Night*, in 1980, and while it did well in the UK hitting the Top 15 on local charts, the record failed to break through in America where the band strongly desired to establish a dedicated following. Most of the album's material was fairly standard rock 'n' roll, but forceful songs like "Wasted" provided a clear view of the group's as-yet untapped potential.

The band managed to catch the eye of respected producer Robert John "Mutt" Lange, who had previously worked with renowned blues-metal kings AC/DC. Lange saw the capacity for promise in the young Def Leppard and agreed to work with the group on their 1981 sophomore release, *High 'N' Dry*. The partnership resulted in a more polished effort and assisted the band as they began to evolve and cement their sound.

Their style emerged to a mix of glam rock and heavy metal, a trait that would help to define hard rock music for the next decade, similar to the influence set forth by Mötley Crüe.

High 'N' Dry didn't light the world on fire from a sales perspective, but it did manage to reach No. 38 on the Billboard Albums chart. "Let It Go" was a legitimate rock anthem, and the band hit upon something decidedly special with the mid-tempo ballad "Bringin' On the Heartbreak," which became one of the first "metal" videos to be played on the burgeoning new television format, MTV. That exposure, along with scoring the opening slot on tour with Ozzy Osbourne, helped Def Leppard establish a stable platform from which they would fully breakthrough from in absolutely massive fashion over the coming years.

The early '80s also marked a few other noteworthy early-beginning moments in hair metal history as well, even if they weren't overly significant at the time. **Kix** and **Dokken** both released their first offerings (*Kix* and *Breaking the Chains*, respectively) and Twisted Sister issued *Under the Blade* while continued to toil away in the clubs working tirelessly in search of a breakthrough moment of their own. **Whitesnake** also released three albums between 1980 and 1982, but the blues-based version of the band that existed during that time bore minimal resemblance to the hair metal giant it would later become.

First formed in 1978, Whitesnake was primarily rooted in classic blues-rock, mostly devoid of the unique elements that would eventually come to define hair metal. Still, their 1982 release, *Saints & Sinners*, contained the first recordings of two songs ("Crying in the Rain" and "Here I Go Again") that would go on to be reimaged and re-recorded five years later on one of hair metal's most successful and beloved albums, *Whitesnake '87*, a record that clearly helped to facilitate the genre's sensational explosion into the mainstream. "Here I Go Again," in particular, would become one of the most famous songs of the *entire era*. But in 1982, hair metal's journey was just beginning, and there was much that still needed to occur prior to that happening.

<u>1980-1982</u>

Best Albums

1. Van Halen – *Fair Warning (1981) (Top 25 in Genre!)*
2. Mötley Crüe – *Too Fast for Love (1981)*
3. Van Halen – *Women and Children First (1980)*

Chapter 4

Cum On Feel the Noize (1983)

While hair metal's seeds had indeed sprouted in the early '80s, it wasn't until 1983 that the genre officially scored its first mainstream commercial "hit," ironically a cover song: "Cum On Feel the Noize," by **Quiet Riot**.

Quiet Riot originally formed back in 1973, and their early lineup included the late, famous guitarist Randy Rhoads prior to him joining Ozzy Osbourne's band in 1980. Quiet Riot had been experimenting with their own unique take on glam metal but failed to really click or see any success until lead singer Kevin DuBrow relaunched the band with three new members after the previous unit briefly called it quits in early 1980.

The revamped lineup signed their first US record deal in 1982 and released the landmark album *Metal Health* on March 11, 1983. The album's stomping title track was issued as the first single and achieved moderate success, reaching No. 31 on the Billboard chart, but it was the second single released to radio that truly shattered the ceiling. "Cum On Feel the Noize," a cover of the 1973 Slade song, proceeded to rocket up the chart becoming the first heavy metal song to break the Top 5 and turning Quiet Riot into a household name.

Ironically, though, when their management first presented Quiet Riot with the proposal to record the track, the band absolutely *hated* the idea. Drummer Franki Banali stated, "We all came up with the idea that we'd tell the producer we were working on that song, although we never did. The inevitable day came when we had to record it, and in theory, it was supposed to be an intentional train wreck. We wanted to make it so the producer couldn't use it even if he wanted to."

In the end, however, the band's plan didn't exactly come to pass (thankfully). Banali started the song from the wrong place and left out both a verse and a chorus, but Quiet Riot just kept going, ramping up in effort as they went along. "Kevin was waiting for it to fall apart, but we just kept playing," Banali recounted. "When we finished, the producer said it sounded great on the first take, and when we listened back, it worked. Kevin was furious!"

The rest, as they say, was history. Buoyed by the success of "Cum On Feel the Noize" and its heavy rotation on both radio and MTV, *Metal Health* rose to the very top of the Billboard 200 Albums chart, becoming the first heavy metal album to ever reach the No. 1 position (famously knocking the Police's iconic *Synchronicity* off its throne). And just like that, the floodgates were officially opened for hair metal to begin marching toward its eventual conquest of commercial popularity in the mid-to-late '80s.

After Quiet Riot's success, the US turned its full attention to the new center of gravity for the hair metal scene, the Sunset Strip in Los Angeles, which would soon spawn an entirely new generation of hair metal maniacs. "Cum On Feel the Noize" was designed to fail but remarkably wound up ushering in a completely new genre of music. Strange how sometimes the most significant things are triggered by the unlikeliest of events.

Speaking of the Sunset Strip, **Mötley Crüe** also unleashed a groundbreaking new album in 1983 that would likewise contribute to the very forefront of hair metal's emergence. *Shout at the Devil* marked the band's first recording with proper label support, and to their credit, the Crüe made sure it was a massive step forward from *Too Fast For Love*. Every aspect of the album was bigger, better and sharper: the songwriting, musical performance, production—even the band's image. Despite the success of *Metal Health*, it is *Shout at the Devil* that is most often referred to as hair metal's "breakthrough album," as Mötley Crüe clearly reset and raised the bar for all that would come thereafter.

The album opened with a sinister, spoken-word monologue set to apocalyptic background sounds before launching into the bombastic, thumping title track, "Shout at the Devil," which was a gigantic fist-in-the-air anthem if there ever was one. If the guitar tone sounded menacing on parts of *Too Fast for Love*, it was downright *fierce* throughout *Shout at the Devil.*

"Looks That Kill" followed and was a moderate hit single, once again packing a considerable punch of a chorus. Primary songwriter Nikki Sixx was less than an accomplished musician at that point in his career but clearly possessed talented writing chops to go along with his undeniable, determined vision for the hair metal genre he would inspire.

Shout at the Devil was consistently more aggressive than *Too Fast for Love*, featuring several relentlessly ruthless, guitar-driven rockers supported by Neil's unique high-pitched wails and Tommy Lee's thunderous drums, including "Bastard," "Red Hot," "Knock 'em Dead Kid," and "Ten Seconds to Love." The album also included the pounding second single "Too Young to Fall in Love" and a cover of the Beatles' "Helter Skelter," a strange choice indeed, but Mötley Crüe somehow managed to seamlessly integrate the classic track among the album's overall mayhem.

Shout at the Devil peaked at No. 17 on the Billboard Albums chart and sold over four million copies. The album is considered by many to be Mötley's Crüe's finest work and a landmark moment for the genre. *Shout at the Devil* was truly a game-changer in terms of just how far it was ahead of the competition on the Sunset Strip at the time, particularly with regard to pure intensity. Mötley Crüe continued to up the stakes for all with their every move.

Mötley Crüe weren't the only band to take a tremendous step forward in 1983, however. **Def Leppard** made perhaps the genre's most prominent commercial breakthrough yet with their third album, *Pyromania.* It was the first record to feature new guitarist Phil Collen (Pete Willis had been dismissed from the band due to struggles with alcohol) and featured a shift away from the heavy metal nature of Def Leppard's first two albums to more hard rock layered with pop-based melodic hooks. If Van Halen wanted to throw you a party, and Mötley Crüe sought to rip your heart out, Def Leppard simply aspired to craft shiny, catchy, hard rock songs.

Perhaps no track was better represented of this approach than lead single "Photograph," a perfect example of what the hair metal genre would move toward as one of its main calling cards: a merger of riff-oriented, guitar-driven rock with melodic pop sensibilities (i.e., pop-metal). "Photograph" was a satisfying rocker but also offered enough melody to be accessible to radio and MTV. This formula proved particularly conducive to mainstream success, with *Pyromania* quickly vaulting to No. 2 on the Billboard Albums chart driven by its "big-three" set of singles: "Photograph," "Rock of Ages," and "Foolin'," all of which became Top 40 hits.

Meticulously constructed under the oversight of Mutt Lange, *Pyromania* sold six million copies its first year alone and would go on to eventually sell over ten million units in total, achieving the rare Diamond certification. (As of 2019, only twenty-two artists *total* have ever had a Diamond record.) The album became a major catalyst for the hair metal movement and officially launched Def Leppard into superstar status as the stage continued to be set for the impending hair metal revolution to come.

Other noteworthy albums released in 1983: Twisted Sister *(You Can't Stop Rock 'N' Roll)*, Kiss *(Lick It Up)*, Kix *(Cool Kids)*

Best Albums 1983

1. Mötley Crüe – *Shout at the Devil (Top 25 in Genre!)*
2. Def Leppard – *Pyromania*

Chapter 5
I Wanna Rock
(1984)

With each passing year, more blockbuster hair metal bands, albums, and singles emerged, further cementing the era's foundational sounds and styles while continuing to pave the way for the genre's eventual commercial takeover.

The success of albums like *Pyromania*, *Shout at the Devil*, and *Metal Health* caught the eye of the major record labels who then proceeded to zero-in on the Sunset Strip, hoping to sign the "next big thing." The pop-metal band **Ratt** had built up a sizable fanbase in Los Angeles, and by 1984, achieved "house band" status at the famed Gazzarri's night club in West Hollywood. Atlantic Records promptly took notice and swiftly snatched them up, and the band quickly banged out their debut album, *Out of the Cellar*, with renowned producer Beau Hill.

Ratt followed the formula of combining catchy hooks with metal guitar riffs while heaping on an extra dose of "sleaze" for good measure. Singer Stephen Pearcy had a unique voice that was both nasally and growling at the same time, and lead guitarist Warren DiMartini offered a style that was decidedly more bluesy than most other mid-'80s hair metal guitar heroes. But overall, Ratt was a perfect reflection of the genre's early years both musically and image-wise.

Out of the Cellar produced four pounding, hard rock hit singles: "Back for More," "Wanted Man," "Lack of Communication," and most importantly, "Round and Round." The latter track, in particular, brought the band their fame as "Round and Round" was a smash hit on radio and received heavy rotation on MTV, where the song's video effortlessly displayed the brash, swagger, and glam-image hair metal would come to adopt as its playbook. The song elevated *Out of the Cellar* to No. 7 on the Billboard Albums chart and turned millions of new fans on to the hair metal movement that was exceedingly picking up steam in Los Angeles. The album sold three million copies and gave Ratt their start on the path to hair metal royalty.

🤘

Twisted Sister also managed to finally catch their big break in 1984 with their third album, *Stay Hungry*. The record contained the two mega-hit singles "I Wanna Rock" and "We're Not Gonna Take It," the latter undeniably remaining one of the most famous hard rock anthems *ever* to this day in 2019. Both songs received what seemed like endless airplay on MTV with their attention-getting, story-based, humor-laden videos, while the band's drag-queen image helped further the public's curiosity.

Stay Hungry was mostly a pop-rock and metal record but also featured an early blueprint of what would evolve to be one of the genre's critical calling cards, the infamous "power ballad." "The Price" gave Dee Snider a chance to display that he could legitimately sing (versus just scream and shout) when called upon to do so. Bolstered by their MTV exposure, Twisted Sister managed to bring hair metal closer into people's homes and one step nearer to commercial domination.

🤘

Meanwhile, the mighty **Van Halen** roared back with their sixth album, *1984*, which served to catapult the band from a place where they were already one of the most popular hard rock bands on the planet to absolute superstardom.

Eddie Van Halen had been not only been dissatisfied with the intentional steering of 1982's *Diver Down* to focus on radio-oriented "hits," but also with David Lee Roth and management's continual rebuking of his efforts to introduce more keyboards and synthesizers into the band's music. From Roth's view, Van Halen was a guitar-oriented rock group, and he was adamant they should stick with their bread-and-butter. In rebuttal, Eddie responded in 1983 by building a recording studio in his own backyard where he was free to compose *1984* in any way he saw fit outside of anyone else's intervention.

When lead single "Jump" was eventually released on December 21, 1983, two weeks before the album dropped, many hardcore Van Halen fans seemed to side with Roth, aghast upon hearing the track's intro keyboards backing the song's first verses devoid of any guitar. Van Halen without guitar? It was sacrilegious to even consider the proposition. Two full minutes passed during the song before Eddie even broke a sweat on his six-string. (To his credit though, the solo was vintage).

The reaction from hardcore fans aside, however, the more pop-oriented nature of "Jump," combined with its absolutely infectious upbeat hooks and chorus, opened up Van Halen to a whole new legion of fans. Alongside an MTV-friendly video that featured Roth and the band in all their glory on stage sparked the song straight to No. 1 on the Billboard Hot 100 chart. Ironically, Eddie had written the synth riff to "Jump" several years prior and had presented it to the band on many occasions, only to have Roth reject it outright time and time again before its appearance on *1984*.

The album's second single, "I'll Wait," was keyboard-oriented as well, but beyond that, the rest of the record was mostly classic Van Halen guitar-driven rock. "Panama" (named after the racecar The Panama Express) was a barnstorming rocker while "Hot for Teacher" was equally intense, featuring a now-famous thirty-second opening drum solo before Eddie's blazing guitar emerged to scorch the earth. Both songs had classic videos that were the darlings of MTV and viewers alike, and along with "Jump," helped propel *1984* to the No. 2 position on the Billboard Albums chart for five consecutive weeks; the only thing preventing it from hitting No. 1 was the entrenched presence at the time of a little album by Michael Jackson called *Thriller*.

On *1984*, Van Halen were seemingly more "Van Halen" than they had ever been while firing on all cylinders from every angle: songs, videos, stage shows, image, attitude—just *everything*. The album went on to be certified Diamond with ten million copies sold in the US and twenty million worldwide. In 1984, Van Halen were the undisputed, heavyweight champion kings of rock.

Whitesnake was another band going through a transformative stage in 1984. Long a classic British blues-rock outfit since the '70s, Whitesnake had experienced some moderate success in the UK but had yet to hit it big in the US despite the relative strength of their 1982 domestic debut, *Saints & Sinners*. Still, lead singer David Coverdale was determined to chase glory and in 1983 marshaled his troops once again to record the new album *Slide It In*.

The record took a decidedly different turn from a musical standpoint. Perhaps influenced by what was going on around them, Whitesnake started to shift from strictly blues-rock material to elements more akin to the hair metal movement. The songs became more guitar-driven, the vocals more dramatic and prominent, and the melodies a little more pronounced. The album was initially released exclusively in the UK, where it managed to break into the Top 10, but Coverdale had already set his sights on a larger landscape.

In preparation for the US release of *Slide It In*, Coverdale worked with A&R-man John Kalodner and new producer Keith Olsen to remix the record and give the album a more hair metal sheen. Hotshot guitarist John Sykes was brought aboard to contribute new guitar parts, adding a few sparks and splashes to the solos, and the entire album was made to sound as "big" as possible while the tracks were resequenced to promote a harder-hitting flow.

Their efforts paid off as *Slide It In* was certified double-Platinum and succeeded in elevating Whitesnake's profile and status in the US both on radio and MTV. Among the album's highlights were the spirited title track, the sultry stomp of "Slow An' Easy," pop-metal "Guilty of Love," and the intense ballad-rocker hybrid "Love Ain't No Stranger." Whitesnake would go on to land a coveted spot touring with Quiet Riot, serving to further expand their rapidly developing fanbase in America.

Slide It In was a pivotal album for Whitesnake in that it drew a clear line in the sand between what came before it and what was to follow. The record symbolically served as a bridge between the '70s blues-rock Whitesnake and what would become the late '80s, full-blown hair metal Whitesnake. How you feel about one side versus the other depends on your personal preference, but for fans of hair metal, *Slide It In* was a breakthrough step in the right direction.

One last notable event in 1984 was the relatively unheralded debut album by a young group of guys out of Sayreville, New Jersey, calling themselves **Bon Jovi**. The band was named after lead singer Jon Bon Jovi, who had written a catchy little tune titled "Runaway" that managed to grab some small momentum on local radio stations. Bon Jovi hooked up with manager Doc McGhee who helped them put together their self-titled debut, including a re-recorded version of "Runaway" that garnered the band critical, much-needed exposure on MTV. The rest of the album was rather unremarkable, but Bon Jovi was successful in at least getting themselves on the board and into the game. From there, they would eventually rise to become perhaps the biggest hair band of them all, and one most successful artists of any genre, period.

Other noteworthy albums released in 1984: Dokken *(Tooth and Nail)*, Quiet Riot *(Condition Critical)*

Best Albums 1984

1. Van Halen – *1984*

2. Ratt – *Out of The Cellar*
3. Twisted Sister – *Stay Hungry*

Chapter 6
Theatre of Pain
(1985)

Hair metal mostly continued to simmer on the stove in 1985 as sporadic sparks occasionally rose up and made their impassioned mark from different directions. The overall pot was just about to boil over, though.

Mötley Crüe, never a band to copy or follow trends (at least during the first half of their career), curiously decided to completely revamp themselves for their third album, *Theatre of Pain.* Coming off the success of *Shout at the Devil,* Mötley surprisingly changed their look, parts of their sound, and even their logo (a trend they would repeat with each album; traditionally commercial suicide, but just another day in the life of the insane circus that was Mötley Crüe).

Before the album's release, however, Mötley Crüe almost met with a premature demise. On December 8, 1984, the band was hosting a party at Vince Neil's residence in Redondo Beach, California. With an inebriated Neil driving, he and Hanoi Rocks drummer Nicholas "Razzle" Dingley headed out for a beer run later that night, resulting in Neil's 1972 Ford Pantera disastrously colliding head-on with another vehicle. Dingley was tragically killed on site, others seriously injured, and an ironically unharmed Neil charged with a DUI and vehicular manslaughter.

Neil spent the next thirty days in court-ordered rehabilitation, undergoing detox while temporarily out on bail prior to his trial. The album's recording sessions took place upon his release from rehab, but a dark cloud hung over the proceedings as there was no guarantee Neil would remain free in the long run to continue as Mötley Crüe's singer, or if he would ever be able to find a way to live with his guilt.

Neil's lawyers convinced him to plead guilty at trial and astonishingly arranged for a truncated jail sentence (only thirty days) to enable him to get back out and tour, earning enough money to pay the assigned fine of $2.5 million. Fair or not, right or wrong (and it was probably both unfair *and* wrong), it appeared Neil would get off easy, and Mötley Crüe would live to fight another day.

So, what of the album then? In true Mötley fashion, *Theatre of Pain* should have been a complete crash-and-burn with the band members other than Neil sinking further into their drug and alcohol fixations, but it was instead a smashing success. The overall quality of the material objectively failed to equal the high standard set forth on *Shout at the Devil* as songwriter Nikki Sixx began to suffer from the effects of a gripping heroin addiction. Still, against all the odds, the album produced the Crüe's first two "hit" singles, ironically both of which were entirely anomalous to everything else on the album (or on the band's first two albums as well).

The first song to hit was a pop-metal cover of the 1973 Brownsville Station tune, "Smokin' in the Boys Room." The lighthearted rocker would have been entirely out of place on either *Too Fast for Love* or *Shout at the Devil* but happily found a welcomed home on *Theatre of Pain*. The song cracked the Top 40 on radio and blew up on MTV with its jokey video featuring the band in all their newfound glam fashion, now wearing just as much lace as they had leather. Mötley Crüe, legitimately one of the most dangerous bands on the planet, were now in people's living rooms.

The album's real commercial breakthrough, however, was the brilliant, landmark power ballad "Home Sweet Home." Power ballads would rise to become a critical component of the hair metal genre over the coming years, and "Home Sweet Home" was perhaps the very first of them all (with apologies to Aerosmith's "Dream On," Kiss' "Beth," Dokken's "Alone Again," Scorpion's "Still Loving You," Twisted Sister's "The Price," or even Led Zeppelin's Stairway to Heaven"). When Mötley first submitted the track, the record company *literally* thought they were joking. The overwhelming sentiment at the time was clear—heavy metal bands did *not* play ballads.

Still, the Crüe fought hard for the song's inclusion, and as it turned out, the ballad saved not only the album, but probably their career as well, along with cementing the format as an integral part of the definitive blueprint for all hair metal albums to follow. After "Home Sweet Home," you simply could *not* put out a hard rock record without the inclusion of at least one major power ballad.

Part of the allure of these softer songs was that they served to practically double the size of any hard rock band's fanbase. Heavy metal was already becoming more assessable outside of just traditional angry males as hair metal began to include more melody and pop-oriented hooks. But the presence of soft, emotional, big-sweeping ballads was enough to draw in *females* as well—most of which were more than happy to swoon over their newfound "sweet, good-natured" pretty-boy heroes as they crooned their love songs (while all the while no doubt secretly plotting their strategy for getting these girls into bed). It would turn into a situation where if you wanted a hit single and a Platinum album, you simply *had* to have a power ballad. And it was "Home Sweet Home" that quite possibly started it all.

The song's video played endlessly on MTV, *literally*. It was the No. 1 most requested video on the Daily MTV Request chart for over three months running, until MTV finally created a new rule (dubbed the "Crüe Rule") mandating that, from that point forward, songs would become ineligible for the countdown after their first thirty days.

"Smokin' in the Boys Room" and "Home Sweet Home" drove *Theatre of Pain* to No. 6 on the Billboard Albums chart with sales of more than four million copies. Aside from the pop singles, however, the remainder of *Theatre of Pain* was full-on, heavy metal glam rock. Many fans considered the album subpar versus the heavy, nasty nature of *Shout at the Devil*, and the vast majority list it as their least favorite Mötley Crüe record of the '80s. Nikki Sixx even routinely refers to it as "trash." Personally? I happened to really like the album. Aside from the singles, *Theatre of Pain* was a solid, meaty (if basic) rock 'n' roll record—no more, no less. The raw, hard-hitting guitar tone, along with Neil's aggressive vocals and the songs' straightforward, chorus-driven structures gave the album an enjoyably mean slant. Songs such as "City Boy Blues," "Keep Your Eye on the Money," "Tonight (We Need a Lover)," "Louder Than Hell," . . . I love them all. To each his own, I guess.

Drama wasn't limited to Mötley Crüe, however, as **Van Halen** seemed to exist in a perpetual state of internal discord and dissent. Tensions between Eddie Van Halen and David Lee Roth had been brewing for years, mostly stemming from the nature of their polar opposite personalities. Despite the massive success of *1984*, Roth was less than pleased with Eddie's newfound fascination with keyboards and still held a grudge stemming from his exclusion from most of the album's composition while Eddie was holed up in his new personal home-recording studio. Roth was also tiring of the enigmatic guitarist's substance abuse. Eddie, on the other hand, had just about had enough of Roth's outrageously outgoing personality, ego, and stage antics.

Further complicating matters, just after the tour for *1984* concluded, Roth released a side-project solo EP of four cover songs, titled *Crazy from the Heat*. Interestingly, however, the album was in a decidedly different style and direction versus Van Halen. The infectious medley of "Just a Gigolo" and "I Ain't Got Nobody" mirrored Louis Prima's 1956 mashup combining two pre-World War II songs, while Roth's fantastic version of the Beach Boys' "California Girls," peaked at No. 3 on the Billboard Hot 100 chart, ironically the same position the Beach Boys' original rendition achieved twenty years before that. Both songs were *major* hits buoyed by relentless video play on MTV. Roth handled the choreography himself, and the combination of his charismatic, larger-than-life presence with the perfectly playful videos launched *Crazy from the Heat* to high levels of success with over one million units sold.

When Van Halen met to discuss their future recording and touring plans post *1984* though, the existence of Roth's solo EP was a significant point of contention for Eddie, who was less-than-approving of the outside venture. Incidentally, Roth was also critical of Eddie's increasing guest spots on other artist's albums, such as the famous guitar solo he contributed to Michael Jackson's "Beat It."

With their relationship seemingly at a nadir, the two simply could not agree on a path forward. Roth wanted to carry on with Van Halen while also continuing with solo side projects, including his plan to write and direct a musical movie that would see him acting in the starring role. Roth even asked Eddie if he would score the film, a request which the guitarist emphatically declined.

Discussions hit a wall, with Roth eventually declaring, "I can't work with you guys anymore. I want to do my movie. Maybe when I'm done, we'll get back together." Despite the acrimony at the time and the high level of ill-will that would exist thereafter, Roth and Eddie shared a tearful embrace before going their separate ways, perhaps recognizing the monumental impact of the moment—Van Halen, the undisputed biggest rock band on the planet, was now over (at least that version of the band, anyway). The group would uncannily break up at the pinnacle of their success. Bizarre, but I guess "that's show business," as Roth would say.

A few other notable albums helped keep the hair metal stove burning as well. **Ratt** followed up their breakthrough *Out of the Cellar* with the double-Platinum *Invasion of Your Privacy*, which included the standout rockers "You're in Love" and "Lay it Down." **Kix** also managed to finally sample a small taste of success with their third album, *Midnight Dynamite*, highlighted by the anthem-type nature of the pounding title track and the steaming "Cold Shower," both of which hit the Top 25 on the Hot Mainstream Rock chart.

Lastly, 1985 saw Bon Jovi issue their sophomore record, *7800° Degrees Fahrenheit.* The album didn't come easy for the developing rock stars as they struggled to find their way as a band and hone their songwriting skills. The music was cobbled together too quickly, attempting to capitalize on the momentum achieved with "Runaway," and Bon Jovi were basically just taking direction from their producer, Lance Quinn. It would be the last time the two parties worked together.

Still, despite containing mostly marginal material (with the possible exception of hit single "In and Out of Love"), *7800° Degrees Fahrenheit* managed to reach an impressive No. 37 on the Billboard Albums chart and achieved Gold certification in the US. The tour to support the record was a convincing success, and fans seem to love the album, but the band was less than pleased with what they felt were marginal results.

The upcoming year would be a completely different story for Bon Jovi, however, and not just them but the entire rock music world as well. Hair metal's seeds were clearly sewn between 1981 and 1985 with bands like Quiet Riot, Def Leppard, Van Halen, Mötley Crüe, and Ratt proving they could compete sales-wise with the many pop-artists that largely ruled MTV and radio at the time, acts like Michael Jackson, Prince, Huey Lewis & The News, Madonna, Duran Duran, Tina Turner, Culture Club, Cyndi Lauper, and Wham!. But much bigger and grander things were right around the corner as hair metal would soon emerge as a premier, dominant genre of music over the next six years—and the spark that would light the explosion would be none other than Bon Jovi themselves.

Other noteworthy albums released in 1985: Dokken *(Under Lock and Key)*, White Lion *(Fight to Survive)*, Twisted Sister *(Come Out and Play)*

Best Albums 1985

1. Mötley Crüe – *Theatre of Pain*
2. David Lee Roth – *Crazy from the Heat*

III

Eruption & Life at the Top

1986 – 1991

Chapter 7
Slippery When Wet
(1986)

Hair metal had been slowly but steadily creeping onto the commercial charts and into the public consciousness since the early '80s, but in 1986 **Bon Jovi** ceremoniously blew the proverbial doors off, officially ushering in a new era with the release of their historic and momentous third album, *Slippery When Wet.*

Despite the moderate success of 1985's *7800° Fahrenheit*, Bon Jovi had hardly been satisfied, fearing the band was stagnating and unable to show any real growth or evolution that could elevate them to their desired "superstar" status. Determined to take the next step, they hired producer-extraordinaire Bruce Fairbairn and his at-the-time protégé Bob Rock while also enlisting the services of famed outside writer Desmond Child. The group then sequestered themselves at Fairbairn's Little Mountain Sound Studios in Vancouver, hell-bent on conjuring up a new album that would change their lives.

Jon Bon Jovi and Richie Sambora consciously drove toward a more mainstream approach on the new songs, focusing not only on heavy guitar riffs but also razor-sharp hooks and huge, sing-along, memorable choruses. And wow, did they ever succeed. *Slippery When Wet* (titled in honor of the Vancouver strip clubs the band frequented where girls frequently performed in showers) turned out to be, at the time, the perfect combination of hard rock, heavy metal, and pop-based melodies for the burgeoning hair metal scene.

The album's first two singles, "You Give Love a Bad Name" and "Livin' on a Prayer," both went to No. 1 on the Billboard chart, the first time any hard rock band had achieved such a feat. The latter tune, in particular, would eventually grow to become one of (if not *the*) genre's most popular songs. "Livin' on a Prayer" was a bona fide classic that has unquestionably endured as one of the most beloved anthems of the era, still resonating strongly with audiences new and old alike nearly thirty-five years later. Ironically, the track almost missed the album's final cut as Jon Bon Jovi didn't feel the song was strong enough! Luckily for the band, Sambora was able to convince him otherwise.

The western-themed power ballad "Wanted Dead or Alive" was released as the record's third single, another instant classic that built upon the popular format put forth by Mötley Crüe's "Home Sweet Home." The song was a massive hit, rising to No. 7 on the Billboard chart and making *Slippery When Wet* the very first hard rock album to produce three Top 10 singles. All three tracks went into heavy rotation on MTV, where Jon's poster-boy good looks served to further expand the band's male audience to include a swarm of swooning females.

Further to the singles, however, the album featured a host of added treasures, including killer pop-rock tunes such as "Let It Rock," "Raise Your Hands," "Wild in the Streets," "I'd Die for You," and the ultra-melodic "Without Love." *Slippery When Wet* ascended all the way to No. 1 on the Billboard Albums chart and remained entrenched in that position for an incredible eight consecutive weeks. The album would wind up staying on the chart in some capacity for *over two years*. The record eventually sold over twelve million copies making it one of the biggest selling albums in music history.

And just like that, the era of glam metal/hair metal was officially launched into the stratosphere.

🤘

Outside of Bon Jovi's big breakthrough, however, 1986 also featured the debut albums from two bands that would eventually go on to prominent representation in the Hair Metal Hall of Fame: the legendary Poison and Cinderella.

First up was **Poison**, a band that would grow to become more representative of (and associated with) the '80s glam metal era than perhaps any other. Poison first originated in Mechanicsburg, Pennsylvania, in 1982, comprised of singer Bret Michaels, bassist Bobby Dall, drummer Rikki Rocket and guitarist Matt Smith, playing under the name Paris in local clubs. The band eventually decided that if they were ever going to make it "big," they needed to move out to the flourishing hair metal scene in Los Angeles. With no money or prospects of any kind, the group packed up a van, changed their name to Poison, and bravely headed west.

Upon their arrival in L.A., the band's poverty proved too much for the homesick Smith, who abruptly decided to retreat back to Pennsylvania. Poison quickly hooked up with flamboyant new guitarist C.C. DeVille, however, and the group's classic lineup was complete. (The band also famously auditioned Slash for the open slot but understandably deemed him a poor fit for the glam image they were seeking.)

Poison worked tirelessly both days and nights, persistently promoting their brand and eventually building a devoted following playing popular clubs on the Sunset Strip. The band finally caught their break in 1986, landing a record deal with Enigma, and proceeded to release their debut album, *Look What the Cat Dragged In*, in August of the same year. The low-budget record was slapped together in just twelve days while costing only $20,000, a pittance even in those times.

The album's cover art was as glam metal as could be, featuring headshots of all four band members looking definitively more like women than men (indeed, Ricki Rocket was a former hairstylist and makeup artist). Musically, however, the album was a giant, pop-metal, party celebration. While the songs could never be mistaken for intricate compositions, their bombastic, hedonistic, festive spirit was utterly perfect for the Sunset Strip atmosphere at the time.

The album's first single, the autobiographical "Cry Tough" (which told the band's story of risking it all while striving for their dreams), launched the record with a thumping, lively, melodic-based energy. Disappointingly, however, the song failed to chart, and the album uneasily stalled out of the gate. The band continued to persevere and push forward, though, playing anywhere and everywhere they could to further cultivate their loyal and growing fanbase.

Then suddenly, almost a full year later, MTV casually decided to give second single "Talk Dirty to Me" a shot and aired the song's ridiculously glam and over-the-top video. The network's phones surprisingly lit up with masses of enthused listeners, and Poison became a household name virtually overnight. The world was finally ready for Poison's brand of rock. "Talk Dirty to Me" became a Top 40 hit and *Look What the Cat Dragged In* blew up in response, surging to No. 3 on the Billboard Albums chart.

Subsequent singles spurred further sales success, including the glam pop-metal rocker "I Want Action" and the sugary power ballad "I Won't Forget You" (written for the girlfriends the band left back home in Pennsylvania). *Look What the Cat Dragged In* ultimately sold more than four million copies establishing itself as the biggest-selling record in Enigma's history. The initially softly-received "Cry Tough" was soon revisited as a classic, and every song on the album flawlessly embodied the band's overarching mission—to throw the biggest, glam-est, most self-indulgent rock 'n' roll party possible (indeed, as the album's raunchy, guitar-driven title track well-chronicled).

Poison promptly hit the road with the likes of fellow hair metal contemporaries Ratt, Quiet Riot, and Cinderella, and just like that, they were off and running living their dreams.

Cinderella also launched their debut album in 1986, and they too would eventually go on to become hair metal legends. The group hailed from Pennsylvania, similar to Poison, but rather on the east side of the state in the suburbs of Philadelphia. Cinderella first caught the eye of Kiss' Gene Simmons while touring the local east coast circuit, but eventually got their big break after Jon Bon Jovi came away from one of their shows impressed and prompted his A&R man to check them out. The band would ultimately sign with Mercury/Polygram Records in 1985 and solidified their lineup with the addition of talented guitarist Jeff LaBar that same year.

Cinderella released their debut album, *Night Songs*, on August 2, 1986. The first thing audiences were hit with was the album's cover, now famous for misleadingly showcasing the band decked out in full-on glam-mode with high-teased hair, spandex, leather, and frilly lace, up against a pink-hued backdrop. At first glance, you would have assumed Cinderella was a glam/pop-metal band similar to Poison, but in actuality, the band was a blazing inferno of heavy metal blues-rock (at least at the start of their career).

Cinderella's unique signature was the powerful, raspy vocals of ultra-talented singer, songwriter, and guitarist Tom Keifer. *Night Songs* was a heavy, AC/DC-type record that spawned three hit singles on both radio and MTV: the fist-in-the-air anthem "Shake Me," hard-hitting "Somebody Save Me," and haunting ballad "Nobody's Fool." It was the latter song that predominantly broke the album, propelling *Night Songs* to No. 3 on the Billboard Albums chart. The record featured quality deep cuts as well, including "Back Home Again," "Nothin' for Nothin," "Once Around the Ride," and the bluesy "In From the Outside." *Night Songs* would eventually sell over four million copies.

Cinderella initially toured with Poison and eventually landed the coveted opening slot on Bon Jovi's massive Slippery When Wet Tour. *Night Songs* would go on to be cemented as an absolute classic of the hair metal genre, even as the band moved away from their early glam rock image and more toward pure blues-rock in the coming years.

Tesla was another significant band first appearing on the scene in 1986. Taking their name from the eccentric early twentieth-century electrical engineer Nikola Tesla, the group titled their tremendous debut album, *Mechanical Resonance*, based on one of his prominent scientific theories.

Tesla were immediately lumped under the heavy metal or glam metal umbrella with regard to style classification, but categorizing them as such was mostly an errant designation. The band admittedly had long hair, and their music indeed bore heavy metal tendencies, but Tesla were truly more of a '70s classic rock band who just happened to "metal-ize" their sound to fit the times. The band had paid their dues not on the Sunset Strip, but rather on the hard streets of Sacramento, California, and their lyrics often atypically focused on subjects other than simply girls and partying. Tesla's music also offered a good bit of deeper substance and diversity, for those willing to look that far.

Still, *Mechanical Resonance* rang true as a pure hard rock/metal album in many places, with blistering, hook-laden rockers like "Cumin Atcha' Live," "2 Late 4 Love," and "Rock Me to the Top." The dual guitar attack of Tommy Skeoch and Frank Hannon provided an intense wall of sound on many tracks, but the record offered several lighter spots of variation as well.

"Gettin' Better" started out softly before ramping up to a raucous finish, and "We're No Good Together" was a stirring, soft paced ballad that also escalated midway through. Other songs such as the intense "Changes" were more dynamic and mood-driven, but it was the album's two singles that really hit home from a commercial success standpoint: "Modern Day Cowboy" was a fabulous, western-flavored hard rock/metal track (as strange as that sounds), while "Little Suzi" was a light, pleasant, up-tempo cover of the 1981 Ph.D. song.

The success of the singles helped drive the critically acclaimed *Mechanical Resonance* to sell over one million copies, but the real strength of the record was its consistency and the power of the overall listening experience spinning the album from start-to-finish.

Tesla would go on to tour with Def Leppard, David Lee Roth, and Poison, likely contributing to their homogenization among other glam and heavy metal acts of the day. Labels aside, however, *Mechanical*

Resonance was simply a fantastic album regardless of whatever designation one chose to apply to it.

🤘

Of course, no year during the '80s was complete without some type of activity surrounding the indomitable **Van Halen**, and 1986 was no exception. Having split with David Lee Roth the year before, the Van Halen brothers were hard at work searching for a new singer when Eddie received an unexpected suggestion from an unlikely source. As it turned out, the guitarist shared a mechanic with Sammy Hagar, whom Eddie had known from Hagar's days fronting the band Montrose. (Hagar had since gone on to a successful solo career.)

An initial audition was arranged, and the guys quickly hit it off. Eddie and Alex were thrilled to have someone with Hagar's range and powerful vocals, not to mention his ability to play guitar. The missing piece that was Roth's overly flamboyant showmanship served as addition via subtraction from their view. From Hagar's side, the temptation to merge with the musical and creative force that was Van Halen and become something more than just a solo act was simply too inviting to pass up.

The new lineup meshed swiftly, and the framework for several songs that would eventually wind up on the new record was laid down during the group's very first sessions together. The full album came about over a few months and was released to a curious but enthusiastic public on March 24, 1986. The record was titled *5150* after the name of Eddie's home studio, dubbed such as 5150 was the California police dispatch code for an at-large mentally disturbed person.

Just a few weeks before the album's release, however, Van Halen issued the lead single "Why Can't This Be Love" to radio. Traditional fans were anxious to hear what the new lineup sounded like, but many were quickly taken aback as the mid-tempo, synthesizer-laden song was extremely "radio-friendly" and seemingly lacking any real teeth or hard rock semblance of Van Halen prior. Still, the tune was super-catchy and featured the combination of an infectious chorus, lush vocals by Hagar, and of course, a classic guitar solo from Eddie. "New" fans ate it up, but the overall "pop" tone of "Why Can't This Be Love" simply proved to be too much sticker-shock for a large segment of the band's hardcore fanbase, who hastily concluded the new version of the band was not "their" Van Halen.

From that point forward, a sharp wedge was driven between many Van Halen fans—you either loved Dave and hated Sammy, or you loved Sammy and disregarded Dave. For most people, there was hardly any space in between. The "new" Van Halen was unofficially dubbed "Van Hagar."

Outside of the first single, *5150* largely continued its stylistic divergence as the album was primarily pop-oriented and keyboard-driven in many places. Make no mistake, though, the record still had its fair share of blistering guitar wizardry provided by Eddie (witness the title track "5150"), and Hagar was indisputably a vocal force with which to be reckoned. Taken on its own merits and avoiding any comparison to Van Halen's past output, *5150* was undeniably impressive. Songs such as "Dreams" and "Best of Both Worlds" were instant classics with their larger-than-life choruses and driving structures, while "Summer Nights" was pure, unadulterated fun.

5150 also featured a couple of genuine, hard-rocking stompers as well—"Good Enough" opened the album in grand fashion with Hagar emphatically shouting "Hello Baaaaby!" and "Get Up" proved to be a fast and furious track that would have held up admirably on an album like *1984*.

Lastly, *5150* featured the syrupy, keyboard-driven ballad "Love Walks In," which, along with hit singles "Why Can't This Be Love" and "Dreams," helped the record surge to No. 1 on the Billboard Albums chart, a hard-to-believe first for the band at that time. It seemed Van Halen had not only managed to somehow survive the departure of their ultra-charismatic lead singer, but they had managed to get *better* (at least commercially).

This evaluation, of course, was strictly in the eye of the beholder, as many hardcore Van Halen fans understandably found it hard to accept Hagar and the band's new sound. At the same time, the commercial nature of *5150* succeeded in opening the group up to legions of new supporters. I myself was one of the minority fans who very much appreciated both versions of the band. I actually found it difficult to make any kind of meaningful evaluation between the two, as each iteration was, in truth, a completely different animal.

What wasn't up for debate, however, was the smashing commercial success of *5150*, as it sold over six million copies rendering Van Halen as popular as ever. Van Halen had performed the rarest of feats for an established, well-liked act, switching out their lead singer and seemingly not losing a step.

Speaking of Van Halen's previous lead singer, **David Lee Roth** wasn't far behind his former bandmates in terms of getting back into the public spotlight. His 1985 *Crazy From the Heat* EP had gone Platinum, and Roth was hard at work and fully engrossed in his upcoming film of the same name. The ambitious project had been greenlit by CBS films with a sizable twenty-million-dollar budget. Countless hours were invested into the movie, and it was nearing 80 percent complete when the project was suddenly and regretfully scrapped at the eleventh hour due to complications associated with the consolidation of CBS studios.

Disappointed but undeterred, Roth promptly put together a solo band consisting of virtuoso guitarist extraordinaire Steve Vai, drum prodigy Gregg Bissonette, and perhaps the best bassist to-be in all of rock, Billy Sheehan (later of Mr. Big). The band quickly went about recording the songs formerly planned to comprise the movie's soundtrack, and the album *Eat 'Em and Smile* was released on July 7, 1986.

The record was mostly a hard rock, guitar-driven masterpiece that had much more in common with traditional Van Halen than *5150*. Of course, Roth still managed to slip in a few surprises, including jazz, big band, and even speed metal, but the album was mostly a glorious celebration of flamboyant and fireworks-driven rock 'n' roll. For Van Halen fans dissatisfied with the commercial, pop-nature of *5150*, they needed to look no further than *Eat 'Em and Smile* for their satisfaction.

First single and lead track "Yankee Rose" was a perfect anthem for the era. Starting with a literal conversation between Roth and Vai's guitar (played to emulate a voice), the song proceeded to explode into a fierce rocker with a massive chorus as Dave shouted the apt, opening verse, "Are you ready for the new sensation?"!

Vai's searing guitar playing was astonishing, while Sheehan and Bissonette held down a thunderous groove. It is worth noting that while the song was undoubtedly filled with its share of sexual double entendres, the "Yankee Rose" referred to in the lyrics was actually none other than Lady Liberty herself, the legendary Statue of Liberty in New York Harbor.

Second track "Shy Boy" was a blazing speed metal song brought in from Billy Sheehan's prior band Talas, but the album then took a left turn taking on Billy Field's 1981 jazz tune "I'm Easy," to which Vai thankfully added some much-appreciated spice. As only Roth could pull off, all three disparate songs flowed seamlessly. The smoldering, mid-tempo "Ladies Night In Buffalo" was next, followed by the fun, radio-friendly second single, "Goin' Crazy."

Eat 'Em and Smile's second side continued the wild ride with a rocking cover version of The Nashville Teens' 1964 hit "Tobacco Road," followed by three fantastic hard rockers before the album appropriately ended with Roth's bombastic, big-band version of Frank Sinatra's "That's Life," which still managed to sizzle.

If there was any doubt whether Roth could shine outside of Van Halen (and really, there was little), *Eat 'Em and Smile* provided a resounding answer. The album represented Roth at the peak of his powers, supported by one of the best backing bands in the world. The Roth-versus-Van Halen debates were officially free to start flowing.

Eat 'Em and Smile went on to sell more than two million copies, spurred along by its fabulous MTV videos that Roth constructed using the props, setups, and characters originally intended for the discarded *Crazy*

From the Heat film. Roth and his all-star band toured the album extensively, much to the great delight of the public.

Ratt continued their assault on the hair metal scene in 1986 with their third release in as many years, *Dancing Undercover.* While not entirely consistent throughout, the album did manage to put forth three solid, sleazy songs that would become staples in Ratt's live set forevermore, "Dance," "Slip of the Lip," and "Body Talk." The latter track would also appear on the soundtrack and in the cult-classic movie *The Golden Child,* starring Eddie Murphy, further proving hair metal was not only experiencing commercial success but ingraining itself into pop-culture as well.

Other noteworthy albums released in 1986: Europe *(The Final Countdown),* Stryper *(To Hell with the Devil),* Great White *(Shot in the Dark),* Quiet Riot *(QR III)*

The year 1986 officially marked hair metal's explosion, driven by several outstanding albums that sold multiple millions of copies, none more so than Bon Jovi's massive *Slippery When Wet.* As hard as it may have been to believe, however, it was just the tip of the iceberg—hair metal would grow immensely more popular over the coming years with even bigger albums, greater influence, and more substantial victories.

<u>**Best Albums 1986**</u>

1. Bon Jovi – *Slippery When Wet (Top 10 in Genre!)*
2. Poison – *Look What the Cat Dragged In (Top 25 in Genre!)*
4. Van Halen – *5150 (Top 25 in Genre!)*
5. David Lee Roth – *Eat 'Em and Smile*
6. Tesla – *Mechanical Resonance*
7. Cinderella – *Night Songs*

Chapter 8
Welcome to the Jungle (1987)

The year 1987 brought us the emergence of one of the biggest bands in all of rock music history and an album that would change the shape and course of the hair metal era forever. The legendary band was none other than **Guns N' Roses**, and the album was their incredible, groundbreaking debut, *Appetite for Destruction.*

Guns N' Roses (often referred to simply as GN'R) emerged as a conglomeration of the earlier '80s bands Hollywood Rose and L.A. Guns (featuring guitarist Tracii Guns). The lineup was shuffled around a few times early on but eventually cemented itself as polarizing lead singer Axl Rose, uber-talented guitarist Slash, rhythm guitarist Izzy Stradlin, bassist Duff McKagan, and drummer Steven Adler.

Rose possessed a reclusive, manic personality, and the singer's perfectionism made him difficult to work with at times, but there was no denying the absolute immense power of his vocal ability. No one, and I mean *no one*, could scream like Axl Rose. Slash, meanwhile, was a guitar prodigy focused on hard rock and blues, while Stradlin brought songwriting talent and a penchant for developing rhythms that perfectly complemented Slash's lead guitar. McKagan added a vital punk element, and what Adler lacked in formal technique he made up for with a driving swing that shaped much of the group's sound. More than just a band, the five of them were an impoverished, reckless gang, living homeless lives of unwavering debauchery in the seedy underbelly of Hollywood.

Guns N' Roses spent years building up their brand and fanbase on the Sunset Strip, shaping the band into the enormous beast it would soon become. After undeniably establishing themselves as the kings of the Hollywood club scene, the group signed with Geffen Records in 1986 and began recording their full-length debut album in January 1987. *Appetite for Destruction* was officially released and thrust upon the world in July of the same year.

I don't have many childhood memories that I remember clearly, but I can vividly recall the first time I heard *Appetite*'s opening track, "Welcome to the Jungle." Our Junior High bus driver would graciously let the "cool" kids (not me, mind you) submit their favorite cassettes for him to play on the ride to school. I will never forget the feeling I had upon hearing the song's dramatic opening and wicked, chugging guitar riff, not to mention Axl's snarling, vicious vocal stylings as he intentionally stuttered the phrasing "watch it bring you to your shun n-n-n-n-n-n-n knees, knees"!

I was instantly captivated and mesmerized. I had never heard anything like it. For sure, Guns N' Roses was something entirely different versus the pop-artists of the time or even the hair metal that had managed to break through up until that point—the music was intense, angry, and ferocious—and it was *real*. The sound simply leaped out of the speakers and demanded my attention. There was a genuine sleaze and darkness to the band's sound that groups like Bon Jovi and Def Leppard could only hint at, but at the same time, the music was still immensely catchy.

Before all this could translate with millions of listeners, however, history tends to forget that while *Appetite for Destruction* would go on to be one of the biggest selling albums *ever*, it wasn't exactly a huge success right out of the gate, far from it, in fact.

Released in June 1987, just before the album dropped, "It's So Easy" was a curious choice for the lead single. The song's verses featured Rose singing in an atypically deep, low register, almost unrecognizable versus his approach on the album's other tracks. Furthermore, the chorus was laced with profanity, making it an impossible sell on radio. On top of all that, the band spent $150,000 making a video for the song that imprudently contained images graphic and violent enough to warrant it being banned on MTV. Not a great start, to say the least.

In fact, by October 1987, nearly three months after its initial release, the album had received so little reception by mainstream radio and MTV that the record company was ready to pack it in and walk away from the record entirely. A last-gasp plea by the band's manager Tom Zutaut (who was convinced *Appetite* was a monster of an album just waiting to be discovered) resulted in the president of Geffen records cashing in a favor with MTV, convincing the station to play the video for the newly released single "Welcome to the Jungle." MTV reluctantly agreed, but to just one airing, and at 4 a.m. on a Sunday, no less.

Well, as it turned out, people were watching, at least enough to change history. By morning the next day, MTV's switchboard *literally* exploded. The channel had never had so many calls, and the board's wiring actually sparked and melted. You couldn't make this stuff up. And just like that, *Appetite for Destruction* was off and running.

"Welcome to the Jungle" led the way, but almost every song on the album was outstanding in its own right. Songs like "Nightrain" (named after the band's favorite cheap liquor), "Out Ta Get Me," and "You're Crazy" were classic, hard rock, sleaze metal with choruses that would easily stick in your head for days.

Many of the songs featured lyrics that were reflective of the band's dark lifestyle versus the typical sex and party themes common to hair metal at the time. "Mr. Brownstown" was a rhythmic rocker centered on the dangers of heroin use, and the vicious "My Michelle" was a true story written about a downtrodden friend of the band. Even "Welcome to the Jungle" was an authentic recount of Rose's traumatic experiences and impressions first getting off the bus in L.A. after growing up in rural Indiana. *Appetite for Destruction* represented the hardcore, depraved world in which the band lived; Guns N' Roses were neither contrived nor an image—for better or worse, they were the genuine article.

Not that the album didn't contain any sincere, heartfelt moments, however (even though they were just as heavy and intense). One of my personal favorites, "Think About You" (penned by Stradlin), was a slightly more tender track lyrically that told the touching story of thankful, lost love. And then, of course, there was the supreme mega-hit, semi-ballad "Sweet Child O' Mine." The song's now-famous intro started bright and melodic, with a guitar part based on a practice exercise Slash would employ while warming up. Rose's clean, piercing vocals followed, focused on his adoring sentiment for then-girlfriend Erin Everly. The track changed keys midway through, progressing to a low minor, while Slash laid down what would become considered by many the greatest hair metal guitar solo of all-time.

Following the solo, during the song's construction, the band briefly lost a sense of where to take things, and the resulting repeated scratch lyric "where do we go now" wound up sticking as the song slowly broke down and dramatically built back up again to a crescendo finish with powerful vocals from Rose and more amazing guitar work from Slash.

"Sweet Child O' Mine" was unstoppable on both radio and MTV, and finally pushed *Appetite for Destruction* to the No. 1 position at the top of the Billboard Albums chart in August 1988, just over a full year since it was first released. The song was included in *Rolling Stone* magazine's "40 Greatest Songs that Changed the World" article published in the late '90s.

Other album highlights included the epic, huge stadium-rocker "Paradise City" and album closer "Rocket Queen," which started dark, brooding, and nasty, but ended with a sentimental, upbeat melody and lyrics that closed out the menacing album on a surprisingly sincere and hopeful note.

Appetite for Destruction went on to become the highest selling debut album in US history, eventually tallying over eighteen million copies in the US and thirty million copies worldwide, making it one of the top ten biggest selling albums of *all-time*. Guns N' Roses were officially a worldwide phenomenon.

Remarkably, 1987 featured not just *one* of the biggest selling albums of all-time, but *two!* In 1984 **Def Leppard** came off the massive success of *Pyromania* in a much different place than where they were before. Now with some financial success to their names, the band members took up residence together in Dublin to begin composing their next record. However, the task proved unexpectedly arduous as writing sessions drug on without tangible results, and producer Mutt Lange dropped off the project due to "exhaustion."

Def Leppard took a shot at recording with Jim Steinman but just couldn't seem to get on the same page. Steinman's vision was a simple, raw, rock record, but the band had their sights set on something positively *monumental*—an album that would not only equal but surpass the performance and production that was already close to perfection on *Pyromania.*

The biggest setback, however, occurred on New Year's Eve 1984. Drummer Rick Allen was driving with his girlfriend outside of Sheffield, England, when he suddenly lost control of his speeding Corvette. The vehicle spun off the road and violently crashed through a drystone wall, flipping over in the process. Allen was thrown from the car and horrifyingly severed his left arm. Doctors would later successfully reattach the limb with surgery, but unfortunately, an unyielding infection quickly set in and Allen eventually lost the arm permanently.

It was a no-brainer to assume that his career as a drummer was over, but Allen was determined to continue on, believing he could instead play his left arm percussion parts with his feet. Def Leppard were fully committed to supporting their bandmate and promptly shut down operations for the better part of a full year while Allen re-learned to play his instrument from scratch, constructing a custom electronic drum kit that would trigger beats from his footwork.

After a tremendous amount of effort and persistence, Allen eventually regained the ability not only play, but play *live.* He made his emotional and successful comeback in front of almost one hundred thousand people at the renowned 1986 Monsters of Rock festival in Leicestershire, England. Allen's tearful release reflected the intense emotion associated with all he had been through in a true watershed moment for Def Leppard, who came off the stage with a renewed sense of joy and confidence.

With Allen back on board and the welcomed return of Mutt Lange as producer, the band was finally getting back on track. It would still be an uphill climb, however, as both Lange and Def Leppard were determined to make the new album a bona fide "classic," no matter how much work or time was needed. Lange's meticulous, perfectionist approach steered the ship, with full morning or evening sessions sometimes resulting in only a few new vocals or a couple of sparse guitar parts, but the point was they were *perfect.*

Def Leppard was convinced the new material had to congeal as a combination of both the band's hard rock roots and a new focus on commercial pop melodies and cutting-edge technical recording techniques, i.e., a rock/pop hybrid. Allen's injury also necessitated style adjustments as his drum hits were now more staggered and dramatic. The group's stated objective was to make the rock-version of Michael Jackson's *Thriller*, where every song was a little different, and each was of such high quality as to all be potential hit singles. Quite an ambition, for sure.

Finally, after almost four years of challenges, delays, adversity, and intense work, the new record, titled *Hysteria*, was at last completed and released on August 3, 1987. Like *Appetite for Destruction*, it would become one of the best-selling albums of all-time; however, also like *Appetite*, *Hysteria* would struggle mightily out of the gates (at least in the US, in the UK it was an instant smash).

Part of the challenge was that, in America, Def Leppard had lost valuable momentum with the short attention span of the public consciousness during the four long years that had elapsed since *Pyromania*. Furthermore, and again like *Appetite*, the first US single selected from *Hysteria* turned out to be less than the best choice.

The pop-metal masterpiece "Animal" had been wisely released as the first single in the UK, where it quickly rose into the Top 10. However, against Def Leppard's suggestion to follow the same path in the US, the record label instead went with the album's first track, "Women." The thought was to build a bridge back to Def Leppard's earlier fanbase as "Women" was more hard rock than the melodic "Animal" (although still nothing like the band's earlier NWOBHM sound). As it turned out, the record label chose poorly. Irrefutably, "Women" was a cool song and a natural choice to lead off the full album as it built a potent, deliberate, grooving atmosphere from which the record could later explode, but it was far from perfect as a stand-alone radio track, and "Women" commercially fizzled as a result.

Realizing the error of their ways, "Animal" was then quickly released as the second US single, but despite the strength of the song with its lush melodies and catchy hooks, it was curiously only mildly successful, just barely cracking the Top 20. Determined to see the record "hit," the amazing semi-ballad "Hysteria" was then unwaveringly issued as a third single. Again, it did reasonably well, but *Hysteria* as an album bizarrely still failed to "break." The insufficient commercial response prompted a good bit of anxiety among the band, as the record had taken so long to complete and cost so much to produce, *Hysteria* needed to sell an intimidating five million copies *just to break even.*

And then, almost twelve full months after *Hysteria* was first issued, Def Leppard finally caught the break they were seeking. Just prior to the album's completion a year earlier, only Mutt Lange and singer Joe Elliott remained in the studio finishing up a few vocal tracks before putting the record to bed. While Lange took a quick break, Elliott casually picked up an acoustic guitar and started strumming a riff he had developed a couple of weeks earlier. Upon hearing it echo from afar, Lange immediately stopped dead in his tracks, feeling sure the idea had tremendous potential.

Although the album was already far behind schedule, Lange insisted they stop everything to work on the tune, believing it had the capacity to be a major crossover hit. Uncharacteristically, the song was quickly completed by the full band in less than two weeks and placed on the record as the final track before shutting down. It was titled "Pour Some Sugar on Me."

Fast forward twelve months, and "Pour Some Sugar on Me" was released as the fourth single in one last attempt to kick-start the album. And as luck would have it, the track absolutely *blew up* on radio and MTV. The song's video showcased Def Leppard's stunning live show as they were currently playing "in the round" concerts to fantastic critical reviews. The ultra-catchy hard rock tune's somewhat rap-like verses had been influenced by the first true rap-rock foray a year earlier when Aerosmith and Run DMC collaborated on a reimaging of Aerosmith's 1976 hit single "Walk This Way."

Evocative strippers all over the world rapidly adopted "Pour Some Sugar on Me" as their theme song, and the track's success on radio drove *Hysteria* to swiftly sell over four million additional copies in only a few months. The album shot to No. 1 and wound up staying on the charts for an astonishing two years running.

After "Pour Some Sugar on Me," Def Leppard and *Hysteria* were essentially unstoppable. The first three singles were "re-discovered" and properly established as the classics they were, and subsequent singles were released to additional success, among them the huge ballad "Love Bites," glam-rocking "Armageddon It," and even the quirky "Rocket," which was driven by African drum loops and included a long, break-down mid-section featuring all sorts of space-age samples and sound effects. Each song was a massive hit that surged into the Top 5. ("Love Bites" fabulously went all the way to No. 1.)

Hysteria eventually sold a whopping twenty-five million copies worldwide and established Def Leppard as one of the most successful hard rock bands of the era, if not in history. The album yielded an unheard-of *seven* hit singles, and the irony was that a couple of the records best songs didn't even get released. The dark, epic "Gods of War" was often cited by fans as their personal favorite, and semi-ballad "Love and Affection" unquestionably had "hit" written all over it had the song been officially sent to radio. Even the simpler, more straightforward rockers "Run Riot" and "Don't Shoot Shotgun" shined brightly and would have been standouts on any lesser album.

While some critics and fans understandably mourned the death of the Def Leppard whose previous sound was based on the NWOBHM style, the success of their newfound pop-metal approach was undeniable and allowed them to reach a much larger audience. The production techniques on *Hysteria* were cutting-edge for the time and served as a sought-after template for hundreds of albums to follow. To this day, you would be hard-pressed to find a more polished record. The sound was simply perfect for what the band was trying to achieve.

Constructed over the most difficult of circumstances over a four-year period, *Hysteria* would eventually more than justify all that went into it, cementing itself as one of rock's greatest achievements and success stories.

Amazingly enough, 1987 had more magnificent hair metal gifts to bear still. In addition to offering two of the biggest selling records of all-time in *Appetite for Destruction* and *Hysteria*, fans would also get one of the most beloved albums of the entire hair metal genre.

David Coverdale acquired his first taste of modest US success with 1984's *Slide It In*, but **Whitesnake** would go on to join the likes of Bon Jovi and Def Leppard as official hair band royalty with their hugely successful 1987 self-titled album, *Whitesnake* (often referred to as *Whitesnake '87*, or simply the *1987* album, as it was officially titled in Europe). Similar to *Hysteria*, however, there were significant challenges to overcome before any success could be realized.

The project began with Coverdale and co-writer/guitarist John Sykes taking up residence in Vancouver along with bassist Neil Murray and drummer Aynsley Dunbar. Initial writing and demo sessions went well enough as several songs began to take shape that appeared destined to become powerful statements and big hits. But just as things were about to kick into high gear, suddenly, out of nowhere, Coverdale developed a dangerously serious sinus infection that robbed him of all vocal ability. The condition was so severe that doctors estimated there was at least a 50 percent chance he would never be able to sing again, describing the infection as the worst they had ever seen.

Antibiotics provided a brief measure of temporary respite but failed to fully cure the issue, and it was eventually decided Coverdale would need to undergo surgery. The outcome was in great question, as there were no assurances he would ever be able to resume his career as a vocalist. The outlook was so grim, Coverdale even suggested his bandmates jump ship and go find another gig.

Coverdale wound up on the sidelines for eight long months as he struggled to recover and come to grips with the fact that someone else may have to sing his songs from that point forward. Under the strain of the difficult situation, his relationship with Sykes deteriorated to the extent the guitarist wound up divorcing from the group.

In fact, by the time Coverdale was recovered enough to try getting back in the saddle, he was the only Whitesnake soldier remaining. Against the odds, though, Coverdale eventually regained his voice, at least enough to move forward with the stalled album. And while that was the good news, the bad news was the project was in serious debt, and Coverdale no longer had a band.

A new lineup was dutifully assembled, including guitarists Adrian Vandenberg and Vivian Campbell, bassist Rudy Sarzo, and drummer Tommy Aldridge. The group put the necessary finishing touches on the album, and *1987* was released on April 7, 1987. The result saw Whitesnake fully complete their conversion from '70s blues-rock to heavy pop-metal, a transformation that had first planted its seeds on *Slide It In.* In fact, Sykes (who was still present on the recordings) had explicitly searched for a guitar tone to align with the popular hair metal sounds of the time, which he eventually succeeded in finding with the help of producer Bob Rock (who had helmed Bon Jovi's *Slippery When Wet*).

The *1987* album featured a marvelous set of absolutely huge-sounding, pop-metal anthems driven by flashy hard rock guitar riffs and solos, Coverdale's remarkable Robert Plant-like vocals, and two of the most famous power ballads ever put to tape. Of course, if you dug deep enough, you could also still hear (very) faint traces of the '70s classic rock and blues as well.

The colossal "Crying in the Rain" launched the US version of the album with dramatic grandeur. Re-recorded and enhanced from its original form on Whitesnake's 1982 *Saints & Sinners* album, the track can only be described as epic, with all the wonderfully bombastic hair metal sounds and styles for which a person could wish.

The real hard rock masterpiece on *1987*, however, was the heavy-hitting, Led Zeppelin-esque "Still of the Night," which featured one of the greatest riffs to emerge from the entire era, period. There was just no escaping the song's chugging groove. The track distinctively included a fantastic breakdown section that saw Sykes using a violin bow (of all things) to play his guitar. "Bad Boys" also provided an imposing hard rock/metal assault, actively employing double bass kick drums to heighten the intensity. *Whitesnake '87* offered its fair share of pop-metal sheen as well, as "Give Me All Your Love Tonight" was just about perfect, and "Children of the Night" and "Straight from the Heart" weren't far behind.

And then, of course, there were the album's power ballads, of which two would eventually go on to be etched in the proverbial Hair Metal Hall of Fame. "Here I Go Again" (originally presented on *Saints & Sinners*) and "Is This Love" were massive hits beyond words and received countless hours of both radio and MTV airplay. The former, in particular, grew to become almost singularly synonymous with the entire hair metal genre, and outside of Journey's "Don't Stop Believing," might possibly be the world's most requested Karaoke song.

Regarding the almost-equally popular "Is This Love" (the song peaked at No. 2 versus the No. 1 chart position achieved by "Here I Go Again"), I once heard a rough demo-track version where Coverdale can be heard breaking in at one point, stating, "and now comes the chorus that will change the world." A little dramatic perhaps, but clearly, the band knew they were creating something special right from the start.

The music videos accompanying the two hit ballads were notably famous in part due to the sultry presence of vixen Tawny Kitaen, who gladly provided the requisite over-the-top sexuality sought after via sensual, choreographed movements in see-thru clothing. Of course, Coverdale and Kitaen wound up dating, and the two were later briefly married.

The *1987* album existed in two distinctly different formats. The initial UK release featured eleven tracks, two of which, unfortunately, needed to be omitted from the US version: the dramatic ballad "Looking for Love" and the hard rocker "You're Gonna Break My Heart Again." Their exclusion had nothing to do with inferiority, as in fact, both tracks were on par with the majority of other fantastic songs on the album. But in 1987, vinyl was music's primary format, and it was inherently subject to physical space limitations. John Kalodner had remastered the album for the US and wanted it to sound "bigger and louder" than the UK release, required more "space," and thus imposing the tighter tracklist consistent with the limitations of a 33" vinyl record. The running order of the songs was also adjusted for the US to provide maximum impact.

In 2017, a Thirtieth Anniversary Deluxe Edition of the album was issued featuring all eleven tracks across both the US and UK versions fully remastered to the fullest, thickest, clearest sound available yet. (Production on the original release admittedly sounded a little "thin," especially after the record was transferred to compact disc format with the limited technology available in the early '90s.) If you own *1987* in any other format than the 2017 release, do yourself a favor—pick it up, rip it to your device of choice, and reorder the tracks to the sequence below. This is possibly the best of both worlds between the original two editions and facilitates the optimal flow among the record (personal opinion, of course):

1. Crying in the Rain
2. Bad Boys
3. Still of the Night
4. Here I Go Again (US radio-mix)
5. Give Me All Your Love
6. Children of the Night
7. Is This Love

8. You're Gonna Break My Heart Again
9. Looking for Love
10. Straight from the Heart
11. Don't Turn Away

Note I referenced the "US radio-mix" associated with "Here I Go Again." Interestingly, there are a few different versions of the now-famous song. A scaled-back adaptation of the track first appeared on Whitesnake's 1982 album *Saints & Sinners*, although it failed to generate commercial interest at the time. On the *1987* album, however, the song was re-recorded at a different pace and in a much grander fashion, mainly featuring Sykes on guitar, although Coverdale had Vandenberg redo the solo just before the album's completion. Lastly, a third version came to be in the form of a "radio-mix" for the US. However, unlike most radio-edits, it was not simply a shorter version of the song (although it is shorter by forty-two seconds).

The album version had an extended keyboard and vocal intro, whereas the radio mix started with the full band. The arrangement differed as well, with the radio mix featuring a more consistent, subdued guitar strum versus the more dramatic album version. Dan Huff performed the guitar solo on the radio mix versus the aforementioned Vandenberg on the album.

Both formats received ample airplay in 1987, although I would wager 99 percent of fans prefer the album version. Personally, I am almost always in favor of a song's album edition, as radio-edits are famous for simply cutting out parts of a song to facilitate a shorter run time. However, in this instance, I tend to most often prefer the radio-mix, as it just seems to flow a little better in the track sequence (or perhaps I simply suffer from overkill, having heard the more theatrical album version about a billion times, or so). Whichever you choose, however, will surely suffice.

Whitesnake '87 was a huge success in any format, eventually reaching the No. 2 spot on the Billboard Albums chart and selling over fifteen million copies. Similar to Def Leppard's transition from *Pyromania* to

Hysteria, though, there was inevitably a certain segment of fans who viewed the album as a sell-out to modern trends (i.e., hair metal) and clearly preferred the late '70s or early '80s version of Whitesnake. That said, if sales were any indicator, those fans were clearly in the minority. In time, even Coverdale himself would come to be somewhat wary of fully embracing the new style, but at the moment, there was no denying he had finally achieved the massive global success he had long sought, and *Whitesnake '87* was a killer album.

Mötley Crüe continued their trend of issuing a new record every other year with the release of their fourth album, *Girls, Girls, Girls*, which once again saw the band reinventing themselves. This time around, the Crüe abandoned the glam fashion they had adopted on *Theatre of Pain* and traded in their makeup and spandex for leather, motorcycles, and strip clubs.

The music was darker and rougher as well, reflecting the shadowy nature of the band's lifestyle at that time, which was steeped in drug addiction, alcohol and general mayhem, debauchery, and dysfunction (even more than usual). Similar to *Theatre of Pain*, Mötley was lucky to even get *Girls, Girls, Girls* out, let alone have it be a success, although this time it was for different reasons.

The most glaring hindrance stemmed from primary songwriter Nikki Sixx's heightening heroin addiction, which had reached its apex in 1987 (although to be sure, the entire group was less than fully functional). With Sixx operating below peak capacity, the band had only eight legitimate new songs to offer, as two of the album's tracks were basically throwaways: the short instrumental "Nona" (which Sixx wrote in tribute to his grandmother, who passed away during the recording of the album), and a fairly weak live rendition of Elvis Presley's "Jailhouse Rock." Additionally, a few of the remaining songs might not have been much more than "fillers." Between the dicey states of the band members combined with the effect their substance abuse struggles had on the music, it would have been no surprise if *Girls, Girls, Girls* had finally been Mötley Crüe's downfall.

However, again in true Mötley fashion, against all the odds, the album was a smash success, again saved primarily by the overwhelming strength of just a few songs, in particular, "Girls, Girls, Girls" and "Wild Side," which probably served to save the band's career as well.

"Girls, Girls, Girls" and "Wild Side" were undeniably inspired, and both should unequivocally earn a place on any Crüe "best of" compilation regardless of fans' different preferences for each varied stage of the band's career. "Wild Side" kicked off the album with a wicked, blues-metal guitar riff and menacing vocals from Vince Neil that clearly laid out the new law of the land:

Kneel down ye sinners to
Streetwise religion
Greed's been crowned the new King
Hollywood dream teens
Yesterday's trash queens
Save the blessings for the final ring, Amen!

The crushing song featured uncharacteristic (for Mötley Crüe) time-changes and blasted along as a perfect opening salvo for the new, rougher, grittier Crüe.

The sleazy "Girls, Girls, Girls," meanwhile, was the album's second track and first single, a driving rocker packing a huge punch of a sing-along chorus. The instant classic was a staple in every strip club in America each night, as it remains to this day, more than thirty years later. It was the ideal song to represent everything the Crüe stood for at the time.

There were admittedly a couple of other cool moments on the album, as well. "Dancing on Glass" was a bruising, bluesy rocker featuring backup vocals by female soul-singer Phyllis Saint James (a first for Mötley at the time), and "All In The Name Of..." was an underrated, straightforward slice of legitimate boogie rock. *Girls, Girls, Girls* did feature one power ballad, "You're All I Need," that was also released as a single, but it failed to make a mark similar to what "Home Sweet Home" had achieved. A beautiful love song in style at first glance, the lyrics actually told the sick story of a man who killed his lover so he could keep her "close" to him. Naturally, in true Mötley self-sabotaging fashion, they shot a disturbing video for the song that MTV, of course, refused to air.

Nevertheless, fans ate up the first two singles, and the immensely popular album eventually went quadruple-Platinum, reaching the No. 2 position on the Billboard Albums chart. *Girls, Girls, Girls* was controversially unable to supplant Whitney Houston's *Whitney* album for the No. 1 spot, as in those days, initially-tallied official weekly album sales were too often somewhat "subjective."

Mötley Crüe toured the record to much acclaim and with great success, at first. Whitesnake and Guns N' Roses would both occupy opening slots at different points, and the stage show featured drummer Tommy Lee's innovative, upside-down spinning drum-kit cage. However, Mötley's peak drug and alcohol use would eventually force their manager, Doc McGhee, to cancel the 1988 European leg of their tour, stating, "if the band went to Europe, one of them was coming home in a body bag."

While McGhee's proclamation may have seemed overly dramatic, it was, in fact, an entirely accurate assessment of the death spiral the group was heading down at the time, particularly Sixx. On December 23, 1987, the Mötley Crüe bassist finally hit the wall. After a hard night of drug-filled partying, Sixx was injected with one last shot of heroin when he suddenly passed out cold. This was no ordinary crash, however. Paramedics were quickly called to the scene as Sixx's heart had stopped and friends were unable to rouse him with mouth-to-mouth—EMTs gloomily pronounced him dead on arrival.

Once in the ambulance, a last-ditch effort was made to revive the shattered rock star as a paramedic shoved two adrenaline needles directly into Sixx's heart. Miraculously, he violently shot back to life.

Sixx finally woke a few hours later, finding himself strapped down in a hospital bed. True to his destructive form, he promptly tore out his IVs, left the hospital against doctors' advice, caught a ride with a couple of fans who had assembled a small vigil in the parking lot to mourn his death, and went directly to his junkie to shoot-up again. He awakened the following morning lying on his floor with a needle sticking out of his bloody arm. Sixx could get no lower it would seem.

It was a miracle Mötley Crüe was even able to function in 1987, let alone have a hit record and a massive tour. As it turned out, the Girls, Girls, Girls Tour would be the last of its kind for the band, at least in terms of lifestyle. Each member of the group would go through rehab together for drug and alcohol addictions in the coming year, and a clean, sober Mötley Crüe would return stronger and better than ever in 1989—but we'll get to that later.

🤘

Speaking of getting sober, 1987 finally saw **Aerosmith** solidify their comeback from a great career almost put to an early death by drug and alcohol abuse during the '70s and early '80s.

Aerosmith first attempted a reunion and revival with 1984's marginally successful Back In The Saddle Tour and 1985's subpar album *Done With Mirrors*, but their overall commercial success failed to return to the extent desired. Another aim at relevancy was then made in 1986 when the band teamed up with the emerging rap group Run-DMC for a modern reimaging of their 1973 hit "Walk This Way." The single was a smash and successfully returned Aerosmith the public eye, prompting the band's full commitment to getting sober for one last shot at a return to glory.

Aerosmith's true reinstatement at the top of the mountain would occur in 1987. As the newly clean group set about putting together a new album, they decided to completely revisit their creative process. For the first time, the band decided to collaborate with outside writers in a bid to regain their popularity and conform to the recent shift of heavy metal to more commercial pop-metal. Aerosmith also had the power of MTV on their side this time around, which had emerged as a vast and critical vehicle to exposure and success for artists of all kinds.

The result of their efforts was the band's ninth studio album, titled *Permanent Vacation.* The new record was the band's strongest offering in more than a decade and resonated with a newfound fanbase (although there was a reasonably large contingent of hardcore Aerosmith fans from the '70s that understandably lambasted it as a sell-out). Still, the album succeeded in successfully returning Aerosmith to their former fame, largely on the backs of three catchy pop-rock singles: "Dude (Looks Like A Lady)," 'Rag Doll," and the syrupy power ballad, "Angel."

Ironically, the album's singles are some of my least favorite songs on the record. I'm not exactly sure if this is the result of an objective assessment of their quality or perhaps simply raw over-exposure, as these songs have ostensibly been played and heard seemingly *billions* of times.

My personal picks from the album were the stomping hard rock punch of lead tracks "Heart's Done Time" and "Magic Touch," the blazing "Simoriah," the fun, island-themed title track "Permanent Vacation," and the bluesy "Hangman Jury." As for the hit ballad "Angel," it was undoubtedly a great song but came off as just a little too contrived for my long-term liking.

Any way you slice it, though, Aerosmith was back on top in a big way. *Permanent Vacation* sold over five million copies, generated three hugely popular hit singles, and re-established the band as a major concert draw.

White Lion also found success in 1987, finally breaking through with their hit album, *Pride.* Interestingly, While Lion came from quite different geographic origins versus the majority of hair metal bands that were launching from the Sunset Strip in Hollywood. Lead singer Mike Tramp had packed up and moved from his home country of Denmark to New York, where he then hooked up with guitar prodigy and songwriting partner Vita Bratta.

The band had released their true debut, *Fight To Survive*, in 1985, but the album proved a rough start to the group's career. Major label Elektra records had optimistically signed White Lion in 1984 but were patently unhappy with *Fight To Survive* and promptly decided against releasing the album. The record was then bought out by a new label and eventually released, but only in Japan. After some time, the album finally received a US-release in 1985, although it was disappointingly met with little fanfare.

White Lion received a fortuitous second chance in 1987 when Atlantic records scooped them up off the scrap heap and funded their sophomore album, *Pride*, issued in June of that year. *Pride* fit perfectly among the hair metal scene with Tramp's emotive vocals and the blistering guitar work of Bratta, a supreme talent not entirely distant from the great Eddie Van Halen. Indeed, Bratta was awarded the title of Best New Guitarist by *Guitar World* magazine that year. White Lion's songs (at least initially) were the perfect epitome of pop-metal—hard rock with ultra-catchy melodies.

The pop-rock masterpiece "Wait" was immediately sent to radio as the first single, but curiously only simmered for a few months until its fortunes dramatically changed for the better upon MTV playing the song's video in early 1988. The added exposure and drawing power of Tramp's poster-boy good looks pushed both the song and album into the Top 10. The fantastic "Tell Me" was released as a second single, but for whatever reason, it didn't fare as well as "Wait." No matter though, as the third single, power ballad "When the Children Cry," followed and received an overwhelmingly tremendous response on both radio and MTV.

The soft, contemplative track was somewhat atypical for a rock ballad, as its subject matter wasn't focused on love or relationships but instead conveyed a remorseful lament that future generations of children would sadly have to bear the brunt of a harsh world shaped by the wars and fighting nations of current times. Despite the unconventional lyrics, "When The Children Cry" soared to the No. 3 on the charts and helped push *Pride* to sales in excess of two million copies and a full-year stay on the Billboard Albums chart.

Lastly, 1987 saw the self-titled debut album of Sunset Strip stalwarts **Faster Pussycat** (named after a Russ Meyer sexploitation film). Hailing from the same breeding ground as Guns N' Roses, Faster Pussycat offered up a brand of hair metal that was equal parts sleaze, metal, and punk, but contained plenty of melodic hooks as well. The album was released the same week as *Appetite for Destruction*, and while it wouldn't go on to experience the same enormous level of success, it quickly became a genre classic. Featuring the uniquely sleazy vocals of lead singer Taime Downe, the record produced the fan-favorite single "Bathroom Wall," along with the entertaining "Don't Change That Song" and rollicking "Cathouse."

Other noteworthy albums released in 1987: Great White *(Once Bitten)*, Dokken *(Back for the Attack)*

All told, 1987 was an absolutely massive year for hair metal and produced three of the best and biggest-selling albums not only of the era but in all of music history as well. Hair metal was now officially in the upper echelon of commercial popularity and success, a place it would continue to occupy and expand upon over the next four years.

Best Albums 1987

1. Guns N' Roses – *Appetite for Destruction (Top 5 in Genre!)*
2. Whitesnake – *Whitesnake (Top 10 in Genre!)*
3. Def Leppard – *Hysteria (Top 10 in Genre!)*
4. Mötley Crüe – *Girls, Girls, Girls*
5. Aerosmith – *Permanent Vacation*
6. White Lion – *Pride*
7. Faster Pussycat – *Faster Pussycat*

Chapter 9
Open Up and Say... Ahh!
(1988)

The hair metal party vigorously steamrolled into 1988, featuring a host of triumphant releases by several hair bands legitimately hitting their stride alongside a few welcomed newcomers to the scene as well.

Coming off the massive sixteen-month Slippery When Wet Tour, which ran from July 1986 to October 1987, **Bon Jovi** took a mere four weeks off before immediately getting back together in New Jersey to begin writing for their next album, attempting to both maintain their momentum and validate the success they experienced with *Slippery When Wet*. The band was determined to make an even bigger, *better* album, if you can imagine that.

By early 1988 Jon Bon Jovi and guitarist Richie Sambora had amassed more than thirty new songs, intending to make the new release a double-album titled *Sons of Beaches*. The record company, however, was dead set against the long format and wisely convinced them to trim the album down to a single disc featuring only the best-of-the-best songs. The band returned to Little Mountain Studio in Vancouver with Bruce Fairbairn and Bob Rock and went about the arduous task of culling down the list with the help of fan focus groups.

Twelve songs were eventually selected, and the new album was re-titled *New Jersey*, chosen to represent more than just the band's home-town geography, as Jon Bon Jovi stated, "It's more than just a place you're from . . . it's an attitude that you carry around with you."

From my view, *New Jersey* indeed seemed bigger and improved over *Slippery When Wet* in almost every way, from the writing to the production, performances, and overall variety and nuance of the songs.

The blasting album opener "Lay Your Hands on Me" featured one of the greatest slow-building, dramatic intros of any song from the era. The band intentionally designed the track to serve as a grand way to open their live shows, channeling two minutes of initial anticipation and excitement followed by an explosion of energy as the group hit the stage. It was the perfect launching off point for the record, which never let up from there forward, as practically every track was a winner.

"Bad Medicine" was the second track and the album's lead single. Opening with keyboards from David Bryant, the song jumped into a classic, pop-metal anthem with a perfect sing-along chorus. If Bon Jovi were looking to equal or better "You Give Love A Bad Name," they had succeeded. The song went to No. 1 on the Billboard Hot 100 chart, and its video served to make millions of girls swoon with desire.

"Born to Be My Baby" was the second single, possibly continuing Tommy and Gina's "trying to make it" story from *Slippery When Wet*'s "Livin' on a Prayer." (The fictional duo would definitively get a nod later into *New Jersey*, during the fun, upbeat rocker "99 In the Shade.") "Born to Be My Baby" featured another standout chorus and rocketed to No. 3 on the Billboard chart.

New Jersey also featured a couple of enormous power ballads, "Living in Sin," which broke the Top 10, and "I'll Be There for You," which went all the way to No. 1. These massive songs were everything power ballads were supposed to be in 1988, with the chorus on "I'll Be There for You" being, in particular, impossibly catchy.

All told, a whopping total of *five* songs from *New Jersey* breached the Top 10 on the Billboard chart! No other hard rock album had ever achieved such success, and none has ever equaled the mark since.

*New J*ersey was much more than just its singles, however, as perhaps the album's greatest song was never even officially released. "Blood on Blood," inspired by the hit film *Stand by Me*, was an epic, six-minute,

Springsteen-like story of lifelong friendship set up against a backdrop of massive guitars and soaring, emotionally-moving vocals. "Hometown Train" was another standout tune that saw Bon Jovi rocking perhaps harder than they ever had before. Possessing a legitimately metallic, hard rock sheen, the diverse song also featured both harmonicas and organs, while Sambora's guitar work was possibly his best effort on the album.

The record also included the haunting, mid-tempo "Wild is the Wind" and the inspirational, cowboy-themed, semi-ballad "Stick to Your Guns." Bon Jovi had first dabbled in Old West themes on *Slippery When Wet's* "Wanted Dead or Alive," and it would be a style Jon Bon Jovi, in particular, would continue to explore further in later years.

New Jersey spent an incredible *four consecutive weeks* at No. 1 on the Billboard Albums chart and stayed in the Top 200 for more than two years. The album sold seven million copies in the US and twelve million worldwide, figures that were short of *Slippery When Wet* but still a tremendous success. Bon Jovi supported the album with their massive New Jersey Syndicate Tour that spanned the globe and lasted into early 1990, finally concluding after a whopping 237 rocking performances. The five blue-collar guys from New Jersey had irrefutably cemented their status as kings of the pop-metal world, and hair metal had officially become a regular and accepted sight at the top of the commercial charts.

Poison, meanwhile, took the momentum they had established with 1986's *Look What The Cat Dragged In* and in 1988 achieved their own breakthrough moment with their high-spirited, energetic sophomore release, *Open Up and Say... Ahh!*.

For four guys fresh off living at poverty levels in L.A. who went straight to overnight national exposure following the MTV-debut of "Talk Dirty to Me," the task of assembling a hit second record seemed, at first, overwhelmingly daunting. It didn't help matters that the chosen producer for the album, Kiss-hero Paul Stanley, unexpectedly bowed out at the last minute.

Poison managed to catch a bit of good luck, however, when the seasoned Tom Werman agreed to step in and steer the ship. Werman had already worked with the likes of Mötley Crüe, Cheap Trick, and others, and was well-positioned to guide the young group. Poison was also elated to learn that, this time around, Capitol Records were more than happy to provide ample funding and studio time as opposed to the meager twelve days and $20,000 that had been allotted for *Look What the Cat Dragged In.*

Armed with a real budget and a capable producer, the self-appointed "Glam Slam Kings Of Noise" rose to the challenge and went about putting together a fresh batch of wild, sordid, party tunes. *Open Up and Say... Ahh!* was released with much anticipation from fans on May 3, 1988, but quickly hit turbulence right out of the gate.

Several major retailers initially refused to stock the record due to what they perceived as indecent cover art. A non-event by modern standards but scandalous at the time due to intense scrutiny by groups like the PMRC (Parents Music Resource Center, formed in 1985 and hell-bent on destroying heavy metal), the album cover featured a cartoonish, devilish-looking vixen with a long, curved tongue. Poison quickly adjusted the picture to hide the extended tongue and blackout everything other than the she-demon's eyes.

With Poison back in business at retail, the music promptly took over from there. *Open Up and Say... Ahh!* was perhaps the ultimate party, completely unapologetic with regard to its hedonistic lyrics and brash musical tone. Bassist Bobby Dall once said, "I didn't want to be a musician growing up, I wanted to be a *rock star*... and that is exactly what I became." That pretty much summed it up as Poison unleashed an album of blistering, decadent, good-time party songs filled with catchy hooks and C.C. DeVille's flamboyant, over-the-top guitar solos. For fans of hair metal, it was no less than glorious.

The record's opening track, "Love on the Rocks," quickly set the tone, launching with an ear-splitting riff and offering the opening verses:

She goes down slow like a shot of gin
She's got an angel's face and a devil's grin
She kinda' stared me down as I looked her up
She said I'm your poison now you drink a cup

Only Poison, it seemed, could offer up such phrasings in such good taste.

The album continued its assault with "Nothin' But a Good Time," the record's second track and first single released to radio, which rose to No. 6 on the Billboard chart. The song's iconic video received ample play on MTV, its famous opening scene depicting a rebellious youth slaving away in the back of a restaurant and getting yelled at by his boss before finally kicking out the back door and (naturally) joyously escaping to an elaborate Poison concert. You can imagine the rest. "Nothin' But a Good Time" was an instant hair metal classic that just possibly summed up everything the entire era stood for in a concise (but extravagant) four minutes.

The second single, "Fallen Angel," was another smash hit and my personal favorite on the album. The driving guitar riff and infectious chorus accompanied lyrics relating the story of a small-town girl who headed off to Hollywood seeking fame and fortune, but alas, times were tougher than she anticipated. The tale drew on the band's personal experiences and was certainly not entirely disconnected from the lives of many who found their way to the famed Sunset Strip in the '80s. Despite the difficult times it conveyed, the song was spirited and upbeat, and of course, featured a blazing guitar solo by DeVille. "Fallen Angel" just missed the Top 10, peaking at No. 12 on the Billboard chart.

But as good as the first two singles were, it was really the record's third song released to radio that truly blew up the album and firmly established Poison as megastars. Regarded by many as perhaps *the* definitive power ballad of the hair metal era (and that's saying something, as there were literally hundreds of them), "Every Rose Has Its Thorn" delivered Poison a cherished No. 1 song. As the story goes, broken-hearted lead singer Bret Michaels wrote the tune in a run-down laundromat after phoning his long-distance girlfriend only to be dejected while overhearing a man's voice in the background.

Ironically, Poison had to fight for the hit song's inclusion on the album, as the record label initially felt the track was too "country" with its opening acoustic guitar, and the style was too severe of a departure from the band's rock 'n' roll calling card. Poison was convinced the track would work, though, and their insistence paid off as they wound up with one of the most recognizable songs of the entire era.

The album's fourth and final single was an exuberant, fired-up cover of the 1972 tune "Your Mama Don't Dance" by Kenny Loggins and Jim Messina, done in the one-and-only style of Poison, of course. Fun stuff for sure, and the song also broke the Top 10.

Similar to Bon Jovi's *New Jersey*, what was particularly impressive about *Open Up and Say... Ahh!* was the strength of the songs that *weren't* released as singles. Several of them could have likely been substituted and legitimately done just as well. The raucous "Back to the Rocking Horse," harmonica-driven "Good Love" and energetic "Look but Don't Touch" were all outstanding on their own and fit perfectly within the album's broader context.

Interestingly, *Open Up and Say... Ahh!* was the very first rock album to be recorded entirely digitally. Producer Tom Werman actually disliked the finalized sound of the album, believing it to be too sterile as a result of the technology. Certainly, the production was a little *thin* for lack of a better word, but for me, it fit the record just fine. And this is coming from someone who is an admitted audiophile when it comes to demanding first-class, full-sounding, beefy, dynamic production.

The simple reality was that most of the albums produced in the '80s were not very focused on bass and bottom-end anyway. The emphasis for rock music at the time was primarily centered on the guitar and vocals. Unfortunately, the format change from vinyl and cassette to compact disc in the early '90s brought out the worst in this approach. The initial technology for transferring analog tape to compact disc was relatively limited and often resulted in a very thin, overly "bright" sound that lacked the warmth and depth offered by vinyl recordings.

By the time computer science evolved to produce better results, many of the '80s original master tapes had been lost, destroyed, or simply degraded by time. Some of this unfortunate circumstance was rectified in the '00s with the emergence of "remastered" re-releases of albums originally recorded in the '80s and early '90s. Some of these remasters successfully brought back some of the missing bottom-end, but many simply increased the volume (resulting in a critical loss of dynamic range) as part of the so-called "loudness wars" that came about as a result of vying for attention on streaming services or digital downloads.

Nevertheless, despite any perceived limitations, the digital recording process pioneered on *Open Up and Say... Ahh!* certainly had no detrimental effect on its success, as the album was a magnificent hair metal marvel that would go on to sell more than ten million copies worldwide and produce four hit singles and videos. The record climbed all the way to No. 2 on the Billboard Albums chart, where it was blocked from the No. 1 spot week after week by Bon Jovi's *New Jersey*. Two hair metal albums at the top of the pop chart—yes, this really happened.

Open Up and Say... Ahh! was a record about Poison's hopes and dreams (even if those dreams were simply to party like rock stars), and with the album's success, all of their dreams came true. Poison landed the coveted opening slot on David Lee Roth's Skyscraper Tour and quickly graduated to headlining arenas on their own. Suddenly, four guys who just a year before were sleeping in laundromats and eating ramen noodles for dinner were kings of the world. Isn't hair metal great?

Another band that took a significant step forward on their sophomore record was **Cinderella**. Their 1986 debut, *Night Songs*, was a straightforward hard rock and heavy metal record and succeeded in bringing the band some initial success, but singer/songwriter Tom Keifer aspired to deeper depths the second time around.

In addition to pivoting his lyrics to subjects other than just girls and partying (no offense to Poison), Keifer wanted to start expanding Cinderella's musical offering, adding more orchestration and instrumentation, including acoustic and pedal steel guitars, pianos, and organs. He also desired to begin shifting more toward the blues elements that comprised an integral part of his musical roots.

Keifer's work resulted in Cinderella's second album, *Long Cold Winter*, released on May 21, 1988. The record was a substantial upgrade from the band's debut in every way, and despite sharing some inevitable similarities, it was also a decidedly *different* album, just as Keifer had intended. The songs were indeed more textured and diverse, although that didn't mean they rocked any less—in fact, quite the opposite in several places.

Lead track "Bad Seamstress Blues/Fallin' Apart at the Seams" surprisingly opened up the record with a twangy, country-tinged, southern swamp-groove before launching into a gigantic blues-metal anthem with a fist-pumping chorus. Pop-metal second track "Gypsy Road" was the album's first single and featured an uplifting, steady beat with yet another supremely catchy chorus.

The album included several other straight-ahead, quality rockers such as "Second Wind," "If You Don't Like It," and Fire and Ice," but the record especially shined on its more diverse material. "The Last Mile" was melodic pop-metal done to perfection, and the album's title track was an authentic, Led Zeppelin-esque, blues-rock number that spotlighted Keifer's impressive vocal chops. At the time, I remember listening to the song with a classically-trained musician-friend who was admittedly not the biggest fan of hair metal, and even she spoke up unsolicited during "Long Cold Winter" expressing a newfound appreciation for Keifer, stating, "now *that* is some impressive singing; that's not easy to do!"

What really caught the public's attention on *Long Cold Winter*, however, were the album's two hit ballads, "Coming Home" and "Don't Know What You Got (Till It's Gone)." Cinderella's power ballads always seemed to be a step up from the standard, generic template, and both on *Long Cold Winter* were no exception, each cracking the Top 20 on the

Billboard chart. Keifer just had a certain way of combining emotive, sentimental verses with broad, sweeping choruses, backed up by his raspy, powerhouse vocals. "Don't Know What You Got . . . " was a great example of this approach, while the sparkling "Coming Home" shined in its own right, possessing legitimate tinges of country music.

Lastly, "Take Me Back" ended the album with yet another super-catchy, riff-oriented, uplifting pop-metal song. *Long Cold Winter* was an impressive offering with no real weak spots top-to-bottom. The album sold in excess of three million copies and served to entrench Cinderella's status among the hair metal rock royalty of the era.

Kix had made significant strides on their third album, 1985's *Midnight Dynamite*, but had yet to experience any real, top-shelf success. Their situation would soon change for the better, however, with the band's superb 1988 release, *Blow My Fuse*. With Tom Werman on board to produce, Kix managed to retain all of their traditional hard rock sound but also seamlessly incorporated the pop hooks required to make the music fully accessible.

Steve Whiteman's vocals were spot-on to deliver good-times party rock, and the album featured a host of blistering, pounding rock anthems with singalong choruses to match. Standouts included "Red Lite, Green Lite, TNT," "Get It While It's Hot," "No Ring Around Rosie," and the thumping title track "Blow My Fuse." Perhaps the very best offering on the album, though, was the glam, romping, infectious "Cold Blood," a perfect arena-anthem if there ever was one.

Still, despite all the album's terrific rock songs, *Blow My Fuse* achieved Platinum status primarily due to the record's one ballad (are you sensing a trend?), the heartfelt and haunting "Don't Close Your Eyes." With lyrics delivering an anti-suicide plea rather than the standard love-song fare, the powerful track reached No. 11 on the Billboard Hot 100 chart, finally giving Kix their first real taste of victory. As Whiteman would later joke, "it gave Casey Kasem a reason to say 'Kix' on the radio!"

All kidding aside, though, "Don't Close Your Eyes" emerged to be one of the most poignant and respected power ballads of the decade.

Ironically, the band hadn't originally intended to release the popular song as a single. Kix was on tour with Great White when the latter group's manager Alan Niven stumbled across the brilliant track and bewilderingly inquired why it hadn't been sent to radio yet. Niven zealously called up the president of Atlantic Records and told him he had a massive hit on his hands if he would just release it. The rest was history.

🤘

Van Halen returned in 1988 with their second offering with lead singer Sammy Hagar, playfully titled *OU812* (taken from the humorous license plate of a delivery truck). The new album was perhaps a more diverse effort than *5150* and continued Van Halen's trend at the time of heavily incorporating keyboards and synthesizers into the mix alongside Eddie's huge guitar licks.

Fans have mixed feelings on *OU812*'s rank in the band's catalog, but for me, the record was a step down from *5150*, a little too varied and inconsistent, and everywhere it tried to do what *5150* did, while it wasn't bad, it just simply wasn't as good. The big, huge, rock sound, along with anthems like "Dreams," or "Best Of Both Worlds," just wasn't there.

Perhaps most troubling was the album's ultra-thin production (particularly exposed on compact disc format). There was practically no bottom-end or bass to be heard at all, and several of the songs seemed to lack any real teeth as a result. It was a shame, as with bigger and better production, many of the tracks could have legitimately come alive into real standouts.

OU812 possibly stands toe-to-toe with Metallica's *And Justice For All...*, ZZ Top's *Afterburner*, and Billy Idol's *Whiplash Smile* as some of the '80s rock albums most desperately in need of a proper remix and remaster to resolve the lack of bass. The driving, opening track "Mine All Mine" was a perfect example. While lacking a standout chorus, the unique synthesizer and keyboard-driven song featured deep, metaphysical lyrics and could have packed a real punch if there was any discernible "thump" whatsoever.

Of course, hardcore Van Halen fans were less-than-thrilled when the first ballad wasted no time popping up as the album's second track. "When It's Love" was a great song, and to its credit had a little edge in certain places, but it was still a sugary, power-pop ballad coated with keyboards and a far cry from classic Van Halen output like "Unchained." Nevertheless, "When It's Love" went all the way to No. 5 on radio and was a huge hit.

OU812 did include a few genuinely explosive rockers that harked back to "old Van Halen" to some extent (particularly with the brilliance of Eddie's blistering guitar work), such as "A.F.U. (Naturally Wired)," "Sucker In A 3 Piece," and "Source of Infection," but for the most part, each just seemed to be lacking a certain "something" that would've put them over the top as proper knockouts.

Ironically, the album's brightest moments were found on some of its most unconventional songs (at least in terms of comparison to the band's history). "Finish What Ya Started" was an acoustic, country-tinged, blues track that was catchy enough to hit No. 13 on the Billboard chart. The song was the last written for the album as *OU812* was basically finished when a drunk Eddie sought out Hagar late one night at 2 a.m. to play him "this great riff I'm working on!"

Elsewhere, there was the terrific, extremely radio-friendly "Feels So Good," which, like "When It's Love," was primarily keyboard-driven but even more pop-oriented in nature. Again, hardcore fans objected to the style change, but was the song really any more "pop" than "Dance the Night Away" from *Van Halen II* a decade earlier?

Lastly was the seven-minute, mid-tempo epic "Cabo Wabo," Van Halen's first foray into a song of that length. Just prior to the album's completion, Hagar had taken a couple of weeks off and set up camp at his residence in Cabo San Lucas to work on the last remaining uncompleted lyrics. The resort city, located on the southern tip of Mexico's Baja California peninsula, is best known for its beaches, water-based activities, and nightlife. The idyllic setting served to inspire Hagar's tribute to the location, which he had grown to love. As the lyrics went:

There's a sleepy town south of the border
You go there once you'll be there twice

The song's title originated from Hagar observing tourists having a good time stumbling around the city in drunken states, doing what he termed the "Cabo Wobble," later adopted to "Cabo Wabo." The grooving, infectious tune is my personal favorite on *OU812.* In later years, Hagar would go on to make Cabo his second home, opening to enormous success the first of his famous Cabo Wabo Cantinas that hosts his gigantic annual birthday bash.

Aside from any musical or production weak spots, commercially, *OU812* was a massive triumph going straight to No. 1 on the Billboard Albums chart and selling over five million copies. Over the years, I have come to appreciate the album a little more than when it was first released, but while it has some objectively great moments, the record still remains a somewhat inconsistent platter plagued by poor production.

Still, *OU812* was a smash hit at the time, and everything was firing on all cylinders in the Van Halen camp as far as chemistry and cohesiveness. Sadly, the good times for Van Halen would not last forever, but in 1988, Van Halen remained firmly rooted among the kings of the rock music world.

Of course, not to be outpaced or outdone by his former bandmates, **David Lee Roth** also dropped a new album in 1988. However, unlike with his debut, *Eat 'Em and Smile*, the new record, titled *Skyscraper,* would take a decidedly different turn musically and hit a few bumps along the way.

Many hardcore Van Halen fans had sided with Roth after comparing the commercial pop-tendencies of *5150* to the blistering, guitar-driven rockers on *Eat 'Em and Smile*, identifying with him as the biggest detractor of Van Halen's attempt to incorporate synthesizers and keyboards during his time in the band. It was highly ironic and somewhat bizarre then to find that *Skyscraper* was *filled* with synthesizers and keyboards. What was Roth thinking?

Perhaps he was thinking about commercial success, as *Skyscraper*'s synth-driven, ultra-poppy lead single "Just Like Paradise" turned out to be a massive hit, breaking into the Top 10 on radio. And to be clear, it was a *great* song, irresistibly fun as only "Diamond Dave" could deliver. The issue was, it just wasn't what many longtime Van Halen fans were searching for.

Skyscraper as a whole was a different kind of animal versus *Eat 'Em and Smile*—not only synthesizer and keyboard-heavy but also exceedingly experimental in places and lacking the previous album's aggressive guitar tone. Where the guitars actually *were* present, they were robbed of their impact by a thin, overly compressed production, ironically similar to the punch-less sound of *OU812*.

Whereas *Eat 'Em and Smile* was basically recorded "live" in the studio, *Skyscraper* was pieced together bit-by-bit using the latest digital technology of the time. The results, unfortunately, proved sterile and harsh in many places, lacking the excitement and power of either *Eat 'Em and Smile* or historical Van Halen.

Bassist Billy Sheehan was so frustrated with the approach that he quickly departed the band after recording was finished. Steve Vai unquestionably delivered an inspired, extraordinary guitar performance on many songs, but it was just a little too unfamiliar and a tad too eclectic for the taste of the average rock fan. Complicated, intricate songs like "Hina" and the pseudo-psychedelic "Skyscraper" were inherently impressive for what they were, but the impact was lost on many listeners absent of traditional hooks and melodies. Vai stuck around for the album's tour, but like Sheehan, also wound up leaving the band shortly after, citing "creative differences."

All that said, *Skyscraper* did, in fact, contain a few notable highlights.

It was almost impossible not to love the aforementioned "Just Like Paradise," and the terrific, slow-paced, nostalgic "Damn Good" was a fantastic acoustic number that sentimentally reflected on Roth's "good old days." I was also convinced "Hot Dog and a Shake" and "Knucklebones" were actually great songs that were just hidden behind horrible production. And of course, Roth's lyrics and vocals were classic "Dave" throughout the album, which was always a good thing to this listener.

Roth's aspirations for *Skyscraper* were admirable, but the combination of synthesizers, experimentation, poor production, and just plain "misses" ("Stand Up," "Perfect Timing") made it somewhat of a disappointment. Still, the combination of "Just Like Paradise," Roth's God-like status, and the fact that practically nothing could derail the hair metal train at the time resulted in *Skyscraper* selling more than two million copies and rising all the way to No. 6 on the Billboard Albums chart. Roth was still king (for the time), and the battle with Van Halen raged on.

The year 1988 also brought new hair metal blood to the table, featuring debut albums from three bands that would firmly establish themselves as significant players in the genre: L.A. Guns, Britny Fox, and Winger.

L.A. Guns were a Hollywood-based hard rock/glam metal band featuring guitar-king Tracii Guns, who had formed the first version of the group back in 1983, only to merge with competitors Hollywood Rose in early 1985 to launch the first incarnation of Guns N' Roses. Guns would leave Guns N' Roses just a few months after, however, as he and Axl Rose couldn't manage to see eye to eye.

Guns would reform L.A. Guns later that year, and after a few lineup changes, the group would go on to become a popular fixture on the Sunset Strip. Their debut album was mostly already written in 1987 when the band signed with major label Polygram Records and parted ways with then-vocalist Paul Black (at the label's "suggestion"). They then teamed up with British singer Phil Lewis (formerly of the band Girl), and L.A.

Guns' eponymous debut album was released on January 4, 1988.

The sound of *L.A. Guns* fit like a glove on the Los Angeles hair metal scene. It was raw, dirty, aggressive and sleazy, but still retained ample pop-sensibilities. Although the album failed to achieve the same level of massive commercial success similar to some of the band's contemporaries, it did produce a few classic songs, including "Sex Action," "One More Reason," and the motorcycle-nomad-inspired "Electric Gypsy." The album as a whole was lauded by fans and critics alike for brilliantly balancing heavy metal with catchy hooks and punk undercurrents. *L.A. Guns* did manage to get certified Gold and spent thirty-three weeks on the Billboard Albums chart, peaking at No. 50.

Also debuting in 1988 was **Winger,** hailing from the opposite side of the country in New York City. The band featured singer and bassist Kip Winger, who had formally studied classical music and composition since the age of sixteen and already played on two Alice Cooper albums prior to forming Winger. Also on board were virtuoso guitarist and Berkley College of Music graduate Reb Beach, accomplished keyboardist Paul Taylor, and prior rock-fusion drummer Rod Morgenstein. The group initially went by the name Sahara but later changed to Winger at the suggestion of Alice Cooper. (If you look closely, you can see the word "Sahara" etched in small print on Winger's debut album cover.)

Winger's self-titled debut was somewhat of a mixed bag, with a few great songs intertwined among others that were a tad generic. The album's style appeared as straightforward pop-metal on the surface, but a deeper listen revealed Winger sneaking in a few more progressive tricks here and there, a trend they would expand further upon as their career progressed.

On the plus side, the album's three singles were particularly impressive. "Madalaine" started the record off with an acoustic intro before launching into a pumping rocker featuring some fantastic shredding by Beach. "Seventeen," meanwhile, was a super-catchy rock anthem with a huge chorus and popular video that drove the song up to

No. 25 on the Billboard chart. While the lyrics gave the appearance of standard fare '80s hair metal, the song's musical structure was actually quite complex. Also boasting a more intricate and textured shape was the hit ballad "Heading for a Heartbreak," with its markedly moody atmosphere and dramatic keyboard parts.

The rest of the album was fairly straightforward, with a few surprises sprinkled in such as the orchestral string arrangement that introduced album opener "Hungry." Winger would expose more of their pedigree and substance on future albums but were happy to play it pretty straight on their debut.

Spurred by the singles, *Winger* reached No. 21 on the Billboard Albums chart and was certified Platinum with sales of more than one million copies. It didn't hurt that Kip Winger's cover-model good looks were all over MTV, fully swaying and swooning the female component of the band's audience. Winger forced themselves into a prominent position among the hair metal bands of the time and were even nominated for an American Music Award for "Best New Heavy Metal Band" in 1990.

One more notable debut act in 1988 also originated on the East Coast: the boisterous **Britny Fox,** from Philadelphia, Pennsylvania. The band's style was brazenly full-blown hair metal, featuring the soaring, screeching AC/DC-style vocals of lead singer "Dizzy" Dean Davidson. Their self-titled debut resonated well with fans of the genre, selling over one million copies propelled by the popular singles "Girlschool" and "Long Way to Love." The album also featured a cool cover of Slade's "Gudbuy T'Jane." The remainder of the record was relatively standard, but Britny Fox fortuitously scored a sought-after opening slot touring with Poison and quickly built up a loyal fanbase from which they would expand upon in the coming years.

Toward the end of 1988, **Ratt** released their fourth album in as many years, titled *Reach for the Sky.* While somewhat lackluster in many areas as Ratt's songwriting evolution had become a little stale and the band was seemingly going through the motions in some spots, the record did contain the impressive hits "I Want a Woman" and "Way Cool Jr.," in addition to the gritty "City to City." *Reach for the Sky* managed to go Platinum but disappointingly did not live up to the sales of Ratt's prior releases.

Guns N' Roses closed out the year by putting out the EP *G N' R Lies* in December 1988, as their management and record label attempted to maintain the band's momentum stemming from mega-album *Appetite for Destruction.* The new record was a mix of older, unreleased material combined with four new acoustic recordings.

Side One of *G N' R Lies* (the first four songs) was really just the independent EP *Live ?!*@ Like A Suicide* Guns N' Roses had released prior to *Appetite* in 1986 (although that wasn't common knowledge to the average fan at the time, as *Live ?!*@ Like A Suicide* had generated virtually no commercial noise at all at the time of its release). It is worth noting the band later freely admitted the songs were not actually recorded live as postured, with the crowd noise dubbed on top of studio recordings for artificial effect.

The "live" recordings featured two raw, early GN'R originals that didn't make the cut while *Appetite* was being assembled ("Reckless Life" and "Move to the City"), along with cover versions of Rose Tattoo's "Nice Boys" and Aerosmith's "Mama Kin," which often closed out the band's live sets back when they were regulars on the Sunset Strip.

Side Two contained four newly recorded acoustic tracks, one of which was a slowed-down reimaging of "You're Crazy," which appeared in a faster electric version on *Appetite for Destruction.* (Truthfully, the more measured version was actually the *original* format of the song when first written; it was later sped up to better fit the overall style of *Appetite.*) Rumor had it the new tracks were put together in only a few sessions and recorded in just one afternoon.

Of the remaining three newly written songs, "Used To Love Her" was a jokey, upbeat number that contained dark-humor lyrics (the full chorus was "I used to love her—but I had to kill her") that either fictitiously referenced one of the band member's ex-girlfriend or represented a real-life recount about Axl's since-deceased dog, depending on who you believed. "Patience," however, was a much more sincere effort. The slow, somber ballad featured love-letter lyrics and possessed a quiet, simple authenticity that reflected a gentler side of Guns N' Roses that had not previously been made available to the public. The track was released as the album's only single and rose to No. 4 on the Billboard Hot 100 chart.

Disappointingly, the last of the new songs and album closer "One in a Million" was marred for many by lyrics that were laced with racism and homophobia. Axl Rose wrote the song solo and claimed he meant no offense being neither a racist nor anti-gay, but instead was only trying to reflect upon specific situations. Nevertheless, the song generated a tremendous amount of debate and controversy.

G N' R Lies served its purpose, however, selling more than five million copies and proving the record label correct that demand for all things Guns N' Roses at the time was so high given the mega-success of *Appetite for Destruction*, the band probably could have released an album of children's lullabies and it still would have sold millions of units.

For fans looking for a continuation of what *Appetite* offered, though, the new release wasn't exactly what they were seeking. Little did everyone know, it would take almost three more long years for Guns N' Roses to release the true follow-up to *Appetite for Destruction*, but more on that later.

Other noteworthy albums released in 1988: Queensrÿche (*Operation: Mindcrime)*, Lillian Axe *(Lillian Axe)*, Lita Ford *(Lita)*, Bulletboys *(Bulletboys)*

The year 1988 was another colossal victory for hair metal, featuring two of the top five releases of the era in addition to several other noteworthy albums from both veterans and newcomers alike. But there was still much more to come, as 1989 would astonishingly prove to be even bigger.

Best Albums 1988

1. Poison – *Open Up and Say… Ahh! (Top 5 in Genre!)*
2. Bon Jovi – *New Jersey (Top 5 in Genre!)*
3. Cinderella – *Long Cold Winter (Top 25 in Genre!)*
4. Kix – *Blow My Fuse*
5. Van Halen – *OU812*
6. L.A. Guns – *L.A. Guns*

Chapter 10
Dr. Feelgood
(1989)

While the year 1989 saw hair metal continue to dominate the musical landscape at possibly its peak potency, it was unique perchance for the sheer volume of *new* bands that jumped on the scene, issuing their first albums in hopes of catching a ride on hair metal's success-train. No fewer than twenty notable debut records all found some level of achievement, ranging from a hit single all the way up to selling several million copies. There were also roughly a dozen new sophomore hair metal albums, each mostly representing a significant step up in quality from their predecessors released between 1986 and 1988. Further, and perhaps most significantly, three of the genre's heavy-weight veterans came back with fresh new records in 1989, each of which represented a critical landmark for the era. The most notable of these latter releases was from none other than Mötley Crüe.

Mötley Crüe had released the commercially successful *Girls, Girls, Girls* album in 1987, but other than the awesome title track, "Wild Side," and a few other noteworthy moments, the record fell short in many ways. The Crüe then basically imploded at the end of the year, as escalating drug and alcohol addictions alongside a never-ending appetite for excess and debauchery essentially drove them into the ground, forcing the early cancellation of their tour. Mötley Crüe, as constituted at the time, were clearly in no shape to continue forward, and no one close to the band would have been even remotely surprised if they had simply faded away, or even died—hell, Nikki Sixx *did* die!

However, in 1988, perhaps motivated by Sixx's dalliance with death or merely responding to their management's overwhelming decree that they clean up their act, each band member formally enrolled in rehab and emerged in 1989 clean and sober for the very first time.

Renewed, re-energized, and focused, Mötley Crüe took up temporary residence at Little Mountain Studios in Vancouver with producer Bob Rock and proceeded to relegate themselves to a strict, regimented, and clean work environment. The studio was no longer simply a place to "party." Rock proceeded to put Mötley through the paces as never before with regard to songwriting quality and performance perfection. The process proved arduous, challenging, and frustrating at times, but the band was committed to delivering something special.

Regarding Mötley's mood during those sessions, Nikki Sixx reflected, "We all said, 'Look, we either have to get it together and become the biggest band in the world, or we're going to knock this thing on the head and go out with more fury than anyone has ever hit the music business with.'"

The new approach and the band's dedication wound up paying off in a big way, as the completed album, titled *Dr. Feelgood*, dropped on September 1, 1989, and hit No. 1 on the Billboard Albums chart just a few weeks later, giving Mötley Crüe their hard-earned, very first No. 1 record.

Dr. Feelgood started with the short, atmospheric intro "T.n.T. (Terror 'n Tinseltown)," setting a fierce, ominous mood before crashing into the bombastic, thumping title track "Dr. Feelgood," which served as the record's first single. Right out of the gate, the first thing that hit the listener was simply how "huge" the album sounded in terms of drums and bottom-end. Indeed, the drum sound Rock managed to capture was one of the very best ever achieved for a heavy rock album. In fact, Metallica sought out Bob Rock to produce their famous self-titled 1991 "Black Album" based solely on the production sound they admired on *Dr. Feelgood*.

"Dr. Feelgood" was an uncompromising hard rock monster that laid down the heavy foundation from which the album would lay waste. The song hit No. 6 on the Billboard chart (a new high for the band) and was followed by no fewer than *four* additional hit singles/videos. "Kickstart My Heart" was a rowdy, punk-based, speed metal anthem with a shout-along chorus built perfectly for arena shows. The song's lyrics were partially inspired by Sixx's earlier near-death experience, when he was revived from an overdose after paramedics jammed two adrenaline needles directly into his heart.

The obligatory power ballad "Without You" followed as the third single and also broke the Top 10. Sixx wrote the lyrics in reference to the adoring relationship between Crüe-drummer Tommy Lee and his then-wife, TV-superstar Heather Locklear. The melodic "Don't Go Away Mad (Just Go Away)" dropped next, featuring a pleasant, pop-based first half followed by a ramped-up, hard rock finish. The song topped out at No. 13. "Same Ol' Situation (S.O.S.)" rounded out the last of the album's singles as a catchy, pop-metal, hard rock masterpiece, with lyrics relating the story of a guy's girlfriend breaking up with him to be with another girl, of course.

The strength of *Dr. Feelgood* wasn't just its singles, however. Each of the record's "album tracks" also offered up their own unique blend of hair metal might. In fact, while recording the album, Mötley had felt certain the infectious rocker "Rattlesnake Shake" might just be the crown jewel of the bunch and had clearly envisioned it as the "hit single." The song was never issued to radio (for whatever reason), but I imagine it would have been a sizable success had it been formally released, as the tune offered another huge, irresistible chorus, and even featured an appealing horn section intertwined among its blazing guitar parts.

"Slice of Your Pie," meanwhile, was a powerful, burning stomper that featured an extended, trippy outro by guitarist Mick Mars based on the Beatles' song "She's So Heavy." And "Sticky Sweet" was a grooving, sleazy rocker that included backing vocals by Aerosmith's Steven Tyler. Ironically, Aerosmith had been working in the same studio as Mötley

Crüe at the time, recording their massive opus *Pump*. The two bands bonded (or commiserated, depending on who you asked and when) over their shared, newly found sobriety after years of drug and alcohol abuse.

Dr. Feelgood was unquestionably one of the landmark albums of the hair metal era. It sold six million copies in the US, featured five hit singles (two of which earned Grammy nominations), and won Best Hard Rock/Heavy Metal Album at the American Music Awards. The record definitively established Mötley Crüe as the clear rulers of the hard rock hill at the time. *Dr. Feelgood* is easily one of my absolute favorite albums, and if you were to remove "Without You" and substitute "Primal Scream" from Mötley's impending 1991 *Decade of Decadence* compilation in its place (which can easily be done in this age of digital playlists), the result could very well be my favorite album ever.

The success of *Dr. Feelgood* spurred a massive two-year world tour during which Mötley Crüe uncharacteristically (mostly) operated like a well-oiled machine, rocking millions of satisfied fans around the globe (I, personally, vividly recall the incredible show to this day). Success for the group, however, would come in the form of a double-edged sword to some extent, as the grueling twenty-four-month tour resulted in inevitable burnout and band tensions that would later come back to haunt them.

Still, in 1989, Mötley Crüe had finally reached the peak of the mountain after ten years surviving a series of ups and downs that would have easily put most bands out of the game, if not six feet under. With *Dr. Feelgood*, the Crüe were the new undisputed kings of the hair metal world.

The aforementioned **Aerosmith** was another genre heavyweight to drop an amazing new album in 1989. Fresh off their newfound sobriety and return to commercial prominence and success with 1987's *Permanent Vacation*, the excited band quickly went back to work in 1988 just as soon as the album's tour had ended. They felt as confident and invigorated as ever going into the writing sessions for the new record, and lead singer

Steven Tyler was convinced the group could take the music to a whole other level.

Aerosmith sought to get much closer to their core sound and roots this time around, while still incorporating the radio-friendly elements that had made *Permanent Vacation* such an outright success. Holed up in Vancouver, in the studio adjacent to Mötley Crüe, they prolifically laid down a ton of new material that was then surgically culled down to just the gems with the help of producer Bruce Fairbairn. The band emerged with the spectacular *Pump* in September 1989. The album's title was, in part, a reference to how "pumped up" the group felt now that they were clean and sober and how thrilled they were with the new songs.

Pump blasted out of the gates with a terrific trio of hard-driving, sleazy rockers, serving as a quick one-two-three punch that was tough to beat. The lively opening number "Young Lust" chugged along at a frenetic pace prior to wrapping up with a riotous drum solo that merged directly into the impressive, hard rock second track, "F.I.N.E." (abbreviated for 'Fucked-Up, Neurotic, Insecure, Emotional'). But it was the third song and the first single "Love in an Elevator" that really launched the album into the stratosphere. The tongue-in-cheek, hip-swaying, groovy rocker hit No. 5 on the Billboard chart, and the tune's video was an absolute smash on MTV.

Pump wasn't all sex and hard sleazy rock, however. The album's biggest singles alongside "Love in an Elevator," both Top 10 hits, were the ballad "What It Takes" and the dark, serious, mid-tempo "Janie's Got a Gun." "What It Takes" wasn't exactly a traditional hair metal power ballad, but, in fact, was actually closer to a country song. While it was a good tune, and Aerosmith would come to be (overly) dependent on ballads in the near future, at the time, the track was almost seen as a necessary evil. "I'll put some ballads on an album," Tyler remarked, "if that's what it takes so that some young kid can get to hear a 'Young Lust' or 'F.I.N.E.'."

It was "Janie's Got a Gun," however, that was the album's highest-charting single at No. 4 and received most of the attention, standing out as something unique in the Aerosmith catalog and resonating sharply with both fans and critics alike. The haunting song dealt with the tragic topic of child abuse and told the poignant story of a victim who chose to fight back. "Janie's Got a Gun" would go on to win Aerosmith a Grammy award for Best Rock Performance.

Pump also had a few other standout songs as well, several of which were tied together by brief musical interludes sonically connecting the tracks and giving the whole album a delightful, natural, organic flow. "The Other Side" was a sparkling pop-rocker that also became a hit single, "Hoodoo/Voodoo Medicine Man" was heavy, spooky and ominous, and "Monkey on My Back" was a terrific groover that warned of the dangers of drug addiction.

If *Permanent Vacation* served to reintroduce Aerosmith as a commercial entity with which to be reckoned, *Pump* succeeded in reestablishing the band in all of their bluesy, hard rock glory. The album was an enormous success, reaching No. 5 on the Billboard Albums chart and selling over seven million copies. Aerosmith had fully completed their comeback and improbably managed to achieve a level of popularity that not only matched but surpassed what they had accomplished in the '70s.

The third big veteran act to release a new album in 1989 was the newly hair metal-minted **Whitesnake**. The *Whitesnake* album had finally broken the band big in the US, but not long after its release, the group that recorded it was surprisingly shown the door by ringmaster and lead singer David Coverdale. In particular, Coverdale had experienced a significant falling out with guitarist John Sykes, who notably co-wrote all of the album's material.

Coverdale recruited an entirely new lineup to tour *Whitesnake*, including guitarists Adrian Vandenberg and Vivian Campbell, bassist Rudy Sarzo and drummer Tommy Aldridge. The same group then came back together in 1989 to begin developing songs for a follow-up record. The initial sessions went fine enough, but just before recording was scheduled to commence, Coverdale had a combative spat with Campbell ("artistic differences") leading to his departure, and Vandenberg suffered an unfortunate injury to his wrist, rendering him temporarily unable to play guitar. Once again, Coverdale found himself without a full band just as he was about to record an album.

Faced with pressure from the record company to finish the project, Coverdale promptly recruited guitarist Steve Vai into the fold, who was fresh off his tenure in David Lee Roth's solo band. Vai was undoubtedly a capable virtuoso guitarist, but a curious choice as his technique and style at the time lent itself more toward the flamboyant and flashy versus the meat-and-potatoes blues-rock for which Whitesnake had been known.

Vandenberg, before his injury, had co-written all of the new material with Coverdale and admittedly wondered how Vai's contrasting style would translate to the songs. Still, Whitesnake had undeniably already started to veer off the blues-based, '70s-rock course with the *1987* album, so perhaps the fit wouldn't be as unintuitive as some surmised.

The new album was titled *Slip of the Tongue*, and the record was finally released on November 18, 1989. The songs definitely proved to be in stark juxtaposition versus the sound Whitesnake had come to be known for prior to 1987, full of all the overabundance and excessive elements hair metal was famous for, made all the more so by Vai's lavish guitar pyrotechnics. That said, it was perhaps a perfect record for its time, even if for some fans it was too much of a change and for others it hasn't aged as well as more traditional Whitesnake albums.

The record detonated right out of the gate with the exploding, overblown production of the intense, vibrant title track, "Slip of the Tongue." Coverdale's vocals were in peak form (and particularly sky-high), and Vai's guitar playing was precisely as advertised—showy and flaming, chock-full of splashy effects and intricate fills (but admittedly brilliant).

As stated, the music fit the hard rock style of the times seamlessly. There were massive rockers such as "Cheap An' Nasty" and "Fool for Your Loving '89," a wildly improved upon, beefed-up version of the song first featured on Whitesnake's 1980 *Ready An' Willing* album. And, of course, there were the ballads, "Now You're Gone" and "The Deeper the Love," both tremendous tracks that wound up being hit singles alongside "Fool for Your Loving."

Meanwhile, "Judgement Day" (the album's fourth single) was a moody, pulsing, Led Zeppelin-inspired rocker drenched in atmosphere, while songs like "Wings of the Storm" were more intricate in composition. Not to be left out, "Sailing Ships" was a positively beautiful ballad that built slowly from an acoustic foundation, ascending to a full-blown corker to close out the album.

While *Slip of the Tongue* failed to equal the commercial success of *1987*, it still sold over one million copies, charted in the Top 10, and served as the foundation for a massive world tour in support. Personally, I have always had a soft spot for the album, despite all of its uncharacteristic idiosyncrasies versus the band's historical output.

Outside of the three titans that were Mötley Crüe, Aerosmith, and Whitesnake, 1989 was notable for the vast number of new hair metal bands emerging on the scene eager to put their own hard rock stamp on the era. Some of these fresh acts managed to hit right away with multi-Platinum releases, while others still succeeded in placing at least one big hit single on the Billboard Top 40 chart as the launching point for their future hair metal tenure. Two of the best of these new bands were Skid Row and Warrant, both of whom were just getting started on a journey that would eventually see them graduate to the Hair Metal Hall of Fame in terms of the quality of their output and their influence and impact on the genre.

Similar to Bon Jovi, **Skid Row** hailed from New Jersey on the East Coast. In fact, Skid Row guitarist Dave "The Snake" Sabo was a good friend of Jon Bon Jovi and even a brief member of Jon's band in one of its very earliest incarnations. When Sabo formed Skid Row a few years later in 1987, Bon Jovi gladly did his old friend a favor, enlisting the aid of his management to help get Skid Row off the ground. Indeed, the band eventually signed-on with Bon Jovi's publishing and record companies.

Alongside Sabo, Skid Row was comprised of bassist Rachel Bolan, additional guitarist Scotti Hill, drummer Rob Affuso, and in their early stages, singer Matt Fallon, with Sabo and Bolan serving as the band's primary songwriters. Skid Row quickly parted ways with Fallon, however, and suddenly found themselves in need of a new frontman to help deliver their fiery songs.

Canadian-born singer Sebastian Bach was only nineteen years old at the time and playing in the Toronto-based band Kid Wikkid. As fate would have it, Bon Jovi's parents ran into Bach singing at a wedding and postulated the dynamic youth might be a good fit for the new band being formed by their son's friend. Bach was undoubtedly an egomaniac and possessed an ADHD-type personality to boot, but very few singers (if any) could match his combination of intensity, vocal range, and overall chops. He was also a natural frontman with the charisma to command full arenas of screaming fans. His pin-up-boy good looks would also serve to attract a large female audience to go along with the male metal-heads who would naturally gravitate to Skid Row's brand of hard rock.

Skid Row wound up sending Bach their demos, and the intrigued singer decided to fly to New Jersey for an audition. He was soon welcomed to the band and quickly went about lending his vocals to Skid Row's self-titled debut album, which with a few exceptions, was mostly already written at that point.

Recorded and produced by Michael Wagner (who had previously worked with Mötley Crüe, Poison, and others), *Skid Row* was a fierce hard rock assault. Many of the songs were decidedly heavier than the music contemporaries like Poison and Bon Jovi was producing, but still contained ample hooks and huge, fist-pumping choruses. The appropriately titled first single, "Youth Gone Wild," was perhaps the perfect illustration of this approach. More than just a great song, however, the track stood as a lyrical symbol for much of what the hair metal genre was all about. Indeed, Bach had the phrase tattooed on his forearm as a flaming, stamped emblem of unmistakable intent.

Skid Row was chock-full of heavy, catchy rockers that sought to blitz the listener with an intense, rock 'n' roll onslaught. Bach's soaring, snarling vocals and the sheer conviction of his delivery made the statement that much more powerful. "Here I Am," "Makin' a Mess," and "Sweet Little Sister" all packed a sizable punch. "Piece of Me" was another raging single that saw Bach openly challenging anyone bold or foolhardy enough to, well, try to get a piece of him.

Ironically, *Skid Row's big* hit singles were the two songs that were exceptions to the rule in terms of the album's overall style. The first was the spectacular "18 and Life," a magnificent semi-ballad that told the dark story of a rebellious teen sentenced to life in jail for an accidental shooting. The haunting song featured intense slower sections alternating with heavier segments, along with a chorus you couldn't forget if you tried. Bach's absolutely amazing vocals were what really turned the track into something special, though. The song went all the way to No. 4 on the Billboard chart.

And then there was the immense power ballad "I Remember You." Starting with gentle, acoustic verses before building into a dramatic rock landscape with soaring refrains, an irresistible chorus, and a blazing guitar solo, the love song featured yet another brilliant performance from Bach that ensured the song would fully recognize its potential. "I Remember You" went to No. 6 on the Billboard chart and was a huge smash hit, although ironically (and similar to "Home Sweet Home" and "Every Rose Has Its Thorn"), the track almost didn't make the album.

The song was written by Bolan and Sabo, but the duo quickly dismissed it as being too "wimpy" for the image and type of hard rock music they wanted to play and represent. Bach was perhaps the biggest metal-head of them all but still recognized a great song when he heard one. The singer fought hard for the track and convinced the band's manager Doc McGhee to check out the tune during rehearsals. McGhee was smart enough to spot a commercial cash cow when it was right in front of him and, upon hearing the tune, laughingly informed the band (against some of the member's wishes) the song was "definitely going on the album."

The combination of the two hit ballads, several catchy hard rock tunes, the twin metal-guitar attack of Sabo and Hill, and Bach's powerhouse vocals shot *Skid Row* to instant success, peaking at No. 6 on the Billboard Albums chart. The record sold over five million copies and scored heavy rotation on radio and MTV. Skid Row literally became an almost overnight sensation as the band was fortunate enough to land prime opening slots on the major tours of the time conducted by Aerosmith, Mötley Crüe, and Bon Jovi. The group also seemed to instantly appear on every other page in popular music magazines such as *Metal Edge*, *Hit Parader*, and *Circus*. Just like that, yet another hair metal band from New Jersey had officially hit the big time.

Warrant would also issue their debut album in 1989 and thenceforth go on to become a pillar of the hair metal establishment. Warrant originated from the country's opposite coast, where they had spent two hard years building the band into one of the most popular acts on the Sunset Strip L.A. club-scene circa 1987-1988. The group featured charismatic lead singer Jani Lane, whose distinctive voice and songwriting ability (Lane pretty much wrote 100 percent of the Warrant catalog) served to elevate the band's impact.

Warrant eventually signed with Columbia Records and released their debut album, *Dirty Rotten Filthy Stinking Rich* (also known simply as *D.R.F.S.R*), on January 31, 1989. Similar to Skid Row, the group was practically an instant overnight success upon the album's release. Warrant were a different flavor of hair metal than Skid Row, however, with more of a pop-metal or glam feel to their upbeat, catchy songs.

That's not to say the band couldn't "rock," though, as the marvelous lead single "Down Boys" showcased their ability to shape one of the era's most famous hard rock anthems. The song also served to provide the group's unofficial moniker.

Again, similar to Skid Row, *D.R.F.S.R.* was largely propelled to success based on the strength of the album's two ballads, "Heaven" and

"Sometimes She Cries," which hit No. 2 and No. 20 on the Billboard chart, respectively. "Heaven" in particular was placed in heavy rotation on radio and MTV, providing critical and much-needed exposure for the burgeoning new band.

Ironically, the initial success of "Heaven" managed to catch Columbia Records off-guard with its pants down. However, once the label realized the smash hit it had on its hands, the executives quickly (and unconventionally) ushered Warrant back into the studio to re-record it with a "bigger radio sound." The song's original version can be found on the initial pressing of the album's first 250,000 copies.

Outside of the singles, however, the remainder of the album's songs were more average, but there was just something about Lane's vocals and delivery, along with the overall flow and vibe of the record, that was uniquely special. The album was highly successful, cracking the Top 20 on the Billboard Albums chart.

Warrant was then off to the races, touring arenas with Poison, Mötley Crüe, and other big-time hair metal acts on their way toward even bigger things in the years to come.

🤘

In an even further contrast in style, 1989 featured the classic debut album by glam kings **Pretty Boy Floyd,** *Leather Boyz with Electric Toyz.* With all due respect to Poison, *Leather Boyz . . .* was undoubtedly the "glammest" hair metal album of them all. Unabashedly so, at that.

Pretty Boy Floyd was named after the infamous bank robber of the same moniker (Charles Arthur Floyd, nicknamed Pretty Boy Floyd), circa the 1920s. While many likely wrote the band off outright stemming from their over-the-top image or the album's ridiculous cover art, Pretty Boy Floyd managed to put out a record that would definitively become a cult-classic among fans of the genre. Indeed, it is quite possibly my personal absolute favorite guilty pleasure.

The album's pop-metal songs were exceedingly and irresistibly catchy in terms of melodies and hooks, along with an interwoven flavor of hard rock, glam, and heavy guitar. I defy anyone to listen to "48 Hours" and not find themselves unconsciously humming the chorus days later.

It was almost impossible to pick a favorite, but other standouts included "Leather Boyz with Electric Toyz," "Rock and Roll Outlaws," "Wild Angels," "Your Momma Won't Know," "Rock and Roll (Is Gonna Set the Night On Fire)," and the power ballad "I Wanna Be With You." The latter two songs had accompanying videos that made welcomed appearances on MTV, with "I Wanna Be With You" becoming a minor hit.

Lead vocalist Steve Summers is probably a love-him-or-hate-him type of option for many people given his unique stylings, but for me, his vocals perfectly suited the band's music, attitude, and style. Summers is the "voice of glam rock" as far as I am concerned.

The timeless album performed only modestly on the charts (it topped out at No. 130), but it splendidly provided the foundation from which Pretty Boy Floyd would operate for the next thirty years and counting, as of this writing.

The different styles and variations on the standard hair metal template kept coming with albums from new bands like Bang Tango, Electric Boys, Enuff Z' Nuff, Dangerous Toys, and Tora Tora. In truth, I'm not entirely convinced the distinctive tones these groups displayed necessarily wholly represented hair metal "variations," but rather likely reflected the reverse correlation that any music sounding even remotely similar to the hair metal standard at the time was simply homogenized and lumped under the same broader category. Nevertheless, each new offering was gladly treated as a much-welcomed addition to the family.

Bang Tango and Electric Boys were among the first to incorporate an authentic "funk" sound into hair metal. **Bang Tango** focused on the unique combination of funky rhythms and prominent bass lines overlapping with heavy, hard rock guitar riffs. The band featured the dual guitar attack of Kyle Stevens and Mark Knight alongside vocalist Joe

Lesté, who could sing (scream) with the absolute best of them.

Although the band had issued an in-concert EP titled *Live Injection* in 1987, they released their first official major label studio debut, *Psycho Café*, on May 29, 1989. The album roared out of the gate with the blistering "Attack of Life," followed by the second song and first single released to radio, "Someone Like You," which received reasonably heavy rotation on MTV and managed to thrust the album onto the Billboard Albums chart where it would peak at No. 58.

Other highlights included the hard rockers "Wrap My Wings" and "Breaking Up a Heart of Stone," along with the extra funky "Love Injection." Every song on the record was solid, and Bang Tango quickly gained the following and allegiance of a sizable segment of the hair metal audience. The album flat-out rocked, and there simply wasn't anything else that sounded like it at the time.

Electric Boys also cropped up with their own take on merging hard rock and heavy metal with funk, although distinctly different from Bang Tango. While Bang Tango combined funk with '80s-Hollywood glam metal, Electric Boys were more a fusion between funk and '70s retro rock. Their sound often included unique elements of pop and psychedelia, as well. Of course, being as it was 1989, the album also had its fair share of the hard rock and hair metal sounds typical of the times, for sure.

Electric Boys didn't originate from L.A. like most bands at the time but instead hailed from the far-reaching spaces of Sweden. Formed in 1988 and led by talented lead singer, guitarist, and songwriter Conny Bloom, the band released their debut album *Funk-O-Metal Carpet Ride* initially exclusive to Europe. The record was a relatively sizable success in their home country and the UK, primarily driven by the fantastic hit single "All Lips n' Hips."

To help launch the band in the US, however, famed producer Bob Rock was brought in to remix the album and give it a more polished, "big-sounding" feel. To ensure the record matched well with the music scene in America, Rock also felt a few songs from the original release should be substituted with new recordings. As a result, some of the more eclectic or "extra funky" songs (indeed, "Party Up" sounded more like Prince than he did himself) were removed in favor of fresh tracks that were slightly more in the L.A. hair metal vein.

Still, there was no changing the overall style or tone of the album, and like Bang Tango (but still different), there was truly nothing else similar to it at the time. And it was objectively pretty awesome. The first time I heard the captivating opening intro to "All Lips n' Hips" (played on an acoustic sitar-guitar of all things), I was certain Electric Boys were something special. Songs like "Psychedelic Eyes," "Rags to Riches," "Who Are You," and "Hallelujah! I'm On Fire" (with its chorus modeled after INXS' "Guns in the Sky") were simply outstanding.

In 2005, *Funk-O-Metal Carpet Ride* was remastered with superior sound and reissued in a deluxe format that included *all* songs from both the EU and US versions of the album—it is more than worth seeking out and picking up.

Despite my enthusiasm (both then and now) for the band, they failed to break big in the US despite MTV adopting "All Lips n' Hips" into favor. Still, the album would launch a series of terrific records from the group over the years. As of this writing in 2019, Electric Boys had just released a brand-new album of great songs, a testament to their talent and longevity.

Enuff Z' Nuff presented yet another distinct style. The group was a marriage between lead singer Donnie Vie and bassist Chip Z'Nuff, who complemented each other perfectly and combined to create a spectacular songwriting team. Many have written that Vie and Z'Nuff are the "Lennon & McCartney" of pop-metal, a flattering comparative I would certainly support. Enuff Z' Nuff unabashedly borrowed heavily from their heroes and influences: the Beatles, Cheap Trick, and David Bowie, among others. The band's music essentially answered the question: "what if the

Beatles played hard rock"?

Of course, again, as it was 1989, their record naturally marketed them as a hair metal band. Vie himself has stated on many occasions he never cared for the group's initial overly glam image and always saw Enuff Z' Nuff as more of a "power-pop" band versus heavy metal. Nevertheless, when their first video, "New Thing," hit MTV, the label made sure the band was decked out in full glam, surrounded by bright fluorescent colors, and wearing all the hairspray their heads could hold.

Image aside, the music was truly something special, mixing insanely catchy hooks with stick-in-your-head-for-days choruses. The pop-based undertones were then "metalized" via the elaborate electric guitar-work contributed by Derek Frigo. Both "New Thing" and the popular power ballad "Fly High Michelle" received steady airplay on MTV. Other personal favorites from Enuff Z' Nuff's 1989 self-titled debut album included the fantastic "For Now" and the boogie-woogie "Kiss the Clown."

The record charted at No. 67 on the Billboard Albums chart but failed to achieve the full commercial impact the band had envisioned. Still, Enuff Z' Nuff were on the board and would be back stronger than ever with their sophomore release in 1991.

Other debut albums issued in 1989 by bands that would go on to significant prominence in the hair metal era included three self-titled releases from Danger Danger, Extreme, and Mr. Big.

Danger Danger were the epitome of pop-metal and scored MTV hits with the sleazy "Naughty Naughty" and bright "Bang Bang." The album also featured the terrific, melodic, mid-tempo ballad "Don't Walk Away."

Extreme showcased the talents of gifted lead singer Gary Cherone and virtuoso guitarist Nuno Bettencourt, who many aptly compared to the great Eddie Van Halen, a fitting association while at the same time Bettencourt possessed a distinctly unique style all of his own.

Similar to Enuff Z' Nuff, Extreme weren't *exactly* hair metal, but they were assuredly advertised as such, and perhaps fairly so. Their debut album featured funky rhythms with fantastic guitar work full of blazing solos. Highlights included "Kid Ego," "Teacher's Pet," and the minor hit "Mutha (Don't Wanna Go to School Today)."

Mr. Big were formed as one of the first "supergroups" of sorts. Bassist Billy Sheehan had recently departed David Lee Roth's solo band a year earlier, following the disappointing recording process for *Skyscraper*. He then quickly sought to assemble a band of all-star (if somewhat unknown) talent.

The first recruit was the exceptional vocalist Eric Martin, who possessed a raspy, powerful, soulful voice. Martin had already released a couple of well-regarded albums as a solo artist and was a known up-and-comer in the industry who was actually invited to audition for both Toto and Van Halen.

Next up was ultra-talented guitar shredder Paul Gilbert, a prior member of the speed-metal band Racer-X and well-known for his virtuoso abilities, particularly the ability to play fast, ripping solos. Finally, there was drummer Pat Torpey, who had performed on renowned albums and tours with the likes of Ted Nugent, Belinda Carlisle, and The Knack. Naturally, the band was quickly signed to Atlantic Records.

Mr. Big's musical style was characterized as melodic hard rock focusing on soulful singing, stunning guitar work, and tons of harmonized vocals (all four band members were more-than-capable singers). Still, similar to Extreme, at the end of the day, the music was shaped as hair metal, and certainly presented as such.

Their debut album did reasonably well, hitting No. 46 on the Billboard Albums chart, and while it was admittedly great in some places (for example, "Addicted To That Rush"), the record overall fell short of having enough "hits" to launch Mr. Big up to the level of success experienced by the more prominent hair metal acts of the time. Mr. Big wouldn't be left out for long, however, as we would see in the coming years.

The year 1989 saw a mass of hair metal debuts beyond even those discussed above, all of which managed to make at least some level of noise with a hit single or video, including *Surprise Attack* by Tora Tora ("Walkin' Shoes"), *Dangerous Toys* by Dangerous Toys ("Scared"), *Babylon A.D.* by Babylon A.D ("Bang Go the Bells"), *Blue Murder* by Blue Murder ("Jelly Roll"), *Saraya* by Saraya ("Love Has Taken Its Toll"), and *XYZ* by XYZ ("Inside Out").

Outside of these new bands and debut releases, though, there were several sophomore albums that surfaced in 1989 from hair metal artists whose initial output first appeared between 1986 and 1988. The majority of these releases represented significant and impressive steps up in quality.

Perhaps the best of the bunch was the second release from **L.A. Guns**, *Cocked & Loaded.* The album reflected the band's meaningful development with regard to songwriting, consistency, and performance. It was an instant classic for the genre.

Cocked & Loaded started off with a short, building intro ("Letting Go") before launching into the scorching rocker "Slap in the Face." The remainder of the album's first side featured a slew of awesome sleaze-rockers, including "Rip n' Tear," "Never Enough," and the driving "Malaria." All three songs were released as singles, with "Rip n' Tear" successfully making noise on the Billboard chart. The record birthed two additional singles as well, the sparkling rocker and album closer "I Wanna Be Your Man" and the touching, ultra-popular power ballad "The Ballad of Jayne."

"The Ballad of Jayne" resonated loudest from a commercial standpoint, propelling the album to Gold status peaking at No. 38 on the Billboard Albums chart. The song was a tribute to Jayne Mansfield, a popular actress and pin-up girl in the 1950s. Often compared to Marilyn Monroe, Mansfield tragically died young in a fatal car accident at the early age of only thirty-four.

Cocked & Loaded certainly stood out among its peers in 1989 and was a perfect slab of what would come to be known as "pop/sleaze-metal."

While on the subject of sleaze-metal, **Faster Pussycat** took a similar step forward in songwriting quality and performance with their second release, *Wake Me When It's Over*. The new album saw a more mature band with better compositions, instrumentation, variety, and overall musicianship.

The overarching tone of *Wake Me When It's Over* was more blues-based, sleazy, hard rock versus the glam metal approach of Faster Pussycat's debut. The guitar work, in particular, was a significant upgrade and improvement. At nearly seven minutes long, the grinding opener "Where There's a Whip There's a Way" was perhaps the album's highlight, but there were plenty of other bright spots as well.

The catchy rocker "Poison Ivy" and power ballad "House of Pain" were both released as singles, with the latter reaching No. 28 on the Billboard chart and driving the album to Gold status similar to what "The Ballad of Jayne" did for *Cocked & Loaded*. The raunchy "Slip of The Tongue" was a personal favorite, along with "Ain't No Way Around It" and the saloon-like, piano-driven "Arizona Indian Doll." *Wake Me When It's Over* was simply a genuinely fun ride from start to finish, and a perfect example of sleazy glam metal.

Britny Fox followed the commercial success of their 1988 self-titled debut with 1989's *Boys in Heat*. Despite failing to capitalize on their momentum and realize an increase in sales, *Boys in Heat* was clearly a superior effort, in my view. Lead singer Dean Davidson began incorporating welcomed "clean" vocals on several songs in addition to the AC/DC-Cinderella-type style Britny Fox had become known for, and many tracks featured acoustic, layered guitars and more serious subject matter among the lyrics. The overall songwriting was also a sizable improvement with tighter arrangements and catchier hooks. Particular standouts included "Dream On," "Long Way from Home," and "She's So Lonely."

Despite the disappointing commercial impact of *Boys in Heat*, Britny Fox still managed to build up an ample fanbase while touring with the likes of Poison, Ratt, and Joan Jett.

On the other end of the spectrum, **Tesla** rocketed to stardom with their second release, titled *The Great Radio Controversy*. As pointed out earlier, Tesla was never truly a perfect fit with the hair metal template, and while *The Great Radio Controversy* admittedly contained a lot of the big-sounding production methods associated with the genre, it also included a significant amount of content more rooted in '70s blues-rock. The album itself was produced at Bearsville Studios outside of Woodstock, New York, an atmosphere about as far removed from the L.A. hair metal scene as you could get (indeed, Tesla would regularly perform in jeans and t-shirts versus the more fashion-oriented glam images of their contemporaries).

Among the record's highlights were the heavy rocker "Lady Luck," riff-laden "Heaven's Trail (No Way Out)," and the spirited "Be a Man," which launched with a long, bluesy, slide-guitar intro before shifting into a robust, melodic rocker. And then, of course, there was the massive hit, "Love Song." The unique-sounding ballad (with its ninety-second acoustic prelude) is often referred to as one of the best power ballads the genre ever produced, and the song hit the Top 10 driving *The Great Radio Controversy* to No. 18 overall and sales of more than two million copies.

Lastly in 1989, **White Lion** released their sophomore record, *Big Game*, having wasted no time getting right back into the studio after their successful year-long tour in support of 1987's double-Platinum *Pride* album. *Big Game* was a distinctly more diverse affair than *Pride* but remained stylistically similar in the overarching vein of pop-metal. The exception in White Lion's case was that several of their songs contained lyrics focusing on more than just partying, girls, and good times, and of course, guitarist-extraordinaire Vito Bratta was in relatively rarefied air in terms of esteemed guitar composition and execution.

"Little Fighter" was the album's first single and high point. The song was an upbeat, catchy rocker written about The Rainbow Warrior, an unrelenting Greenpeace boat that was intentionally sabotaged and sunk by the French Secret Service. Other highlights included the nostalgic personal favorite "Goin' Home Tonight," "Baby Be Mine," and "Cry For Freedom." The record also featured White Lion's grandiose popular cover of Golden Earing's 1973 hit, "Radar Love."

Although *Big Game* failed to achieve the overall sales of *Pride* (mainly because it lacked a true smash hit like "Wait" or "When the Children Cry"), it still attained Gold status, peaking at No. 19 on the Billboard Albums chart and serving to continue the band's upward arc. White Lion continued to ride the success-wave and immediately went back on tour after the record's release, not an unusual approach and cycle for many acts of the era, at the time.

Other noteworthy albums released in 1989: Michael Monroe *(Not Fakin' It)*, Kiss *(Hot in the Shade)*, Great White *(...Twice Shy)*, Shotgun Messiah *(Shotgun Messiah)*, EZO *(Fire Fire)*, Sea Hags *(Sea Hags)*, Shark Island *(Law Of The Order)*, Cats In Boots *(Kicked & Klawed)*, Junkyard *(Junkyard)*, Vain *(No Respect)*

The year 1989 certainly delivered the most substantial volume of hair metal albums of any year up to that point. The mighty triumph of Mötley Crüe and Aerosmith, alongside the many notable debut artists (particularly Skid Row and Warrant) and uplift in quality that shined through on several band's sophomore releases marked the year as a glorious triumph for the hair metal genre, which further cemented its status as a commercially dominant musical and cultural style.

Best Albums 1989

1. Mötley Crüe – *Dr. Feelgood (Top 5 in Genre!)*
2. Skid Row – *Skid Row (Top 10 in Genre!)*
3. Pretty Boy Floyd – *Leather Boyz with Electric Toyz (Top 10 in Genre!)*
4. L.A. Guns – *Cocked & Loaded (Top 25 in Genre!)*
5. Warrant – *Dirty Rotten Filthy Stinking Rich*
6. Whitesnake – *Slip of the Tongue*
7. Electric Boys – *Funk-O-Metal-Carpet Ride*
8. Aerosmith – *Pump*
9. Faster Pussycat – *Wake Me When It's Over*
10. Bang Tango – *Psycho Cafe*
11. Britny Fox – *Boys in Heat*
12. Tesla – *The Great Radio Controversy*
13. Enuff Z'Nuff – *Enuff Z'Nuff*
14. Lillian Axe – *Love + War*
15. White Lion – *Big Game*
16. Danger Danger – *Danger Danger*
17. Extreme – *Extreme*

Chapter 11
Cherry Pie
(1990)

The hair metal party continued to pick up speed as the train feverishly sped down the tracks into 1990. Poison and Warrant had the highest-profile albums, while several new hair bands emerged to become some of the very last to join the scene while it was still thriving, before the dark emergence of grunge music in the years that would follow.

Warrant became an overnight sensation after releasing their double-Platinum debut album and receiving ample radio and MTV support for the hit songs "Down Boys" and "Heaven," all the while touring extensively with the likes of Mötley Crüe, Poison, and Cinderella. When the band came off the road in June 1990, the record company made sure to capitalize on Warrant's momentum by forcing them right back into the studio to begin writing and recording sessions for what would become their sophomore release, *Cherry Pie*.

Singer/songwriter Jani Lane was beginning to mature his craft and branch out with song structure while Warrant worked hard to polish and perfect their performance. The band was enjoying a newfound approach of starting off songs with light, acoustical intros prior to blowing them up into full-blown, pop-metal rock anthems. Although Lane would later lament the lack of a longer timeline to further refine the new tunes (*Cherry Pie* was released in September 1990), the songs were still plenty strong in most places.

The group was most proud of the new track "Uncle Tom's Cabin," which indeed is one of the best songs Warrant ever laid down to tape and an unquestioned standout for the hair metal genre. The song began with a bluesy, acoustic guitar intro recorded by Lane's brother, Eric Oswald. Oswald had been absent-mindedly doodling away, warming up in preparation for the formal take, but the eavesdropping band liked what they heard so much they simply used the recording as-is. A banjo and harmonica then joined the fray post-intro before the song eventually launched into a huge, hard rock bonanza. The lyrics related the story of a silent witness to a double murder—the song's original title was "I Know A Secret."

Warrant had fully finished and turned the completed album in to the record company, eagerly suggesting it be titled *Uncle Tom's Cabin* and requesting the title track be released as the first single. Upon listening to the record, however, the label decided it lacked a clear "anthem" consistent with the party-oriented hair metal mega-hits of the era. Lane was told the executives wanted a "hit party song, something sexually tongue-in-cheek, similar to Aerosmith's 'Love in an Elevator.'"

Frustrated with the label's narrow-minded take on the album, Lane responded by writing the salacious, jesting "Cherry Pie" on the back of a pizza box in just under twenty minutes. The band then returned to the studio the following day and quickly put the track to tape. Lane has since stated he angrily wrote the song almost as a joke to spurn the record company, but to his shock, the label enthusiastically took it and ran. Suddenly, almost overnight, and with little of the band's input, "Cherry Pie" became the album's new title, first single, and center of the group's marketing campaign. The rest was history.

"Cherry Pie" hit radio and exploded up the charts, quickly breaking into the Top 10 on Billboard. Warrant rather sought to shine the spotlight instead towards some of the album's more matured songwriting, but at that point, nothing could stop the runaway train that was "Cherry Pie."

In retrospect, Lane claimed the song was both "a blessing and a curse" in that it undeniably brought the band a heightened level of fame and success, but also had the adverse effect of labeling Lane with its juvenile style, which was deeply unfortunate as he genuinely had so much more to offer as one of the most gifted songwriters of the genre. Further, the lighthearted but sexist nature of the video rubbed many women the wrong way. Sadly, Lane would later battle clinical depression stemming from becoming known only as "The Cherry Pie Guy."

But back at the time in 1990, it was hard to focus on anything other than the song's dramatic and overwhelming success. The accompanying video was a smash hit on MTV and became one of the most memorable images of the hair metal era. The clip featured actress and vixen Bobbie Brown, who would also go on to her own personal fame as a result of the song. Lane had seen her on the TV show *Star Search* and insisted she was the perfect fit for the role—indeed, Brown did a more than adequate job acting out the sexual innuendo laced among the song's lyrics. Naturally, Lane began courting her shortly after the video was filmed, and they were married roughly a year later. The couple would undergo a difficult divorce two years down the road, but at the time, everything was bliss.

Interestingly, "Cherry Pie" opened with a slow-building scream that the average listener would understandably assume was Lane's vocal, but it was actually Dee Snider, as producer Beau Hill lifted the snippet directly from the song "I Want This Night (To Last Forever)," from Twisted Sister's 1987 album *Love is for Suckers* (why he chose to do that I still have never learned). Strangely, Snider was not credited anywhere on the *Cherry Pie* album. The song also featured a blistering guest solo from Poison's C.C. DeVille, although, curiously, the guitarist did not appear in the song's video.

"Cherry Pie" was widely polarizing and divisional in nature. To many at the time (and many still), the song was simply exactly what the record label was looking for—a hit party anthem that was loads of fun. To others, and especially in retrospect, it symbolized all that those who were not fans of the hair metal genre actively derided—perceived silliness bereft of musical legitimacy (however one defined legitimacy, that is). Still, the one undeniable truth was that the song was a *massive* hit, and fans simply couldn't get enough of it at the time.

"Cherry Pie" aside, the rest of the album featured several fantastic songs, almost all of which were marked improvements over half the material on Warrant's debut album. Apart from the terrific, aforementioned "Uncle Tom's Cabin," *Cherry Pie* contained excellent, pop-metal rockers such as "Bed of Roses" and the criminally underrated "Mr. Rainmaker," along with the more intricate and textured "Song and Dance Man," a great example of Lane's songwriting starting to evolve to include different formats and styles. Of course, there was also the very much still-welcomed standard hair metal fare such as "Sure Feels Good to Me" and "Love in Stereo" (a story about Lane experiencing his first threesome upon initially arriving onto the craziness of the L.A. party scene at the time).

And surely, there were the requisite power ballads. Only these weren't just *any* power ballads. The magical "I Saw Red" was the album's second single released and managed to break into the Billboard chart's Top 10. The lyrics told of Lane's feelings a year earlier after appallingly walking in on his then-girlfriend in bed with his best friend. The beautiful piano-driven ballad was all over radio and quickly became one of Warrant's most recognizable songs. The tender "Blind Faith" was the album's additional hit ballad, slightly more subdued in nature than "I Saw Red," but exquisite just the same.

At a time when the party-never-stops attitude still reigned supreme, *Cherry Pie* was precisely what the doctor ordered—a fantastic pop-metal celebration full of groove and uplifting energy that also offered a few surprises along the way. The album sold over two million copies and broke the Top 10 on the Billboard Albums chart. Lane was clearly beginning to come into his own as both a songwriter and a singer. His distinctive tone was easily identifiable, and his vocal performance was one of the record's highlights. For me, admittedly though, Lane could have sung the phone book and I still would have enjoyed it.

Warrant immediately hit the road again in support of the album, teaming up to tour with fellow hair metal kings Poison, who, incidentally, would release 1990's other most prominent hair metal album.

🤘

Similar to Warrant, **Poison** were also looking to take a few steps forward on their third album, steering several (but certainly not all) songs to more mature and serious subject matter.

As it was, the '80s were a relatively flashy and gaudy affair, particularly when it came to music and fashion. Few groups personified this style more than Poison. However, all trends eventually run their course (for better or worse), and as the calendar flipped to the '90s, a subtle change began to seep into hair metal. The rise of grunge was still off in the distance, as yet unforeseen and unexperienced, but nevertheless, many bands seemed to (perhaps unknowingly) sense that some type of change was indeed brewing, and made distinct efforts to replace *some* of the glitz and glam with more serious subject matter, bluesier songs, stripped-back production or some combination of all three.

For Poison, this attempt at evolution resulted in their 1990 release, *Flesh & Blood.* And if commercial sales were any indication, the band was highly successful. Personally, I will always hold *Open Up and Say... Ahh!* in higher regard, but there are legitimate arguments on both sides.

A good friend of mine and an equally big Poison fan shares a different perspective, however. Our conversation (disagreement) on this topic always seems to take the same shape. Inevitably, she will ask me the following questions, and I will offer the following responses:

"Which album has the better overall songwriting"?
--*Flesh & Blood,* I respond.
"Which album has better musicianship"?
--*Flesh & Blood,* I respond.
"Which album features the better vocal performance"?
--*Flesh & Blood,* I respond.
"Which album has the better production"?
--*Flesh & Blood,* I respond.
"Which album do you like better"?

--*Open Up and Say... Ahh!*, easily, I tell her.

I know, it seems to be an inconsistent evaluation. But for me, *Open Up . . .* just had the better vibe—it was unabashedly one big, glam party. *Flesh & Blood* simply had too many "filler" songs, in my opinion, or perhaps Poison's attempt to be something other than a full-time party-band rang hollow for me. Maybe I missed the "gaudiness" or perhaps the giant hooks. Or possibly we can just chalk it up to personal opinion. David Lee Roth perhaps said it best: "music is like girlfriends—there's just no accounting for people's taste."

In any case, Poison's newfound "maturity" (if you could truly call it that) did seem to fit well in some places. The melodic, pop-metal "Ride the Wind," for example, was one of the albums finest moments and clearly belonged on any Poison best-of compilation. "Life Loves a Tragedy," meanwhile, was another standout, featuring a bluesy, melancholy introduction that transitioned to an upbeat, optimistic rocker. As for performances, the ballad "Life Goes On" featured what C.C. DeVille stated (at the time) was his "greatest guitar solo to-date."

And of course, there was the emotionally moving, mega-hit power ballad "Something to Believe In." Bret Michaels found himself in difficult spirits during the song's construction, dealing with the tragic death of his best friend and security guard, James Kimo Maano. Michaels would later state that while he was happy with how the track turned out, he never again wanted to be in a place of such sadness required to produce such a stirring result.

In addition to the death of Maano, the song's verses also dealt with difficult subjects such as PTSD-laden Vietnam veterans, evangelistic con men, and the widening gap between the rich and the poor. The lyric "sometimes I wish I didn't know now, things I didn't know then" perhaps best summed up the track's melancholy sentiment. Still, the song optimistically sought hope at the same time, with Michaels' pleading for "something to believe in." The stunning ballad was released as the album's second single and went all the way to No. 4 on the Billboard chart.

Of course, while *Flesh & Blood* did represent an evolution of sorts, it was definitely not entirely devoid of the party-glam, light-hearted image and style for which Poison had become famous. Nowhere was this more evident than on the nonsensical lead single, "Unskinny Bop."

"Unskinny Bop" was a polarizing song in that most listeners either loved or hated it—there seemed to be no in-between. It was distinctively the album's only track that truly harked back to Poison's previous works. The band admitted the song probably didn't register very high on the "substance scale," but felt it was the perfect reintroduction to Poison after the seemingly long two years that had elapsed since *Open Up and Say... Ahh!*.

Indeed, "Unskinny Bop" was pure silliness, but there was no denying its hook-laden catchiness. Detractors of the hair metal genre frequently use the term "cheesy" to characterize the era's style. While this label is highly offensive and considered decidedly errant by hair metal enthusiasts, even the most hardcore fans, in retrospect, view some of the songs as just that. "Unskinny Bop" is perhaps the best example of this (possibly along with Def Leppard's "Let's Get Rocked").

That said, "Unskinny Bop" was a smash hit, climbing all the way to No. 3 on the Billboard chart, and I certainly remember digging it in a big way in 1990. I admittedly still have a keen fondness for it thirty years later, but in truth, it doesn't always find a home on my Poison playlists.

Much has been discussed regarding the actual meaning of the song's title. C.C. DeVille would later confess the phrase "unskinny bop" had no particular meaning at all, and was only inserted as a lyrical placeholder and phonetic match to the music during the song's assembly. DeVille went on to convey that the phrase "wound up sticking" as the band felt it fit the congenial nature of the song perfectly. That said, on the track "Home (Bret's Story)," appearing on Poison's 2012 release *Hollyweird*, the lyrics state that "unskinny bop" is "slang for C.C. banging a porno queen." So, who really knows?

Unfortunately, outside of the songs already discussed, *Flesh & Blood* contained several compositions that either fell flat in their attempt to capture something special or were just plain filler. Lead track "Valley of Lost Souls" certainly rocked hard enough, but at the end of the day felt more like a poor man's "Fallen Angel," at best. "(Flesh & Blood) Sacrifice" just seemed to plod along, and "Come Hell or High Water" simply failed to offer anything memorable. The album ended with the track "Poor Boy Blues," which was, of course, Poison's attempt at a country-blues song (done in the style of Poison, of course). If that's your thing, great, and props to the band for continuing to broaden their palate, but it was a far cry from the favored style of *Look What the Cat Dragged In.*

All told, however, there was simply no denying the demand for *Flesh & Blood* and its massive commercial success. The album peaked at No. 2 on the Billboard Albums chart while going triple-Platinum and spinning off four Top 40 hit singles. Poison, in 1990, were undoubtedly bigger and more popular than ever.

Keeping with the theme of hair bands attempting to evolve as they entered the '90s, **Cinderella**'s third album, *Heartbreak Station,* bore little resemblance to the glam and heavy metal stylings of their 1986 debut, or even to most of the blues-based hard rock found on their 1988 release, *Long Cold Winter.*

Instead, *Heartbreak Station* featured a stripped-back, raw, organic sound with multi-layered instrumentation and several songs that ventured into either country territory or played out as slower, more bluesy tracks. Many hardcore Cinderella fans didn't, at first, easily warm up to the new sound, (although the record still sold more than one million units and hit No. 19 on the Billboard Albums chart), but in terms of songwriting, performance, and breadth of offering, the album was undeniably impressive.

Lead singer and songwriter Tom Keifer has since stated the songwriting process for each of Cinderella's first three albums was basically the same, but the difference with *Heartbreak Station* was the production approach. Something never quite sat right with him on the first two albums, and he eventually decided it was the use (abuse) of heavy reverb, a technique commonly employed on hair metal albums at the time intended to promote a "bigger" sound.

On *Heartbreak Station*, the band pursued a raw, dry production absent of the slick processing found on many releases of the era. For Keifer, the change was consistent with his initial vision of the band from the onset—it had just got pushed in a slightly different direction earlier in Cinderella's career as the record label nudged them toward the shape of all things glam metal.

That's not to say *Heartbreak Station* didn't manage to rock in its own way, however, because it certainly did. But where in the past Cinderella's early songs were shaped around "metal guitars," they were now often replaced with acoustic and blues-slide guitars (Keifer might be one of the top five slide-guitar players, ever—no kidding).

The album's first single, "Shelter Me," was the perfect example of the band's new approach, launching with twangy, organic guitar riffs and Keifer's raw, raspy vocals before evolving into a chorus best suited for a Sunday church choir. According to Keifer, this was the *real* Cinderella, it would seem, or at least it was in 1990. *Heartbreak Station* was truly an album you had to hear to properly understand, as it was relatively far removed from the classic hair metal template (but still somehow related, in a peculiar way).

Other "rockers" included personal favorite "The More Things Change, the More They Stay the Same," "Make Your Own Way," and "Love's Gone Bad." Beyond that, "Love's Got Me Doin' Time" was a super-funky blues jam while "One for Rock and Roll" was undeniably 99.9 percent country. "Sick for the Cure" (another favorite), meanwhile, was based on a piano line fit for a western saloon, while "Electric Love" and "Dead Man's Road" were pure blues. You get the picture—this was a different kind of album.

And, of course, there were two power ballads. The album's emotive title track was a hauntingly beautiful composition with a fantastic chorus that charted at No. 44. Finally, the album ended with the introspective ballad "Winds of Change," which saw Cinderella perhaps looking in the mirror to determine a different path forward for themselves versus their traditional hair metal history.

Heartbreak Station was a phenomenal slate of music and a terrific achievement for the band, even if it was somewhat different from what had come to be expected.

Speaking of things different from what had come to be expected, 1990 marked a significant year in the history of **Bon Jovi**. The band was coming off more than four years of constant global touring amid a whirlwind of success and frenzy surrounding their mega-albums *Slippery When Wet* and *New Jersey*. The group was simply burnt-out, both physically and mentally. After so much time on the road, internal tensions understandably began to rise, and after the final performance on their New Jersey Syndicate Tour in February 1990, the band unceremoniously parted ways, with no clear plans for the future. Bon Jovi was officially "on hiatus." John Bon Jovi has said in retrospect, "if there was ever a good time for the band to break up, that was it."

Both Jon and Richie Sambora then took some needed time off for creative exploration and wound up issuing their first solo recordings in 1990 and 1991, respectively. Jon had always maintained a keen interest in the "Old West," a theme he had previously explored on both *Slippery When Wet* and *New Jersey* with songs like "Wanted Dead or Alive" and "Ride Cowboy Ride." In 1990 Jon was initially approached by his friend Emilio Estevez, who was interested in licensing "Wanted Dead or Alive" for use in the upcoming sequel movie, *Young Guns II*. Jon didn't believe the song was a good fit, however, as its lyrics centered on touring and life on the road as opposed to the pertinent themes of the Old West.

As an alternative, during a dinner with Estevez and Kiefer Sutherland, Jon nonchalantly scratched out the song "Blaze of Glory" across three napkins. At the end of the meal, he pushed them over to Estevez and told him, "there's your first single for the new film."

The epic, western-tinged rock song would go on to be a No. 1 smash-hit upon the movie's release and won an award for Favorite Pop/Rock Single at the American Music Awards while also capturing a Golden Globe as well. "Blaze of Glory" additionally earned Jon Bon Jovi nominations for both a Grammy and Academy Award.

In the end, Jon would end up writing the full soundtrack for the film and delivering it as his first solo album. The songs were quite different in style from Bon Jovi's recent records, representing a change more along the lines of what Cinderella had done on *Heartbreak Station*. The tracks were more organic and stripped-down in nature, and, of course, centered on the Old West subjects and characters explored in the movie (primarily Billy The Kid and Pat Garrett).

Blaze Of Glory soared to No. 3 on the Billboard Albums chart while the album's second single, the melodic, pop-rock "Miracle" also garnered significant success, making its way to No. 12. Other standout tracks included the dramatic, epic "Santa Fe," and the uplifting, straightforward rocker "Never Say Die." The record also featured a slew of notable guest appearances, including Elton John, Jeff Beck, and Little Richard.

The year 1990 was also significant in that it was the last year a wave of *new* hair metal bands would emerge and still manage to taste a brief period of success before the era dissolved in commercial popularity around late 1992. Five of the most prominent of these newcomers were Slaughter, FireHouse, Steelheart, Nelson, and Trixter.

Slaughter was formed by singer/rhythm guitarist Mark Slaughter and bassist Dana Strum. Both were prior members of Vinnie Vincent Invasion but had not particularly enjoyed their time there, struggling to get along with Vincent's rather massive ego. As it turned out, Chrysalis Records wound up revoking the eccentric Vincent's contract due to breach of terms and transferring it to Slaughter and Strum, who had convinced the label they were fully capable of forming a successful band on their own. The two then quickly recruited lead guitarist Tim Kelly and drummer Blas

Elias, and the Slaughter lineup was complete.

Slaughter and Strum made for a terrific songwriting team with a penchant for crafting impeccable melodic, pop-metal rock songs. Slaughter himself possessed a near-nuclear vocal ability in the higher registers that distinctly differentiated him from his peers. The band swiftly wrote and recorded their debut album, *Stick It To Ya*, and became an overnight smash success upon its release on January 23, 1990.

The pounding lead single "Up All Night" was a colossal stadium rocker and became one of the most recognized anthems of the era, reaching No. 27 on the Billboard Top 40 chart. But it was the immense power ballad "Fly to the Angels" that truly cemented Slaughter's initial success. The song, with its touching lyrics centered on the loss of a loved one, flew to No. 1 on radio, and the accompanying video played endlessly on MTV.

The album also featured the sizzling "Burning Bridges" (seemingly a negative nod to Slaughter and Strum's previous employer, Vincent), excellent hard rockers "Eye to Eye," "Mad About You," and "Desperately," and perfect pop-metal, mid-tempo tracks such as "Spend My Life," "Gave Me Your Heart," and "You Are the One."

With sales of over two million units, *Stick It To Ya* was one of the biggest selling albums of 1990 and was nominated for Best Metal Album of the year at the American Music Awards show. The record was a true hair metal treasure for fans of the genre.

FireHouse (originally named White Heat) got their start in Richmond, Virginia, signing with Epic Records in 1989 and releasing their self-titled debut album on September 11, 1990. Much like Slaughter, FireHouse was basically an overnight success as their first record quickly sold more than two million copies. The band diligently followed what had become the go-to template for hair metal albums at the time, first releasing a hard rock song to prove their worth to the core fanbase, followed by the ubiquitous power ballad to rope in the females and capture seemingly boundless radio and MTV airplay.

Also comparable to Slaughter, FireHouse's style was very "pop-metal" in nature; the songs were hard rock, but still plenty commercially accessible, including a plethora of radio-friendly pop hooks and catchy choruses. In a further parallel, FireHouse also featured a vocalist (C.J. Snare) seemingly capable of shattering glass at the higher spectrums of his vocal range.

The album's first single, "Don't Treat Me Bad," led the way, starting off with an extended acoustic intro followed by a full-blown, electric hair metal chorus as catchy as any ever written. And then, unsurprisingly, there was the *enormous* power ballad "Love of a Lifetime." The lush, heartwarming love song rocketed to No. 3 on the Billboard chart and became famous for serving as the official "wedding song" at countless ceremonies.

Beyond the singles, the record also featured a consistent string of solid, hard rock, pop-metal songs. Driving tracks like "Rock on the Radio," "Shake & Tumble," "Oughta Be a Law," and "Lover's Lane" showed the harder edge of the band while the earnest "Home Is Where the Heart Is" and "All She Wrote" were more melodic. And as was seemingly becoming mandatory for hair metal bands as time wore on, there was the "must-include, overly blues-based number," which for FireHouse was "Don't Walk Away," an impressive, slow-churning burner.

Like Slaughter's debut earlier during the year, *FireHouse* perfectly represented and reflected the hair metal style of the time, and the band would go on to win the award for Favorite Heavy Metal/Hard Rock New Artist at the American Music Awards of 1992. In *extreme* irony (in retrospect), the band was chosen over fellow nominees Nirvana and Alice In Chains.

Steelheart also rose to prominence in 1990 to stake a successful claim in the hair metal universe. And guess what? The band's style was pop-metal, the lead singer sang in an atmospheric upper register, the first single was a rock song, and the second track released to radio was the "huge power ballad" that drove the album to commercial success. Can you sense a trend developing?

Later we will explore the common belief that the emergence of grunge music was what killed hair metal, and to some extent, that is certainly true. However, hair metal was undoubtedly beginning to hammer the nail into its own coffin even before the arrival of grunge, with the template becoming increasingly predictable and the large volume of new acts jumping on the bandwagon following paint-by-number recipes clearly beginning to dilute and sterilize the soup.

That said, there was no denying the formula was working at the time. Additionally, there should be no disputing the marvelous talent some of these newer bands possessed regardless of the style they applied that talent to at the time.

But back to Steelheart, speaking of talent—wow, could that guy *sing*. That "guy" in question was Croatian-born Miljenko Matijevic. Granted, Matijevic's high-end register certainly wasn't for everyone (especially outside of the hair metal fanbase), but it was undeniably impressive. Matijevic would go on to become one of the true "voices of pop-metal," supplying the singing voice of Mark Wahlberg's character, Chris (Izzy) Cole, in the 2001 movie *Rock Star*, which portrayed a relatively spot-on version of the hair metal scene back in the late '80s and early '90s.

Steelheart's self-titled debut album naturally went Gold, featuring a standard string of solid pop-metal songs with a few particular standouts, including "Everybody Loves Eileen," "Love Ain't Easy," and "Like Never Before." The first single, "Can't Stop Me Lovin' You," didn't manage to make a whole lot of noise on radio, but second single and power ballad "I'll Never Let You Go" was a rousing success, reaching No. 24 on the Billboard chart and breaking the album into the Top 40. While it wasn't entirely different from any other ballad from the era, Matijevic's vocals set it apart with soft, emotional verses set against an utterly soaring chorus. Make sure to tune in for the song's very last note for an excellent example of Matijevic's crazy range.

Next up was **Nelson**, a group that was notably more "pop" in nature than their hair metal peers but were lumped into the broader hair metal category just the same. The band was founded and led by Matthew and Gunnar Nelson, twin sons of the late Ricky Nelson, who himself had a very successful music career generating over fifty hit singles from 1957 through 1975. (Ricky Nelson would die in a tragic plane crash in 1985.)

The brothers assembled a band that included drummer Bobby Rock from Vinnie Vincent Invasion, and after many months of effort and persuasion, secured a major label record deal with Geffen Records in the late '80s. Nelson released their sparkling debut album, *After the Rain*, on June 26, 1990, and it was an instant success driven by the enormous first single, "(Can't Live Without Your) Love and Affection."

The song featured lush dual vocal harmonies by the brothers (an approach reflected in most all their output), an insanely catchy chorus, and, of course, a guitar solo entirely representative of the hair metal genre. Whether or not you loved or hated hair metal at the time, you had undoubtedly heard " . . . Love and Affection." With lyrics based on a crush the brothers bore for supermodel Cindy Crawford, the song went all the way to No. 1 on the Billboard chart and played constantly on MTV and radio.

The album featured several other highlights as well, including the perfect pop-rock hit singles "After the Rain" and "More Than Ever," along with the requisite ballad "Only Time Will Tell." The twins were clearly talented songwriters; indeed, they had come from a musical family and, according to them, had been writing songs together since the tender age of six. *After the Rain* would eventually sell more than three million copies, and the success of the album would launch Nelson on a massive world tour that included over 300 concert dates.

The final notable band of the new bunch was **Trixter**, hailing from the suburbs of Paramus, New Jersey. The band members were still just teenagers upon signing their first record deal with MCA Records in 1989, but in many ways, they were already veterans of the scene having played countless shows over the four years prior, including appearances with Skid Row, Kix, and several other well-established hair metal acts.

Trixter released their self-titled debut album on May 29, 1990, and somewhat naturally, the album was very similar in style to the debut records offered by Slaughter and FireHouse: radio-accessible pop-metal. Opening track and lead single "Line of Fire" didn't exactly light up the charts but did land the band vital touring slots with Stryper and Dokken. MTV then soon picked up the video for the colossal second single "Give it to Me Good," and suddenly the band was full speed off and running.

In its first week, the video went straight to No. 1 on the MTV Top 10 countdown and stayed in the top position for the next month and a half. "Give it to Me Good" was similar to FireHouse's "Don't Treat Me Bad" in that it started off with an acoustic intro before launching into a full-blown, electric, pop-metal masterpiece with another one of those choruses that just seemed to get stuck in your head. And if the tune ever did somehow manage to escape your consciousness, all you had to do was turn on MTV, and bam, there it was in your face again.

I distinctly remember driving with a high school friend of mine upon the song's release, and although this particular acquaintance was far from a fan of hair metal, when the tune came on the radio, I recall him somewhat reluctantly admitting, "Hey, it's objectively a good song." Coming from a guy who looked down upon everything that hair metal stood for at the time, it was high praise indeed. I will always associate this fun, rocking song with the memory of driving around on that sunny day in a beat-up (but beautiful) red '67 mustang convertible. Good times.

But back to the album. The more pop-oriented third single "One In a Million" followed the success of "Give it to Me Good," again becoming the most requested video on MTV in February 1991. Power ballad "Surrender" was next, giving Trixter their third consecutive No. 1 song on MTV and helping to drive the album to No. 28 on the Billboard Albums chart while achieving Gold sales status. *Trixter* also featured the epic anthem "Only Young Once," although it was never officially released as a single.

The success of the album soon landed Trixter high-profile gigs with Poison and Scorpions, and later they would participate in the famous "Blood, Sweat & Beers" tour with Warrant and FireHouse in 1991.

Unfortunately for Trixter, however, they joined the party just a little too late to maintain their momentum, as the musical climate would suddenly and violently change in the coming years. Even MTV would completely abandon the hair metal era in the early '90s after serving as an essential part of its lifeblood in the '80s.

Trixter's "Surrender" was No. 1 on MTV for two weeks running during the summer of 1991 when the channel abruptly chose to abolish both its popular dial-MTV show and the Top 10 countdown in favor of a programming shift steered more toward the emerging wave of grunge. Trixter officially had the last No. 1 video *ever* to be played on MTV. On top of that, shockingly, the band was never to be played on MTV again! This wasn't related to any drop-off in the band's output, mind you, but rather reflected a reality where the hair metal scene was about to be almost entirely extinguished by the impending tidal wave of grunge.

For bands like Trixter and their peers who had been riding high on success from a commercial standpoint (the Blood, Sweat & Beers Tour was routinely selling out venues with thirty thousand-plus in attendance), the unexpected and violent change in popular music sentiment that was about to fully unfold in 1992 was surely difficult to understand. But more on that later.

Back in 1990, however, hair metal was still joyously charging full steam ahead. Genre kings **Ratt** even managed to release perhaps their best album, in my view, *Detonator.* While I was admittedly never the biggest Ratt fanatic (although I did recognize and enjoy the strength of many of their singles), I *was* a big fan of *Detonator.* Versus much of Ratt's previous output, the album just seemed to have more to offer in terms of songwriting, polish, production, and sound. Not coincidentally, the band co-wrote several of the tracks with super-songwriter Desmond Child (who had contributed to the success of Bon Jovi's *Slippery When Wet*), which likely played a role in the high quality of the material.

The record's overall tone was a noticeable shift away from some of the raw, unrefined energy associated with Ratt's earlier releases and more toward the recognizable style of template-driven pop-metal. For me, it was a welcomed evolution, but for other hardcore fans of the band, perhaps not so much.

Detonator began with the slow, bluesy, atmospheric guitar piece "Intro to Shame" before blasting into my personal favorite Ratt song, the scorching "Shame Shame Shame." The album then kept pace with second track and hit lead single "Lovin' You's a Dirty Job." The song featured heavy, sleazy verses and a huge, anthemic chorus. The record contained several other great rockers as well, including "Can't Wait on Love" and the smoldering "Top Secret."

The new album was also notable for the inclusion of a couple of songs quite different from Ratt's past output. In an era where every rock record was required to have at least *one* big power ballad, Ratt curiously never had *any*— it just wasn't their style, and lead singer Steven Pearcy's overly rough, sleazy and raspy vocals didn't exactly lend themselves to that type of song format. *Detonator*, however, featured the band's first official ballad, "Giving Yourself Away" (co-written with Child and Dianne Warren, of all people). It was undoubtedly a good song but failed to fully light up the charts like so many other power ballads of the era (although it did register as a minor success reaching No. 39 on Billboard).

The album also included the melodic "One Step Away," which was the most pop-metal, radio-friendly song Ratt had recorded up until that time. It was a terrific track, but not exactly what some Ratt purists were looking for at the time.

Although sales results didn't live up to past Ratt records, *Detonator* could still be considered an overall success, achieving Gold status and reaching No. 23 on the Billboard Albums chart. Hardcore Ratt fans would probably point to 1984's *Out of the Cellar* or 1985's *Invasion of Your Privacy* as the band's best work (and they might not be wrong), but for me, *Detonator* was Ratt's finest moment.

Winger released their sophomore album, *In the Heart of the Young*, on July 24, 1990. The record was a significant commercial success shifting almost two million copies. While the songs were similar in nature to the band's 1988 debut, they also featured a few noticeable differences, namely the inclusion of more progressive elements and a focus on two big power ballads (naturally).

Lead single "Can't Get Enough" was a huge rocker much in the same vein of Slaughter's "Up All Night." Unfortunately, the song didn't do much to help Winger escape critics who deemed their output superficial (not that it was intended to), but it did succeed for what it was, which was simply a terrific hard rock song. The accompanying video received plenty of exposure on MTV and expectedly reflected all the hair metal clichés of the time.

The gritty "Loosen Up" followed as the album's second track, and again it was a forceful statement with tons of attitude and energy. The album's momentum then slowed to accommodate the smash second single, power ballad "Miles Away." The tune was everything a hair metal power ballad had come to be known to need to be and hit No. 12 on radio while playing in constant rotation on MTV. The third single from the album, pop-rocker "Easy Come Easy Go," finished off an impressive four-song start to *In the Heart of the Young.*

After that, the album began to explore new territory. "Rainbow in the Rose," for example, was an intricate composition with progressive tendencies and sophisticated layering not previously heard from Winger. The band knew it needed to have straightforward songs like "Can't Get Enough" and "Easy Come Easy Go" to ensure continued commercial success, but also desired to start expanding their wings in an attempt to garner the musical credibility they felt had thus far been lacking in relation to their talent and backgrounds.

In fact, Winger originally turned in the completed album *without* both the songs "Can't Get Enough" and "Easy Come Easy Go," as the band was intentionally trying to move away from that style of writing, but the record company insisted the album needed more "straight-ahead rockers." And so, the songs were written and recorded at the eleventh hour, similar to the situation Warrant ran into with "Cherry Pie." Clearly, the record label was correct in its assessment of what was needed to sell albums in 1990; however, the constraints of this limited style would prove to represent the downfall of many hair bands in the coming years.

The back half of *In the Heart of the Young* was less prominent in terms of highlight material, but the record did end on a strong note with the album's title track, a deep, stirring, and again more musically progressive composition. Overall, *In the Heart of the Young* assuredly improved upon Winger's debut but still contained a few too many underwhelming tracks such as "You Are the Saint, I Am the Sinner" and "Baptized by Fire." That said, the record was a demonstrable commercial success (driven mostly by the hit singles) and reached No. 12 on the Billboard Albums chart. It was more than enough to keep Winger on the upper levels of the music scene at the time and drove a prosperous thirteen-month world tour with bands like Scorpions, Kiss, and Slaughter.

Extreme also released their sophomore album in 1990, and not unlike Winger, it was a significant step forward from their debut, but to a much greater degree. The album was titled *Extreme II: Pornograffitti (A Funked Up Fairy Tale)* (often referred to simply as *Pornograffitti*). While the songs generally still revolved around hard rock riffs combined with funky bass lines and the expected brilliant guitar work of Nuno Bettencourt, the album was musically much more diverse than its predecessor and took the advantage to explore thoughtful, connected, conceptual themes lyrically.

The driving lead track "Decadence Dance" was perhaps the album's highlight and seemingly a good choice as the first single, but surprisingly did not perform all that well in the US. The second single, "Get the Funk Out," stayed true to its title, representing the perfect example of Extreme's signature "funk-metal" style, but alas, it too failed to cause any commercial stir domestically. Both songs were significant hits overseas, however.

The record label made one last push as the album was falling off the charts, releasing the soft, acoustic ballad "More Than Words." While the nature of the song was in stark contrast to the band's heavy, hard-hitting rock/metal styling, it, in fact, turned out to be the record's savior, immediately rushing all the way to the No. 1 position on the Top 40 chart.

"More Than Words" was a straightforward but beautiful tune focused primarily on the vocal harmony between lead singer Gary Cherone and Bettencourt alongside only an acoustic guitar. Its simple structure didn't stop it from becoming a mega-smash hit, however, as the song's widespread exposure and saturated airplay reached almost ridiculous proportions.

Despite the track's commercial triumph, Extreme has often referred to the song as both a blessing and a curse (see "Cherry Pie"; Warrant). On the one hand, the song brought the band immense success and made possible a grand, worldwide tour. It also gave them the necessary freedom to steer their subsequent album in whatever direction they wanted, which would turn out to be an even bigger swing at an intricately orchestrated concept record. However, due to the song's singular worldwide recognition in contrast to the group's more rock-oriented material, the average listener came to think of Extreme as only "the ballad band," a stigma that did not sit well with the group.

This perception was only further reinforced when the record label naturally proceeded to seek out the only other song on the album somewhat analogous to "More Than Words" for the record's fourth (and final) release: "Hole Hearted." The track was decidedly more upbeat but still sparsely structured with only an acoustic guitar to back the vocals. It was definitely a great tune but further perpetuated the casual fan's characterization of Extreme as a soft, acoustic ballad-band. Still, "Hole Hearted" rose all the way to No. 4 on the Billboard chart and was another huge hit.

Outside of those two outliers, however, the rest of *Pornograffitti* was an eclectic mix of hard rock and other unusual styles (for hair metal, that is). "It ('s A Monster)" and "Pornograffitti" were terrific, heavy rockers, while "When I'm President" undeniably featured rap verses and "Song for Love" was more a traditional power ballad versus the acoustic singles. Meanwhile, "Li'l Jack Horny" was a funky, blues-rock song about fairy tale characters, of all things. And perhaps furthest out in left field was "When I First Kissed You," best characterized as a jazzy, big band-style piano sonnet with orchestral strings similar to the type of music popular during the 1940s.

Also included was Bettencourt's absolutely amazing take (with liberties) on the famous orchestral interlude "Flight of the Bumblebee," written by Nikolai Rimsky-Korsakov for his opera The Tale of Tsar Saltan, in 1899. Indeed, Bettencourt's talent did not go unnoticed as he was named "Most Valuable Guitar Player" of 1991 by *Guitar World* magazine.

In the end, the diverse set of songs managed to blend together seamlessly to create a fantastic front-to-back listening experience unique to the hair metal world at the time. *Pornograffitti* would end up climbing all the way to No. 10 on the Billboard Albums chart and establishing Extreme as a world-wide name.

Also notable in 1990 was the successful debut from a band known at the time as **The London Quireboys** (titled afterward only as **The Quireboys**). Hailing from the UK, the group enjoyed a fair amount of good fortune overseas before signing with EMI Records in the US. Sharon Osbourne was promptly put in place as their manager, and they released their debut album, *A Bit of What You Fancy.*

It was somewhat curious that The Quireboys were lumped into the hair metal category. Listening to their music, you would absolutely swear you were hearing The Faces or Rod Steward. Indeed, Jim Cregan, who played with Stewart, co-produced the album and lead singer Spike Gray's vocal style was a dead ringer for the famous crooner. That said, if Cinderella's *Heartbreak Station* was considered hair metal in 1990, then why not The Quireboys as well, I guess.

A Bit of What You Fancy did much better overseas than in America, reaching No. 2 on the UK Top Albums chart. Still, four singles were released in the US, with the superb "7 'O Clock," in particular, receiving ample play on MTV. The album featured terrific songwriting with catchy hooks and choruses layered upon rootsy, blues-based, piano-driven melodies. Highlights included the aforementioned "7 'O Clock," "Hey You," "Sweet Mary Ann," and "Roses and Rings."

The Quireboys brought something relatively unique to hair metal in 1990, and they would go on to have a long, extended career, still actively recording and touring as of this writing in 2019.

One last album of particular interest in 1990 was **Tesla**'s *Five Man Acoustical Jam.* The record was recorded live in Philadelphia, Pennsylvania, at the famed Trocadero Theatre during a short run of shows Tesla performed using only acoustic instruments.

The album surprisingly developed into a huge success, climbing all the way to No. 12 on the Billboard Albums chart. In addition to featuring some of Tesla's most popular original tracks, the set included covers of The Rolling Stones' "Mother's Little Helper," Creedence Clearwater Revival's "Lodi," and the Beatles' "We Can Work It Out." The biggest hit from the album, though, was Tesla's take on "Signs," a folksy tune originally recorded by Five Man Electrical Band, who also found success with the song in 1971. Radio played Tesla's live version of "Signs" endlessly, helping it to reach No. 8 on the Billboard chart.

The success of the acoustic shows and the album helped spawn the hugely popular MTV Unplugged series, which ran for more than a decade thereafter. It soon became trendy for every band (including many hair bands) to do some type of "unplugged" event or recording, but *Five Man Acoustical Jam* may have legitimately been the phenomena's origin. In truth the legendary acoustic performance by Jon Bon Jovi and Richie Sambora at the 1989 MTV Video Music Awards show a year earlier was perhaps the actual *first* time any such performance was attempted by a band of that nature, but *Five Man Acoustical Jam* was the inaugural *album* of that nature during the hair metal era.

Other noteworthy albums released in 1990: Scorpions *(Crazy World)*, Salty Dog *(Every Dog Has Its Day)*, Sweet F.A. *(Stick to Your Guns)*, Damn Yankees *(Damn Yankees)*, AC/DC *(The Razor's Edge)*, Bruce Dickinson *(Tattooed Millionaire)*, Queensrÿche *(Empire)*, Tigertailz *(Bezerk)*, Electric Angels *(Electric Angels)*, Every Mother's Nightmare *(Every Mother's Nightmare)*, Jetboy *(Damned Nation)*, Lynch Mob *(Wicked Sensation)*, Beggars & Thieves *(Beggars & Thieves)*, Love/Hate *(Blackout in the Red Room)*, Bang Gang *(Love Sells)*, Spread Eagle *(Spread Eagle)*, Steve Vai *(Passion And Warfare)*, Hericane Alice *(Tear the House Down)*, Blue Tears *(Blue Tears)*, Sleeze Beez *(Screwed Blued & Tattooed)*

The year 1990 featured a massive volume of high-quality hair metal that succeeded in keeping the genre at its peak but was also notable for the subtle changes that began to creep into the music, such as the style modifications by bands like Cinderella and Poison, and Jon Bon Jovi issuing a record that sounded very little like classic Bon Jovi.

Perhaps more impactful, it was also clear (in retrospect) that what can only be described as a "saturation" effect began to emerge with the vast sea of new bands suddenly popping up, all focused on following the well-established hair metal blueprint that had been clearly documented by that time.

A good illustration of this overload fallout can be found with the 1990 self-titled debut from **Heaven's Edge**. The band had the backing of major label Columbia Records and released what could objectively be considered a classic hair metal album. It had all the elements of success: strong vocals, an amazing guitarist who could produce ripping riffs and solos, catchy songwriting, a huge power ballad perhaps as good as any other released that year, and a mid-tempo rock song perfectly tailored to radio. Along with the band's impeccable image, there was simply no reason the album wasn't at least on the same commercial level as records from bands such as FireHouse, Trixter, and Slaughter.

However, for whatever reason, Heaven's Edge failed to achieve a comparable level of success, or anything remotely close. There was simply too much similar material beginning to souse a market that, while happily absorbing as much as it could, frankly, did not contain an infinite amount of demand. Regretfully, there were many other talented bands that emerged during that time who also went relatively unnoticed and unfairly fell by the wayside.

Despite this phenomenon, however, and regardless of the transformations that began to move some of the music astray from the more glam metal aspects of its roots, in 1991 hair metal would manage to see one final year as a dominant style of music for the mass commercial public.

Even while the genre remained at the top over the next several months, however, it would continue to reflect more pockets of change and interesting development. Of course, there would thankfully still be a substantial incremental heaping of classic, traditional hair metal to come, as well.

<u>Best Albums 1990</u>

1. Warrant – *Cherry Pie (Top 25 in Genre!)*
2. Slaughter – *Stick It To Ya (Top 25 in Genre!)*
3. Cinderella – *Heartbreak Station*
4. Poison – *Flesh & Blood*
5. FireHouse – *FireHouse*

6. The London Quireboys – *A Bit of What You Fancy*
7. Extreme – *Pornograffitti*
8. Nelson – *After the Rain*
9. Trixter – *Trixter*
10. Ratt – *Detonator*
11. Jon Bon Jovi – *Blaze of Glory*
12. Heavens Edge – *Heavens Edge*

Chapter 12
Use Your Illusion
(1991)

The last of hair metal's "peak" years was 1991, and while there were still several high-profile, big-selling albums and singles, not to mention numerous ultra-successful tours, many hair bands began to see a drop-off in commercial sales success despite releasing new material that was some of the strongest they had put out to date. Between the sheer amount of overkill present in the genre and the emerging tidal wave of grunge music that would soon fully envelop the mass-public and make all things hair metal entirely obsolete, the winds of change were definitely beginning to stir.

It is important to note, however, that while much of this perspective is clear when viewed in retrospect, at the time, and in the moment, it was significantly less perceptible. Make no mistake—hair metal in 1991 was, in many ways, more popular than ever (at least among the A-list bands) and still a major force with which to be reckoned.

But deeper down, in addition to changing commercial tastes, hair metal itself continued to evolve more naturally. While there were still a decent number of bands and albums that stayed reasonably true to hair metal's mid-to-late '80s stylings, the genre continued to shift, most prominently reflecting a harder, rougher, heavier edge, with less emphasis on the "glam" aspects of both the music and image. One of the albums that explicitly pushed these new boundaries was the sophomore release from **Skid Row**, *Slave to the Grind.* It was an absolute monster of a record and among the top five albums of the era, from my personal view.

Skid Row had achieved significant success with their self-titled debut in 1989, which was mostly a pop-metal album (albeit in a relatively heavier league versus bands like Poison or Warrant) with sales primarily driven by two ballads. However, in a somewhat counter-intuitive move on their follow-up release, Skid Row purposely chose to abandon the approach that brought them their fame. The band took a substantial risk with *Slave to the Grind*, releasing a brutal, ruthless set of aggressive songs soaked in fierce hard rock and heavy metal. There wasn't a single pop-metal "party-tune" to be found.

Similar to the unwanted characterization with which Extreme had been painted as a result of their soft-sounding hit "More Than Words," Skid Row sought to avoid enforcing the existing misperceptions of many listeners who only knew them for "I Remember You." Suffice it to say, *Slave to the Grind* more than quashed any sentiment held in that regard.

Aside from any image concerns, however, the new musical direction genuinely reflected the honest headspace of the band members during that period, particularly lead singer Sebastian Bach, who was busy loving Pantera's vicious release, *Cowboys From Hell*, at the time. Bach admittedly desired to do something more "rugged," proving to people just exactly who Skid Row was—a band of intensely heavy rock 'n' rollers. Skid Row didn't need to force or calculate anything; the new approach was simply who they were.

The album's lead track and first single was the crushing, kick-to-your-face "Monkey Business." The track ominously began with a restrained vocal simmering over bluesy, subdued guitar chords before exploding into a primal scream of which only Bach was capable, accompanied by a massively heavy guitar riff that drove the piercing anthem. "Monkey Business" was one of the greatest songs the genre had produced, although in retrospect it is admittedly somewhat difficult to characterize the bloodthirsty track as hair metal. That said, it must be remembered that, in 1991, the term hair metal still hadn't really been invented yet; the music mostly all remained "heavy metal."

But back to the album, as if "Monkey Business" wasn't heavy enough, the ferocious speed metal of second track "Slave to the Grind" absolutely blew the record's doors off. The extremely intense nature of the powerful song made it the perfect choice to open Skid Row's concerts from that point forward (replacing "Makin' A Mess").

Interestingly, "Slave to the Grind" was the album's only inclusion where the band chose to use the demo-take from the pre-production sessions rather than the more polished recordings from the official studio cuts. Skid Row actually recorded several formal versions of the tune during the album sessions but didn't feel any of them were able to match the raw ferocity of the rough demo, so they simply kept the track as it was.

The furious, fierce rockers continued throughout the record, all featuring utterly massive vocals from Bach and blistering guitar work from Scotti Hill and Dave Sabo. Other forceful, heavy metal highlights included "The Threat," "Psycho Love," "Living on a Chain Gang," and the burning, savage, mad-for-mosh-pit "Riot Act." *Slave to the Grind* never let up and was remarkably consistent—there was simply no filler or lowlights to be found.

Of course, Skid Row were smart enough not to entirely abandon their money-maker, also including three slower, ballad-type songs on *Slave to the Grind*, assuming you could truly characterize them as such. These weren't "love" songs by any stretch, but rather highly intense, dramatic anthems. Album closer and standout "Wasted Time" was an epic, six-minute crusher centered on the perils of losing a loved one to drug abuse, with soft, contemplative sections alternating with soaring, dramatic segments. Meanwhile, the powerful tracks "In a Darkened Room" and "Quicksand Jesus" also reflected deeper themes, including child abuse and the Gulf War.

The record also featured the controversial, head-bashing "Get the Fuck Out" (contestable for obvious reasons). A "clean" version of the album was proactively issued to retail chains wary of such tracks, on which the provocative tune was replaced with the infectious "Beggar's Day," a song more than worth seeking out as it was equally as impressive as most other material on the record.

Slave to the Grind became the very first hard rock/heavy metal album to debut in the No. 1 position on the Billboard Albums chart. Amazingly, it sold over two million copies without any significant "radio hits" (a reflection of the fact that "heavier" material was not exactly what radio was looking for at the time). Skid Row had succeeded in making a brilliant heavy metal record, but the two million in sales versus the five million achieved on their first album was a clear result of the aggressive style change.

Still, the commercial figures didn't appear to faze the band even a tiny bit as critical praise for the album was high, they had a No. 1 record on their hands, and Skid Row quickly scored the coveted opening slot on the impending mammoth Guns N' Roses Use Your Illusion Tour. Not bad at all for four punks from New Jersey and a vocally gifted Canadian hell-raiser.

Speaking of **Guns N' Roses**, they were, undoubtedly, by far and away, the biggest hard rock story in 1991. It had been four long years since the release of their record-breaking debut album, *Appetite for Destruction.* The band had toured continuously from August 1987 through December 1988, and the life-changing fame that enveloped them during that period clearly threw them for a loop.

Guns N' Roses went from living as homeless street rats to seventeen months of endless touring and debauchery, returning "home" as legitimate superstars with no ability to put their newfound fame and fortune into context. Alone in their big, new, fancy houses, the band members were isolated, confused, and rudderless, and several sank dangerously deeper into drug and alcohol addictions.

Clearly, Guns N' Roses were hardly in any position to pull it together and begin writing and recording a follow-up album. Their manager, Alan Niven, had wisely bought the group some time with the 1988 EP release *GN'R Lies*, but outside of that, spent most of his days simply trying to keep the band members alive as they managed their drug dependencies among the constant chaos stemming from their newborn celebrity.

Unfortunately, drummer Steven Adler was perhaps struggling the most and just couldn't seem to get his demons under control, specifically with regard to heroin. In the summer of 1990, under intense pressure from the record label, the band finally managed to assemble and start laying down initial recordings; however, Adler simply could not function or perform his duties while working on the new track "Civil War." Guns N' Roses had to face the harsh reality that Adler just might not be able to get himself together, and they reluctantly fired him from the group on July 11, 1990.

Slash quickly recruited The Cult's Matt Sorum to fill the open vacancy, but while Sorum was undoubtedly a capable drummer, Adler's absence clearly removed an integral part of the band's delicate ecosystem. Adler was far from the world's most technically proficient percussionist, but his unique "swing" was what many believed gave the songs on *Appetite for Destruction* an essential part of their magic and feel. In contrast, Sorum's style was more akin to a metronome (ironically, a change that was more than welcomed by the band as they had grown tired of Adler's inconsistencies). And as far as change went, Adler's departure would prove to be just the beginning.

The one thing Guns did have going for them, however, was an overabundance of new material from which to work. For starters, there were several "holdovers" still remaining from the *Appetite* sessions, including "You Could Be Mine," "Back Off Bitch," "Bad Obsession," and "The Garden." There was also even older material, such as "Don't Cry" (the first song the band ever wrote together) and, of course, "November Rain," which Axl Rose had been shaping and tinkering with long before *Appetite for Destruction.*

In addition, each band member had been writing on their own and bringing mostly-finished new songs to the table. This approach was another alteration to the dynamic, though. During the writing for *Appetite*, the band collectively worked up the songs as a group, with one member bringing in a riff or melody and all five of them then building upon it together until the full composition was finished. That was part of the Guns N' Roses magic—each member brought something unique to the table that made the whole vastly more than just the sum of its parts. This time around, however, that critical element was missing, and in my view, many of the songs suffered as a result.

While it was almost impossible to get everyone together in the same room during the years between the Appetite for Destruction Tour and 1991, when the band did come together, the work was surprisingly done rather expediently. In the end, the group had a whopping thirty songs they wanted to develop. Axl, for his part, envisioned a grand double-album, but management devised a more creative and lucrative solution to the abundance of material: the new album would come out as not one, but rather *two single standalone records*, to be released on the same day. The unorthodox strategy was an unprecedented stroke of genius that would not only create an additional revenue stream but further distinguish the release as more than just a "new album"—it was now an official "event."

And what an event it was. On the night of September 17, 1991, precisely at midnight, retail stores everywhere made special arrangements to open their doors at 12 a.m. to launch the sales of the much-anticipated new albums, titled *Use Your Illusion I* and *Use Your Illusion II.*

It was a music industry first. I vividly remember my friends and I standing in a line more than four blocks long that night, anxiously awaiting the chance to purchase the records (cassettes actually, as they were the primary musical format at the time). The releases were among the most anticipated in rock 'n' roll history.

In another unrivaled precedent, the albums debuted at No. 1 and No. 2 on the Billboard Albums chart, the first time in history the same artist had occupied both slots. *Use Your Illusion II* came in at No. 1 driven by the presence of the pre-released lead single, "You Could Be Mine," which was by far the best song on the set in my opinion and ironically the only track to really sound anything like *Appetite for Destruction* (indeed, it was written back during the *Appetite* sessions; lyrics from the song actually appear on that album's insert).

Over five hundred thousand copies were sold in the first two hours alone (which was entirely unheard of), and both albums would go on to sell more than seventeen million units combined worldwide. On September 17, 1991, Guns N' Roses were undeniably the biggest band on the planet (a further nod to hair metal's immense drawing power and popularity at the time).

Aside from the enormous commercial success of the albums, however, a more critical eye exposed a few cracks in the foundation. While the new songs inevitably shared some similarities with *Appetite for Destruction*, they were also markedly different in many ways. First was the sheer variety of material across the records. There were balls-out rockers, epic ballads with intricate orchestral arrangements, cover tunes, five songs featuring lead vocals by band members other than Axl, and the inclusion of a host of synthesizers and instrumentation—everything from piano to strings to choirs and banjos.

Many considered the albums to be "overproduced" in relation to the raw energy that was *Appetite for Destruction.* During the construction of the *Use Your Illusion* albums, Axl could be found in the studio alone each night from 2 a.m. to 7 a.m., layering all kinds of computer technology and other knife-ins on top of the basic tracks, mixes which Slash has since indicated were much closer in style to *Appetite* prior to Axl's transformations.

Axl also campaigned hard for the inclusion of a trilogy of dramatic, symphonic piano ballads that collectively told an interconnected story, "Don't Cry," "November Rain," and "Estranged." Axl was no doubt influenced by Elton John as a young boy and amazingly convinced the band to adopt a sixth member to support these types of songs, pianist Dizzy Reed. Whether you loved or hated this new side of Guns N' Roses, there was no debating it was relatively far removed from the sound present on *Appetite for Destruction.*

At the end of the day, for myself, the bloated albums simply contained what I considered to be too much "filler." Remember, these were indulgent records created by a group of individuals that, at the time, weren't really held to any structural boundaries due to their immense fame and power of influence. Had the production been different and the material limited to just one single album, I suspect it could have perhaps been closer on par with *Appetite*, although, in truth, we will never know for sure.

Many have shared this view and put together their own "single-album" playlist. What always strikes me about these suggested composites is their wildly different takes versus one another. Many of the lists (and I have seen plenty of them) only share two or three songs between them. I guess this speaks to the diversity of both the material and the audience—or perhaps Guns N' Roses were on the right track after all. For the record, my ideal single album is below, sequenced as such. Apologies in advance to those who will wonder, "how could he leave off *that* song?"

1. Right Next Door to Hell
2. Dust N' Bones
3. Perfect Crime
4. Pretty Tied Up
5. Double Talkin' Jive
6. Back Off Bitch
7. Yesterdays
8. You Could Be Mine
9. Breakdown
10. Locomotive
11. Dead Horse
12. November Rain

Mind you, none of this critique is to suggest the records weren't victorious. For the ambition they represented, and what the band set out to achieve up against the obstacles in their way, the end result was unquestionably phenomenal. And certain songs *were* legitimate standouts. "You Could Be Mine" was a blistering rocker. "November Rain," for all its bloated grandeur, was amazing. At ten minutes long, it was and still is the longest song ever to break the Top 10 on the Billboard chart. The song's epic video officially surpassed one billion views on YouTube in 2018, at that time, the only music video released before the year 2000 to achieve such a feat. Other tracks such as "Back Off Bitch," "Yesterdays," "Breakdown," and "Double Talkin' Jive" were all impressive in their own way.

An entire book could probably be written further dissecting and assessing the making and impact of these complex records, but suffice it to say, the albums were a *huge* event and would launch a beyond-massive four-year GN'R world tour in support, a trek that would be unlike any other in rock history (for both better and worse).

The coming months and years would see massive change for Guns N' Roses, and in the end, nothing would ever be the same. We'll get to that story later, though. Back in late 1991, Guns N' Roses could legitimately be considered the biggest "rock" band in the world (Metallica and U2 notwithstanding).

Outside of the massive shadow cast by Guns N' Roses, many other standout hair metal albums were released in 1991 as well. That said, the musical climate had already started to slightly sour on the genre with the early arrival of grunge. Several hair bands released new albums that were clear upgrades over their previous output but failed to achieve similar levels of commercial success. Some of the most notable examples of this circumstance surrounded the bands White Lion, Bang Tango, Danger Danger, and Britny Fox.

White Lion had been writing for two years post their successful 1989 *Big Game* album and released their fourth record, *Mane Attraction*, in 1991. In my view, the new album was a sizable step up for White Lion's offering more consistency with regard to quality writing, greater diversity, and a higher number of standout songs.

The first single, "Love Don't Come Easy," was a classic radio-friendly, mid-tempo hair metal anthem that would have easily been a smash success two years earlier, but with the changing musical landscape already beginning to seep in, the song stalled at No. 24 on the Top 40. Ditto for second single "Broken Heart," a much-improved re-imaging of the melodic song first featured on White Lion's 1984 release *Fight to Survive.* The new version topped out at a disappointing No. 64.

The record label then tried going in a different direction with the third single, "Lights and Thunder." The lead track on the album, the eight-minute rock song could only be described as a massive, epic, monster with multiple dramatic ups, downs, and time signature changes. The tremendous track simply had to be heard to be fully appreciated. Alas, much like the first two singles, the general populace just wasn't having it anymore.

The album had several other standout moments as well, including the rockers "Out With the Boys" and "Leave Me Alone," power ballads "You're All I Need" and "Till Death Do Us Part," blues tunes "It's Over" and "Blue Monday," and another blistering, epic, rock anthem, the seven-minute, anti-war protest track, "Warsong." Finally, the record fittingly wrapped up with the ultra-melodic "Farewell to You," the band's ode to relationships and life on the road.

Mane Attraction was quite possibly White Lion's finest overall album, and while it received rave critical reviews, the sales simply weren't there as with previous multi-Platinum sellers *Pride* and *Big Game.*

Perhaps sensing the hard times to come, Greg D'Angelo (drums) and James Lomenzo (bass) left the band soon after the album's release. Tramp and Bratta had always been the songwriting engine behind White Lion and benefitted most from the royalty checks, while D'Angelo and Lomenzo had been inequitably left out in the financial cold, feeling they couldn't afford to continue with the set-up as it was.

White Lion promptly recruited a couple of replacements and briefly toured in support of *Mane Attraction*, but difficulties and frustrations abounded, and the band finally reached the end of the road. When White Lion arrived in Boston for tour's final date, an exhausted Tramp took Bratta aside and simply told him, "This is our last show." Bratta, never really the band's driver like Tramp, aloofly offered only a one-word reply: "Okay." The record company that had pocketed millions off of the band only years before was happy to put up no fight at all, and just like that, White Lion was over.

While there would be much more from Mike Tramp over the coming decades, he and Bratta would unfortunately never play together again, and the ultra-talented Bratta would drop off the music scene entirely. Still, in 1991, *Mane Attraction* was an amazing album for fans of the band and undoubtedly represented some of the best White Lion had to offer.

🤘

Bang Tango, meanwhile, unfortunately found themselves in a similar situation to White Lion. While their 1989 debut, *Psycho Café*, was surely a solid album and had certainly been a commercial success, it perhaps lacked a little diversity and polish. This was more than remedied on Bang Tango's sophomore release, *Dancin' on Coals*, in 1991.

Dancin' on Coals was a terrific accomplishment as a wide-ranging, funky, blues-metal rock album. There unequivocally wasn't anything else at the time sounding anything like it. Opening track "Soul To Soul" began with a funky, atmospheric baseline and subtle vocals prior to launching into a boisterous, catchy rock anthem complete with horns alternating among metal guitar riffs. "Emotions in Gear," on the other hand, was a unique, radio-friendly pop-metal track containing hints of both a ballad and a funky rocker strewn together with orchestrated strings.

The album was chock-full of hook-laden, funk-metal blues songs, some with more hints of hair metal guitars than others. Most all tracks were winners, but particular highlights included the aforementioned "Soul To Soul" and "Emotions in Gear" in addition to "Big Line," "Dressed Up Vamp," and the moving ballad "Midnight Struck."

Alas, *Dancin' on Coals* failed to equal the commercial success of Bang Tango's debut and topped out at No. 113 on the Billboard Albums chart. That said, I loved the album in 1991 and still do today.

Danger Danger and Britny Fox, regretfully, fell victim to the same trap with their new releases. Both were great records that exceeded the quality of their earlier albums but fell well short of sales as a result of the changing musical tide threatening hair metal's grip as a commercially dominant style of music.

Danger Danger released *Screw It!* on October 1, 1991. The album was originally set to be dubbed *Monkey Business* in tribute to the title of the first single, but at the time, Skid Row was having success with their own song of the same name, and Danger Danger sought to avoid any unnecessary confusion. Frustrated that their preferred title was seemingly unavailable, the band wound up just saying "fuck it!" which innately led to the new title, *Screw It!*.

The album's style was classic hair metal, featuring wonderful pop-metal party-rock songs such as "Monkey Business," "Crazy Nites," and "Get Your Shit Together," along with the beautiful power ballads "I Still Think About You" and "Comin' Home." Musically, the album didn't necessarily break any new ground, but it was a consistent source of fun throughout featuring fantastic vocals from Ted Poley and amazing guitar work contributed by Andy Timmons (reference guitar-solo track "Puppet Show"). *Screw It!* was a definitive hair metal classic that shouldn't be skipped over by anyone who even remotely considers themselves a fan of the genre.

At the same time, **Britny Fox** were undergoing challenges of their own. The band had released *Boys In Heat* to critical acclaim in 1989, but, unfortunately, sales lagged behind their 1988 self-titled debut.

In response, lead singer Dean Davidson aspired to take Britny Fox in a new direction with less "screaming" and a more rootsy, stripped-down sound versus the band's traditional hair metal past. While the remainder of the group was not necessarily opposed to exploring a more "mature" sound, they felt strongly the magnitude of change Davidson was seeking would make them unrecognizable as the Britny Fox their fans had come to expect.

In the end, the band just couldn't get on the same page, and the embattled Davidson disappointingly wound up leaving the group as a result of personality differences and the lack of alignment on musical direction. Britny Fox was determined to carry on, however, and after hosting several intense auditions, they decided to bring aboard animated new singer/rhythm guitarist Tommy Paris (formerly of the band Jilson).

Paris was not only capable of successfully replicating the powerful screams of Davidson (in many ways, he was possibly a superior vocalist with greater range and energy) but also brought to the table a good measure of valued songwriting contributions. The band quickly put together their third album, *Bite Down Hard*, and while the style was still very much rooted in hair metal, it was also noticeably heavier and more aggressive, along with an uplift in the quality of its compositions.

Most of the songs were flat-out, balls-to-the-wall rockers, although many retained a melody and chorus melodic and catchy enough to be easily accessible and radio-friendly (had radio not stopped being amicable to hair metal music just about that time). Among the best of these tunes were "Six Guns Loaded," "Liar," "Louder," and "Closer To Your Love." The album also included two fabulous power ballads, "Over and Out" and "Look My Way."

Bite Down Hard is often recognized as Britny Fox's best work, but as with many other hair metal acts at the time, it failed to achieve any mainstream success. In the impending aftermath of the grunge takeover, Britny Fox would regrettably disband the following year.

Davidson, meanwhile, wasted no time forming the new band Blackeyed Susan and released the exact type of album he had envisioned for Britny Fox, the more stripped-back and organic *Electric Rattlebone*. Highlights from that record included the enjoyable pop-rockers "Satisfaction" and "None of It Matters."

While on the subject of lead singers that had branched out on their own, 1991 saw the illustrious **David Lee Roth** attempting to once again step into the hallowed rock 'n' roll spotlight. But before that could be accomplished, Roth needed a new band. Coming off the controversial *Skyscraper* album, both guitarist Steve Vai and bassist Billy Sheehan had gone their separate ways leaving substantial holes to be filled. In response, Roth substituted Vai's with nineteen-year-old guitar virtuoso Jason Becker and brought aboard Matt Bissonette to handle bass duties (brother of Roth's drummer, Gregg Bissonette).

While *Skyscraper* had been undeniably commercially successful, even Roth seemed to realize the pitfalls of its over-produced nature and craved a return to the rough, live energy associated with early Van Halen and the *Eat 'Em and Smile* album. To facilitate his quest, Roth and his band shacked up in one of the most rundown hotels in Vancouver (prostitutes, dealers, criminals, etc.) to write the new record, attempting to create the perfect ambiance to foster his blue-collar, "dirty" vision.

The resulting album, *A Little Ain't Enough*, was released on January 15, 1991. For the most part, it was a straight-ahead rock album with little of the diversity and experimentation present on *Skyscraper*. And this was a good thing, by and large. As far as Roth desiring a "rougher" sound, though, he perhaps both succeeded and failed at the same time. The new material was definitely much more aligned with the raw, energetic vein of old Van Halen, but with producer Bob Rock on board, the songs were clearly quite polished as well. The combination was a success, in my view, even if others didn't necessarily share the same sentiment with the somewhat glossy tunes presenting as slightly "generic" versus Roth's previous output.

The tracks were loud, powerful, blues-based rock songs, sung as only David Lee Roth could sing them, with lyrics to match. Not all were standouts, but the combined impact of the full album was formidable. Lead track and first single "A Little Ain't Enough" was easily the record's bright spot—a good-times rock anthem possibly as great as any Roth had produced in the past. Other energetic, attitude-soaked highlights included "Shoot It," "Baby's on Fire," "Last Call," and the sizzling "40 Below."

The record's second single was the ultra-bluesy, slide-guitar driven "Sensible Shoes." I could perhaps relate to the song's unique appeal, but it never really quite hit home for me. However, on the other end of the spectrum, "It's Showtime" was a welcomed, full-blown burner with guitar work undeniably comparable to early Van Halen.

Overall, the album was a fun listen for fans of Roth, and the band's performances were unquestionably top-notch. However, outside of the title track, there really weren't any "hit singles" for radio to easily embrace, and combined with the changing musical tastes of the public, the album (and Roth) was quickly doomed to lackluster sales and reception. *A Little Ain't Enough* did manage to achieve Gold status but it was a sizeable step down versus Roth's historical figures.

On top of the disappointing sales, sadly, just after joining the band, the talented Becker was tragically diagnosed with amyotrophic lateral sclerosis (ALS), also known as Lou Gehrig's disease. He courageously managed to complete the recording but was regrettably unable to participate in the forthcoming tour as a result of his quickly deteriorating health.

Speaking of the tour, it was unfortunately a disappointing financial failure, with low attendance and nearly half the shows canceled due to poor ticket sales as Roth and all he represented had become "unfashionable" in the wake of grunge. What had seemed impossible for so many years had suddenly and surprisingly come to pass—Roth had lost his divine place on the throne and been officially unseated as rock 'n' roll royalty. A dire circumstance, to say the least.

Outside of Roth, his former bandmates in **Van Halen** also dropped a new release in 1991, craftily titled *For Unlawful Carnal Knowledge.* Sammy Hagar had initially wanted to simply call the album *Fuck* in protest to the heavy emphasis on music censorship at the time but wisely settled instead for what was believed to be the word's phrasing origin.

Van Halen had come under heavy fire from a specific segment of their fanbase in recent years for their shift toward synthesizers and keyboards as opposed to maintaining their focus on the guitar-driven approach that had made the band famous. Happily, *For Unlawful Carnal Knowledge* represented a welcomed return to Eddie's guitars at the front and center and was almost entirely devoid of keyboards outside of the piano-driven "Right Now."

This much-desired shift should have heralded a triumphant return to form for the band (not that they needed it, as commercially they were as successful as ever, keyboards or not), but *For Unlawful Carnal Knowledge* disappointingly wound up a being mixed bag, at best.

When the album was good, it was great, with fantastic songs like "Poundcake," "Judgement Day," "The Dream Is Over," "Top of the World," and 'Right Now." "Poundcake" was a driving rocker that some found a little bland, but it definitely packed a solid punch. And yes, that's a real power drill Eddie was using on his guitar strings. Meanwhile, "Judgement Day" and "The Dream Is Over" were faster-paced rockers that represented some of the best Van Halen had to offer. "Top of the World," however, was a more radio-friendly, pop-oriented track with its origins tied to recordings for the band's *1984* album, where the song's main guitar riff can be heard tagged onto the outro for "Jump."

It was "Right Now," though, that truly scored significant success on radio and MTV. A contemplative, upbeat, piano-based number that also featured great guitar work, the song focused on living for the moment and embracing change. Hagar has since stated the lyrics were among the best he ever put to paper for a Van Halen song. "I was tired of writing cheap sex songs. Eddie and I wanted to get serious and talk about world issues."

However, when the album wasn't good, it was really just average (at least compared to historical Van Halen output), or at some points, even worse. "Spanked" should have been an embarrassment based on lyrics alone, but even the music was somewhat dull. "Pleasure Dome" featured impressive playing by the band, but the chorus and lyrical verses were weak, and the song really went nowhere. "In 'n' Out" and "Man on a Mission" were slightly better but mostly forgettable. "Runaround" was certainly catchy enough but a little too radio-friendly and formulaic to really excite the average Van Halen fan.

One thing the record did have going for it was its outstanding production. The album had taken over a year to make, and apparently it was worth the wait as the sound featured a thick, strong bottom-end to support the guitars and vocals, something that had been sorely lacking on *5150* and especially absent on *OU812*.

While *For Unlawful Carnal Knowledge* may have been an inconsistent affair, at best, to the discerning Van Halen fan, it continued the band's string of commercial success debuting at No. 1 on the Billboard Albums chart and eventually selling over three million copies. It should be noted, however, that *5150* and *OU812* had sold six million and four million units, respectively. The lower sales of *F.U.C.K.* may have reflected the album's weak spots, or more likely the fact that even the mighty Van Halen was not entirely immune to the changing musical climate.

One band that implausibly succeeded in bucking the trend of hair metal's partially declining status in 1991 was **Mr. Big**. Despite coming out in grunge's "year-zero," the group's second album, *Lean Into It*, found the band in vast public favor. It was an excellent record, for sure, but its commercial success was largely tied to one specific song representing the equivalent of finding a Willy Wonka Golden Ticket inside the album. More on that in a minute.

Mr. Big's 1988 self-titled debut featured amazing performances, but the songs generally lacked the necessary hooks and melodies required to generate any real radio or MTV success. *Lean Into It* suffered from no such malady, however, and included three bona fide hit singles alongside several other fantastic songs, climbing all the way to No.15 on the Billboard Albums chart.

Lead track "Daddy, Brother, Lover, Little Boy" was a blistering rocker featuring the unique stylings of guitarist Paul Gilbert and bassist Billy Sheehan harmoniously running Makita cordless drills over their guitar strings, creating an unusually fast solo not likely possible to be replicated with only human hands. (Along with Van Halen's "Poundcake," what was it with drills and guitars in 1991 anyway?)

The second single, "Green Tinted Sixties Mind," was the real pop-metal masterpiece, starting out with a melodic two-handed tapping riff before diving into smooth vocal verses and an ultra-catchy chorus. Written by Gilbert, the lyrics referenced a modern girl with dreams of living in the 1960s. The album's liner notes yield insight into the song's title: "Did you ever notice how old movies from the '60s have sort of a green tint to them? Strange but true."

Other outstanding rockers included the girlfriend/boyfriend runaway track "Alive and Kickin," the metallic (but still melodic) "Never Say Never" and the Jeff Paris-penned "CDFF-Lucky This Time." *Lean Into It* also contained the beautiful power ballad, "Just Take My Heart."

Ironically, though, it was the soft, acoustic ballad "To Be with You" that was the record's golden ticket. The album's second single went all the way to No. 1 on the Billboard chart and found *massive* success in over twenty different countries. Similar to Extreme's situation with "More Than Words," it was the only song if its kind on the album, but quickly came to define the band among casual observers. Mr. Big were suddenly "the ballad band" or the "guys that sing that 'To Be with You' song." Much like with Extreme, the success of the song became a double-edged sword.

That said, Mr. Big certainly enjoyed the victory at hand. Suddenly, the band, "workhorses for so long," as Martin put it, were all over radio and MTV. "It was like going from black and white to color," he stated. "It was a wonderful time." Mr. Big proceeded to embark on a successful world tour that even included three incredible nights opening for Aerosmith at London's Wembley Arena.

Most other hair metal bands in 1991 weren't as lucky as Mr. Big, though. **Kix** were coming off the very successful *Blow My Fuse* album in 1988, but it took them three long years to issue their follow-up, *Hot Wire*. Much like Ratt's *Detonator*, *Hot Wire* was Kix's most hair metal-sounding album. Some fans felt it was too derivative and got away from a few of the things that made Kix unique, but from my view, I found it took the band's sound and polished it to hair metal perfection. To each his own, I guess.

Hot Wire possessed fantastic production and was mostly a straight-ahead, heavy rock record. *Hot Wire* is probably my favorite Kix album, although fans of *Blow My Fuse* no doubt find that assessment blasphemous. Standout tracks included the blistering opener "Hot Wire," the pounding "Girl Money," energetic "Luv-A-Holic," and the rock 'n' rolling "Same Jane." *Hot Wire* also included the terrific power ballad "Tear Down the Walls," which two years earlier would have been a huge hit but was passed over without much to-do in 1991. *Hot Wire* peaked at No. 64 on the Billboard Albums chart in October 1991 and disappointingly only managed to sell about two hundred thousand copies.

L.A. Guns were coming off the Gold success of 1989's *Cocked & Loaded* when they resurfaced with their third album, *Hollywood Vampires*, on June 25, 1991. The new record was, in many ways, a considerable departure from the bombastic hair metal sound associated with the band's first two releases, although it was still distinctly L.A. Guns. The album saw the band branching out to explore several different musical styles other than the standard glam and sleaze metal for which they were known, but whether this approach truly worked or not was debatable, with the results largely being hit-and-miss.

Hollywood Vampires had a dark, semi-gothic theme on top of what was actually engineered to be a very commercial album. The songs were meticulously crafted, and the record included no fewer than three power ballads in an attempt to recreate the success of "The Ballad of Jayne." The writing and performance style were more organic, mellow, and stripped-down in nature (more acoustic guitars), fairly similar to the perceived "maturation" that Poison had undergone on their 1990 release, *Flesh & Blood.* That's not to say, though, that the album didn't contain an ample amount of blazing guitar work.

Right from the start of opening song "Over the Edge," it was clear this was a different kind of L.A. Guns. Buddhist gongs and Asian laments echoed hauntingly over an eerie, atmospheric orchestration with Indian percussion and a synth-string section (really). The intro then proceeded to morph into a deliberately trudging, blues-based, guitar-driven rocker with lyrics centered on coming down from a drug high. The track was likely the album's highlight and a fantastic new achievement for the band. The song also earned a spot in the hit-movie *Point Break,* starring Keanu Reeves and Patrick Swayze.

From there, the album spun off three terrific, stripped-back rockers: "Some Lie for Love," "Kiss My Love Goodbye," and "Here It Comes." Vocalist Phil Lewis was at the top of his game, and the songs had a natural spark. Had the record been able to maintain its momentum thereafter, it would have truly been something special, but regretfully, it was an inconsistent affair the remainder of the way.

"Crystal Eyes" was the first of the three power ballads, and while it was a good song, it admittedly lacked the magic of "The Ballad of Jayne." Make no mistake, though, similar to Kix's "Tear Down the Walls," had the track been released two years earlier it would have surely been an instant classic. "It's Over Now" fared a little better, being more upbeat and even "country-ish" in some parts, if you can believe that. The song received modest radio play and was a minor "hit" (and a personal favorite). The last ballad, the 1950s-style "I Found You," mostly just fell flat, however.

The rest of the album's rockers were less impressive, with only "Dirty Luv" having a little extra bite to it. Overall, the record represented an impressive spreading of L.A. Guns' wings, if admittedly a little monotonous in style at times. *Hollywood Vampires* was a great listen if you were in the mood for its distinct atmosphere, but for those looking for the L.A. Guns that wrote "Sex Action" and "Rip and Tear," they were not to be found in 1991, at least on album.

Another band who found themselves scaling back their sound away from the traditional grandiose hair metal template was **Great White**, who released their fifth album, *Hooked*, on February 26, 1991. *Hooked* featured a very stripped-back, bluesy tone with plenty of southern rock stylings. The production and overall mix of the album was, in my view, the best of any Great White record to-date at the time. The album had a perfect flow and made for a delightful, easy listen. While *Hooked* didn't replicate the massive success of *...Twice Shy* two years earlier, it was still certified Gold and managed to hit No. 18 on the Billboard Albums chart. It remains my favorite Great White album to this day.

Opening track "Call It Rock N' Roll" has often been designated as an attempt to clone the success of "Once Bitten, Twice Shy." The song is admittedly very similar in structure, and while it didn't quite hit the same mark for many fans, I actually considered it the stronger of the two tracks. Most every song on *Hooked* was a winner—highlights included "The Original Queen of Sheba," "Cold Hearted Lovin," and "Can't Shake It," in addition to the beautiful ballads "Lovin' Kind" and "Afterglow" (a cover of the Small Faces song). Also notable was the funky, southern bayou styling of "South Bay Cities," a track that saw the band having some earnest, laid-back fun.

Great White as a band seemed to come together perfectly on *Hooked*, with Jack Russel turning in one of his best vocal performances and each instrument perfectly complementing one another in the mix. It's a shame the average fan knows Great White only through songs like "Once Bitten, Twice Shy" or "Rock Me," as opposed to the band that shined through on either *Hooked* or their 1994 release, *Sail Away*.

In 2005 *Hooked* was remastered and reissued in Japan with four bonus tracks also recorded during the 1991 album sessions. Of these, "Train to Nowhere," a Savoy Brown cover, is a particularly necessary addition to the album that perfectly complements the record's overall easygoing vibe.

Enuff Z' Nuff released their sophomore album, *Strength*, on March 26, 1991. It was a huge step forward from their first record in terms of songwriting, depth, and diversity of material but failed to achieve the same commercial success similar to so many other new albums in 1991.

The record was mostly a continuation of the power-pop, hard rock sound present on the band's self-titled debut, only this time with a darker, moodier, and more textured tone in many places. Still, it was clearly rooted in a foundational sound derived from bands like the Beatles and Cheap Trick.

Lead track "Heaven or Hell" was explicitly written to duplicate the success of "New Thing," but as it was 1991 and not 1989, it did not. Not that the song was any less impressive, mind you. Likewise, "Goodbye" was the power ballad designed to mimic the accomplishments of "Fly High Michelle," but again, it did not. Still, it was also just as great a song. Commercial tastes were changing—it was as simple as that.

Other album standouts included the ultra-catchy "Baby Loves You," the light and airy "Hollywood Ya," the Beatles-esque "Mother's Eyes," and the epic "The Way Home / Coming Home."

At the time, Enuff Z' Nuff actually had a good bit of momentum on their side with *Strength* being released to rave critical reviews and *Rolling Stone* magazine naming the group "The Hot Band of the Year 1991." Further, hotshot celebrity Howard Stern publicly proclaimed Enuff Z' Nuff his favorite band, and the group even scored an appearance on the Late Show with David Letterman. Despite all this, however, nothing could stop the hair metal train from slowing down, and *Strength* fell far short of commercial sales expectations. Make no mistake, though, the record is still a gem waiting to be properly discovered someday.

Mötley Crüe in 1991 were coming down from the immensely

successful Dr. Feelgood Tour that ran from October 1989 to August 1990. To help maintain momentum before getting to work on their next "official" album, the band decided to put out their first compilation record, *Decade of Decadence '81-'91*, on October 13, 1991. This book doesn't focus on greatest hits albums as a general rule, but *Decade* was notable for being more than just the average "best of" release.

The collection featured two songs from each of the band's first five albums (three of which were remixed for *Decade*) in addition to a soundtrack contribution, a compilation album track, a live recording, and most notably, three newly recorded songs: the powerful, rumbling "Primal Scream," pop-metal "Angela," and punk-oriented "Anarchy In The U.K." (a Sex Pistols cover).

Decade of Decadence ascended all the way to the No. 2 position on the Billboard Albums chart, demonstrating the mighty power of Mötley Crüe at the time. The remix version of "Home Sweet Home" actually broke the Top 40, climbing higher than the original had back in 1985 on the same chart.

"Primal Scream," though, was particularly significant, taking all the best elements from *Dr. Feelgood* while adding a snarling, mean, nasty groove on top. It was the perfect song to re-energize Crüe-heads and elevate hope the band could continue the massive success of *Dr. Feelgood* (or even top it). Alas, this would sadly not come to pass, but more on that later in 1992.

Tesla released their third studio record, *Psychotic Supper*, on August 31, 1991, an album the band still proclaims to this day to be their best work. While many Tesla fans share that view, Personally, I do not hold it on quite the same level as, for me, it simply strayed a little too far from the hard rock, hair metal stylings of *Mechanical Resonance* or even *The Great Radio Controversy* in many places. That said, there are a few admittedly great songs on *Psychotic Supper*, including the groovy "Change in the Weather," hard-rocking "Edison's Medicine," and scorching "Had

Enough."

The big, popular semi-ballads "Call It What You Want" and "What You Give" didn't exactly ring my bell for whatever reason, but these generally well-liked songs undoubtedly helped push the album to a very impressive (for 1991) Platinum sales status.

🤘

The year 1991 also featured what was perhaps the very last hair metal band to join the fray and get a brief taste of success before the genre collapsed: **Tuff**. The group had spent several long, hard years establishing their brand on the Sunset Strip in L.A. before finally landing a major record deal and releasing their excellent debut, *What Comes Around Goes Around*, in May 1991.

The album was 100 percent hair metal and featured several cool rockers such as "The All New Generation," "Ruck a Pit Bridge," "Lonely Lucy," and "Forever Yours," alongside the hit single power ballad "I Hate Kissing You Goodbye" which reached the No. 3 position on Dial MTV, behind Guns N' Roses and Metallica. Regrettably, though, Tuff's timing was less than ideal, and unfortunately, they hit the scene just a couple of years too late to fully partake in the genre's remarkable run of commercial success.

🤘

Speaking of **Metallica**, while they fall just outside the hair metal scope and focus of this book, it would be remiss to fail to at least briefly note and acknowledge their 1991 self-titled release (affectionately known as *The Black Album*, in reference to the simplistic cover art) for the sheer titanic impact it had on the periphery of all things hard rock and heavy metal.

The Black Album represented a dramatic shift for Metallica from long, complicated, progressive arrangements to more straightforward, one-dimensional rock/metal songs. This change served to open up a new level of accessibility for the average listener and promptly thrust the band into the upper stratosphere of success with the album debuting at No. 1 in ten different countries and going on to sell a whopping si copies in the US alone.

"True" Metallica fans bristled at the perceived (and nc commercialization of the band's sound (heck, the record even featured two songs that could legitimately be characterized as ballads), but there was no denying the overwhelming success of the album. It didn't hurt that the record contained some genuinely amazing songs ("Enter Sandman," "Sad But True") in addition to an incredible overall sound, courtesy of the pristine and powerful production by Bob Rock.

In 1991, it was hard to find a fan of hair metal that wasn't also a huge fan of *The Black Album*. Remember, at the time, the lines that would later be so conveniently drawn to differentiate various subgenres of hard rock weren't as clear as they would be in retrospect, and they were certainly much less of a focus point. In 1991, Skid Row, Guns N' Roses, and Metallica all had albums that debuted at the No. 1 position on the Billboard Albums chart, and it was all homogenously "hard rock" or "heavy metal," for the most part.

Similar to this point, one last release in 1991 that deserves special recognition despite not categorizing very well into the hair metal genre is **Ozzy Osbourne**'s *No More Tears*. Ozzy-purists will no doubt point toward *Blizzard of Ozz* or *Diary of a Madman* as the best works from the outlandish frontman's solo career, but for me, it was *No More Tears*, which was demonstrably Osbourne's most hair metal release in terms of style and sound.

Penned with axeman extraordinaire Zakk Wylde, *No More Tears* was a huge rock record with several standouts ("Mr. Tinkertrain," "I Don't Want to Change the World," "Desire," and the epic "No More Tears") alongside other prominent groovers and stompers ("S.I.N.," "Hellraiser," and "Zombie Stomp"). The album even included two successful hit ballads: "Mama I'm Coming Home" and "Time After Time."

No More Tears soared to No. 7 on the Billboard Albums chart, producing four singles in the Top 40 and recognizing sales of more than four million copies. Akin to *The Black Album*, in 1991, it was almost impossible to find a hair metal enthusiast who wasn't also a big fan of *No More Tears.*

Outside of new music, 1991 was notable for two additional happenings representing especially significant events in hair metal history. The first was the tragic death of Def Leppard guitarist **Steve Clark.** Clark was one of the band's principal songwriters (from a riff standpoint) and had a unique talent for writing catchy, melodic and complex hooks. Unfortunately, as Def Leppard's success had grown over the years, so did Clark's alcohol addiction.

The band conducted a formal intervention for Clark in 1989 when doctors warned of the significant harm the troubled guitarist was doing to his body. Clark enrolled in proper rehab as a result, but regretfully, the therapy didn't stick, and he continued to struggle with the addiction both physically and mentally. On January 8, 1991, Clark peacefully died in his sleep from a lethal combination of alcohol and prescription pain medication. The death was ruled accidental. He was only thirty years old. Many say the "real" sound of Def Leppard also died that day, and in a lot of ways, that is probably true.

Tesla, who had opened for Def Leppard on the *Hysteria* tour, included the moving "Song & Emotion" on their *Psychotic Supper* album in dedication to Clark, as stated on the liner notes: "To Our Friend, Steve 'Steamin' Clark."

The second high-profile event involved Poison and guitarist **C.C. DeVille.** Poison was at their commercial peak in 1991 and were an obvious choice to perform at the MTV Video Music Awards. However, the band had good reason for concern when DeVille showed up clearly intoxicated with a colossal coif of bright pink hair. Poison was scheduled to play their successful new single "Unskinny Bop," but DeVille became confused at the start of the song and precariously launched into "Talk

Dirty to Me" instead. Poison recovered (somewhat), but it was clearly an awkward moment and a rough performance.

Once backstage, singer Bret Michaels and DeVille got into a serious fistfight as frustrations that had been building between them for years finally boiled over. Soon after the incident, DeVille was fired from Poison, and just like that, the entire dynamic was changed for one of the rock 'n' roll's principal bands at the time; some would argue for the better, others for the worse. More about this when we come back to Poison in the following years.

🤘

Other noteworthy albums released in 1991: The Scream *(Let It Scream)*, Poison *(Swallow This Live)*, Aldo Nova *(Blood on the Bricks)*, Dangerous Toys *(Hellacious Acres)*, Armored Saint *(Symbol of Salvation)*, Contraband *(Contraband)*, Lita Ford *(Dangerous Curves)*, Richie Sambora *(Stranger in This Town)*, Tyketto *(Don't Come Easy)*, XYZ *(Hungry)*, Kik Tracee *(No Rules)*, Shotgun Messiah *(Second Coming)*, Bulletboys *(Freakshow)*, Sweet F.A. *(Temptation)*

The year 1991 saw a ton of fantastic, high-quality new albums, and groups like Guns N' Roses, Mötley Crüe, Poison, and Metallica were clearly among the biggest bands in the world. However, there was no denying the start of hair metal's commercial decline, initially and primarily affecting what some would consider the so-called second and third-tier bands.

The impending grunge movement was already making its presence felt with regard to the changing musical climate and preferences of the general public. Still, *no one* could have predicted how completely, abruptly and violently the bottom was about to drop out with the full explosion of grunge that was right around the corner.

Best Albums 1991

1. Skid Row – *Slave to the Grind (Top 5 in Genre!)*

2. Danger Danger – *Screw It!*
3. David Lee Roth – *A Little Ain't Enough*
4. Britny Fox – *Bite Down Hard*
5. Mr. Big – *Lean Into It*
6. Bang Tango – *Dancin' On Coals*
7. White Lion – *Mane Attraction*
8. Guns N' Roses – *Use Your Illusion I & II*
9. L.A. Guns – *Hollywood Vampires*
10. Kix – *Hot Wire*
11. Ozzy Osbourne – *No More Tears*
12. Enuff Z'Nuff – *Strength*
13. Metallica – *Metallica*
14. Van Halen – *For Unlawful Carnal Knowledge*
15. Tuff – *What Comes Around Goes Around*
16. Great White – *Hooked*
17. Tesla – *Psychotic Supper*

IV

A Different Kind of Truth

1992 – 1998

Chapter 13

Interlude

The Rise of Grunge (Smells Like Teen Spirit)

"Grunge killed hair metal." That's how the story goes, right? More specifically, "Nirvana killed hair metal" seems to be the more precise retrospective sentiment among many. But is that really what happened? In reality, there is legitimately a lot of truth to that perspective, but it is certainly not the *whole* truth or adequate enough on its own to explain the violent, dramatic shift in musical tastes that seemingly happened virtually overnight in late 1991 and early 1992.

It has already been noted that hair metal was experiencing turbulence even before grunge first reared its ugly head. The market was becoming oversaturated via the sheer number of bands signed to new record contacts, all basically following the exact same hair metal template with regard to style and sound. That's not to necessarily say hair metal music in aggregate was lessening in quality; in fact, it was just the opposite in many cases, but some consumers inevitably began to view the output as somewhat stale.

In other instances, we saw that hair metal had indeed begun to change on its own. Bands like Cinderella and Poison took their third albums in a decidedly different direction from the pure hair metal aspects associated with their previous releases. Warrant had tried to do some of the same with their second album in 1990 and might have succeeded if the record company hadn't made it all about "Cherry Pie." L.A. Guns and Great

White shaped their 1991 albums with much more organic, stripped-back styles versus the bombastic hair metal tendencies that marked their earlier records. Jon Bon Jovi's 1990 solo album sounded very little like *Slippery When Wet* or *New Jersey*. And Skid Row's *Slave to the Grind* was far too heavy to really be characterized as hair metal. Even Guns N' Roses' *Use Your Illusion* albums contained a great deal of material that distanced itself from the standard template.

That said, the impact of grunge was clearly the tipping point. Grunge music and the immensely popular subculture associated with it was essentially the polar opposite of everything hair metal stood for, and quickly found itself in definitive favor.

The grunge movement originated in the Pacific Northwest in the very late '80s, primarily in Seattle (it was perhaps fitting that it came from a location famous for its dreary weather). The music drew influences from many places, including punk and heavy metal, but the result was actually a sludgy conglomeration of many disparate sounds.

The raw musical styling was characterized by down-tuned, distorted guitar riffs, pessimistic/nihilistic lyrics, and a deep, low vocal that was in stark contrast to the powerful, high-energy, upper-register approach employed by hair metal bands. This specific vocal mannerism came to be known as "yarling." (At the time, I admittedly referred to it simply as "whining," but, you know . . . details.) The style was first made popular by Eddie Vedder of Pearl Jam and Layne Stanley of Alice In Chains and was defined by a nasal, baritone drone, with lyrics that were often slurred or un-enunciated. The overall aesthetic of grunge was objectively slow, dark, depressing, and ugly. Like I said, pretty much the exact opposite of hair metal.

Also in stark contrast was the simplified or lower level of musicianship associated with grunge music. Intricate guitar solos were replaced with simple, messy, distorted power chords. While this was seen as a drawback to some, the higher level of accessibility the new sound offered actually turned into a driving, attractive element to millions of listeners. Suddenly, the barriers to entry associated with being in a rock band were demolished;

three guys in a garage could get together over a weekend and suddenly be in "a band."

Illustrative of this effect, Def Leppard played an unplugged, on-air radio event circa the grunge era during which they performed several songs featuring lush, layered, three-part vocal harmonies. Upon witnessing the performance, the surprised young DJ commented, "the vocals were "incredible!"; Def Leppard singer Joe Elliot casually replied, "You must be a product of '90s grunge—there is nothing incredible about three guys singing in tune."

The accessibility of the music, however, went further than just the level of difficulty required to play. It was also a matter of relatability. Grunge bands didn't "look" like rock stars. The new subculture carried a fashion trend paradoxical to everything previously offered up by hair metal. Feathered hair, makeup, and flashy outfits were replaced with dirty flannel shirts, ratty sweaters, baggy jeans, knit caps, and unkempt hair. Suddenly, it was now stylish to dress like a homeless bum. Grunge bands looked like punk kids that simply shambled out of their parents' garage, and in many cases, that's precisely what they were.

Further to this, the youth of the emerging generation was starting to feel a fundamental sense of detachment from all things hair metal. Rock concerts during the '80s were larger-than-life spectacles that were surely an extraordinary sight to behold, and while new Generation Y teenagers still admired this (to an extent), they also began to feel an inability to connect with it, being so different from the world in which they lived day-to-day. In contrast, grunge concerts featured artists dressed just like average-Joes, playing songs that were relatively easy for the common person to learn on guitar.

There's also the undeniable fact that rock music throughout history has centered on rebellion. Hair metal had simply been at the top for so many years that it naturally began to lose its innate ability to represent that dissidence. There was no insurgency associated with kids linking themselves to a style of music that received tons of commercial exposure and already ruled the pop charts. It also went against the inherent teenage desire to be a contrarian.

Grunge was also more connected to a generation that was experiencing a distinctly different political and socio-economic climate versus what was present during hair metal's birth and ascension during the '80s. The '80s were a bright time of economic rebuilding, where deregulation was prevalent and everything cultural was becoming bigger and more inflated with an emphasis on flashy spectacle. Across the board, the theme of the decade was unquestionably "excess"—more fun, more drugs, more money, more power, more flash. Hair metal was a natural extension and reflection of this.

But as the '80s came to a close, times began to shift towards the grim and somber, both economically and socially. There had to be a crash to accompany the high. The average American just couldn't relate anymore. Suddenly, an entirely new generation of kids had very little interest in having "Nothing But a Good Time." They instead felt angst, alienation, and depression. And grunge music was right there ready to swoop in and satisfy all their needs.

Grunge felt more "real" to the new generation. It was the perfect medium if you were angry, sad, confused, or depressed and wanted to embrace those feelings. It allowed you to "connect." Hair metal offered nothing along those lines. Personally, I was still seeking the exact opposite. Hair metal was my mechanism to escape those negative feelings. Grunge music was admittedly a giant, pessimistic downer. For myself and other hair metal enthusiasts, at the time, we didn't need or want our music to remind us how difficult life was, let alone exacerbate that feeling. We simply desired an escape to bigger, brighter, and better things, i.e., hair metal. I didn't listen to music to embrace being depressed—I listened to it to lift me up!

Angst and depression were things grunge could deliver in spades via a guy in his grandfather's sweater, whining onstage while strumming three simple chords and staring at his shoes. I and others like me who sought something more fun and positive were quickly becoming the minority. The average listener wanted to see their music reflect their feelings. Bands like Nirvana made it "cool" to be depressed and "serious," and to talk about how "life sucked" all the time.

This new outlook then began to feed off itself until it became an unstoppable monster, as the sentiment and cultural embracing of grunge only intensified after the suicidal death of Nirvana lead singer Kurt Cobain in 1994. Tragic as it was, it served to martyr Cobain in a way that deified him along with everything for which grunge had stood. Record labels immediately and desperately reached out in all directions to find the "next Nirvana." Suddenly, every underground garage-band act in Seattle seemingly received a record deal overnight.

In addition to grunge pioneers Nirvana, Pearl Jam, Soundgarden, and Alice In Chains, tons of knockoffs and copycat bands began to emerge, such as Candlebox, Stone Temple Pilots, and Creed. And these bands proceeded to sell millions of records and dominate the music scene. Ironically, the explosion of grunge wasn't all that different in format from when hair metal exploded in the late '80s. As stated, everything is cyclical.

The siloed approach and inherent behavior of the music industry also severed to exacerbate this transition. In 2011 Warrant guitarist Erik Turner was asked his thoughts on Nirvana's *Nevermind* album, as it was the twenty-year anniversary of the record widely associated with the "death" of hair metal. His response (edited):

> *"I loved that album. It was a great record. What I didn't like was the fact that the industry had to sell only one type of music: grunge. Too bad that the world is big enough for all kinds of music, whether it's grunge, rap, dance, pop or rock. In America, music isn't promoted on merit, it's more based on selling a brand, a brand that is created by the industry. They might as well be selling toothpaste. It's just a product to the record labels. 'It's the new, improved Crest! Now whiter! We no longer sell that other Crest. That other Crest sucks! Now we're selling this new Crest.' They just don't have any soul. If the music industry was a church, we (hair bands) would've all been excommunicated. 'You are no longer welcome to come bow at the*

altar.' We were branded as harlots. Bam! 'You're no longer wanted or needed around here.'"

Indeed, the music industry fully turned its back on hair metal to instead embrace grunge. Never before in history had the establishment just outright dropped a cash-cow moneymaking genre as sweepingly as it did with hair metal.

The resulting impact on hair bands was profound, seemingly driving immediate and outright death. "You sold three million records last year? Well, this year you'll be lucky to sell three hundred. Never mind that your new album is much better than your last. And oh, by the way, we're dropping you from the record label."

Symbolizing this industry phenomenon, Warrant cut a demo song during the grunge era and had their manager strategically present it to the record label with the artist name blanked out to avoid any negative stigma associated with their brand. The label executive was reportedly "thrilled" to hear the "amazing new song" and insisted the band be presented immediately to be swiftly signed to a record deal and marketed to achieve fortune and fame. When the artist was revealed to be Warrant, however, the record label suddenly wanted nothing to do with the song. Hair bands were blacklisted, plain and simple.

To be fair, there were a few notable partial-exceptions to this new world order; Van Halen and Aerosmith were, to a limited extent, somewhat immune to the grunge virus compared to the average hair band, but those groups were never really traditional hair bands anyway. Guns N' Roses may have also fared not so terribly during the grunge era, but we'll never know as they managed to implode fully on their own terms.

Also to be clear, there were assuredly several genuinely great albums released by the so-called hair bands during the grunge era (to be outlined in the coming chapters), but for the most part, anything that even gave off the faint scent of hair metal after 1992 really had no chance at commercial success before it even got out of the gate.

In reality, though, it was quite possible hair metal would have gone out of fashion with or without grunge. Every music genre throughout history has generally run its course in a defined period of time. Young people become tired of the current fad and move on to the next, just like the generations before them did.

Additionally, hair metal may not have been built to last merely due to the defined nature of what it was. The tremendous spectacle these bands grew to encompass really left no space for evolution. At some point, there was simply no more room for any additional excess—you couldn't play guitar any faster, sing any higher, or party any harder. And when these bands did try to evolve, the average listener found it hard to take them seriously based on the larger-than-life reputation they had built up in the '80s. Grunge was likely just in precisely the right place at exactly the right time to pounce.

So, it shouldn't have been any real surprise that hair metal would eventually lose its foothold as a dominant style of music, but the shock, however, was that the change would seemingly occur so suddenly and with such violent force as to immediately brand all things hair metal the most unfashionable matter of substance ever known to man. (Truly, there isn't much exaggeration to that statement with regard to what actually happened.)

Hair metal's organic decline in the absence of grunge would have likely been a long, extended ramp-down; however, in the presence of grunge, hair metal experienced a near extinction-level event previously reserved only for the dinosaurs (and perhaps, disco). It was, frankly, unprecedented in music history.

At the end of the day, likely via some combination of all the factors discussed here, grunge music was undeniably an unstoppable force that exploded onto the scene in the early '90s contributing mightily to the abrupt end of hair metal's commercial popularity. Even if it didn't exactly happen "overnight" as popular sentiment would hold (although it was pretty close), when Nirvana's "Smells Like Teen Spirit" was released to radio on August 27, 1991, a seismic shift occurred that would generate reverberations forever into the future.

Fortunately, however, hair metal is a fickle and resilient beast, and unlike the dinosaurs, while admittedly "down" (or at least out of the commercial eye) for some time, the genre would thankfully refuse to all-out die or simply fade out of existence, as we will see.

Chapter 14
Keep the Faith
(1992)

By 1992, even though it was clear the musical landscape had begun to change, many hair bands, for the most part, steadfastly continued to generate new music, even though some of them continued to evolve their sound outside of traditional hair metal stylings. There was a genuine feeling at the time that hair metal and grunge didn't necessarily have to be mutually exclusive, although that would soon prove to be mostly incorrect.

Van Halen was touring in support of their *For Unlawful Carnal Knowledge* album during this period and had ironically chosen grunge pioneers Alice in Chains as their opening act. It was all just rock 'n' roll, right? However, attending the show in Philadelphia, Pennsylvania, I distinctly recall an arena of frenzied hair metal fans zealously booing the unknown newbies off the stage, having absolutely no appetite for their muddy, droning, lifeless persona. Little did we know the tables would soon be turned.

Despite the impending transition that would shortly surround them on all sides, hair bands had yet to fully accept or acknowledge most new hair metal albums were simply not going to sell millions of copies like before. A portion of this naiveté stemmed from the fact that the musical change was, in reality, a little more drawn out than it is given credit for through a historical lens, while, at the same time, some of it was just plain, staunch denial.

In addition to the evolution of their sound, hair bands continued to adjust their image as well. Mostly gone was the "glam" look characterized by make-up, spandex, bright colors, and flashy clothes. I remember discussing Warrant's upcoming album with a fellow fan of hair metal in early 1992. I related to her seeing new pictures of the band in a recent issue of *Metal Edge* (a popular magazine dedicated to hair metal coverage at the time; remember, this was *before* the internet), clearly showing the band members had traded in their famous glam look for straight hair, leather, jeans, and a general "black" tone. You should've seen her face; she was absolutely mortified! You would have thought I just told her a family member had died. And perhaps that hyperbole was closer to the figurative truth than we realize, with many hardcore fans living and dying by the hair metal sword at the time.

Outside of ditching the glam look, however, for other hair band heroes, the absolute unthinkable even happened—they cut their hair! Much to the dismay and disappointment of millions of female fans, Jon Bon Jovi was the most prominent example of this. Now, I'm quite sure Jon was still near the top of most of the girls' wish lists, but one of hair metal's upper-crust royalty cutting their hair? The event *literally* made headlines on CNN. (I kid you not; look it up.) Times they were a-changing it seemed.

Bon Jovi actually had one of the most prominent album releases in 1992, appropriately titled *Keep the Faith.* The band had been on "hiatus" since early 1990 after more than four years of nonstop writing, recording, and touring to support the enormous *Slippery When Wet* and *New Jersey* albums. The workload and lifestyle had taken a substantial physical and mental toll on the band. Frustration and infighting naturally developed among the group's members, and unthinkably, Bon Jovi's future was suddenly somewhat in doubt.

During the hiatus, the musical climate had moved on to a completely different place from the sound of *Slippery When Wet* that practically launched the entire hair metal genre in the first place. Jon Bon Jovi and Richie Sambora had released solo albums in 1990 and 1991, respectively, both of which had little in common with the traditional Bon Jovi sound.

However, the new sonic explorations, combined with the refreshing nature of the break, served well to rejuvenate the band and spark new avenues of creativity. Guitarist Richie Sambora claimed the band members needed to “find themselves individually,” and the experiences they had during that time different from the endless grind of life on the road served to open up fresh new writing ideas.

Bon Jovi had become excited to start a new era for themselves, but before it could begin, there were outstanding issues to be addressed, lest they continue to plague the group’s future. First, the band fired longtime manager Doc McGhee, with Jon Bon Jovi assuming full command forming Bon Jovi Management. The band also employed outside counseling to assist them in working through their issues together as a group.

Once the house had been cleaned and the air cleared, the band began to rekindle their relationship and turn their focus toward a new album. In January 1992, Bon Jovi retreated to Little Mountain Studios in Vancouver, British Columbia, to begin work on *Keep the Faith*, officially starting a new chapter in their career.

As could be expected, the album represented a significant change in terms of songwriting and sound. *Keep the Faith* began to turn away from the extravagant hair metal tendencies of the past and instead adopted a more “mature” tone, with fewer crazy guitar solos and more profound lyrics (songs like “I’ll Sleep When I’m Dead” and “Woman in Love” being recognized exceptions).

“When we got back together in a room in Vancouver," noted Jon Bon Jovi in 2007, "we closed the door and ignored what had happened to our genre of music. We'd been kicked in the teeth by Nirvana, but we didn't pay attention to that. We got rid of the clichés, wrote some socially conscious lyrics, and got a haircut. I didn't do a grunge thing, and I didn't do a rap thing. But I knew I couldn't re-write ‘Livin' on a Prayer’ again, so I didn't try.”

Inspired by the Los Angeles riots of 1992, “Keep the Faith” was the album's first single, featuring a driving bass line that pushed the song along at a fairly metered tone, only to be subsequently amplified by a mighty, uplifting chorus. While the track in contrast versus much of Bon Jovi's past output, the song was met with critical praise and commercial success, peaking at No. 29 on the Billboard Albums chart. For me, however, album opener "I Believe" was much more energetic and exciting, with its slow intro crescendoing into a massive vocal shout and unfolding into a propulsive anthem of optimism.

"In These Arms" was a fantastic mid-tempo blend of pop and rock, and, of course, the album featured two colossal power ballads. Of these, "I Want You," unfortunately, came off as slightly uninspired, but "Bed of Roses" became the record's biggest hit climbing all the way to No. 10 on the Top 40 chart. The six-minute, piano-driven track featured wailing guitars, introspective verses, a soaring, emotionally anguished chorus, and all the melodrama one could muster. Jon Bon Jovi supposedly wrote the song while nursing a hangover and feeling down in the dumps.

The remaining material on *Keep the Faith* was rather pedestrian, though, along with two tracks that were a little bit of a left turn. "If I Was Your Mother" included guitar riffs that wouldn't necessarily have been out of place on a Metallica album (seriously) along with soft strings in sections, while "Dry County" was a ten-minute epic referencing the decline of the US domestic oil industry and its effect on those whose had come to rely on its income. The song contained several dramatic rises and falls along with varied instrumental sections. "Dry County" was many a fan's favorite tune on the album, but for me, it never really resonated even though I admired the aspirations behind what the band was trying to achieve.

From my view, two of the absolute best tracks recorded for *Keep the Faith* surprisingly didn't make the final cut upon the album's completion. "Starting All Over Again" was an amazing, upbeat song that fully represented where the band members' heads were at the time, and "The Radio Saved My Life Tonight" was equally uplifting and catchy. The former song would appear as a bonus track on the Japanese pressing of *Keep the Faith,* and thankfully both songs would later be included on Bon

Jovi's incredible 2004 box set, *100,000,000 Bon Jovi Fans Can't Be Wrong.*

Keep the Faith made it all the way to No. 5 on the Billboard Albums chart but sold only two million copies, a considerable step down from Bon Jovi's past success. Still, given the commercial focus on grunge at the time, it was a terrific comeback. More importantly, the album showed Bon Jovi they could survive anything—changing musical trends, business turmoil, personal dust-ups—and they could still come out ahead.

"The genre of music that we were a part of was now going away, and, you know, here was this sign of faith, which is all we really had to go forward with," Bon Jovi told NPR in 2009. "We went into the '90s with a clear objective, and that was to believe in each other and what it was that we were all about." Keep the faith indeed.

The other highest-profile release in 1992 was **Def Leppard**'s long-awaited follow-up to their groundbreaking *Hysteria* album, *Adrenalize.* It would be the very last of the big "blockbuster" hair metal records to generate substantial commercial success, with the band just managing to beat the ticking clock that was grunge. However, in what was becoming true Def Leppard fashion, while the album was a substantial victory, it was made under a backdrop of uncertainty, difficulty, and tragedy.

Def Leppard had reunited with longtime producer and integral "sixth member" of the band, Mutt Lange. At the time, however, Lange was predominantly consumed working with Bryan Adams on what would become his *Waking Up the Neighbors* album (which, incidentally, sounds *a lot* like Def Leppard if you notice), With Lange unable to make himself as available or invested as with past efforts, Def Leppard made the risky decision to co-produce the album on their own.

Adding to the challenge, similar to Bon Jovi, Def Leppard had toured extensively behind *Hysteria* and the effect was predictably draining. Everyone was simply exhausted. Not to mention the band faced the immense pressure of having to follow up one of the biggest selling albums of all-time. Most of all, though, Def Leppard was still reeling from the loss of guitarist Steve Clark, who passed away in early 1991 following a long, painful struggle with alcoholism. (Prior to his death, Clark did co-write six songs that would appear on *Adrenalize*, however). The band was tired, numb, confused, and admittedly and in a daze. They were going to have to dig deep for this one.

Def Leppard had faced tragedy before, though, particularly in 1984, when drummer Rick Allen shockingly lost his arm. "Whenever anything negative happens to us, it always pulls us together, personally and musically," Allen said after Clark's death. "You batter on with the record and it takes your mind off whatever bad is happening." And that's precisely what the band did, recording as a four-piece with Phil Collen playing both rhythm guitar and the lead parts previously handled by the much-missed Clark. Def Leppard was determined to carry on.

It a lot of ways, the finished product took up right where *Hysteria* left off, but *Adrenalize* was truly more of a straightforward pop-rock album, with prominent guitars and songwriting that was concise and to-the-point. On the downside, though, the record lacked some of the adventure and diversity boasted by *Hysteria*.

Among the album's most notable tracks was "White Lightning," the next-to-last song written for the record (both in memory of and dedicated to Clark). The tune was both somber and powerful at the same time, a truly stunning piece of music. "So much emotion went into 'White Lightning,' by the time we put it to bed it was like we'd done group therapy," Elliott recalls. "After that, we needed something completely ridiculous."

Cue the final song penned for *Adrenalize*, the lead single and opening track, "Let's Get Rocked." It was a simple, silly (yet effective), upbeat, catchy rock song. (Elliot supposedly wrote the lyrics after watching an episode of *The Simpsons*.) You could possibly say it was Def Leppard's "Unskinny Bop," although I'm not sure how the band would feel about that analogy. Def Leppard was shooting for a shameless, celebratory rock song fit for a stadium performance, and they no doubt more than succeeded along those lines. The track's opening stand-alone lyrics set the tone for both the song and the album as an event: "Do you wanna get rocked?"

And that was really it in a nutshell. Coming from a backdrop of tragedy and difficulty, *Adrenalize* emerged as a triumph over that adversity and an escape portal for not only the band but their fans as well.

The first side of *Adrenalize* featured the great one-two-three punch of "Let's Get Rocked," "Heaven Is," and "Make Love Like A Man," all perfect rock songs for what Def Leppard was seeking. In addition to "White Lightning," Side One also included the terrific ballad "Tonight," a track with origins dating back to the *Hysteria* sessions that would emerge as one of a whopping *six* singles to be released from *Adrenalize*.

The album's second side was slightly less inspired in some places but did feature the fantastic, lush, mid-tempo "Stand Up (Kick Love into Motion)" and album closer "Tear It Down," a balls-out rocker also with origins tied to the *Hysteria* recordings.

The biggest commercial hit from the album, however, was the full-on power ballad "Have You Ever Needed Someone So Bad," which reached the No. 12 position on the Billboard chart. Personally, it felt a little too "standard" from my perspective after the creativity of "Love Bites," but the song was a smash hit, nevertheless.

Adrenalize debuted at No. 1 on the Billboard Albums chart and stayed in that position for six consecutive weeks. The album sold over three million copies in the US alone and went to No. 1 in more than thirty different countries.

Shortly after the album's release, the band introduced Vivian Campbell as their new guitarist in early April 1992, and the new-look Def Leppard performed together for the first time at the Freddie Mercury Tribute Concert For Aids Awareness at Wembley Stadium in front of an audience of eighty thousand people with more than one *billion* others watching on live TV. The event launched an absolutely massive world tour for Def Leppard that would run throughout the entire calendar year, as both the band and their fans made good on their promise to "get rocked."

As successful as *Keep the Faith* and *Adrenalize* were, given the times, ironically, the very *best* album released in 1992 (in my view) turned out to be a colossal commercial flop.

Extreme had been riding high thanks to the success of their 1990 album *Pornograffitti* with its smash hit single, "More Than Words." However, rather than try to repeat that style, Extreme ambitiously set out to craft their third album as an elaborate concept record with three distinct yet interconnected "Sides."

The album was to cover a multitude of themes and layers, including war, racism, politics, religion, self-introspection, alienation, spiritual rebirth, and everything in between. Aside from the lyrical content, the music would be shaped just as deep and diverse, comprised of all-out rockers, rap, soft experimental pieces, big ballads, and finally, an integrated, three-part, twenty-two-minute grand finale revolving around a classical composition utilizing a seventy-piece orchestra. Quite a robust vision, indeed.

The album was fittingly titled *III Sides to Every Story*, with the "Sides" being "Yours," "Mine," and "The Truth," each featuring a distinct musical style and lyrical theme. The new set of songs was over eighty minutes in length, which fit just fine on the cassette format it originally occupied (the dominant music delivery mechanism of the time) but eventually had to be trimmed by one track to fit within the constraints of the newly emerging compact disc technology. The average hair metal album, it certainly was not.

The first side ("Yours") consisted of six "rock" songs, mostly heavy, funky, and true to Extreme's signature style, but with great musical variety among them. "Warheads" opened the album as the heaviest track, with lyrics rallying around an anti-war theme. A quartet of strings then introduced "Rest in Peace" before giving way to the song's rock-steady beat continuing Extreme's call for peace. The tune ultimately wrapped up with a soft, sixty-second acoustic epilogue similar in style to "More Than

Words."

An edit of "Rest in Peace" (the album version clocked in at over six minutes) was the first single released from the album. It received modest play, hitting No. 96 on the Top 40 chart, but its unique characteristics didn't seem to resonate particularly well with traditional hair metal fans.

"Politicalamity" (a combination of the words "politics" and "calamity") was up next and presented itself as a funky blues-rocker loaded with horns and focused on the ills of social injustices along with other hot political topics. "Color Me Blind" followed as one of the more straightforward rock songs on the record, this time choosing to target the pitfalls of racism.

Side One's penultimate song was the spirited "Cupid's Dead," one of my personal favorites on the platter. A driving rock song at its root, it also featured rap-rock verses by lead singer Gary Cherone and a full rap overture during the song's final minute presented by guest John Preziosa Jr. The track included an impressive, blistering, two-minute guitar-bass-drums breakdown in its middle section.

Closing out the rockers was "Peacemaker Die," an initially funky groover that eventually changed time signatures to a heavy metal guitar onslaught and culminated with an overlay of Martin Luther King's "I Have a Dream" speech. The song was a tribute to King and his vision.

For the listener that survived the content-driven blitz of directives that represented Side One and was ready for more, Side Two ("Mine") offered a somewhat of a respite of sorts, changing gears to a softer, more contemplative tone. "Seven Sundays" opened the set with a dramatic string arrangement before settling into a slow waltz driven by textured keyboards. I'm pretty sure Extreme was the first hair band to attempt a waltz.

If there was one moment on *III Sides . . .* that harked back to any of Extreme's previous work or passed for a relatively "standard" song, it was "Tragic Comic," the album's second single. It was a lighthearted, upbeat, acoustic track with clever comedy lyrics similar in musical style to "Hole Hearted" from *Pornograffitti.* Unlike "Hole Hearted," however, it regretfully failed to make an impact on radio, where it would have been dramatically out of place with the popular grunge style of the time.

"Our Father," a pseudo-ballad with stunning guitar work, dealt with child abandonment, while "Stop the World" followed more in line as a traditional power ballad but with a melancholy focus on the dangers of forgetting history's past sins lest they be repeated. "Stop the World" was also given a shot as a single but failed to generate success similar to other big ballads of the era. The shortfall was tied not only to the year it was released but likely also as a result of its relatively serious lyrical content that wasn't exactly every hair metal fan's cup of tea. It was a considerably beautiful song, however.

From there, the album shifted to a much darker, somber tone with the piano orchestration of "God Isn't Dead," a quiet, stark, contemplative interlude. The cassette version of the record featured one additional track on Side Two, "Don't Leave Me Alone," a climactic, emotional piano-ballad with Moog synthesizers, soaring guitars, and vocals centered on alienation and a dramatic plea for companionship.

Regretfully, the song had to be omitted from the compact disc version of the album due to physical space limitations. As *III Sides to Every Story* was very much a concept album with all parts connected and integrated, guitarist Nuno Bettencourt was horrified having to choose which track to remove, saying at the time that eliminating the song was like "cutting off my own arm."

As if Sides One and Two alone weren't exhausting enough of a journey (indeed, the album would have been plenty complete had it just ended there), the most ambitious and grandiose section of the record was yet to come.

Side Three was titled "The Truth" and was comprised of one massive, twenty-two-minute song titled "Everything Under the Sun," split up into three distinct sub songs (with overlapping segments): "Rise 'n Shine," "Am I Ever Gonna Change," and "Who Cares?." Each song featured multiple musical styles, varying time signatures, and an intricate, interconnected arrangement strewn together via the seventy-piece orchestra Extreme had employed.

"Rise 'N Shine" represented the "awakening" after the somber tones of Side Two. Bettencourt and Cherone traded versus on the beautiful duet as the instrumentation built up a bright and hopeful mood. A short interlude followed that would later become the primary component of "Who Cares?," but instead immediately dove into the melodic and moving "Am I Ever Gonna Change," with its powerful chorus and enlightening message. "Who Cares?" was the final piece, beginning softly with existential questions and religious overtones before rising in structure and coming full circle to a powerful melody combining and connecting all three songs, bringing Side Three to a dramatic and triumphant summation.

Extreme took a *huge* swing with *III Sides to Every Story* and achieved nothing less than a masterpiece, in my view. Unfortunately, the combination of bad timing and the simple fact that the album's aggressive reach and depth may have been lost on the average hair metal fan (translate: no obvious radio-singles) resulted in the record underselling to expectations—only 750,000 copies compared to the two million units *Pornograffitti* had sold.

Still, the album was praised by critics and hardcore fans alike, and it should still be deemed a success even if it is still out there waiting to be discovered. *III Sides to Every Story* is a complicated endeavor that is difficult to do justice to in text. The album really needs to be heard to be properly appreciated for the tremendous achievement that it was. I hope you get the opportunity (if you haven't already).

Warrant returned in 1992 with their follow-up to the successful *Cherry Pie* album, titled *Dog Eat Dog*. Jani Lane had been yearning to present Warrant in a more "credible" light (particularly after achieving unwanted notoriety as the "Cherry Pie-Guy"), and had actually started to steer Warrant away from the glam image of their debut in places on the *Cherry Pie* album with songs like "Uncle Tom's Cabin" and "Song And Dance Man."

Dog Eat Dog was a decidedly much heavier and darker record compared to the first two Warrant albums, both sonically and lyrically. The album is not entirely "un-Warrant," but very little of it would have fit with the band's previous material with the possible exception of "Bonfire," which was standard rock featuring the famous gang-vocals for which Warrant had come to be known. The album's new direction might have been perceived as a strategy aimed at keeping up with grunge, but in fact, the shift was independent of anything happening around or outside the band. The album was a prime example of hair metal's organic evolution.

Opening song and lead single "Machine Gun" immediately informed the listener that *Dog Eat Dog* was indeed not *Cherry Pie*. The track was a heavy, grooving rocker, easily harder than anything Warrant had done before. At the time, a friend of mine who pretty much despised all things hair metal perhaps put it best, stating, "I'd love to hate the song, but I just can't because it rocks so damn hard."

Other heavy hitters included the distorted "Hole In My Wall" (lyrically based on voyeurism), stomping "April 2031" (a super-heavy grinder focusing on a possibly bleak, apocalyptic future stemming from mankind's wars and abuse of the planet), and "Inside Out," which uncharacteristically bordered on speed-metal, a style that was certainly not what people had come to expect from the Down Boys.

Other parts of *Dog Eat Dog* saw Warrant branch out in different directions aside from just "heavier." A small child sang the opening lines of "Andy Warhol Was Right," and the song's soft sections thereafter bled into a dramatic overture with an orchestral arrangement. The lyrics told the tale of a young boy growing up obsessed with the rich and famous, "dying for attention," and ultimately committing murder.

"Bitter Pill," meanwhile, was a huge ballad (for lack of better characterization), but unlike any "traditional" hair metal ballad Warrant had produced in the past. The epic song focused on internal struggles (quite possibly Lane's himself) and included quiet verses, a dramatic German rock-opera middle-section, and an intense closing segment.

That said, there were a thankfully a few lighter moments on *Dog Eat*

Dog as well. "Hollywood (So Far, So Good)" was a pleasant, breezy affair, and "Let It Rain" was an absolutely beautiful power ballad more in line with "I Saw Red." And the marvelous, pop-oriented "Sad Theresa," would have fit perfectly on a John Cougar Mellencamp record.

From a commercial standpoint, while *Dog Eat Dog* managed to go Gold and sell over five hundred thousand copies, it was a significant letdown versus the sales figures of *Cherry Pie.* Jani Lane frequently told the story of him walking into Columbia Records' main office just before the new record's release and in place of the towering *Cherry Pie* print that previously hung in the lobby now rested a picture of Alice In Chains. Lane solemnly saw the harbinger for what it was. Indeed, Warrant was dropped by Columbia not long after *Dog Eat Dog*'s was issued.

Still, *Dog Eat Dog* is often hailed as Warrant's best work by both critics and fans alike. Many people cite "Andy Warhol Was Right" and "The Bitter Pill" as two of the best songs Lane ever wrote. Without question, Lane achieved a higher level of depth and intricacy on *Dog Eat Dog* versus any prior Warrant album. The songs undeniably possessed more texture and were composed with a deeper weight than the lighter fare of the first two records. But at the end of the day, personally, it just wasn't the Warrant I was seeking. At the very least, it wasn't the Warrant I had come to know and love. Sure, "The Bitter Pill" may have been Beethoven's 5th Symphony compared to "Down Boys," but please, give me "Down Boys" any day of the week and twice on Sunday.

And that sentiment of mine was perhaps illustrative of the root problem fostering the downfall of hair metal's glory days as much as anything. The bands *had* to evolve (most of them anyway), but the growth and progression that was so critically called for were in stark contrast to what made fans love those bands in the first place. That's not to say there weren't examples of change that managed to impress, but with several of them, and in particular *Dog Eat Dog*, the change just came off as a little bland and boring. In the end, grunge made the point moot anyway.

All told, though, Warrant achieved what they set out to do with *Dog Eat Dog* (other than continue their commercial success that is). It would have been interesting to see how the album was received had it been released just two years earlier. For me, I might include "Machine Gun" or "Let It Rain" on one of my Warrant playlists, but other than that, I am unashamedly happy just to give another spin to *Cherry Pie.*

🤘

Slaughter also returned with a new album in 1992, but unlike Warrant, stayed primarily faithful to the hair metal tone of their 1990 debut, *Stick It To Ya,* with possibly just a couple of new twists. Titled *The Wild Life,* the album debuted at No. 8 on the Billboard Albums chart (higher than the No. 18 peak position achieved by *Stick It To Ya*) and produced three moderately successful singles. However, similar to Warrant's sales experience, *The Wild Life* went on to sell only about five hundred thousand copies versus the two million achieved by *Stick It To Ya.* Again, though, I suspect new songs like "The Wild Life" and "Days Gone By" might have been just as successful as "Up All Night" and "Fly To The Angels" had they been released in 1990 rather than 1992. It just goes to show the seismic nature of the musical shift that had occurred in a relatively brief eighteen months.

In reality, though, while *The Wild Life* was a solid, enjoyable slice of hair metal, it just seemed to lack the overall "magic" of Slaughter's debut. It was perhaps a little too formulaic, missing the prior record's spark and energy. That said, there were certainly a few great songs that stood out and belonged on any Slaughter "best of" compilation. "The Wild Life" was a great rocker, and "Days Gone By" was a graceful, emotive ballad. Meanwhile, "Streets of Broken Hearts" and "Hold On" were definitely pop-metal perfection.

None of the other songs fully fell flat, but perhaps dropped a little too far into the "average" category. The band did take an admirable reach with the intended-epic "Times They Change," a seven-minute semi-ballad that dealt with modern political themes, but the track unfortunately fell a little short of living up to expectations. Slaughter also released a music video for the ballad "Real Love," starring the at-the-time very popular Shannon

Doherty of the hit TV show *Beverly Hills, 90210*, but unfortunately, none of it was enough to compete against the invasion of grunge.

🤘

Grunge had cast a planetary cloud over hair metal in the early '90s, and outside of Warrant and Slaughter, there were several other less-prominent music releases in 1992 that suffered from the same commercially ill-fate

Trixter released their sophomore album, *Hear!*, titled as such because the band members were convinced if they could just get people to listen to the album among the sea of grunge saturating the airwaves, they would be turned on to how strong of a record it really was.

And in truth, the album was a significant step forward from their debut in many ways, featuring the fantastic rockers "Damn Good," "Rockin' Horse," "Power of Love," and "Wild Is the Heart," alongside melodic gems "Road of a Thousand Dreams" and "Nobody's a Hero." However, also in truth, despite the band's literal plea, most people simply had no desire "hear" hair metal anymore, and Trixter's style of fun, party-rock 'n' roll was clearly no longer in fashion. The same band that scored multiple No. 1 songs on MTV for several consecutive weeks just two years prior was promptly and callously dropped by its record label.

🤘

FireHouse had slightly more success with their sophomore release, *Hold Your Fire*, which along with Def Leppard's *Adrenalize* the same year, was really one of the very last true hair metal albums to make a significant commercial impact. The record produced three hit singles and went Gold in the US, selling more than nine hundred thousand copies.

For me, however, *Hold Your Fire* was a tangible letdown versus FireHouse's self-titled debut, seeming to lack the latter album's spark and energy similar to Slaughter's *The Wild Life*. The new songs were also relatively uninventive in places and largely derivative of their first record, just not quite as good. The single "Sleeping with You" sounded almost *exactly* like former success "Don't Treat Me Bad," and the biggest hit from the album, the power ballad "When I Look into Your Eyes," was basically nothing more than "Love of a Lifetime" part-two. That said, "When I Look into Your Eyes" rose all the way into the Top 10 on the Billboard chart and was primarily responsible for the overall success of the new album.

By 1992, however, we had simply heard all of these songs before, and much of the music was becoming a little bland and generic. In other words, exactly the opposite of what hair metal had first offered fans back in the early '80s. *Hold Your Fire* was, regrettably, a great example of the genre beginning to dig its own grave (although grunge was undoubtedly the force that drove it into the ground).

On the other hand, **Steelheart**'s sophomore release, *Tangled in Reins*, was much more impressive than their 1990 debut. The songs were tighter and of higher overall quality while the style was still pure hair metal.

"Loaded Mutha" and "Sticky Side Up" opened the album with a hard rock bang followed by the slow, heavy, perfect late-night drinking song 'Electric Love Child." "All Your Love" was a beautiful ballad, while "Take Me Back Home" was a melodic, pop-metal personal favorite. The remainder of the record was relatively strong as well.

The story remained the same, though, as *Tangled in Reins* was unable to duplicate the commercial success of Steelheart's debut album in the US. The album did do very well in Asia, however, as the ballad "Mama Don't You Cry" reached No. 1 on the charts in many East Asian countries, including Hong Kong.

The international success provided Steelheart the valuable opportunity to launch a successful tour of Asia in September 1992. Upon the close of the victorious overseas run, the group was invited to open one last show for Slaughter in Denver, Colorado, on Halloween night. Little did they know tragedy would strike the band that evening as they performed the song "Dancing in the Fire."

Lead singer and band architect Miljenko "Mili" Matijevic had climbed a huge lighting truss taking a dramatic position to belt out his powerhouse vocals when the improperly-secured structure suddenly broke loose. The thousand-pound steel contraption collapsed, violently striking Matijevic in the back of the head and crushing him face-first down into the ground. Matijevic somehow found the strength to get up and walk off the stage under his own power before being immediately rushed to the hospital.

The initial diagnosis was grim—a broken nose, cheekbone, and jaw, along with a twisted spine and traumatic brain injury that resulted in severe memory loss. Just like that, Steelheart was over.

Matijevic endured a long, painful, steep road to recovery over the next four years as his brain had been damaged far worse than initially known. He was left in a constant state of dizziness and confusion, forced to fight the condition mostly alone. Still, he never gave up, and the resilient singer fought hard to recover.

Thankfully, Matijevic would triumphantly resurface with a revamped version of Steelheart four years later, in 1996. He explained, "One day the fog just seemed to miraculously lift. I had lost my family, my home, and my money, but I had found myself." It would still take further time before Matijevic would fully heal, but in 1996, it was heartwarming to see him back in action.

Faster Pussycat dropped their third album, *Whipped*, on August 4, 1992. The record included several styles different from either the pure glam rock of their debut or the more blues-based hard rock of their 1990 sophomore release, *Wake Me When It's Over*. *Whipped* turned out to be a rather inconsistent affair that featured a few legitimate bright spots alongside a good deal of "average," in addition to a couple of downright misses. The album's uneven nature was partly influenced by the internal strife that had developed among the band members, as financial concerns had led to an unhealthy competition for songwriting credits.

The album wasted no time informing the listener it was clearly something other than the Faster Pussycat of the past, with the first song and single "Nonstop to Nowhere" opening with the solo vocals of a female choir. The tune then morphed into a melodic, mid-tempo, pop-metal track much more commercial than anything the band had attempted on their first two records.

The track did have one brief section where it briefly broke down into a style and vocal more reminiscent of Faster Pussycat's traditional sleaze rock mannerisms, and, at the time, I remember thinking that those thirty seconds were the best part of the song. Of course, consistent with the day and hair metal's rapid fall from favor, when the single was released to radio, the half-minute detour that had provided a temporary hard rock respite had was and dropped out, naturally.

Nevertheless, "Nonstop to Nowhere" was a great song overall and, in my view, the highlight of the album. The tune managed to reach No. 35 on the Billboard Mainstream Rock chart.

Second and third tracks "The Body Thief" and "Jack the Bastard" rounded out the best *Whipped* had to offer. The songs were considerably heavier, with the former including some of the industrial sounds and stylings Faster Pussycat would further explore in future years. Outside of that, though, the album contained a few compositions that were more run-of-the-mill, along with others that were decidedly more "skip-worthy" ("Loose Booty," "Mr. Lovedog").

Whipped peaked at No. 90 on the Billboard Albums chart, and the band launched a semi-successful tour in support of the record, but the grunge writing was on the wall, unfortunately, and Faster Pussycat broke up and went their separate ways in early 1993.

🤘

As the peak years of hair metal came to a close and bands started to break up in response, many of them had amassed enough clout to facilitate individual members securing record deals for solo or side-projects. Two of these solo albums issued in 1992 came from former members of hair metal heavyweights Guns N' Roses and Twisted Sister: guitarist **Izzy Stradlin** and singer **Dee Snider**, respectively.

Stradlin had departed Guns N' Roses back in 1991, having become entirely un-enamored with the unrelenting spotlight, drama, and chaos that consistently surrounded the biggest rock band in the world at that time. His newfound sobriety had also played a role in his decision to exit.

Stradlin headed back home to Indiana and formed the band Izzy Stradlin and the Ju Ju Hounds, who released their self-titled debut album on October 13, 1992. True to Stradlin's roots and influences, the record sounded nothing like typical Guns N' Roses but was instead a very stripped-down, laid-back affair much akin to an early '70s Rolling Stones album. Stradlin not only handled rhythm guitars but also took the mic to provide lead vocals.

The album was praised by critics and even spawned a couple of modest hits, despite failing to make any real dent in the commercial landscape as could have been expected. I very much enjoyed the record for what it was, even if it was admittedly a universe away from the standard hair metal style. Highlights included "Somebody's Knockin," "Shuffle It All," and "Time Gone By."

Dee Snider also decided to move in a different direction versus his former band, but instead of scaling back like Stradlin, he gravitated more toward rock 'n' roll's heavier side. Snider formed the band Widowmaker and released the pummeling album *Blood and Bullets*, a genuine hard rock and heavy metal-based affair.

Dee's vocals were top-notch, and the band was on fire producing massive, powerful rockers like "Emaheevul" and "The Widowmaker." The album was unquestionably solid, but naturally a commercial flop in the face of grunge.

I remember watching Dee Snider perform a solo concert in the late '90s; unsurprisingly, the setlist was primarily comprised of crowd-pleasing hits from his Twisted Sister days. However, at one point, Snider stopped the show to address the audience, informing us he was about to play a song from a band we probably never heard of (Widowmaker). Lamenting the fact that most people indeed had no knowledge of Widowmaker's existence, Snider dejectedly explained that "sometimes things fail not because of their quality, but just because of bad timing." That pretty much summed up the *Blood and Bullets* album, along with countless other hair metal releases in the '90s, for that matter.

Nevertheless, the ultimately undeterred Snider and his band proceeded to launch into the massive "Widowmaker." I excitedly thrust my fist in the air, head-banging my heart out while most of the disillusioned crowd headed off for a temporary bathroom break. Alas, such were the times.

Electric Boys followed up their marvelous 1990 album, *Funk-O-Metal Carpet Ride*, with sophomore release *Groovus Maximus*, recorded at Abbey Road Studios in London. As the title suggested, the band's latest slate of songs was a collection of hard, funky groovers done in the style unique to Electric Boys. The music was heavier and less commercial than their debut, but still possessed tons of melody and huge choruses.

"Groovus Maximums," "Knee Deep in You," "She's Into Something Heavy," and "Bad Motherfunker" were massive rockers with plenty of swagger to spare. There was also the very melodic, Beatles-esque, psychedelic single "Mary in a Mystery World," along with several other more experimental tracks.

Groovus Maximum was a terrific album even if not perhaps as excellent as its predecessor, but it unsurprisingly failed to generate any commercial success. By the end of the tour to promote the record (opening for Mr. Big), Electric Boys had, unfortunately, lost the services of both their drummer and lead guitarist. The determined band would persist, however, and resolutely return with a new lineup in 1994.

Nineteen ninety-two was also the year that saw singer **Vince Neil** shockingly split from **Mötley Crüe**. This was a monumental occurrence as Mötley was unquestionably one of the biggest bands in the world at the time, coming off the No. 1 charting *Dr. Feelgood* album in 1989 and the successful *Decade of Decadence* compilation in 1991. Similar to when David Lee Roth departed Van Halen in 1985, Mötley Crüe would stupidly split up at the absolute peak of their fame.

Tensions between Neil and the band had been building for quite some time, going all the way back to the aftermath of the tragic 1984 car accident that killed Hanoi Rocks drummer Razzle. (Vince was charged with drunk driving and vehicular manslaughter and spent nineteen days in prison.) The extensive and exhausting Dr. Feelgood Tour was particularly challenging as Nikki Sixx was forcing and policing the band's sobriety, much to Neil's dissatisfaction.

When it came time for the group to reconvene in early 1992 and begin writing and rehearsing for a new album, Neil struggled to get on the same page with the rest of the band regarding the song's musical direction. The turmoil and unrest finally came to a head on February 10, 1992. Neil was late to a rehearsal, and the band had already come to be angered by the disgruntled singer's inconsistent participation and slip backward from sobriety (in truth, both Nikki Sixx and Tommy Lee were also drinking again, as well). Sixx and Lee felt Neil was holding the band back and they had admittedly already been contemplating getting a new vocalist for some time.

A blow-up quickly ensued upon Neil's delayed arrival at the studio, and before anyone knew what happened, Neil either quit or was fired (depending on who you ask) or both. Neil angrily stormed out of the building as a barrage of expletives was launched in both directions. The door abruptly slammed shut behind him, and suddenly there was no going back.

Four days later Mötley Crüe and their management issued a misleading press statement (this was pre-internet) announcing their split with Vince Neil: "Racecar driving has become a priority in Neil's life," the report read, "His bandmates felt he didn't share their determination and passion for music."

As Mötley Crüe was my absolute favorite band at the time, I will never forget where I was when I first heard the surprising, upsetting news break on the radio. Undramatically, I was on the driveway of a friend's house, but still, the weight of the moment was enough to cement a permanent memory. One of the greatest forces in rock music was unexpectedly and abruptly no more.

Neil was quick to dispute the "charges" in an interview a few days later. "Despite what everybody heard, it had nothing to do with me choosing racing over music," Neil stated. "That was the announcement the band put out, and that's all some people ever heard. I wanted the band to continue in a straight hard rock direction, but they wanted to go in more of a blues direction. It just wasn't sounding good to me. I'm not a blues singer, and Mötley is a rock band, not a blues band. I think it's a stupid idea that will alienate the fans."

At the end of the day, there were precious few details available to sort out what really happened and provide any objective truth. All fans knew was that Vince Neil was no longer the singer for Mötley Crüe. It was virtually unfathomable at the time.

For his part, Neil seemed determined to prove he was still focused on music and a force in the industry. He quickly released a blazing solo single in the summer of 1992 titled "You're Invited (But Your Friend Can't Come)" that was included on the *Encino Man* movie soundtrack. The song was co-written with Jack Blades and Tommy Shaw from Damn Yankees, and it rocked in perfect hair metal fashion not entirely dissimilar from the sounds of *Dr. Feelgood.*

While Mötley Crüe plotted their next move and life without their longtime singer, Vince Neil would go on to fully launch his solo career onto the scene in 1993.

Other noteworthy albums released in 1992: Skid Row *(B-side Ourselves)*, L.A. Guns (*Cuts*), Heavy Bones *(Heavy Bones)*, Great White *(Psycho City)*, Kiss *(Revenge)*, Jackyl *(Jackyl)*, Jerusalem Slim *(Jerusalem*

Slim), Slik Toxik *(Doin' The Nasty)*, Lillian Axe *(Poetic Justice)*, Damn Yankees *(Don't Tread)*, Faster Pussycat *(Belted, Buckled and Booted)*, Tora Tora *(Wild America)*, Electric Angels *(New York Times)*, Wildside *(Under the Influence)*, Lynch Mob (*Lynch Mob)*

Best Albums 1992

1. Extreme – *III Sides to Every Story (Top 25 in Genre!)*
2. Def Leppard – *Adrenalize*
3. Slaughter – *The Wild Life*
4. Bon Jovi – *Keep the Faith*
5. Trixter – *Hear!*
6. Electric Boys – *Groovus Maximus*
7. Steelheart – *Tangled in Reigns*
8. Warrant – *Dog Eat Dog*
9. Roxy Blue – *Want Some?*

Chapter 15
Exposed
(1993)

If 1992 was the year the nails were being hammered into hair metal's coffin, 1993 saw it officially dropped six feet underground. Many bands lost their record deals, split apart, or simply called it quits altogether due to lack of album sales or underwhelming tour attendance. Still, just because the genre was no longer commercially viable didn't mean *every* hair metal band stopped touring and putting out music. Some of the new releases were resplendently terrific, while others openly failed to match the quality of their '80s output with bands continuing to evolve or simply hitting the wall in certain aspects. It is also notable that there *were* still tiny pockets of success to be found, even if smaller in size and less frequent in occurrence. Most importantly, outside of any sales figures, there was still some great new music to be enjoyed and celebrated—critical successes, if not necessarily commercial.

Vince Neil had split from Mötley Crüe in 1992 determined to forge a prosperous solo career, and quickly. Fresh off placing the single "You're Invited (But Your Friend Can't Come)" on the *Encino Man* movie soundtrack, Neil swiftly inked a record deal with Warner Brothers and went about putting together a new band.

Jack Blades, from Night Ranger and Damn Yankees fame, was the first to sign up, serving both as Neil's manager and co-writer. Blades and Neil then recruited ex-Ozzy Osbourne bassist Phil Soussan to help develop the new songs and assemble the remainder of the band. At the urging of the record company, guitar virtuoso Steve Stevens (famous for his playing with Billy Idol) was brought aboard (Stevens would also co-write) in addition to rhythm guitarist Dave Marshall and Enuff Z' Nuff drummer Vik Foxx. Robbie Crane eventually slotted in on bass after Soussan resentfully left the band following arguments with Stevens regarding creative control and who would perform on the record (five of Soussan's songs were still used on the album, though).

The resulting record was titled *Exposed*, referencing Neil moving into the spotlight alone and away from Mötley Crüe, and was released on April 27, 1993. The album was a glorious platter of pure hair metal and debuted on the Billboard Albums chart at No. 13. The year may have been 1993, and grunge was clearly in favor, but apparently Vince Neil couldn't be bothered to care. And thank goodness he didn't. The style was strictly guitar-driven party-rock, not entirely different from the sound of Mötley Crüe (in particular, *Dr. Feelgood*). It was exactly what Mötley fans wanted, and Neil delivered in spades.

Neil was at the top of his game vocally, and the album was absolutely *smothered* with Stevens' distinctive guitar style (which was a good thing, if you asked me). If you ever looked up "what does hair metal guitar sound like," I wouldn't be surprised if the first reference was to Stevens on the *Exposed* record (after the obligatory nod to Poison's first two albums, of course). For those who might have thought Stevens went overboard, in his defense, every time he presented Neil with a new solo, the singer typically had only one piece of feedback: "Great; now make it longer and faster." Undoubtedly, though, Stevens' out-of-this-world guitar work was a primary force behind the album's flash and quality.

Most of the songs were in the tried-and-true hard rock and hair metal vein, along with two ballads (naturally), a blistering cover song (Sweet's "Set Me Free"), and a slight twist on the jazz-rock infused "Living Is A Luxury," which allowed Neil to sing in a style previously unexplored during his time in Mötley Crüe.

Three singles were released to radio and MTV (not that either format wanted them): the huge-sounding, bombastic "Sister of Pain," rocker

"Can't Have Your Cake," and the power ballad "Can't Change Me," which was perhaps a nod to Neil's former bandmates, including the line "you're somewhere in tomorrow, I'm stuck here in today" along with the refrain "you can't change me into something I can never be."

"You're Invited (But Your Friend Can't Come)," previously found on the *Encino Man* soundtrack, was re-recorded with the new lineup and included on the album but not selected for re-release as an official single.

Other highlights include the fiery opener "Look in Her Eyes" (a six-minute song with at least three minutes of scorching space-aged soloing by Stevens), "The Edge" (lyrically centered on race car driving, and inclusive of some fantastic flamenco guitar work by Stevens), and the touching ballad "Forever" (written for Vince's then-wife Sharise, who had filed for divorce earlier in 1993).

The Vince Neil Band were fortunate to score the coveted opening slot on Van Halen's 1993 Right Here, Right Now Tour, but despite the prominent exposure and fan-pleasing songs, *Exposed* flopped big-time from a commercial standpoint, failing to achieve even Gold certification, a far cry from the multi-Platinum status Neil had routinely achieved with Mötley Crüe. Still, the poor sales were unquestionably a direct result of the times—without a doubt, had *Exposed* been released in 1989, it would have been a *huge* success.

The album was also a clear victory in ways other than just the quality of the material, perhaps most importantly in that Neil emphatically proved he didn't need Mötley Crüe to put out a great album.

Mötley Crüe wasn't the only high-profile band navigating lineup change in 1993, however, as Poison was attempting to deal with the loss of their original guitarist, C.C. DeVille.

DeVille had been ousted from the Poison back in September 1991 following the infamous incident at the MTV Video Music Awards. The band went on to audition several new axe-slingers, and the choice came down to two virtuoso players: Richie Kotzen and Blues Saraceno; Bret

Michaels preferred Kotzen while Bobby Dall and Rikki Rockett preferred Saraceno.

Michaels wound up winning out, and Kotzen was installed as Poison's new lead guitar player (we will get back to Saraceno later). Kotzen had released three accomplished solo albums of his own, including one upon which he handled lead vocals himself. The newest member of Poison possessed a style that was soulful, laid back, and bluesy—in other words, the exact opposite of DeVille.

The revised lineup went forth and created the band's fourth studio album, *Native Tongue*. The result was predictably dramatically different from anything Poison had done before. In truth Michaels had wanted to move the group in a bluesier direction for some time, a topic which had contributed to the split with DeVille, who was steadfast in his belief Poison should stick to the glam rock approach that made them famous.

Kotzen's presence, however, only served to exacerbate the desired shift in style. In fact, Kotzen later claimed he had already fully completed several songs that would appear on the album prior to him joining the band. "*Native Tongue* could have easily been my next solo record," he stated. Of course, writing credits were split evenly four ways, as was Poison's tradition, but it was clear it was Kotzen's bluesy composition that dominated the album.

Curiously, the first single issued to radio, "Stand," was as un-Poison-like as anything on the record. It was *miles* away from party-rock, instead being a soulful, bluesy, mid-tempo song that employed a gospel choir to sing the choruses. Props to Poison for branching out and everything, but for my tastes—please, no. Not that it was a bad song, far from it, in fact. But in 1993, when I heard a new Poison record was coming out, I was naively looking forward to having "Nothing But a Good Time," not singing along with a group of church carolers. And I'm pretty sure I wasn't the only one who felt that way.

Still, similar to Warrant's *Dog Eat Dog*, there are many fans and critics (*especially* critics) who, to this day, swear *Native Tongue* was Poison's absolute finest hour. And from a musically technical standpoint, perhaps it was (depending on your point of view), but as something that best represented where the band had cut their teeth or what its fans had come to appreciate about the group, most definitely not.

Don't get me wrong; there were moments on *Native Tongue* that clearly had *hints* of Poison-past with regard to upbeat rock songs, among them personal favorite and horn-tinged "Seven Days Over You," "Blind Faith," and "Ride Child Ride." But even those tunes were soaked with Kotzen's bluesy, soul-oriented style. Michael's vocals were sometimes the only thing that identified most songs on the album as Poison.

In addition to shifting to the blues, other songs on the record incorporated a harder and heavier style, including opening stomper "The Scream" and the driving "Bring It Home." *Native Tongue* also featured the obligatory ballads, of course, but they were certainly not traditional hair metal power ballads. "Theatre of the Soul" was a touching, emotional song based on the band's split with DeVille, while "Until You Suffer Some (Fire and Ice)" was super soulful and just screamed 100 percent Kotzen. Incidentally, the latter was probably the best song on the entire album.

And then there were the blues songs that were even bluesier than the others: "Ain't that the Truth" (which was actually pretty cool), and the not-so-cool album closer "Bastard Son Of A Thousand Blues," which was *Native Tongue*'s answer to *Flesh & Blood*'s final track, "Poor Boy Blues."

Did I mention that *Native Tongue* was soulful and bluesy?

At the end of the day, from a commercial standpoint, grunge made sure none of it really mattered anyway. *Native Tongue* did manage to go Gold and peak at No. 16 on the Billboard Albums chart, but it was a long way off from Poison's prior success. In reality, even if Poison had released *Open Up and Say... Ahh!*-Part Two, as it was 1993, I'm pretty sure the sales results wouldn't have been much better.

For the band, the album objectively displayed an impressive evolution with regard to musicianship, diversity, and depth of songs, but it just wasn't the Poison we had come to know and love.

As it turned out, Kotzen didn't last long with Poison anyhow. In November 1993, the band discovered Kotzen had been sleeping with

Rockett's fiancé and promptly kicked him out of both the group and the tour bus (literally in the middle of nowhere). Ironically, Blues Saraceno was chosen to replace him.

Michaels would later admit Kotzen was likely a choice too far in the inverse direction of DeVille, stating, "I was so fed up, I wanted someone completely opposite of everything that was C.C., and that is exactly what I got." Saraceno was probably a more appropriate "middle ground" solution. More on Saraceno and Poison later, though.

Elsewhere in 1993, **Def Leppard** was busy conducting their massive "in the round" tour in support of *Adrenalize* when the producers of the movie *Last Action Hero* contacted the band requesting a song for the film's soundtrack. Def Leppard's busy tour schedule didn't permit a new studio session, so the band submitted an existing acoustic track they had first demoed and put to tape back in 1989, titled "Two Steps Behind." Conductor Michael Kamen subsequently added a string arrangement, and the final version was chosen to be included on the movie's album.

Unexpectedly, the somewhat sparse song became a *huge* hit, reaching No. 12 on the Billboard chart. The surprising success of "Two Steps Behind" inspired singer Joe Elliott to move forward with an idea he had been kicking around for some time—shaping a new album out of a conglomeration of older B-sides, rarities and other leftovers that had been hanging around collecting dust in Def Leppard's closets.

The new record was to serve two primary purposes, the first of which was to reward longtime fans with something special—quick new material. As a result of Rick Allen's unfortunate accident in 1984, four long years had gone by between *Pyromania* and *Hysteria*. Then, Steve Clark's tragic passing in 1991 contributed to a five-year period between *Hysteria* and *Adrenalize*. Ideally, Def Leppard didn't want to make their fans wait yet another few years in between albums.

Second, the band wanted to "wipe the slate clean," putting all things associated with their traumas behind them (specifically Clark's death, to the extent that was possible). Def Leppard felt this was the only way to treat new guitarist Vivian Campbell fairly, ensuring he would not have to be continually haunted by musical ghosts from the group's past forever into the future. The record would also serve to help the band achieve a sort of closure regarding Clark. Def Leppard was going to empty the vaults.

Elliott came up with the title *Retro Active*, and the project soon began to take shape. Among the songs included were unfinished outtakes from the *Hysteria* sessions, re-recorded and polished-up tunes from very early in the band's career, and touched-up tracks previously released as B-sides or singles that appeared only on Japanese pressings of their albums (primarily *Hysteria* and *Adrenalize*).

As a result of its origins, *Retro Active* was a highly diverse platter but somehow felt naturally cohesive at the same time. It was quite a statement that Def Leppard could patch together a bunch of old material and still manage to assemble a finished album that was head and shoulders above what the average band could generate with a formal new record. And the finished production was still extensive and pristine—after all, this *was* a Def Leppard album.

The opening two tracks were among the album's best, both being completed versions of songs that were partially explored during the *Hysteria* sessions. "Desert Song" was a dark, brooding, powerful riff-rocker, while "Fractured Love" was a slow-building, dramatic burner that evolved into a walloping anthem similar to "Foolin" from *Pyromania.* These tracks were clearly not throwaways and were very much deserving of seeing the light of day.

There were also more pop-metal-based songs such as "She's Too Tough" (originally written in 1985), "I Wanna Be Your Hero" (a re-recorded B-side from *Hysteria*) and cover song "Only After Dark" (the B-side to the "Let's Get Rocked" single). Further, "Ride Into the Sun" was a fantastic rocker that originally dated all the way back to *The Def Leppard E.P.* from 1979, while "From the Inside" originated from the *Adrenalize* sessions taking the shape of an Irish-tinged sing-song tale cautioning of the dangerous addictions that had plagued Steve Clark.

And, obviously, there were the mandatory ballads, "Two Steps Behind" and "Miss You in a Heartbeat," both of which became smash hits and appeared in both acoustic and electric versions on the album. A cover of Sweet's "Action" was also released as a successful single.

Retro Active was a sizable success both critically and commercially, reaching No. 9 on the Billboard Albums chart and eventually achieving Platinum status in the US and earning similar acclaim overseas.

Perhaps more important than its commercial triumph, however, *Retro Active* served to re-energize Def Leppard, and as bassist Rick Savage stated, "got the band back to a more earthy feel." This would be an essential step for the group moving forward given their intent to produce a more stripped-back, organic-sounding album for their next formal release (in contrast to the super-polished, immense production associated with the trilogy of *Pyromania*, *Hysteria*, and *Adrenalize*). The world would see the results of their effort three years later, in 1996.

Also managing to experience a good bit of commercial success in 1993 was **Aerosmith**. To an extent, bands like Aerosmith, Van Halen, and Metallica were seemingly partially immune to the grunge infection that infiltrated the US in the early '90s (at least from a sales perspective). This was perhaps driven by the fact that these bands never fit perfectly into the hair metal category anyway, with Aerosmith's and Van Halen's origins firmly planted in the '70s and Metallica being more of a thrash/heavy metal band.

Aerosmith had concluded a twelve-month tour in support of their excellent *Pump* record in October 1990 and taken a brief break before re-emerging with their eleventh studio album, *Get a Grip*, in April 1993. As with their recent two releases, the new record featured several collaborations with outside writers to help give the songs more commercial appeal. While this approach continued to prove successful, in my view, it actually served to water-down the pure rock 'n' roll that Aerosmith represented so well in the '70s on albums like *Rocks* and *Toys in the Attic*.

But the strategy was undeniably effective from a sales perspective as *Get a Grip* debuted at No. 1 on the Billboard Albums chart and went on to tie *Pump* as Aerosmith's second-best-selling album in the US, moving just over seven million copies.

Outside of the extensive commercial sales, however, *Get a Grip* was not quite as impressive critically. The album basically took over where *Pump* left off from a style standpoint, but plainly wasn't as good. In my opinion, other than a couple of songs, even the best material on *Get a Grip* was decidedly weaker than the worst material on *Pump*.

Get a Grip started off in fine enough fashion as the first three songs were all winners. The driving "Eat the Rich" was a pleasing, rowdy rocker followed by the groovy "Get a Grip" and the hot-burning "Fever." Unfortunately, those three tracks represented the best the album had to offer, with everything pretty much going downhill from there. "Living on the Edge" was released as the album's first single and was met with much critical acclaim, but just never seemed to do much for me personally, coming off as a little bland, at best.

The real commercial success-driver of the album, however, was the trifecta of power ballads that saturated the back half of the record. "Cryin'," "Crazy," and "Amazing" were all massive hits on both radio and MTV, but to many longtime Aerosmith fans (myself included), the songs came off as lame, boring, interchangeable sell-outs. The videos for all three songs were immensely popular, each featuring the at-the-time hot, sexy up-and-coming actress Alicia Silverstone.

The remainder of *Get a Grip* was comprised of average songs at best or dull filler at worst. The entire affair just seemed uninspired and overly commercially focused after the fantastic effort that was *Pump*.

Still, *Get a Grip* went on to sell over twenty million copies worldwide and earned Aerosmith two Grammy Awards in the category of Best Rock Performance for "Livin' on the Edge" and "Crazy." Aerosmith may have sold out, but they certainly managed to preserve their ride on the high seas of sales success.

On the other end of the spectrum, **Winger** found it much harder to maintain their run of commercial prosperity in 1993 in the face of strong headwinds both musically and culturally. For whatever reason, Winger was an extremely popular (and somewhat easy) target for opponents of hair metal. Whether it was Kip Winger's pin-up-boy good looks, the juvenile lyrics on songs like "Seventeen," or the sugary coating that smothered hit ballad "Miles Away," hair metal antagonists loved to pick on Winger.

In truth, though, none of these attributes put forth by Winger were really any different than the preponderance of their hair metal contemporaries. It was also of the utmost irony that Winger objectively possessed more musical talent than the overwhelmingly vast majority of their peers (although the band didn't necessarily establish the most conducive platform for their members' diverse classical training to fully shine through on Winger's first two albums).

A peculiar and particular point of attack came from the TV show *Beavis and Butt-Head*, of all places. The MTV cartoon was hugely popular in the early '90s, and the show's two main "cool" characters (Beavis and Butt-Head) wore shirts with the band names Metallica and AC/DC on them. Even at the height of grunge, these two bands maintained their immense popularity and were, for the most part, still deemed "credible."

However, the show's "un-cool" character, the nerdy Stuart, wore a Winger shirt. Beavis and Butt-Head mercilessly and relentlessly mocked the band, and as a result of the show's massive audience, Winger soon became a primary poster child for hair metal haters everywhere.

The topic may sound trite, but it indeed had a profound influence on the sharp downward arc of the band's career at the time. Radio DJs, for example, immediately dropped Winger from their playlists, afraid of the inevitable public shaming and negative backlash they would receive otherwise.

Despite all of this, though, in 1993, Winger released by far their best album yet. Similar to Warrant, Winger changed their sound for their third release, steering away from traditional hair metal to a much harder, darker, diverse, and serious-toned style. Unlike Warrant, perhaps, Winger managed to do so with triumphant success (at least critically).

The new album was originally to be titled *Blind Revolution Mad* in tribute to the album's first song; however, despite the band believing the record was indeed their finest moment to-date, the members were keenly aware of the overwhelmingly anti-hair metal music scene at the time and the battering their image had taken. In the end, they decided to tongue-in-cheek title the album *Pull*, consistent with their vision of critics dismissing the album out of hand and using it as a skeet-shooting target.

Winger recorded *Pull* as a three-piece, as Paul Taylor (keyboards) had left the band citing exhaustion after Winger's year-plus tour to support the *In the Heart of the Young* album. The trek had seen the group play roughly 250 dates with Scorpions, Kiss, ZZ Top, Slaughter, and Extreme.

The new album was a distinct evolution for Winger, with the band beginning to mature beyond basic hair metal stylings. Kip Winger stated, "In many ways, *Pull* was the real birth of the band. There were things that happened on the first couple of records that were absolutely fantastic. But there were also some things in there that didn't quite represent who we were as a group. When the third album came about, I was able to work with a couple of different people, and I was able to refocus the sound of the band back to what I originally hoped for in the beginning. Add to that the fact that we were better as songwriters, better as lyricists . . . it was kind of like the perfect storm for us."

The songs were clearly harder and more aggressive, also featuring an ample amount of socio-political commentary among the lyrics. The material was still guitar-oriented but also more diverse, containing elements of a progressive nature as well (an approach Winger would continue to explore to a much greater extent on future releases).

The first track, "Blind Revolution Mad," began with two minutes of acoustics and soft verses before exploding into a heavy metal riff that drove the rest of the song's hard rock, anthem-like structure. Kip Winger proudly stated, "'Blind Revolution Mad' represented Winger perfectly."

A harmonica then kicked off second song and lead single "Down Incognito" before the tune launched into a heavy, swampy groove that carried the rocker alongside an upbeat, acoustic-tinged chorus. The tune was one of Winger's best and even reached No. 15 on the Billboard Mainstream Rock chart prior to overwhelming backlash from the continued *Beavis and Butt-Head* exposure.

"Spell I'm Under," meanwhile, was a beautiful ballad that featured significantly more depth than earlier softies like "Miles Away." The song was written for Kip's loving wife Beatrice, who he would tragically lose in an auto accident in the late '90s. Conversely, "Junkyard Dog (Tears on Stone)" was a massively heavy rocker with riffs that could have easily been mistaken for Metallica (seriously; this was not the Winger known for lighter pop-metal songs like "Easy Come Easy Go"). "Junkyard Dog . . ." was an epic, seven-minute blast that alternated between soft, emotive verses and rough, heavy metal riffs. The lyrics told the story of a friend's heroin addiction (heroin represented by the "junkyard dog") and his eventual death as a result of the drug ("tears on stone" symbolizing the sorrow of friends and family left behind on the deceased's gravestone).

The album also included a couple of more standard (but still excellent) rock tracks such as "In My Veins," but there was also the starkly lovely album closer "Who's the One," an intricate acoustic arrangement that many have claimed is Winger's singular standout achievement.

Pull was a magnificent accomplishment for the band and is often cited as their best work. However, given the musical climate and fire the band's image was under at the time, the album sputtered commercially and only reached No. 83 on the Billboard Albums chart. Not surprisingly, Winger was dropped by Atlantic records after the album's release, and the band broke up shortly afterward in 1994.

Mr. Big was coming off the absolutely massive success of "To Be with You" from their excellent 1991 *Lean Into It* record when they released their third album, *Bump Ahead*, during the summer of 1993. Similar to

Aerosmith's *Get a Grip*, *Bump Ahead* basically followed the same formula as its predecessor album but was a step down in overall quality (albeit a much smaller step than *Get a Grip* was from *Pump*).

Bump Ahead's lead track, "Colorado Bulldog," was the album's high point, a furious ass-kicker that started things off with a bang prior to the album settling in thereafter. "Price You Gotta Pay" followed close behind with its terrific, super-heavy groove. Those two songs were great rockers for sure, but let's face it, Mr. Big had achieved their stardom with the ballad "To Be with You," and they tried hard to replicate that success on *Bump Ahead*, with the album featuring *four* ballads.

Among these softer tracks, "Promise Her the Moon" and "Ain't Seen Love Like That" were fantastic even if they failed to replicate the success of "To Be with You." By 1993, the musical climate had simply shifted far too much to accommodate a hit single by Mr. Big, even if the songs were just as good if not better than "To Be with You."

That said, *Bump Ahead* also featured a stunning cover of Cat Stevens' "Wild World" that did reasonably well on radio, reaching No. 27 on the Billboard Hot 100 chart. The band executed a faithful but still inspired version of the beautiful song.

All told *Bump Ahead* featured four or five songs that belong on any Mr. Big "best-of" playlist, but outside of that, most of the tunes were closer to just average, unlike *Lean Into It*, which warranted a full listen from top to bottom. These less prominent songs weren't bad by any stretch, but they simply weren't as catchy or commercial perhaps as earlier material. Of course, in all cases, the level of musicianship was beyond reproach given the caliber of talent present in the band. And Mr. Big still remained *immensely* popular in Asia, if not the US.

As hair bands continued to splinter apart as an inevitable consequence of the market for their music drying up, we continued to see an emerging trend of individual band members moving on to solo projections, entering into side-ventures, or forming new bands entirely. There were three of these such instances of particular note in 1993, featuring the lead singers of Whitesnake, Ratt, and White Lion.

Whitesnake had wrapped up their tour for 1989's *Slip of the Tongue* album in the fall of 1990. **David Coverdale**, exhausted from multiple years of nonstop recording and touring, had become disillusioned with not only the music business in general, but with what, in his eyes, Whitesnake had managed to become.

His once '70s blues-based rock band had been converted to a full-blown hair metal monster in the late '80s, and, in his words, Coverdale felt the whole "spectacle" of the thing had just gone too far. He was also struggling with his separation from wife Tawny Kitaen and was in dire need of a break to regroup and reassess both his career and future. In late 1990 Coverdale proceeded to disband Whitesnake indefinitely, intent on taking some take time off from the music industry.

At the same time, Led Zeppelin had recently released their first box set in 1991 but failed to mount a tour in support. Zeppelin guitarist **Jimmy Page** was itching to get back in the studio and out on the road, but singer Robert Plant was seemingly unavailable. It was legendary A&R man John Kalodner that then came up with the idea to pair Coverdale and Page together. It was not such an unintuitive stretch, really; Coverdale had long been labeled a Robert Plant clone by Whitesnake critics, and songs like "Still of the Night" undeniably shared similarities to Led Zeppelin.

Coverdale was subsequently coaxed back on the rock 'n' roll bus and he and Page were matched together in the spring of 1991. The duo then spent more than a year writing and recording before the collaboration eventually birthed the *Coverdale-Page* album in early 1993. And as it turned out, the record sounded pretty much exactly as you would expect—a mix of Led Zeppelin and Whitesnake.

Page's classic, textured guitar offerings were fully layered throughout the album and Coverdale was in great form on vocals, combining the higher registers and screams of '80s Whitesnake with the opportunity to get back to some of his more bluesy, rock roots, something he had been seeking for some time.

Lead track "Shake My Tree" was the perfect example of the Led Zeppelin-Whitesnake mix, a slowly building crescendo that exploded into a hard rock anthem. Page had actually developed the song's key riff back during the sessions for Zeppelin's final album, *In Through the Out Door*, in 1978.

First single "Pride and Joy" was similar, starting out with acoustic riffing prior to launching into a full-blown corker. "Easy Does It," meanwhile, could have comfortably fit on Led Zeppelin's *Houses of the Holy*, while at the same time, the ballad "Take a Look at Yourself" would have been right at home next to "The Deeper the Love" from Whitesnake's *Slip of the Tongue*.

"Don't Leave Me This Way" was the album's most epic and ambitious track, clocking in at eight minutes and showcasing some of Page's best post-Zeppelin guitar work and Coverdale's most accomplished vocals. The remainder of the album was straightforward '70s/'80s bluesy hard rock as only the Coverdale-Page combination could have produced.

Coverdale-Page was a sizable hit, reaching No. 5 on the Billboard Albums chart, and was certified Platinum in the US. Critics mostly lavished heaps of praise on the album while others simply saw Coverdale as a cheap Robert Plant clone. The album was admittedly stunning in some places as it succeeded in merging the best of Whitesnake and Led Zeppelin together.

However, disappointingly, the record just seemed to be missing something for me. It was bizarrely as if the album as a whole was somehow less than the sum of its parts. Each song and section was spectacular in its own isolation, but the full listen left *something* to be desired.

Maybe the songs were a tad too long? Or perhaps the material just left Led Zeppelin fans wishing the Whitesnake elements weren't there while '80s Whitesnake fans wished the Led Zeppelin elements weren't there (blasphemous, I know). Or maybe the album just needed a decent remastering to beef up the sound a little, similar to the treatment given to *Whitesnake '87* in later years (Coverdale talked of this potentially happening during a 2018 interview, but it disappointingly hadn't come to fruition yet as of this writing in 2019.) In any event, suffice it just to say that *Coverdale-Page* was a "good" album with some truly "great" moments.

Coverdale and Page did a limited tour for the record in Japan but the US leg regretfully wound up canceled due to poor ticket sales. The hard rock stigma (mostly attributed to Coverdale's vocal stylings) that permeated the US at the time due to grunge was simply too much to overcome. High-energy, high-shriekers like Coverdale had fallen out of fashion in favor of mellow, yarling growlers like Pearl Jam's Eddie Vedder and Soundgarden's Chris Cornell.

The plug was soon pulled on the overall pairing as a result of the underwhelming concert response, but the experience did serve to revitalize both Page and Coverdale, with the former soon going on to reunite with Plant and the latter moving on to reform Whitesnake for a successful Greatest Hits album and tour in 1994.

🤘

Ratt's **Stephen Pearcy** was the second example of a prominent lead-singer forming a new band in the early '90s post-break-up of his original '80s hair metal group. Ratt had come off the road from their *Detonator* Tour in 1991 and released the terrific one-off single "Nobody Rides for Free" on both the *Point Break* movie soundtrack and their greatest hits compilation, *Ratt & Roll 81–91*. Regretfully, the song was the last recording to feature guitarist Robbin Crosby as he had fallen deep into substance abuse over the years and was no longer able to serve as a functioning member of a band.

After Ratt's break-up in February 1992, Stephen Pearcy formed the new band **Arcade**, which also featured drummer Fred Coury, who had exited Cinderella after their *Heartbreak Station* album.

Driven by the presence of multi-Platinum seller Pearcy, Arcade was signed to a major record label deal with Epic and released their self-titled debut, *Arcade*, in 1993. The music style was very much in the same vein as Ratt, perhaps just a tinge sleazier with a heavy nod to the Sunset Strip scene in the late '80s. Similar to Vince Neil, for whatever reason, it seemed Pearcy didn't get the memo about grunge in the early '90s, and thank goodness he didn't as *Arcade* was a welcomed trip back to classic hair metal.

Opening track "Dancing With the Angels" absolutely smoked and was perhaps up there in quality with anything Ratt had done, while "Nothin' to Lose" and "Calm Before the Storm" continued the sleazy, hard rock onslaught with the latter's lyrics focused on the drug addictions suffered specifically by both Nikki Sixx and Fred Coury. The album continued in the same vein throughout with a couple of ballads thrown in for good measure.

Perhaps surprisingly, in the face of grunge, the record proved to be a moderate success, managing to hit No. 133 on the Billboard Albums chart and generating two singles that climbed into the Top 30 on the Mainstream Rock chart: the pulsing "Nothin' to Lose" and ballad "Cry No More."

Ex-White Lion singer **Mike Tramp** had also moved on to a new outfit by 1993 as well. Just days after White Lion broke up in September 1991, Tramp met up with longtime friend Oliver Steffensen, whom he had played with in the band "Danish Lions" before forming White Lion. The two friends wrote and recorded several new songs that would eventually form the foundation of the new band **Freak of Nature**, whose sound would be far removed from the hair metal stylings of White Lion, primarily coming across harder, leaner and darker.

A full band was soon put together and the self-titled album *Freak of Nature* was recorded entirely live in less than a week, with Tramp wanting to ensure the group's raw, organic energy translated accurately in the studio. The music was powerful and the musicianship was strong, but the tunes just weren't as catchy or smooth as Tramp's earlier work with White Lion. "Turn the Other Way" and "Rescue Me" were among the album's distinct highlights.

Steffensen wound up leaving the band due to a disagreement with Tramp just before the album's release, but a replacement was soon found and Freak of Nature went out and toured behind the album for eight full months, mainly in the UK. The tour was only scheduled to last a brief thirty days, but the band persisted and the trek became unofficially dubbed the "put us in any shithole and we'll play there" tour. Tramp had assembled a formidable band of brothers, but the album failed regrettably to generate any commercial success.

The London Quireboys (as dubbed on their first album *A Bit of What You Fancy* in 1990) were now titled only as The Quireboys in 1993. Their sophomore release, *Bitter Sweet & Twisted*, had a few great songs but mostly failed to duplicate the consistency and overall magic of the band's debut.

The first three tracks were all fantastic, blues-based, '70s-style pop-rockers: "Tramps and Thieves," "White Trash Blues," and the catchy "Can't Park Here," while the mid-tempo ballad "Hates to Please" also stood out as an album highlight. Some fans thought highly of the slow, emotional "King of New York," but while it was an admittedly beautiful song, it was just never my cup of tea.

Bitter Sweet & Twisted failed to produce any meaningful sales, and despite a good run opening for Guns N' Roses on a leg of their Use Your Illusion Tour, The Quireboys would regretfully split up soon after.

Enuff Z' Nuff also hit the end of the road in 1993, at least with regard to major record label support. The band was coming off their 1991 critically acclaimed *Strength* album, but due to underwhelming sales, Enuff Z' Nuff were forced to file for bankruptcy while they split with Atco Records. With a last gasp breath of air, the band managed to latch on with Arista Records for one final major label release, 1993's *Animals with Human Intelligence*.

The album was markedly darker and heavier in several places versus previous Enuff Z' Nuff material. "Master of Pain" was borderline heavy metal, while other songs featured deep lyrical themes such as abortion and substance abuse. The new style didn't particularly seem to suit the band, from my view, but there were admittedly a few welcomed brighter spots as well. The poppy, melodic "These Daze" was one of the best songs in the group's catalog, and "One Step Closer to You" was perfect power-pop. The band did try releasing the ballad "Right by Your Side" as a single but the track was a little too generic and ill-timed to make any commercial impact.

Enuff Z' Nuff did have pockets of opportunity, however, appearing on *Late Night with David Letterman* to perform the track "Superstitious" while "Bring It on Home" was commissioned for the Tom Cruise movie *Jerry Maguire.* As it turned out, however, the latter song was played only over the movie's end-credits, as its featured scene wound up on the cutting room floor at the eleventh hour. Such was the luck of Enuff Z' Nuff, it would seem.

Animals With Human Intelligence received a decent amount of critical acclaim but failed to sell any significant numbers; grunge was just too much to surmount. The band did manage a moderately successful tour in Japan where they still had a sizable following, but Enuff Z' Nuff were quickly dropped from the label directly afterward. The group also lost drummer Vikki Foxx just before the album's release as he chose to join Vince Neil's new solo band for the *Exposed* album. Enuff Z' Nuff was far from done, however, and would soldier on mostly independently for the remainder of the decade.

Danger Danger also fell upon turbulent times in 1993. The band had released the amazing *Screw It!* in 1991 and toured the record into 1992 with prominent artists such as Kiss and Alice Cooper. By 1993 they had fully completed their third album, titled *Cockroach* (in reference to the fact the band simply wouldn't agree to die despite grunge's best efforts).

Singer Ted Poley, however, was having "creative differences" with the group, and in a sudden and surprising move, the band fired Poley just before the album's release, notifying him of the sacking by mail of all things (email was not yet a widely adopted technology).

Danger Danger's remaining band members proceeded to hire singer Paul Laine and tasked him with re-recording *Cockroach's* vocals in 1994. The band then attempted to release the album, but Poley blocked its delivery, countering from his side with lawsuits claiming infringement violations. By this point, Epic Records no longer had any interest in the project given the impact of grunge and decided to simply shelve the record rather than make any investment to battle or settle any lawsuits that would've facilitated the album's release.

Cockroach remained in limbo for several years, much to the great dismay of fans. However, in 2001, the lawsuits were dismissed, and Epic finally released the record as a two-CD set, one disc with the vocals originally recorded by Ted Poley and another with the re-recorded vocals provided by Laine. It was a unique situation and a genuine treat for fans to be able to hear and contrast both versions. The *Cockroach* album will be discussed in greater detail later on in the chapter dedicated to the time frame during which it was eventually released, 2001.

Back in 1993, however, Danger Danger continued as a three-piece with Paul Laine, Bruno Ravel, and Steve West (keyboardist Kasey Smith had departed just before *Cockroach* was originally recorded and lead guitarist Andy Timmons left to pursue a solo career). From his side, Ted Poley formed the new band Bone Machine that would go on to release its debut album, *Dogs*, in 1994.

🤘

Lastly, **Guns N' Roses** surprised fans in 1993 by unexpectedly released a new record. Back in May 1991, GN'R had kicked off the absolutely massive Use Your Illusion Tour in support of their new hit albums. The tour would turn out to be one of the longest in rock history, running more than two years with 194 shows in twenty-seven countries.

The concerts were marked by a great deal of infamy due to riots, late starts, cancellations, and Axl Rose's unpredictable behavior. By the time the tour had officially wrapped in July 1991, a total of seven million fans had seen the show. The band was beyond burnt out, naturally.

Despite their exhaustion, GN'R managed to release a cover-songs album consisting of older punk and hard rock songs in November 1993. The album was titled *"The Spaghetti Incident?"* in reference to Steven Adler's code word for his drug stash. During a past legal proceeding for one of the myriad lawsuits brought against the band for all manner of incidents, a lawyer stoically prompted the band in court to "tell us about the spaghetti incident." The band members found the situation hilarious and adopted the prosecutor's verbiage as the name of the record.

Several songs on *"The Spaghetti Incident?"* were originally recorded during the *Use Your Illusion* sessions back when the project was being considered as a three or four-disc set rather than just the double-album release it ultimately became. The band then planned to release a few of the tracks as an EP in 1992, with new guitarist Gilby Clarke replacing Izzy Stradlin's parts, but eventually decided to record a few more songs to facilitate the full album release in 1993.

As for the songs themselves, to me, they were discouragingly mostly underwhelming. The performances were adequate, for sure, but the song selections just never did much for me (probably because I have never been much of a fan of punk music), and the recordings seemed to lack any urgency or spark. It's not an album I would necessarily suggest is a must-own for any GN'R enthusiast, but some fans did seem to appreciate the raw nature of the record compared to the bloated production employed on the *Use Your Illusion* albums. Liner notes on *"The Spaghetti Incident?"* stated, "A great song can be found anywhere. Do yourself a favor and go find the originals—GN'R."

The album did manage to debut at No. 4 on the Billboard Albums chart and eventually went Platinum (it *was* Guns N' Roses, after all), but sales were a far cry from the *Illusion* albums (not that it would have been expected a cover-songs record would generate the same level of interest).

The most distasteful thing about the album, though, was the presence of the hidden "bonus track," a cover of Charles Manson's song "Look at Your Game, Girl." Why the band (i.e., Rose) chose to do this and give any publicity to the horrific acts committed by Manson is hard to explain, other than their (Rose's) natural gravitation toward controversy. Naturally, the song's inclusion caused a great deal of contention with law-enforcement and victims-right groups. Then again, by that point in their career, being embroiled in controversy was the overarching norm for Guns N' Roses.

In related GN'R happenings at the same time, bassist Duff McKagan took the opportunity to release a solo album, appropriately titled *Believe in Me*. The record was truly a mostly individual endeavor as McKagan handled the vast majority of the effort himself, including lead vocals, rhythm guitar, bass, piano, and drums. The album featured a host of prominent guest appearances as well, including GN'R bandmates Slash, Matt Sorum, Dizzy Reed, and Gilby Clarke, in addition to members of Skid Row, Lenny Kravitz, and others.

Whether or not you liked the record largely depended on your feelings toward McKagan's vocals, which to me, were certainly serviceable but overall a weak point. Mostly containing songs in the punk-rock/metal vein, *Believe in Me* sold a modest one hundred thousand copies.

Other noteworthy albums released in 1993: Lillian Axe *(Psychoschizophrenia)*, Harem Scarem *(Mood Swings)*, Every Mother's Nightmare *(Wake Up Screaming)*, Shotgun Messiah *(Violent New Breed)*, The Scream *(Takin' It to the Next Level)*

Overall, 1993 was no picnic as the popularity of grunge and shaming of all things related to hair metal really started to take hold. Hair bands bore the brunt directly, and the sharp decline in commercial support forced many to either break up or head out in different directions, struggling to find their place in the "new world" as emerging trends continued to influence the scene. Still, quite a few hair metal acts defiantly did their best to preserve and keep the faith, even if their style would mostly continue to evolve toward a harder and heavier sound versus the pop and glam metal of the era's origin.

The year 1994 would offer much of the same, but also be particularly notable for the long-awaited return of an absolute titan of the genre and perhaps hair metal's founding entity—the question was, what would it sound like upon its return?

Best Albums 1993

1. Vince Neil – *Exposed*
2. Winger – *Pull*
3. Def Leppard – *Retro Active*
4. Mr. Big – *Bump Ahead*
5. Poison – *Native Tongue*
6. The Quireboys – *Bitter Sweet and Twisted*
7. Coverdale-Page – *Coverdale-Page*
8. Lillian Axe – *Psychoschizophrenia*
9. Enuff Z'Nuff – *Animals with Human Intelligence*

Chapter 16
Power to the Music
(1994)

By 1994, it had been five long years since hair metal giants Mötley Crüe issued their last full-length studio album, *Dr. Feelgood*, which had gone all the way to No. 1 on the Billboard Albums chart and spawned a massive two-year world tour that firmly established the band alongside Guns N' Roses as kings of the hair metal and hard rock world, at the time. Mötley Crüe then kept their momentum active by releasing the No. 2 charting greatest hits compilation *Decade of Decadence* in 1991. Mötley had finally reached the top of the mountain ten years after first coming together during hair metal's onset in 1981.

However, after Vince Neil departed (or was ousted) from the band in February 1992, Mötley Crüe suddenly found themselves without a singer at the peak of their fame. Neil forged ahead with his solo career, dropping the terrific *Exposed* album in 1993 along with a somewhat successful tour in support. All the while, however, things back at the Mötley camp were quiet as a church mouse.

Finally, in late 1993, an unconfirmed report surfaced that Mötley Crüe had hired a relatively unknown singer by the name of John Corabi. (Remember, this was before the internet and social media, so news and details were sparse and hard to come by for the average fan.)

It was also rumored the band was busy hard at work on a new album. But so much had changed in the five years since *Dr. Feelgood* (not just

Mötley's singer, but the entire musical and cultural landscape), many wondered what the Crüe would even sound like when (if) they reemerged in 1994. As it turned out, the band could not have chosen a new frontman more different than Neil.

In truth John Corabi wasn't exactly an unknown to those close to the scene. He had led the hard rock outfit Agora in the late '80s, a popular outfit that succeeded in establishing a fairly big following on the Sunset Strip. Corabi then went on to form The Scream in 1989, and the group released their very cool debut, *Let It Scream*, in 1991.

Upon hearing the *Let It Scream* album in 1993 and coming away impressed, Nikki Sixx reached out to Corabi to see if the underground singer might be interested in auditioning for the mighty Mötley Crüe. Corabi was clearly talented, but the fit could be understandably questioned as both his style and approach were starkly different than what Neil had brought to the table.

Neil was always the blonde, party-boy, chick-magnet, good-times guy with the high-pitched, clean vocals. Corabi, on the other hand, was more on the dark and reserved side, with a gravelly, coarse, blues-based, raspy sound. That said, Corabi did possess a more powerful, versatile voice and was assuredly more technically proficient. Further, the singer also played rhythm guitar and was an accomplished songwriter, adding a couple of exciting new ingredients to Mötley Crüe's traditional formula.

In addition to the change that was Corabi, the musical landscape had mutated into a completely different animal in 1994 versus what it had been just a few years prior. Largely gone was the pop-metal style for which Mötley Crüe had come to be known, replaced with the gloomy, grungy "Seattle Sound" and bands like Soundgarden and Alice In Chains, along with the aggressive outside stylings of heavy metal groups like Pantera. All of these changes and fresh influences would combine to shape an unmistakably "new" Mötley Crüe.

As Corabi put forth in Mötley's 2001 autobiography, *The Dirt*, "Mick Mars had never worked with a second guitarist, Nikki had never worked with a second lyricist, and the band had never written songs together through just jamming." The band members were decidedly ecstatic over both the modified dynamic and the initial shape of the new material. Tommy Lee appropriately likened it to the "honeymoon phase that occurs when you get a new girlfriend."

Outside of the band, fans were also in great anticipation of what was to come. The "return" of Mötley Crüe was announced to coincide with the release of a new album to be issued in March 1994. Promotional pictures appearing in magazines piqued curiosity by strategically omitting not only the band's image but even their name, choosing instead to display only a large, cryptic "MC" logo simply stating, "They're Back."

In early 1994 I remember happening upon a large cardboard poster-stand of that same enigmatic ad in a local record store (yes, these used to exist, really). Being a *huge* Mötley Crüe fan, I excitedly inquired as to its availability with the clerk, hoping to be able to take it off his hands after the album was eventually released. Of course, as it was 1994 and grunge in full swing (especially on college campuses), the clerk just rolled his eyes at me and said, "you can take it *now.*"

I'm pretty sure he was happy to have it out of his establishment, if he even knew what it referred to anyway (actually, *especially* if he knew what it referred to). My non-hair-metal-loving roommate, however, was decidedly less excited to see my newfound treasure as I proudly displayed it back at our apartment. Anyway, I digress.

The new album possessed the working title *Till Death Do Us Part* for quite some time, but the name was changed at the last minute to simply *Mötley Crüe* (of course, not until after Corabi had the former title tattooed on his arm). Self-title aside, perhaps unsurprisingly given all we now know in retrospect, but seemingly a humongous surprise to the fanbase at the time, *Mötley Crüe* sounded absolutely nothing like Mötley Crüe. And I do mean *nothing.*

Not that this was necessarily a bad thing, at least in my view. Sure, there is little more I would have loved than *Dr. Feelgood*-Part Two, but that simply wasn't in the cards for a multitude of reasons. For what it *was,* however, *Mötley Crüe* was an absolute *monster* of a record.

To say the album was heavy would be a gross understatement. The songs were also longer, darker, moodier, and undeniably *huge*. The addition of a second guitarist helped give the material a fuller, thicker landscape while Corabi's powerful, abrasive vocals were 180 degrees away from Vince Neil in terms of both pitch and sound.

The record's production, contributed by Bob Rock, was near perfection. In my view, the drum sound he managed to capture was among the very best ever recorded for a rock album. And although Mötley had tuned down their guitars similar to other popular music at the time, Rock was somehow able to still capture their crisp power without having them sound "muddy," as was the style with grunge.

From a songwriting standpoint, aside from "Poison Apples" (incidentally the only song on the album to feature the input of outside writers), *Mötley Crüe* contained barely a trace of anything even remotely related to hair metal. As Nikki Sixx stated, "with Vince out, it allowed the darker side of Mötley to breathe."

The crunchy, heavy, opening riffs to album-starter "Power to the Music" immediately signaled the listener this was something entirely different than the Mötley Crüe they had come to know. The hulking song was an absolute beast and flawlessly set the tone for the rest of the album's ferocious assault. "Uncle Jack" followed, an equally heavy, dark tune with angry reference to Corabi's convicted, child-molesting relative, including directed lyrics proclaiming the band wanted to "rip (his) goddamn heart out!"

"Hooligan's Holiday" was the album's first single, still heavy but also featuring a bit of a catchy chorus as Corabi wailed away up against all the aggression the band could muster. The epic, seven-minute "Misunderstood" then offered an interesting change, starting off acoustic and somber and proceeding to tell the tale of an old man whose "life has passed him by" before launching into an angry rocker backed by a full orchestra. It was the type of song Mötley Crüe would have never even considered attempting in the past.

"Loveshine," which would have been right at home on *Led Zeppelin*

III, proceeded to offer a brief respite with its bright and cheery guitars prior to the album going full-on heavy again with "Hammered," a song with lyrics that sounded an awful lot like an attack on Neil although officially the band denied any similarities. The massive riff that drove the track dated all the way back to a tune Corabi had been tinkering with while fronting Angora, and in fact, "Hammered" was the first song Mötley's new lineup wrote together upon Corabi's introduction into the band.

The album continued with a few more dark, heavy, huge rockers (including speed/thrash-metal monster "Smoke the Sky") before allowing the listener to unwind on the final track and record's only ballad, the contemplative "Driftaway." Not a power ballad in the traditional sense, the beautiful song began with just Corabi on acoustic guitar and vocals before evolving against a broader musical landscape and finally closing out the album on a slow, reflective note. By the end of the full listen, you genuinely felt as if you had been run over by a truck (in a good way, of course).

Mötley Crüe was a fantastic accomplishment and easily the band's most impressive musical performance. A certain segment of supporters claimed it was also Mötley's best album, overall. Nevertheless, the majority of fans viewed it as a massive disappointment being so far removed from the band's signature style. Me? I *loved* the album. But the key was, I avoided comparing it to any other Mötley Crüe material. It was just too much of a different animal that truly needed to stand on its own.

Naturally, though, the album was a *colossal* commercial flop. Mötley Crüe had changed their style demanding to be taken seriously (album liner notes stated "No Cheese"), but of course, practically no one did. Most traditional fans simply dismissed the record outright given the absence of Neil. Grunge fans dismissed it just as quickly without even listening, as all they needed to know was the album was "Mötley Crüe." No doubt, however, had Soundgarden released the same record, it would have been a smash success, and a song like "Misunderstood" would have garnered significant radio and MTV airplay.

Further, in true Mötley Crüe self-destruction mode, the band promptly sabotaged whatever slim chance they had of MTV embracing the record when they famously walked out of a live interview on the channel after becoming emphatically irritated by questions about hair spray and their previous image.

In retrospect, Sixx stated, "the smartest thing we could have done would have been to change the name of the band. That would have let us have complete and utter acceptance or denial based on the music, not the name." Fair enough in hindsight, but there was no realistic chance the record label would have ever allowed such a decision. I'm pretty sure it wouldn't have mattered either way, unfortunately.

Mötley Crüe initially toured the album to much failure after its release. Not only was grunge at its peak, but the majority of fans simply weren't interested in a Mötley Crüe without Vince Neil. Mötley instantly went from sold-out arenas to half-full theatres and woodsheds. I saw them on that tour, of course, and while I loved the show, even I found Corabi singing the older Crüe material a somewhat peculiar mismatch (and I was a Corabi fan, for sure). Of course, the new material played by the band during these shows absolutely rocked.

The poorly-attended tour was eventually canceled midway through, and Mötley Crüe would, unfortunately, be left with no choice but to head home with their tails tucked between their legs, lick their wounds, and ponder the unclear next steps and uncertain future of the band.

Mötley Crüe, however, weren't the only band in 1994 that swept away their hair metal past and released a different-sounding and overall heavier album. **L.A. Guns** had taken their time (against a backdrop of growing internal discord) following 1991's *Hollywood Vampires* and eventually emerged with their fourth studio album titled *Vicious Circle*, a diverse fourteen-song platter with a prominent emphasis on a newfound hard and heavy sound in many places. The music's overall production was fantastic, and despite the style change, the record sounded like a million bucks.

"Face Down" opened the set as L.A. Guns' heaviest song to-date at the time, a fast and aggressive stomper that demonstrably set the tone for much of what was to follow. Other songs in a similar vein included "No Crime," "Kill that Girl," and the brutal "Killing Machine."

Vicious Circle also featured a few tracks that were much more experimental in nature versus anything L.A. Guns had attempted in the past. "Long Time Dead" was acoustic and trippy, while "Fade Away" was more mellow and borderline psychedelic. "Nothing Better to Do" (sung by bassist Kelly Nickels) was pure boogie, and songs like "Kiss Of Death" were an attempt at a dramatic, epic ballad.

L.A. Guns also unconventionally gave "Crystal Eyes" from *Hollywood Vampires* another shot on *Vicious Circle,* believing the song somehow missed getting its proper due on the former release and was too good not to warrant a second chance at success. Overall, *Vicious Circle* was a little uneven, but for me, the diversity worked. Admittedly, the album may have been a tighter, superior statement had it been trimmed down to ten songs versus fourteen, but that was just nit-picking.

Of course, the year was 1994, so the album naturally failed to chart or generate any significant commercial sales whatsoever. At the end of the day, similar to Mötley Crüe, L.A. Guns, who were unquestionably hair metal royalty selling millions of records only a few years before, were left to ponder a hazy future after releasing perhaps the best album of their career.

Bang Tango would also return with a new, awesome, heavier album, but would somehow fare commercially even worse than L.A. Guns, hard as that might be to believe. Titled *Love After Death,* the record saw Bang Tango really come into their own from a songwriting and performance standpoint. Tracks like "New Generation," "My Favorite Nine," "Don't Count Me Out," and "So Obsessed" were among the heaviest and best in the band's catalog. Not every song was a standout, but there were no losers in the bunch while the overall album flowed perfectly.

Many fans proclaim *Love After Death* to be Bang Tango's finest moment. Twenty-five years later, the band feels the same, even if the album was somewhat of a departure from the more glam-influenced, funky metal that comprised their more successful first two records.

Continuing with the regretful theme, however, hair bands, regardless of the musical style employed on their latest albums, had virtually no chance of success in 1994. In Bang Tango's case, this was the literal truth. Upon the album's completion, MCA records surveyed the musical climate and abruptly decided it didn't make good financial sense to promote or even try to release the record. Luckily for hardcore fans, *Love After Death* was picked up by Music for Nations and saw the light of day released in the UK and Japan. To this day, though, the album has remarkably never been issued in the US.

Left without any true direction or options, Bang Tango sadly dissolved in 1995 following a brief European tour in support of the record and would not be heard from again until 2003.

Not all hair metal bands went in a heavier direction in 1994. **Great White** was certainly on board with a departure from their traditional sound, but unlike Mötley Crüe, L.A. Guns, and Bang Tango, at the suggestion of manager Alan Niven, they went in a *softer* direction. Having split with Capitol Records and assessed the musical landscape, Great White sensed the opportunity to do something a little different compared to their hair metal past.

The band's seventh album, *Sail Away*, was a very mellow affair, mostly unplugged and decidedly laid back. It was dominated by stripped-down, acoustic rockers and several soft ballads—an enormous departure from the loud guitars, heavy drums, and extensive production associated with Great White's earlier records.

Despite the shift in direction, *Sail Away* was a winner, in my view, and a classy, critical success. Jack Russell was at the top of his game, and his amazing vocals carried the record alongside songs that were organic, bluesy, emotional, spirited, and flat-out magnificent in many places.

After beginning with the brief "A Short Overture," *Sail Away* curiously launched the album with unusually morose subject matter, as the soft, haunting "Mother's Eyes" told the tragic story of a mother suffering the accidental death of her infant child. While the topic was decidedly unappealing, the tune was indeed moving. The lovely "Alone" was also quiet and sentimental, while the hopeful "All Right" possessed a spark and tempo that was more uplifting; both tracks were fantastic and definitively album highlights. Also included was the epic, bluesy "Sail Away," and Great White's cover of Tony Joe White's 1972 "If I Ever Saw a Good Thing," which was one of the most beautiful songs I had ever heard.

Sail Away was undoubtedly not what fans of Great White had come to expect, but taken for what it was, the album was quite an accomplishment. Naturally, regretfully, the record was utterly and entirely ignored by the general public.

Cinderella had released the acclaimed *Heartbreak Station* album in November 1990 and successfully toured the record through the summer of 1991. However, tragedy unexpectedly struck shortly after the tour ended when lead singer and primary songwriter Tom Keifer suddenly lost his voice. Keifer struggled for an extended time to obtain a proper diagnosis, but it was eventually determined he had paralysis of the left vocal cord. The vocal cord paresis was a neurological disorder, a relatively uncommon ailment likely resulting from a random virus. The outlook was decidedly grim as the condition typically ended a professional singer's career.

Still, Keifer was determined to fight and underwent several surgeries attempting to improve the affliction, including the complicated repair of a vocal cyst and hemorrhage. Unfortunately, the operations were to no avail, and Keifer was left still unable to vocalize properly.

Dr. Rick Fornelli, a specialist in the condition, was convinced Keifer would have to start from scratch, stating, "a paresis patient literally has to learn how to talk again, this time using technique and form that was never a conscious consideration in the past. It's often a tough assignment to get back to speaking normally, let alone singing professionally."

Many months of intense physical therapy and vocal coaching followed with a marginal degree of success, but the results were unpredictable, and Keifer was told it was probable he would never be able to resume his profession. For every ounce of improvement, there were occasions where he would experience sudden, uncontrollable changes in pitch and tone, or not be able to sing at all. The frustration was unbearable.

Miraculously, after much additional work, Keifer managed to write and contribute vocals to Cinderella's fourth album, *Still Climbing*, in 1994, even as he often had to piece his parts together one word at a time. The album was a more straightforward, heavy, blues-rock affair versus the stripped-back and often country-tinged *Heartbreak Station*.

The album featured some great material, including the standout rockers "Bad Attitude Shuffle" and "All Comes Down," both of which should earn a place on any Cinderella greatest hits compilation. Additionally, "Talk Is Cheap" was an awesome, heavy groover that dated all the way back to 1987 while "Freewheelin" flat-out smoked, and "Easy Come Easy Go" was more melodic pop-metal. The record also contained the fantastic "Hot & Bothered," originally released on the *Wayne's World* movie soundtrack in 1992.

That said, a great deal of Cinderella's past success (at least on radio and MTV) had been generated via power ballads, and unfortunately, the three included on *Still Climbing* failed to match the magic of the band's earlier works, leaving the group without a primary vehicle for commercial welfare. Not that radio or MTV generally wanted anything to do with hair metal power ballads in 1994 anyway, regardless of their quality (Aerosmith and Bon Jovi notwithstanding).

Not surprisingly, Mercury Records had zero interest in the album and gave it absolutely no promotion or exposure at all, as grunge continued to rule the day. Even many dedicated hair metal fans had no idea the album even existed (again, there was no real internet, yet). *Still Climbing* entered the Billboard 200 Albums chart at No. 178 but quickly dropped out altogether. Cinderella was then promptly ditched by their record label and sadly broke up (went on hiatus) in 1995.

Electric Boys had carved out a nice little hair metal niche for themselves on their first two records with their fairly unique brand of funk-metal. However, by 1994 several other bands had consumed the spotlight featuring a similar style (Faith No More and Red Hot Chili Peppers, of particular note). Electric Boys felt the market for their brand of music was becoming saturated and responded with a new batch of songs primarily focused on simple, heavy, groove-laden, riff-based melodies. While not as "funky" as their past output, it was still clearly Electric Boys, just a little meaner and rougher around the edges. The result was the formidably impressive *Freewheelin'* album. The style change wasn't necessarily better or worse (mainly just *different*), but it was objectively awesome, just the same.

Recorded at Abbey Road Studios, the new songs were raw and powerful, with less extravagance placed on the production. Still, the overall sound of the album remained "big." "Ready to Believe" opened the record with a smashing, steady groove before personal favorite "Straight No Chaser" officially rammed the door down. Conny Bloom's vocals were on fire, and the album's guitar work was particularly heavy.

The record contained other fresh elements as well, many of them harking back to a '70s-vibe, including the groovy "Mountains and Sunsets" and stoner-ish "Sad Day." Most of the songs were straightforward, hard rock, though, such as the mighty "Nothing for Nothing" and angry "My Knuckles Your Face." Interestingly, the title track "Freewheelin" was initially left off the album for whatever reason, only to be added back on subsequent reissues decades later as a bonus track. Bloom, from his view, could never explain how it managed to get overlooked in the first place, as it was one of the album's stronger selections.

Despite the strength of the record, however, similar to Bang Tango, Electric Boys couldn't get a US label to even remotely consider releasing the album, restricting its availability only to Great Britain. *Freewheelin'* was an imposing statement, but the US market for Electric Boys and all things hair metal in 1994 was simply too barren, and the band unfortunately dissolved in 1995 as a result.

Consistent with the period, many other hair metal groups and alumni fell on hard times in 1994, witnessing their bands and projects dishearteningly fizzle and expire.

Mike Tramp's **Freak of Nature** released their second album, *Gathering of Freaks*, but after it failed to generate any sales momentum whatsoever, the band would later break up in 1996 after issuing a final collection of earlier B-sides. *Gathering of Freaks* continued Tramp's darker direction post-White Lion, and while strong musically, lacked the hooks to garner any commercial interest. Make sure to check out "Enemy" and "Stand Back," though, as the fierce rockers will knock you on your behind.

Similarly, Dee Snider's **Widowmaker** gave it one last shot in 1994 with their sophomore release, *Stand By for Pain*. The material was *much* darker, crunchier, and heavier than prior record *Blood and Bullets*, but overall, it was a weaker album with regard to song-quality. Regretfully, it would be the last Widowmaker release.

Stephen Pearcy's **Arcade** issued their second album *A/2*, which also featured a much heavier and less hair metal sound. "Angry" and "Get Off My Back" were intense rockers, but the hooks were missing and the songs lacked the overall structure and melody present on Arcade's self-titled debut. Sales of *A/2* were less than a fifth of their previous album, and Epic Records quickly dropped the band. Arcade broke up for good in 1995.

Tuff had arrived late to the hair metal party in 1991 but managed to attain a small taste of success with the power ballad "I Hate Kissing You Goodbye" (the video reached No. 3 on Dial MTV behind Guns N' Roses and Metallica). By the time 1994 rolled around, however, the window of opportunity for bands of their ilk had regrettably closed.

Having been dropped by their record company and unable to secure a new deal in the darkness of grunge, Tuff attempted to hang on by independently releasing their new album, *Fist First*, but the effort was to no avail as the record went largely unnoticed by the mass public. Even I was surprised by it when I first spied a rare copy that had been instantly relegated to the bargain bin of my local record store (I recall even wondering if it was indeed the same band given the "un-glam" nature of the album's artwork.)

Fist First wasn't as strong as Tuff's earlier debut, but it was still thankfully mostly trademark Tuff hair metal, only a little heavier and decidedly less glam. The record did feature the excellent track "Tied to the Bells," and the album was eventually picked up by BMG records and officially issued in 1995 under the revised title, *Religious Fix*. The updated printing also added the awesome "Daddy's Money," which remains on my gym playlist to this day. From a new-material albums standpoint, however, that was sadly the last of Tuff.

Texas-based rockers **Dangerous Toys** got around to releasing their third album in 1994, appropriately titled *Pissed*. The record was the first to feature new lead guitarist Paul Lidel, whose style aligned perfectly to the more aggressive nature of the material the band was seeking at the time. *Pissed* was Dangerous Toys' best record yet, in my view, although as it was 1994, sales, of course, did not support that position. But make no mistake, *Pissed* was a solid effort, coursing with hard, heavy, angry venom. "Pissed" and "Strange" were the album's highlights, and Dangerous Toys even delivered a sweet, uncharacteristic ballad in "Promise the Moon."

Enuff Z' Nuff had been dropped from their record label after *Animals with Human Intelligence* failed to achieve success in 1993.

Talented songwriters Donnie Vie (vocals, guitars) and Chip Z'Nuff (bass) were in dire straits in the mid-'90s, having come down from the success and high of the '80s only to see themselves broke and mired in substance addictions by the time 1994 rolled around.

In 1985 Enuff Z' Nuff recorded their first set of demos, titling the collection *Hollywood Squares.* However, upon finally securing their record deal in 1989, the band wound up writing an entirely fresh, new batch of songs to celebrate the joyous occasion. Fast forward to 1994, and Enuff Z' Nuff thankfully decided to dust off those original demos and package them up as a new album, simply titled *1985.*

However, these weren't just your average demos—much of the previously passed-over material was surprisingly terrific. The songs' style was significantly more pop-rock versus the harder edge recently presented on *Animals with Human Intelligence*, and the tunes were amazingly catchy in the true Enuff Z' Nuff-roots vein of Beatles-based power-pop. The production was excellent and there was no doubt at least a couple of the songs would have been significant hits had they been unleashed on the public back in the mid-'80s.

The *1985* album was all-original material with the exception of the opening track, a spirited rendition of Smokey Robinson's "Tears of a Clown." Among other enjoyable, ultra-catchy pop tracks were "Catholic Girls," "Day by Day," "I'll Be The 1 2 Love U," "Fingers on It," and "Marie." Each song brilliantly displayed what Enuff Z' Nuff was truly all about at its core and would certainly be worthy of a spot on any best-of compilation that focused on the band's immense catalog.

Liner notes for the album were written by Enuff Z' Nuff uber-fan and radio shock-jock Howard Stern, who pronounced that if he could bring only three albums to a deserted island, they would be the first three Enuff Z' Nuff records. High praise indeed, but as with everything else hair metal at the time, certainly not enough to mount any meaningful resistance against the mid-'90s grunge onslaught. Sadly, *1985* racked up hardly any sales at all, although, for true fans, the album was a decidedly special treat.

Tesla released their fourth studio album, *Bust a Nut*, in 1994, their final record with Geffen Records. Amazingly, the band found some moderate success with record selling more than five hundred thousand copies in the US. Undeniably, a Gold record paled in comparison to Tesla's former efforts, but in 1994, for a band the general populous had no issue casually lumping under the hair band umbrella, it was a notable achievement.

The style of the new material was not entirely dissimilar to Tesla's previous works but was unquestionably more diverse and less bombastic in places than the tone of their more metallic debut, *Mechanical Resonance*, back in 1986. The evolution seemed natural and unforced, though, and the result was a more modernized version of the band's sound.

"The Gate / Invited" was a heavy-building, hard rock opener, while the second track, "Solution," was a full-blown metal blaster. After that, *Bust a Nut* moved into more mid-tempo tracks featuring plenty of acoustic guitars and melody prior to "Action Talks" bringing back the heavy metal once again before the album finished with a few lighter and more organic tunes, including the southern-sounding "Wonderful World" and Joe South cover song, "Games People Play."

When I'm in the mood for Tesla, I admittedly always reach for *Mechanical Resonance* or *The Great Radio Controversy* first, but *Bust A Nut* assuredly saw the band in fine form in 1994.

Sadly, Tesla had to fire guitarist Tommy Skeoch shortly after the album was released due to his continuing struggles with substance abuse, and the unfavorable musical climate for Tesla's brand of music forced the band to break up (temporarily) in 1995.

Gilby Clarke had first joined Guns N' Roses in 1991 after being called upon to replace departed original rhythm guitarist Izzy Stradlin. Clarke was still officially a part of GN'R in 1994 (if by contract only) when he used the fame brought by his tenure in the band to release his debut solo album, *Pawnshop Guitars.*

Every member of the GN'R lineup at the time made a guest appearance on the record, even Axl Rose, who duetted with Clarke on a faithful, spirited cover of the Rolling Stones' "Dead Flowers." Clarke handled all lead vocals for the record, and while not a powerhouse singer by any means, his voice held distinction and he was more than capable of carrying a good tune. The real surprise was what a truly excellent record *Pawnshop Guitars* was from a songwriting standpoint!

While Izzy Stradlin's solo album was all about the Rolling Stones, the material on *Pawnshop Guitars* was equal parts the Stones, Beatles, and '70s blues-rock mixed in with a few modern twinges.

"Cure Me…Or Kill Me" gave the record a welcomed jump-start as the only song to truly feature metal-based guitar riffs similar to Guns N' Roses. "Tijuana Jail," meanwhile, was a barnstorming romper that was legitimately both parts heavy metal and punk. Both songs featured classic hard rock guitar solos contributed by none other than Slash himself. Several other terrific tunes ventured outside of the heavy rock category, though, as "Skin & Bones" was vintage Stones, "Johanna's Chopper" was trippy, psychedelic, and groovy, and "Let's Get Lost" flowed with sing-along, Beatles-esque melodies. *Pawnshop Guitars* was a welcomed surprise and a pleasure to behold.

Guns N' Roses, meanwhile, were unsurprisingly mired in drama toward the end of 1994 as they prepared to contribute a cover of the Rolling Stones' "Sympathy for the Devil" to the soundtrack for the much-anticipated blockbuster film *Interview With The Vampire*, starring Tom Cruise and Brad Pitt.

Already absent original members Izzy Stradlin and Steven Adler, Axl Rose decided not to utilize Gilby Clarke and instead brought in childhood friend Paul "Huge" Tobias to lay down the song's rhythm guitar parts. Not only did Rose make the unilateral decision to bring the new guitarist aboard, but he would often secretly instruct Tobias to overdub some of Slash' lead guitar after the legendary axe-slinger had left the studio for the night. Naturally, Slash was outraged over Rose's bold decision to bring in a new band member and plot the group's course without the full band's input, let alone the fact that Slash felt Tobias was a poor creative fit for GN'R, in any event.

The finished song itself was released as a single in December 1994, and all told, the results were more than underwhelming. The performance certainly held true to the original song just fine, but it was utterly devoid of any energy or spark. Slash would later state, "if you ever want to hear the sound of a band breaking up, just listen to that recording."

Indeed, Clarke's contract went unrenewed and he was gone from the band by early 1995. Further, "Sympathy for the Devil" proved to be the final Guns N' Roses track to feature original members Slash and Duff McKagan, and replacement drummer Matt Sorum. Slash, finally fed up with Rose's behavior, left the band in 1996. Rose then fired Sorum in early 1997, and finally, McKagan threw in the towel later that same year no longer wanting to deal with the overarching chaos and whatever it was Guns N' Roses had devolved into.

Rose then proceeded to take sole ownership of GN'R afterward (he had already forced Slash and McKagan to sign away their rights to the band's name and trademark years earlier) and went about rebuilding the group as he saw fit. We will see that it would be a very long time indeed before anything substantive would come of his efforts.

David Lee Roth resurfaced in 1994 with his new release, *Your Filthy Little Mouth*, an album the struggling singer recorded with mostly studio musicians as his solo band members had gone their separate ways by that point. Roth was coming off the commercially underperforming *A Little Ain't Enough* album in 1991, and, unfortunately, *Your Filthy Little Mouth* only served to push the one-time legend and king of the rock 'n' roll world further down to his critical and commercial nadir.

Not that *Your Filthy Little Mouth* was necessarily a *bad* album per se (although it definitely wasn't *good*), but rather it was perhaps unwisely overly diverse to the extent it likely served no single master and was just too far removed from Roth's Van Halen-based hard rock roots to satisfy longtime fans. I guess "eclectic" was the most favorable way to describe the record overall, but admittedly, a lot of the songs just simply couldn't hold a candle to anything from Roth's past.

The album's first three tracks were actually pretty decent: "She's My Machine" was a cool, groovy, mid-tempo rocker while "Everybody's Got the Monkey" and "Big Train" were more up-tempo and not entirely distanced from early Van Halen. After that, however, things managed to get pretty dicey fairly quickly.

The further the album went along, the less rock 'n' roll the music seemed to be, as no less than *all* of the following styles were present at one point or another: country, R&B, big band, jazz, dance, reggae, and even fusion (really). On the one hand, you could've said it was an admirably ambitious endeavor, but on the other hand, you could've characterized it as an ill-advised hot mess, and you probably wouldn't have been wrong. At the end of the day, *Your Filthy Little Mouth* was simply not going to satisfy anyone that picked up a David Lee Roth album expecting to hear something even remotely similar to Van Halen or his early solo career—and that was *everyone*, by the way.

Given the musical climate at the time, though, it was entirely probable Roth would have been challenged to sell a legitimately proper rock 'n' roll album even if had he made one. Perhaps that justified the attempt at something unconventional, but at least he could have satisfied whatever small number of hardcore fans remained (versus taking a chance on something seemingly destined to fail across the board). Or maybe Roth was just honestly expressing where his creative juices were running at the time, and if so, more power and credit to him for sticking to his guns.

Either way, sales were practically non-existent as *Your Filthy Little Mouth* was quickly relegated to the bargain bins and came to represent Roth's first real taste of failure up to that point in his career. The subsequent tour to support the album saw Roth demoted to mainly small, insignificant venues limited to the US.

In 1995, Roth would curiously transition to a full-time, adult lounge act performing almost exclusively in Las Vegas casinos. While that platform actually fit Roth's style and personality perfectly, it was still a long, far fall from his undistributed position as sultan of the rock music world with Van Halen back in the early '80s.

Perhaps the only hair metal act to really find significant commercial success in 1994 was, naturally, none other than **Bon Jovi.** The band had toured extensively through December 1993 in support of 1992's *Keep the Faith*, visiting thirty-seven countries along the way and playing almost 200 shows in total. The group then quickly got back to the task of writing, but as of October 1994, they still weren't ready to release their sixth record despite having penned close to sixty new songs. In an effort to tide over their anxious fanbase, Bon Jovi instead decided to release their first greatest hits album, *Cross Road*, featuring two freshly recorded studio tracks.

Cross Road was a relatively straightforward best-of compilation, but was particularly notable for the new single "Always." The classic hair metal power ballad became an *enormous* hit, turning into Bon Jovi's highest-selling single *ever*. The song stayed in the Top 10 on the Billboard Hot 100 chart for six consecutive *months* and managed to hit No. 1 in thirteen different countries. From my view, "Always" was just another standard '80s power ballad (it was decent enough), but for whatever reason, it resonated as all the rage with the majority of the commercial public. The album's other new tune was also a winner, the catchy pop-rocker "Someday I'll Be Saturday Night."

Driven by "Always" and the immense popularity of Bon Jovi's back-catalog of mega-hits, *Cross Road* went on to sell over twenty million copies making it one of the biggest-selling records of all-time.

Notably, the new songs on *Cross Road* were the last to be recorded with original bassist Alec John Such, who was unceremoniously fired from the band in late 1994. Jon Bon Jovi had grown weary of Such's troubles keeping up while performing live and felt his commitment to Bon Jovi's exhaustive schedule no longer matched that of the rest of the band. Such was replaced by Hugh McDonald for the foreseeable future.

Other noteworthy albums released in 1994: Jackyl *(Push Comes to Shove)*, Slik Toxic *(Irrelevant)*, Erotic Suicide *(Abusement Park)*, Bone Machine *(Dogs)*

If 1994 was seemingly a dark time for hair metal, that's because it really was. Several hair bands evolved to harder, heavier, or otherwise different styles generating some of the best albums of their career (while others fell decidedly short), but, unfortunately, grunge and alternative music had slammed the door shut to any commercial success either way. Many hair metal acts either broke up or were left with uncertain futures (at best) as a result.

Hair metal's hard times would sadly persist for the next four years, possibly even getting worse along the way, but thankfully there was still plenty of activity yet to come and even a few bright spots to be savored, as we will see.

Best Albums 1994

1. Mötley Crüe – *Mötley Crüe (Top 25 in Genre!)*
2. Bang Tango – *Love After Death*
3. L.A. Guns – *Vicious Circle*
4. Electric Boys – *Freewheelin'*
5. Great White – *Sail Away*
6. Cinderella – *Still Climbing*
7. Enuff Z Nuff – *1985*
8. Talisman – *Humanimal*

Chapter 17
These Days
(1995)

The longer the '90s wore on, the less popular hair metal became. Grunge was running full force, wretchedly buoyed by the suicide of Nirvana's Kurt Cobain in 1994. Hair bands, for the most part, struggled to adapt, and many found themselves broken apart or struggling to move forward in the absence of support from labels, promoters, radio, or MTV. The year 1995 saw a relatively smaller number of new hair metal albums, and a good chunk of the material that did emerge showcased questionable style changes as artists attempted to evolve or keep up with the times.

Bon Jovi was coming off their uber-successful greatest hits compilation, *Cross Road*, when they finally unleashed their new studio album, *These Days*, on June 27, 1995. Stylistically, the record was light-years away from the hair metal nature of *Slippery When Wet* or *New Jersey*. Bon Jovi was fully aware that the musical climate had become entirely inhospitable to albums like those, and the band simply couldn't (or wouldn't) continue in that vein. But as it turned out, even under a scenario where the musical climate hadn't changed, Bon Jovi, as both individuals and a band, *had*.

For Bon Jovi, the period from 1986 through 1990 was pure excess at the height of the '80s hair metal scene, but like everything, it simply wasn't built to last. People (typically) grow, mature, and move on as they get older, and the members of Bon Jovi had burnt themselves out on the party lifestyle a long time ago, a circumstance that had led to the band's hiatus after the New Jersey Syndicate Tour came to a close in 1990. It was a classic "innocence-lost" transition.

Bon Jovi had written the fantastic song "Miss Fourth Of July" for *Keep the Faith* (the track didn't make the record's final cut, but did appear on the 2004 box set *100,000,000 Bon Jovi Fans Can't Be Wrong)*, with lyrics centered on Bon Jovi's '80s party/circus environment packing up and leaving as the band grew to deal with family, finances, maturity, and other life-challenges. Bon Jovi were forced to "wave goodbye to Miss Fourth of July." There was simply no going back to that carefree atmosphere, and the band's music and lyrics had to grow to reflect their new reality.

That said, *These Days* took things pretty far down a dark road. *Keep the Faith* had started the band's progression away from hair metal in 1992 but still managed to include lighter, good-times fare such as "Woman in Love" and "I'll Sleep When I'm Dead" among more in-depth material like "Dry County." *These Days*, however, was much murkier and more soulful, featuring a simple, stripped-back, organic instrumentation and production. I know a great many fans (and even more critics) who strongly feel *These Days* is Bon Jovi's best album. And while I certainly appreciated the high quality of the record musically, at the end of the day, I couldn't seem to get around this one simple fact—if you weren't depressed before you listened to *These Days*, you certainly were after.

One of the reasons I could never get on board with grunge was its attachment to the central themes of "life sucks" and "it's cool to be depressed." I listened to music to be uplifted away from life's daily challenges, not to further immerse myself in them. And in 1995, during a tough time when most Bon Jovi fans were in desperate need of another festive "You Give Love a Bad Name" (as unpractical as that would have been in hindsight), Bon Jovi delivered exactly the opposite.

The band that ostensibly always managed to offer "hope" had seemingly succumbed to the mood of the times. Of course, critics loved this because the music was deemed more "serious." Personally, I will never understand the critical association between "serious" music and "quality" music. In the '90s, however, one thing was spectacularly clear—if you played good-time, fun, party-songs, you were a joke; if you sang about hard times and depressing topics, you were legitimate.

These Days opened up with the six-minute, bitter, brooding, angry "Hey God." The lyrics spoke of people who had fallen on various hard times while Bon Jovi wondered if God ever even bothered to think about those who were struggling:

Hey God, tell me what the hell is going on
It seems like all the good shit's gone
It keeps on getting harder hanging on
Hey God, there's nights you know I want to scream
These days you're even harder to believe
I know how busy you must be, but Hey God...
Do you ever think about me?

Good times, right? The song was tight musically with some terrific guitar work by Richie Sambora, but it was tough to come away from the tune feeling cheery if that's what you were seeking. Not that *all* music needs to make us feel good, for sure, but you could forgive people if that was what they had in mind when they bought a Bon Jovi album.

"Something for the Pain" continued the bleak outlook as Jon sang, "happiness has been no friend to me" and "loneliness has found a home in me." The ironic thing was that the music accompanying the song's lyrics was actually fairly bright and upbeat. Too bad it couldn't overtake the tune's overarching sentiment, however, as things were apparently so bad that Jon literally needed something to "dull the pain."

"This Ain't a Love Song" followed, but despite its misleading moniker, the composition was very much a depressing love song focused on a lost relationship. Then, just when you thought the album might have bottomed out from a lyrical standpoint, the title track took things to a new low, with Jon singing about people trying to commit suicide, having his cross to bear, stars that "seem out of reach," heroes dying, and the characterization of the current time as "a graceless age." Good grief.

If you managed to make it to track five, "Lie To Me" was a stunningly beautiful ballad, but again, the theme was miles away from the hope inherent in Bon Jovi's past. "Lie To Me" told the story of a relationship that had gone so sour that Jon simply gave up, numbly asking his partner to lie to him in an attempt to convince him everything was really okay.

Side Two of *These Days* somehow managed to turn even darker, with slow, languishing, and lamenting songs like "My Guitar Lies Bleeding In My Arms" and "It's Hard (Letting You Go)." "Something to Believe In" then kept the party going with the lyrics:

I lost all trust in my friends
I watched my heart turn to stone
I thought that I was left to walk this wicked world alone
Tonight I'll dust myself off
Tonight I'll suck my gut in
I'll face the night and I'll pretend
I got something to believe in
Though I know I won't win
I'll take this one on the chin
We'll raise a toast and I'll pretend
I got something to believe in

Well, okay then. *These Days* was polarizing for me because, really, to the extent you can perhaps measure music objectively, it was, in large part, a great record. The songs were beautifully crafted, the vocals were emotive and powerful, and the performances and production were undeniably top-notch. But all that aside, it just wasn't the album I wanted to hear from Bon Jovi in 1995, and I suspect I wasn't alone in that regard (although as stated, I have heard tons of fans and critics insisting *These Days* was Bon Jovi's finest hour; to each his own I guess).

Either way, the record was a sizable commercial success, not necessarily in America (you know, grunge) but definitely overseas. In the United Kingdom, for example, *These Days* displaced Michael Jackson's

HIStory album from the top slot and spent four consecutive weeks at No. 1. Over the years, I have developed more of an objective appreciation for *These Days*, but I can't honestly say it's the first Bon Jovi album I reach for when I'm in a hair metal kind of mood, although that would seem consistent with its intent, however.

🤘

Bon Jovi weren't the only New Jersey-based hair band wrestling with the changing musical tide in 1995. **Skid Row** had been uncompromising when they moved away from the successful pop-metal style of their 1989 debut to the full-blown, heavy metal assault of 1991's *Slave To The Grind*. However, when it came time to put together their third album, *Subhuman Race*, the band faced an uphill battle not only with their management and new producer Bob Rock but also amongst themselves.

Skid Row had taken an extended break after *Slave to the Grind* with their manager Doc McGhee suggesting the band wait until the grunge movement faded away before getting back to business (good luck with that, as it turned out). However, upon returning to the studio in 1994, the group was hampered by continual conflicting interests and internal turmoil between lead singer Sebastian Bach and the rest of the band, a situation that had, in fact, been building for years.

Bassist Rachel Bolan stated, "*Subhuman Race* was a nightmare. Internally the band had fallen apart, but we were forced to go in and do another record, and it was a nightmare with the recording, writing, and producing. We worked with someone we had not worked with before after being so successful with Michael Wagner, and we were used to the way he did things."

Indeed, Rock made a concerted effort to convince the band their style should be conformed to align with the more prevalent musical trends of the day. Bach would later recount he had to "fight for every scream on the record," with Rock suggesting Bach try to sing more like Scott Weiland from Stone Temple Pilots (could you imagine!?).

Rock also influenced a very different production sound that was seemingly a complete mismatch for both the band and their material. Skid Row's once razor-sharp, clear riffs and solos were replaced with a muddy, sludgy guitar tone, and the thunderous drum sound on *Slave to the Grind* was traded for an effect making it sound as if drummer Rob Affuso was cooped up in a small closet banging on trash can lids.

The stripped-back, altered production failed to do justice to what was actually some very heavy, viscous material in places. Songs like "Beat Yourself Blind," "Subhuman Race," and "Medicine Jar" could've sounded huge instead of simply punk-thrashy. Without exaggeration, I found the production on *Subhuman Race* nearly made the album unlistenable.

Outside of the subpar production, though, with a few exceptions, the songs just simply weren't there as they were on previous Skid Row records. The tunes were fairly uninspired as a whole, and there was almost a complete lack of hooks. Further, many of the tracks contained elements that were definitely more grunge or alternative versus the traditional Skid Row sound.

The internal tensions that had mounted over the years during the band's relentless touring schedule had simply disabled the group as a unified, creative force. Even the album's disjointed cover art was simply an ugly conglomeration of five entirely and distinctly different ideas and themes. Skid Row couldn't even agree on the band's logo, as the cover featured the new block-based lettering stamped over an outline of the old logo in an attempt to satisfy both opinions. Bach stated, "No one really wanted to be there. We wrote the songs halfheartedly. It was more of a commitment to get a new record out than really wanting to do it."

As an example, the album featured the framework of what could have possibly been a fantastic ballad, the new song *Breakin' Down*. However, the band apathetically recorded only a rough demo and simply sent it away to Bach to apply vocals (the other members didn't want to be in the same room as him). Bach sang to the demo once, returned it back to them, and that was what appeared on the album (as opposed to a polished final recording).

Subhuman Race was really a missed opportunity, as when Skid Row was firing on all cylinders, they were one of the absolute very best bands of the hair metal era. That said, Bach's vocals were still utterly amazing on the record even if the production and songs didn't lend the same quality.

The album did manage to go Gold based on name recognition alone, but sales were a far cry from what Skid Row had achieved in the past. Atlantic Records would indeed promptly drop the band directly after the album was issued.

Tensions continued to escalate, and Sebastian Bach was fired from Skid Row in 1996 as a result of disagreements over both the group's creative direction and an incident that saw Bach blow up at the band for turning down an opportunity to open for his idols, Kiss, at a show in December 1996. Bach stated, "I thought we should be doing material that stands next to 'Youth Gone Wild' or 'In a Darkened Room,' not stuff that was just *okay.*"

The remaining members of Skid Row, minus Bach and Affuso, would go on to form other bands in the late '90s before relaunching the Skid Row name in 1999 with a new singer and drummer. Bach, for his part, would move forward with various projects and a solo career. Sadly, as of 2019, there has still been no reunion with Bach, and it does not appear likely there ever will be.

Another group dealing with internal tensions and on its last legs (again) in 1995 was **Van Halen**. The band had been conspicuously quiet after 1991's *For Unlawful Carnal Knowledge* album, and much had changed by the time the members reconvened together more than two years later. Grunge and alternative music were all the rage, but thankfully Van Halen (mostly) stuck to their historical guns on their fourth and, as it turned out, last studio album with Sammy Hagar, *Balance.*

In an interview with Guitar International in 1995, Eddie Van Halen stated, "Van Halen has always just done our thing, taking it wherever we could, without changing because of what was on the radio. We got signed during punk and disco, and it's the same thing now, only with rap and grunge. But we're not changing. I've never changed the way I write; I play what I like."

And *Balance* mostly reflected that statement, although it was apparently impossible to avoid letting at least some of the darker sound that dominated the musical landscape of the mid-'90s seep into the new material, specifically on lead single "Don't Tell Me (What Love Can Do)." The song featured a grinding, down-tuned guitar riff quite representative of the "Seattle-Sound" popular at the time (Eddie would later admit that it seemed like every song on the album was written in D-minor), but the mammoth chorus accompanying the verses was pure Van Hagar, no doubt.

One thing *Balance* did have going for it was the best production on any Van Hagar album to-date. While the band's first two records with Hagar were horribly "thin" sounding, and *F.U.C.K.* was a marked improvement, *Balance* had the clearest, thickest production yet. Some hardcore fans saw it as over-polished, but for me, it was a welcomed change.

From a songwriting perspective, *Balance* didn't have any tunes quite as impressive as the absolute best material on *F.U.C.K.* ("Judgement Day," "The Dream Is Over," "Poundcake," "Right Now"), but it also didn't have any tracks that were quite as awful as that album's worst songs ("Spanked," "Pleasure Dome," "In 'n' Out").

Balance opened with atmospheric, polyphonic Gregorian chants by The Monks of Gyuto Tantric University (really) as it launched into a dark, steady, heavy guitar riff that comprised "The Seventh Seal." The driving rock song was probably the album's highlight as it pulsed along featuring Hagar in top form vocally (as he was for the entire album, for that matter). The track's mystical textures were an output of Eddie's recent sobriety and his first attempt to write clear-headed in more than twenty years.

"Can't Stop Loving You," however, followed in a distinctly different style—the song was as "pop" and commercial as Van Halen could possibly get. Hardcore David Lee Roth fans saw the song as an embarrassing sell-out, and even some Hagar fans squinted a little upon first listen, but the track was the only single from *Balance* to chart in the Top 40. Producer Bruce Fairbairn had specifically commissioned the band to write a more "radio-friendly pop song" to help drive commercial success, and for better or worse, as it turned out, he knew exactly what he was doing.

Most of the songs on *Balance* were modest, mid-tempo numbers with the exception of "Big Fat Money," a blitzing boogie-rocker that could have fit musically on any of the band's classic late '70s or early '80s albums, but for some reason fell just a little flat in its final form on *Balance*. Aside from "The Seventh Seal," my favorite tunes on the album were the chugging "Amsterdam," underrated rocker "Aftershock," and the whimsical, island-type semi-ballad "Take Me Back (Déjà Vu)."

Outside of the stronger material, a couple of instrumentals served as filler, while the soft ballad "Not Enough" failed to resonate and the dramatic album closer "Feelin'" was just a touch too morose and dark for this listener (although many fans claimed it was the best song on the record).

As Van Halen were always somewhat immune to the commercial impact of grunge, *Balance* debuted at No. 1 on the Billboard Albums chart and eventually sold over three million copies. However, Van Halen were, unfortunately, not immune to themselves.

Internal tensions had been building between Hagar and the Van Halen brothers (notoriously difficult with whom to get along) for some time, and many *Balance* songwriting sessions were plagued with anxiety and arguments. The troubles came to an apex in 1996 as the band was planning a greatest hits album that Hagar vehemently opposed. Hagar felt strongly that hits compilations were only for bands that had nothing left to offer, and he firmly believed Van Halen still had plenty of creative spark left in the tank.

The breaking point surrounded the band's contributions to the movie soundtrack for the film *Twister*. Eddie wrote the music for what would become the song "Humans Being" and sent it to Hagar to add lyrics and vocals. But when Eddie heard the finished product, including the exact lyrical themes he had explicitly requested Hagar avoid, he became enraged.

A second song for the soundtrack had been planned but was relegated to only a brief instrumental, as Hagar was unavailable dealing with his wife's pregnancy and wasn't jumping to do it anyway, not being keen on contributing to the soundtrack in the first place. And for Eddie, that was possibly the straw the broke the camel's back.

Frustrations between Hagar and Eddie boiled over, and suddenly Hagar was out of the band. Similar to Mötley Crüe's split with Vince Neil in 1992, Hagar claimed he was fired while Eddie insisted he quit. For the second consecutive decade, Van Halen had lost their lead singer and faced an uncertain future. As amazing as Van Halen were, they just couldn't seem to get out of their own way sometimes—a development that would, unfortunately, continue to haunt them throughout their career.

Continuing the trend of heavy-weight hair metal bands facing uncertainty, glam rock kings recently turned blues/soul-rockers **Poison** were also at a crossroad in 1995. Having split with original guitarist C.C. DeVille in 1991, Poison had brought aboard Richie Kotzen and released the very un-glam and bluesy *Native Tongue* in 1993. They then found themselves without a guitarist once again later that year after discovering Kotzen was having an affair with drummer Rikki Rocket's fiancé; the band promptly kicked him out of the group right on the spot.

Ironically, Poison replaced Kotzen with Blues Saraceno, who was the alternate finalist to replace DeVille back in 1992. Saraceno represented perhaps a middle ground between the flamboyant glam stylings of DeVille and the more serious blues side of Kotzen. Plus, Saraceno was a talented guitar virtuoso in his own right and more than capable of providing anything the band desired.

In 1994 Poison began recording a brand-new album, to be titled *Crack a Smile*. The musical direction was evenly split down the middle between their earlier glam metal output and the stripped-back, blues-rock of *Native Tongue*. Unluckily, however, recording and progress on the album came to an abrupt halt in May when Bret Michaels crashed his

Ferrari and suffered a serious set of injuries, including a broken nose, ribs, jaw, and fingers, along with several lost teeth.

Over time, Michaels would recover, and the band managed to finish the record in 1995. But upon its completion, Poison's label, Capitol Records, decided to put the album "on hold" after surveying the unwelcoming nature of the grunge and alternative music scene and deeming it altogether inhospitable to a new Poison record.

The label decided instead to release a Poison greatest hits album in 1996 that included two fresh songs from *Crack a Smile*, while the full new album would wind up on the shelf collecting dust for the next four years until it was finally released in March 2000. We will revisit *Crack a Smile* later on during the chapter focusing on the time period coinciding with its formal release.

Poison wasn't the only band to see an album long-delayed due to the music trends of the '90s. **Nelson** had released their triple- Platinum debut, *After the Rain*, in 1990 and played over 300 concerts in support of that record into 1992. Production on their sophomore album began later that year and saw Gunnar and Mathew Nelson heading in a markedly different direction versus the lighter pop-metal sound of *After the Rain*.

Nelson observed that the musical landscape had fiercely abandoned the hair metal style that had brought them their prior success. Upset with the state of affairs, they wrote a concept album they described as "really dark, brooding and angry." The records' theme revolved around the concept of manufactured trends tending to manipulate people's feelings. The lyrics focused on the need for society to shed its dependence on both technology and the media by taking control of its own thoughts, emotions, and choices. Nelson also wanted to break free of their overly "sugar-coated" image and showcase their genuine writing aptitude alongside the talented musicianship of the band.

The album was written and recorded entirely on the band's own, as produced John Kalodner found his time consumed with the making of

Aerosmith's *Get a Grip*. Nelson put the finishing touches on the new record in 1993, titling it *Imaginator*. The brothers were thrilled with the results and excitedly delivered the new set of songs to the label, confident their management would share a similar assessment.

However, upon hearing the album, Kalodner and Geffen were shocked and mortified by the style change and wanted absolutely nothing to do with the record. They had been expecting another radio-friendly, pop-metal album that would hopefully spawn a couple of singles as successful as *After the Rain*'s "(Can't Live Without Your) Love and Affection" or "More Than Ever." The dark, heavy nature of *Imaginator* "scared the hell out of them," according to Gunnar Nelson. Geffen quickly offered Nelson the choice (ultimatum) to write and record an entirely different album more in line with their expectations or be dropped from the record label altogether.

Nelson left the meeting feeling "frustrated and helpless," but, seeing as they were out of options, reluctantly decided to return to the studio and produce the album Geffen wanted. The result was *Because They Can*, released in 1995, a full five years after Nelson's debut in 1990. The sound of the record was exactly as the label requested, light and pop-oriented, mostly acoustic, and very close to "country" in many places.

To its credit, the album featured several very catchy and beautiful songs, such as "(You Got Me) All Shook Up," "The Great Escape," "Five O'Clock Plane," and tear-jerker "Love Me Today." Gunnar Nelson stated, "I'm proud of *Because They Can*. I think it's a great record for what it is. But I was given the mandate by John Kalodner, 'You're not allowed to play any crunchy guitar on this record at all. It's got to be acoustic and organic, and that's it'."

Of course, the mandate from Geffen dictating the album's style (in an attempt to generate commercial success) was entirely in vain. Let's face it—Nelson could have released the Beatles' *White Album* in 1995 and it wasn't going to sell three million copies like *After the Rain*, let alone three hundred thousand. Making matters worse, Kalodner wound up leaving the label a week before the record's scheduled release, and the remaining management completely ignored the record from a promotional standpoint. Not long after, Geffen predictably wound up dropping Nelson from their contract, which Gunnar referred to as "one of the best days of my life."

Nelson went on to form their own independent label, Stone Canyon Records, and partnered with Japanese label JVC Victor to give the previously shelved *Imaginator* a formal release in Japan in 1996, and later an official US release in 1998.

Imaginator was indeed relatively dark and heavy versus what someone might have expected from a Nelson record, but it wasn't without its share of catchy hooks and big choruses either. "Kiss Me When I Cry" and "Sooner or Later" were particularly memorable, while "Tell Me" was an absolutely beautiful ballad. *Imaginator* was an ambitious effort by Nelson, and it was easy to see why they were so proud of it in the first place.

Hair metal kings **Warrant** were also embroiled in flux and disarray in 1995. The band had moved away from its glam metal roots with their 1992 release *Dog Eat Dog*, and while many felt it was the group's best album yet, the record was a commercial flop in the face of grunge and Warrant was dropped from their record label later that year.

Band leader Jani Lane, meanwhile, was going through a painful divorce with then-wife Bobbie Brown (of "Cherry Pie" fame) and also coping with the death of Warrant's longtime manager, Tom Hule. Depressed and disenchanted in the face of grunge, Lane temporarily quit Warrant to start a solo career, but wound up quickly returning to the group in September 1993. A short club tour commenced, but disillusioned guitarist Joey Allen and drummer Steven Sweet then left the band during the spring of 1994.

Lane attempted to jump-start Warrant once again in late 1994, signing a new record deal with underground label CMC Records and onboarding three new members: guitarist Rick Steier and drummer James Kottak (both formerly of the band Kingdom Come) and keyboardist Dave

White. The latest version of Warrant (still featuring Lane writing 100 percent of the songs) began recording their fourth studio album, titled *Ultraphobic*, in November 1994, and the record would see its release on March 7, 1995.

Sadly, *Ultraphobic* was considerably more grunge than it was hair metal, as Lane had tried to respond to the changing musical tide by "updating" Warrant's sound and merging grunge-inspired themes and riffs into his traditional songwriting. It didn't hurt that his depressed headspace at the time lent itself perfectly to the specific elements in which grunge specialized (lyrically, a good bit of the album focuses on Lane's difficult divorce).

Much of *Ultraphobic*'s sound was unquestionably squarely in the "alternative/Seattle" camp. Perhaps Lane was thinking, "if you can't beat 'em, join 'em." Indeed, most of the songs featured many of the grunge clichés of the time: gloomy, heavy guitar riffs, lyrics centered on violence or sadness, and droning, depressing music. In other words, everything that was the complete opposite of what most Warrant fans loved.

Warrant was certainly not the only hair band to change their style in an attempt to remain commercially viable in the mid-'90s, and while I get what they were trying to do, I never really understood how they could have possibly thought it would work. On the one hand, if a band genuinely appreciated the new sounds of grunge and desired to incorporate those stylings into their existing toolkit, you couldn't exactly blame them for a sincere attempt at evolution. However, when the change was merely driven by motivation to remain relevant, the approach came off as shallow, insincere, and disingenuous. Of course, on some level, you couldn't really blame these bands as commercial success was their source of livelihood.

But the real confusion point was how they could be so misguided to think such a dramatic shift would be successful, especially considering their musical heritage. If anything, the strategy would *backfire*. Let's say Warrant (or any other hair band for that matter) actually did manage to release a great grunge album. First, grunge fans would never give the record even a fleeting chance based on the name of the band alone. Hair bands should have known this. Second, true supporters would most likely hate the record, as hair metal enthusiasts were generally *not* fans of grunge.

And this lucid viewpoint doesn't entirely stem from having the benefit of hindsight. Even at the time, the inevitable outcome of such a venture should have been spectacularly clear. Commercial success was simply no longer an option for the average hair band in the mid-'90s, regardless of what path they chose. It is genuinely hard to believe they couldn't see (or accept) that truth. Perhaps bands were simply blinded by past success, or, more likely, surrounded by short-sighted, naïve managers and producers convincing them the transformation would work.

If hair bands had at least stayed true to their hair metal roots, they likely could have, at least, retained the small number of true fans that remained. Instead, with releases like *Ultraphobic*, bands like Warrant managed to please NOBODY. Certainly not grunge fans who couldn't be bothered to give them the time of day, and most assuredly not the hair metal fans who brought them their success in the first place.

Again, if the change was truly representative of what they felt in their musical hearts, then more power to them, but if the shift was motivated solely by commercial aspirations, then it was not only a complete waste of time but also damaging. As fans, it was bad enough we were surrounded by grunge on all sides, it was even worse to see some of our heroes jump ship. And to be fair, Warrant weren't the only band to walk down that road, but *Ultraphobic* was a prime example. Perhaps the only better illustration was Warrant's follow-up album, in 1996, but we'll get to that later.

Back to *Ultraphobic*, there's really not all that much to say regarding the songs other than most were largely deprived of any hooks or overly inspiring elements. The angry, brooding track "Family Picnic" (about family violence and spousal/child abuse, of all things) was released as a single, but radio and MTV literally avoided it like the plague. Some of the tunes admittedly possessed faint traces of Lane's classic melodies ("Sum of One," "Chameleon," "High"), but to the extent the songs were also infiltrated with grunge stylings, these elements quickly lost their ability to shine through. "Crawl Space" was perhaps the closest thing to traditional Warrant, but even it would have been considered only average (at best) had it been placed on either of the band's previous records.

The album's lone standout was the closing track "Stronger Now," which Lane many times thereafter referred to as the best song he ever wrote. And on some levels, it's difficult to argue with that statement. "Stronger Now" was a simple, acoustic ballad with emotive lyrics both sad and uplifting at the same time (focused on Lane's split with Bobbie Brown). The song was objectively beautiful. Had it been released by Christina Aguilera or some other pop star at the time, it would have undoubtedly been an enormous success. "Stronger Now" was actually promoted as the second (and final) single from *Ultraphobic*, but outside of a few of us, no one was listening, which in this specific case was everyone else's loss, never mind the rest of the album.

As mentioned, Warrant weren't the only artists to shift styles during the '90s in an attempt to match the alternative music wave. Surprisingly, **Vince Neil** also put out a record that was legitimately about as far away from his hair metal roots as it could possibly get.

Ironically, Neil had achieved a moderate level of success with his 1993 *Exposed* album by sticking to his rock 'n' roll roots, but by the time 1995 rolled around, Warner Bros. Records succumbed to the temptation to try and modernize Neil's sound and hooked him up with The Dust Brothers to produce and help write his new album. The Dust Brothers were best known for hip-hop and street music and had just finished working with the Beastie Boys on their breakthrough release, *Paul's Boutique*.

Further, guitarist extraordinaire Steve Stevens, who had shaped much of *Exposed's* hair metal sound, was no longer a part of the band. From Neil's perspective, he was indeed up for trying something different, just perhaps not as different as it turned out.

And make no mistake, it *was* different. Titled *Carved in Stone*, the album's first track, "Breakin' In the Gun," raced out of the gate immediately hitting the listener with an air raid siren followed by grungy guitar riffs, hip-hop beats, industrial samplings, record-scratching, street rhythms, and vocals that were barely identifiable as Vince Neil. And all of that went down in just the first sixty seconds. For real.

The remainder of the record followed suit with plenty of dark, sludgy, droning moments interspersed with hip-hop elements, techno, and rare instances where there were small hints of rock-guitar solos and traces of vocals that were *almost* recognizable as Vince Neil. Oh, and the group threw in some big band-type moments along the way, just for good measure. If it all sounds like a giant, disjointed mess . . . well, that's precisely what it was.

It's hard to know, however, if Neil truly supported the stark hair metal departure The Dust Brothers had engineered, given he was understandably distracted by personal tragedy at the time. In 1987 Neil married mud wrestler and fashion model Sharise Ruddell after a brief courtship spurred by a chance meeting at the famous Tropicana in Los Angeles. The pair separated four years later in 1991, but not before Ruddell would give birth to their first child, a baby girl named Skylar. Neil remained close to Skylar as an essential part of her life even though he was remarried to Playboy Playmate Heidi Mark by 1995.

Early that year Neil unexpectedly received a panicked phone call from Ruddell. Skylar had been hospitalized with what doctors thought was a burst appendix, but the truth was far worse. A malignant tumor around her abdomen had exploded, spreading cancer throughout her body. Neil's beautiful little girl who had seemed perfectly healthy only days before was now facing the direst of circumstances.

Months of pain and torment followed as doctors performed no fewer than six different operations trying to get the condition under control. Horribly, each procedure revealed the situation to be worse than previously believed. Neil would sit by Skylar's side for as much time as the hospital permitted each day, then drown himself in sorrow and alcohol each night on the Sunset Strip. Tragically, Skylar passed away at the young age of four in August 1995.

So, needless to say, Neil was understandable less than fully engaged during the production of *Carved in Stone*. During the initial studio recordings, Neil often headed home pleased with the day's output only to come back the next morning to find the material had been completely reworked and rearranged by The Dust Brothers the night before. That said, you couldn't so much as blame him for not really caring at the time.

After the album's initial completion, but following Skylar's passing, Neil co-wrote one last tune titled "Skylar's Song," in loving memory of his late daughter. It was a beautiful, uplifting, piano-driven ballad entirely unlike anything else on the record, a small beacon of light on an otherwise strange and often dreary affair.

Naturally, Neil's fanbase did not take well to the album (neither did anyone else for that matter), and it sold fewer than one hundred thousand copies. Ironically, the rise of rap-rock and successful artists like Kid Rock and Limp Bizkit was just around the corner only a few years away. In some ways, *Carved in Stone* was really just ahead of its time. In other ways, it just wasn't what fans were looking for when they bought an album with Vince Neil's name on it, plain and simple.

Another hair metal act to turn alternative in 1995 was **Danger Danger**. The band was in shambles versus its glory days, with original singer Ted Poley fired in 1993 and guitarist Andy Timmons and keyboardist Kasey Smith since departed, as well. Meanwhile, the re-recorded *Cockroach* album with new vocalist Paul Laine was seemingly in permanent limbo, held up by multiple lawsuits and lack of interest from Epic Records.

Still, Laine, Bruno Ravel, and Steve West forged on with the Danger Danger name as a three-piece and released the brand-new album, *Dawn*, in 1995. Compared to the good-times party-rock for which Danger Danger had become known, *Dawn* was a dark, somber, and dreary affair that, much like Warrant's *Ultraphobic*, very much reflected the popular grunge stylings of the time. For fans of hair metal, regretfully, there simply wasn't anything to like on the album, at all. Enough said.

Dangerous Toys also gave it one last shot in 1995, radically changing their sound and even their name, to a certain extent. In truth, the band had already begun transitioning away from their hair metal roots on 1994's *Pissed* album, but the new material was something else entirely.

The record was titled *The R*tist 4*merly Known as Dangerous Toys*, a reference that marked their updated style and also served as a tongue-in-cheek parody poking fun at the name-changing antics of the artist Prince. The album's music was best described as alternative, industrial metal, similar in many places to the approach that Nine Inch Nails was employing at the time, just with more metal guitars in the mix.

In the case of Dangerous Toys, however, the change wasn't so much about keeping up with the times but rather a more natural evolution. Singer Jason McMaster had been through the proverbial ringer leading up to the album, enduring the death of a friend, a relationship gone sour, and a rotating Toys lineup that left only McMaster, guitarist Scott Dalhover, and drummer Mark Geary as original members of the band. "I suppose you need sorrow in your life before the happiness so you can tell the difference," posited McMaster, "The personal tragedies started me writing songs I was finally feeling good about. It may have been 'Teas'n, Pleas'n' and 'Scared' that got us on MTV, but we can't rewrite those songs over and over. That was then, and it certainly isn't where we are now."

The album was a little rough around the edges and lacked overall polish and accessibility, but there was no denying the power and impact certain songs possessed. Among the best songs on offer were the heavy, ultra-aggressive rockers "Share the Kill," "Take Me Swiftly," and "New Anger." Of course, the record's grungier moments I could have done without.

Predictably, though, there was no mainstream audience for what Dangerous Toys were offering, and *The R*tist 4*merly Known as Dangerous Toys* would, unfortunately, become the last album recorded by the band.

Also seemingly jumping aboard the alternative music train in 1995 was **Extreme**. After the immense ambition and production that went into 1992's *III Sides to Every Story*, Extreme scaled everything way back on their fourth album, *Waiting for the Punchline*, which was a very raw affair incorporating many of the grunge elements popular at the time.

Outside of lead single "Hip Today," the album contained barely any traces of Extreme's past stylings, aside from the consistently incredible guitar work of Nuno Bettencourt (although his contributions this time around didn't come in the form of typical '80s hair metal blazing solos, but rather more subtle and intricate compositions).

The disappointing record would prove to be the temporary end of the band. Sales were non-existent, and the group amicably decided to part ways after its release, with the talented Bettencourt wishing to split off and pursue a solo career.

Fortunately for hair metal fans, however, some bands stuck to their guns and continued to pump out classic hair metal in spite of the inhospitable musical revolution surrounding them, perhaps recognizing that change was futile anyway.

Kix was always one of the most "good-times" bands of them all, and despite being dropped from Atlantic Records after the underwhelming sales of the fantastic *Hot Wire* in 1991, the group managed to hook up with CMC International in 1995 and release the super-fun *Show Business* (stylized as *$how Bus$$ine$$*). Gloriously, Kix seemingly existed in a cocoon as if grunge had never happened, doing things the only way they knew how to do them—in spectacular hair metal style.

Show Business featured awesome, high-energy, party-rock, including the standouts "Ball Baby," "9-1-1," and "Baby Time Bomb." Each of these was as strong as anything in Kix's historical catalog, even if the album as a whole wasn't necessarily as consistent as *Blow My Fuse* or *Hot Wire*. Still, the record was a wonderful breath of fresh air given all the grungy gloom that surrounded it. Of course, *Show Business* was a huge commercial failure, going almost entirely unnoticed and, unfortunately, serving as Kix's last album prior to a long, extended break-up.

Slaughter had completed their third studio album, *Fear No Evil*, in early 1994 but were disappointingly dropped from Chrysalis Records after the label merged with EMI, effectively shelving the record temporarily. The band would eventually sign with CMC International (the same label Warrant and Kix went with that year), and *Fear No Evil* was officially released on May 2, 1995.

The album featured a rawer, heavier sound than Slaughter's first two releases but was still mostly rooted in traditional hair metal. Curiously, the album's first (and only) single was the one song most unlike anything Slaughter had done before, the fairly modern-sounding "Searchin'." The track saw Mark Slaughter singing in a more subdued vocal style over what, unfortunately, could only be described as generic rock.

Outside of the disappointing "Searchin'," however, "Live Like There's No Tomorrow" was a ferocious rocker, "It'll Be Alright" was a dreamy, mid-tempo tune that sounded like it could have been right at home with the Beatles' "Strawberry Fields Forever," "Breakdown N' Cry" was Slaughter's first authentic "blues" song (and a good one at that), and "Yesterday's Gone" was a pleasant, up-tempo ballad. The remainder of the album was less notable and the record as a whole wasn't as strong as the band's first two releases, but at least Slaughter were still flying the hair metal flag high.

FireHouse released their third studio album in 1995 as well, simply titled *3*. Similar to Slaughter's *Fear No Evil*, *3* wasn't as strong as either of FireHouse's first two albums, but hey, at least it wasn't grunge. Overall the record was still very much hair metal, but mostly softer and less metal compared their earlier work. Personally, I found the majority of the songs rather uninspired with the exception of the mostly acoustic, ballad-like tunes "Here for You" and "No One at All." There really wasn't any solid "rock" on the album to be found, unfortunately.

Of course, as it was a FireHouse record, it wouldn't have been complete without a big, traditional power ballad. Just as FireHouse had struck gold with "Love of a Lifetime" from their debut and "When I Look Into Your Eyes" from *Hold Your Fire*, they again managed to score a massive hit with "I Live My Life for You," from *3*. Lead singer CJ Snare remarked that despite the drastic changes in the industry, FireHouse was, in fact, the *only* band from the hair metal genre to have a Top 20 hit as late as 1995 without abandoning their hair metal sound.

The album as a whole failed to find much success in the US but achieved impressive sales results overseas, particularly in Asia, where it was certified Gold in many countries.

Enuff Z' Nuff soldiered on with their independent record label and in 1995 brought fans the new album, *Tweaked*. The record clearly showed signs of more modern stylings in some places, but at the end of the day, the band thankfully couldn't manage to stray too far from its Beatles/Cheap Trick influences. Highlights from included the classic EZ'N tracks "My Dear Dream," "Has Jesus Closed His Eyes," and "We're All Alright," in addition to moving tunes like "Stoned" and "If I Can't Have You." The music's overall tone much more stripped-back than the band's previous efforts, likely due in part to the absence of former lead guitarist Derek Frigo, who had left the group earlier during 1993.

And of course, no year would be complete without some type of Guns N' Roses activity or drama. By this time, Slash had finished writing a bunch of songs intended for the next Guns N' Roses album, but upon being presented with them, Axl Rose promptly and callously deemed them "not good enough." Undeterred, Slash formed his own band, assigned it the moniker **Slash's Snakepit**, and promptly recorded the tunes for his first solo album, titled *It's Five O'Clock Somewhere.*

Joining the determined lead guitarist were GN'R bandmates Gilby Clarke and Matt Sorum, along with bassist Mike Inez from Alice In Chains and Jellyfish's Eric Dover on vocals. The album sounded much as you would have expected, not too far removed from Guns N' Roses but unquestionably not as strong. Personally, I found most of the material somewhat unremarkable; perhaps Rose's cold assessment had been correct. It didn't help that Dover's vocals grated on me a little, seemingly more alternative versus classic rock.

Still, it would not have been hard to imagine the same set of songs comprising the core of a great new GN'R record had they benefitted from the input and contributions of the full band alongside Rose's vocals. For the most part, the tracks were basic blues and hard rock that undeniably possessed potential had they been adequately fleshed out. Outside of the slightly subpar songwriting, though, Slash's fantastic guitar work throughout the record was a welcomed highlight.

Perhaps not surprisingly, carrying Slash's name and the GN'R stigma, *It's Five O'Clock Somewhere* sold relatively well, shifting over one million copies in the US alone and serving to support a successful tour by Slash and his new side-project.

The year 1995 was clearly a rough time for hair metal. Many hair bands attempted to update and evolve their sound to more closely match the popular grunge and alternative musical landscapes, but their efforts were often ultimately futile and, in many cases, served only to alienate the small volume of true fans they had remaining.

Many bands splintered or broke up as a result of turmoil related to the unfavorable climate, shamelessly left for dead by record labels, radio, and MTV. Any instances of commercial success were few and far between, mainly limited to Slash's solo record (which likely sold on the basis of name recognition rather than the quality), a ballad from FireHouse, and a couple of minor hits from Bon Jovi and Van Halen. Things were so bad MTV even canceled the popular music program *Headbangers Ball*, the one remaining bastion of refuge where hair metal fans could still celebrate, even if they had to stay up until midnight to do so.

Still, there were definitely some bright spots to be found if you looked hard enough. Take Kix's *Show Business* album, for example. It was a colossal commercial failure, and I'll wager even many of the most hardcore hair metal fans were unaware of its existence in 1995 (or even now for that matter). But find it and check it out. Granted, it's not *Sargent Peppers*; heck, it isn't even Kix's best output, but take it for a spin, appreciate it for what it is, and I guarantee you're in for a great time and a fun ride. And isn't that what hair metal was really all about at its core?

Nevertheless, hair metal would stay sparse and mostly underground for the next few years, but there would still be a great deal of new music to enjoy if you worked hard to seek it out. And that's the thing, really—hair metal never truly *went away* in the '90s, even if that's how it appeared to the majority of the population. Sure, commercial success was undeniably no longer within reach for most, and several bands clearly tried to update their sound to a more modern place, but several not-so-much, and many that did still maintained their hair metal roots alive and well lurking somewhere underneath the surface, just waiting for the right time to re-emerge.

Best Albums 1995

1. Van Halen – *Balance*
2. Kix – *Show Business*
3. Nelson – *Because They Can*
4. Bon Jovi – *These Days*
5. Skid Row – *Subhuman Race*

Chapter 18
Slang
(1996)

When **Def Leppard** released *Adrenalize* in March 1992, it was a classic hair metal album all the way despite the fact that Nirvana and other grunge contemporaries had already radically altered the music scene that had come to exist over the past decade. *Adrenalize* was the last of the big blockbuster hair metal records to achieve substantial commercial success, hitting No. 1 on the Billboard Albums chart and selling over seven million copies worldwide.

The colossal tour that followed in support of *Adrenalize* was immense, bigger even than the massive *Hysteria* jaunt, and routinely drew full capacity crowds upwards of twenty-five thousand fans at each stop. When the final show ended in late 1993, however, Def Leppard had no choice but to take stock of the new landscape. "I remember being on our private plane," singer Joe Elliot said, "flying over Manhattan at two in the morning, having just finished a bunch of sold-out shows, and going: 'Yeah . . . about this grunge thing . . .'"

In truth, Def Leppard were in dire need of a change regardless of the public's evolving musical tastes. The prior trilogy of *Pyromania-Hysteria-Adrenalize* all featured the same enormous, overblown production (not that that was a bad thing), and the band had become both tired and bored with the consistent "formula" employed on those albums.

The intention the next time out was to strip the music back to a more organic and natural format. At the same time, the new material would be influenced in different directions by changes in the lives of the band members themselves. Similar to Bon Jovi, Def Leppard had now reached the point where other aspects of life started to creep in outside of the party landscape that was the fun-filled '80s: marriages, divorces, children, deaths of parents, etc. The band naturally allowed these new experiences and outlooks to influence their songwriting. The attitude toward their former sound was very much "been there, done that," according to Elliot. A change was needed.

That's not to say the group wasn't aware of the new grunge movement and the shifting musical tides, however. In fact, the band made a conscious effort to take a hard listen to albums by Nirvana, Alice In Chains, and Soundgarden when they first reconvened, not necessarily to embrace or incorporate those types of sounds, but merely to "be aware of them," said Elliot. At the end of the day, Def Leppard firmly decided they unequivocally had no desire to jump on grunge's bandwagon, feeling it would be entirely disingenuous if they did. They just wanted to make a more "honest" Def Leppard album without necessarily all the pomp and circumstance that accompanied their past output. And if that meant stylistic changes in accompaniment, then so be it.

And so, in mid-1994, Def Leppard gathered together in the Spanish town of Marbella to begin writing and recording sessions for what would eventually become their 1996 release, *Slang*. The album's initial working title was jokingly put forth as *Commercial Suicide*, seeing as the band were well aware of the risks associated with deviating from the proven formula millions of fans had grown to know and love. Still, the Leps were determined in their mission. The group would later state that had they not made *Slang*, being the necessary departure that it was, they would not have been able to continue at all.

And true enough, *Slang* was indeed different. Very different in many ways. That said, in other ways, once you took a step back and really looked at it, the record was still very much a Def Leppard album at heart, just as the band had intended.

Thunderous opener "Truth?" was a mid-tempo track with relatively restrained vocals from Elliot, featuring mammoth, crunching riffs and industrial-electronic, modern-sounding samples and drum beats. "Turn to Dust" followed, employing an Indian sarangi to generate foreign rhythms with hypnotic overtones, all up against a classically-layered Def Leppard-like chorus. These dark yet catchy tracks were nothing like anything put forth by the band before, but while they were indeed disparate, make no mistake—these were *terrific* songs. Just because the style had been altered didn't necessarily mean the quality had to suffer.

Next up was the poppy title track, "Slang," which was contrastingly upbeat and bouncy, featuring Latin rhythms, rap-like verses, salsa/mambo sections, and a big, anthem-like chorus. The mixture of styles might have seemed like a hot mess similar to recent albums from David Lee Roth (*You're Filthy Little Mouth*) and Vince Neil (*Carved in Stone*), but Def Leppard somehow made it "work." Sure, it was different, but to my ears, it was fantastic (even if I admittedly would have preferred to hear "Pour Some Sugar on Me"-Part Two in my heart of hearts; maybe part of me just wasn't as aware as Def Leppard that perhaps change was needed for all of us at that time).

Slang also featured three gentler, ballad-type tracks, although none were in the exact vein of a classic hair metal power ballad. "Breathe a Sigh" was legitimately R&B/jazzy, "Blood Runs Cold" was soft and atmospheric, and "Where Does Love Go When It Dies" was contemplative and somber. Without a doubt, each was marvelous, though, to be sure.

"Deliver Me" was *Slang's* only real foray into grunge-styling (purposeful or not), but "Gift of Flesh" more than made up for that outlier, representing the only authentic, high-energy "rocker" on the album. Interestingly, Elliot states his favorite *Slang* song didn't even make the album's final cut; "Move with Me Slowly" was a very Rolling Stones-ish, R&B-type track written by guitarist Phil Collen that was omitted from the album's first issuance. Notably, the tune finally made its appearance on the deluxe reissue of *Slang* in 2014, which is worth seeking out.

Slang as a whole seemed to add up to more than the sum of its parts, making for a gratifying listening experience top-to-bottom. The production and orchestration were incredible even as a stripped-back exercise, and Elliot's vocals were a particular point of strength as the record saw him truly *singing* seemingly more so than in the past. The album didn't feature a ton of blazing guitar solos a-la Steve Clarke, but the guitar riffs were still unquestionably huge. Despite not being what people expected, I enjoyed the album immensely in 1996, and it has only aged better with time, in my view.

That said, a great many fans just simply did not "get it," and blasted *Slang* for either being a sell-out or just plain *bad.* Sales reflected the general discontent, with *Slang* failing to generate the multi-Platinum sales status of their prior releases (it went Gold only). That said, I am fairly certain *Adrenalize* would not have come anywhere close to the seven million copies it managed to move were it released in the unfriendly hair metal days of 1996 rather than 1992.

Slang is generally written off as the black sheep of Def Leppard's catalog, but I believe it is a spectacularly unique point of excellence, similar to the characterization of Mötley Crüe's self-titled album back in 1994.

Steelheart's rising career was abruptly cut short in 1992 following the tragic stage accident that saw lead singer Mike Matijevic suffer significant brain trauma and other serious injuries. During the four years that followed, Matijevic endured a long and challenging road filled with countless hours of strife, struggle, and seemingly endless physical therapy. While he was still less than fully recovered in 1996, he was gratifyingly well enough to put together a fresh version of Steelheart (Matijevic was the only remaining original member) and release a new album, titled *Wait.*

Wait was a significant departure from the hair metal sound of Steelheart's previous two records. The initial Asia-only release of the record was split into two distinct parts: the first "side" ("Heart") was made up of soft ballads and/or mostly lighter acoustic songs, while the second "side" ("Steel") was comprised of more up-tempo, intense, electric songs.

That said, the record's running order differed significantly in each region where the album was eventually released.

The one characteristic shared by every song, however, was a general lack of having anything in common with Steelheart's previous hair metal past. And as beloved as Steelheart's earlier records were, this wasn't necessarily a bad thing. The new material was diverse, adventurous, quite complex, and very intricate in terms of songwriting and orchestration. *Wait* had a lot of hidden layers. Admittedly, there wasn't much there for fans dedicated to earlier Steelheart songs like "Loaded Mutha" or "Love Ain't Easy," but for those with an open mind, *Wait* was a treasure trove of musical delights.

"All Your Love" was the only song not newly written for the album, having been previously put forth on *Tangled in Reins*, but the lovely track was presented in a more stripped-back, slower form on *Wait*. "Shangrila" was beautifully sung and orchestrated, possessing the unique ability to transport the listener away to a quiet, special place. "Garden of Delight," meanwhile, was a hopping, acoustic track reminiscent of Led Zeppelin, as was "The Ahh Song" (albeit with a more modern twist in some parts). Conversely, "Say No More" was heavy, dark and hypnotic, while "We All Die Young" was more anthem-like in nature.

Additionally, the album's title track, "Wait," was a soft, moving ballad that hit No. 1 in several Asian countries, where Steelheart still maintained a strong following. Other tracks also each managed to present something distinguished and the album as a whole took the listener on an elaborate journey both musically and spiritually.

Naturally, *Wait* made no commercial noise in the US whatsoever, where it was almost entirely unknown and unavailable even had Americans possessed the appetite for it, which the majority of them most definitely did not. Still, I like to think *Wait* offered something special for fans of *any* genre of music, and certainly for hair metal enthusiasts who were open to expanding their palate.

Speaking of expanding palates, while *Wait* could have been viewed as a welcomed hair metal diversion, two other famous hair bands presented style changes in 1996 that were decidedly more difficult to swallow.

First up was **Warrant**, who just a year earlier had released the relatively unrecognizable and grungy *Ultraphobic*, and now came to the plate with a new album that was somehow even *more* alternative in nature. The record was titled *Belly to Belly: Volume I.* (I admittedly have no idea why "Volume I" was included as part of the title; I can only surmise there was a planned Volume II, but there has never been any evidence of such an intention.)

It is almost impossible to express just how far removed the album was versus Warrant's original hair metal sound. Of all the '90s albums by hair bands that saw artists going in a different direction, *Belly to Belly* was one of the furthest out there. While *Ultraphobic* was clearly grungy, most of it was at least still "rock," but *Belly to Belly* was something . . . *different.* The band even adopted an official new moniker, "Warrant 96," to solidify and formalize notation of their style change.

The album started off with the dreary, droning "In the End (There's Nothing)." Both the song's music and lyrics were as dull and depressing as its title suggested. Kurt Cobain would've been proud, I guess. Next up was "Feels Good," which Lane explained represented how "good" it felt to finally be able to write songs without any record label pressure to produce "radio hits" (seeing as record labels wanted nothing to do with Warrant anymore, anyway). And that brings us to the critical point that, this time around, Lane wasn't just writing songs to try and "fit it"—he truly *believed* in his new material.

I remember seeing Warrant in concert around this time. In between songs, Lane took a break to announce the band would be playing a long show and fully planned to deliver all the classic hits we wanted to hear (that he probably didn't want to play), but also stated they intended to play some of the new, different stuff as well. He literally *begged* us to listen with an open mind and give the latest tunes a chance. Regardless of my opinions on the new material, I had to respect what he was trying to do.

Sadly, I was in the minority, as disappointingly, it seemed like at least half the crowd had shown up only to hear "Cherry Pie."

But back to *Belly to Belly,* the album was *very* "alternative" in style and overall mostly drab and uninteresting, in my humble opinion. There were virtually no hooks, melodies, or guitar riffs to latch on to. "Vertigo" and "A.Y.M. (Angry Young Man)" were at least heavy rock songs, but they were decidedly grungy and bore absolutely no resemblance to traditional hair metal. Ironically, the lyrics to "A.Y.M." were a tongue-in-cheek satirical commentary on some of the more ridiculous and hypocritical aspects of the '90s alternative/grunge music movement. Go figure.

To be fair, for the style it was trying to represent, Lane's songwriting was actually quite good, and his vocals were a high point along with lyrics that were indeed meaningful, assuming you could tolerate the subject matter. But as a fan, if you were looking for the Down Boys, you certainly weren't going to find any trace of them on *Belly to Belly.*

🤘

Another hair band that took a significant left turn style-wise in 1996 was **L.A. Guns**. The band had released the fantastic *Vicious Circle* album in 1994, but after it caved commercially in the wake of grunge, singer Phil Lewis disappointingly decided to pack up and leave the group. Guitarist Tracii Guns was quick to bring aboard new vocalist Chris Van Dahl and L.A. Guns promptly set forth to write a new record, albeit this time with a drastic design change. Rather than adhere to the pop/sleaze hair metal sound of traditional L.A. Guns, the new material was focused more on just brutal, heavy guitar riffage, very similar to Pantera at the time.

In the past, songwriting for L.A. Guns had always taken the shape of Guns contributing the riffs while Lewis built melodies and song-structure around them. However, before his exit, Lewis frequently complained Guns had become laser-focused on only super-heavy riffs, choosing to ignore and abandon the melodic sensibilities of the band's historical output.

Adding to the turmoil, PolyGram Records dropped L.A. Guns from the label during the new album's writing sessions, as the executives were still perturbed by *Vicious Circle's* complete lack of sales success. At that point, disenchanted original bassist Kelly Nickel's left the band as well.

Still, L.A. Guns continued as a four-piece and finished recordings for their fifth album, titling it *American Hardcore*. Similar to Warrant, the group adopted a slightly modified moniker, "*The* L.A. Guns," to suitably mark the style change. The group then hooked up with the popular label for abandoned hair bands at the time, CMC International, to give the new record a proper release.

American Hardcore was very Pantera-like indeed, just an absolutely vicious assault of chugging, heavy, simplified guitar riffs over mostly mid-tempo structures and brooding bass lines, with heaps of backing gang vocals to top it off. Interestingly, there were hardly any of the blazing, intricate guitar solos of which Guns was both famous and capable.

Either luckily or by intent, Van Dahl's style fit the album perfectly for what it was. The raw vocalist was quite adept at deep-voiced, guttural growling and screaming, and that was exactly what the material required. It was quite the contrast to the more polished approach of Phil Lewis. Even the album's cover art was wildly unlike anything hair metal-related, featuring a cartoonish, gun-toting, punk-gangster kid posing in front of hardcore wall-graffiti depicting the band's name in harsh lettering.

Some of the songs were actually relatively decent, assuming you were in the mood for ferocious savagery (a few of them remain on my gym playlist to this day). "Give" and "Pissed" were super-intense, and "Mine" was pretty cool as well, with lyrics telling the tale of a vampire taking a human's life without mercy, subsequently transforming them to eternal darkness. "Unnatural Act" was particularly ruthless in terms of riffs and lyrics centered on the unnerving act of necrophilia. Thankfully, several of the songs featured short, welcomed breakdown interludes to offer a little mercy and a brief breath of air between the violent assaults.

Honestly, if you didn't know *American Hardcore* was L.A. Guns, you would've never guessed it upon listening. As with Def Leppard and

Warrant, props to L.A. Guns for trying something different (I guess), but it wasn't at all what their fans wanted, and it certainly didn't earn them any new followers. *American Hardcore* was barely noticed for its existence, and most who did give the album a try quickly wrote it off. It was quite a fall from when L.A. Guns and their contemporaries were on top of the music world just a few years earlier.

Mr. Big returned in 1996 with their fourth record, the comically titled *Hey Man* (reference the album's artwork). Unlike several other hair bands at that time, however, Mr. Big stuck with their tried-and-true blueprint, and *Hey Man* was not entirely dissimilar from the band's earlier records, just perhaps a little less hair metal, as simply had to be the case with anything in 1996, it appeared. Overall, *Hey Man* wasn't as strong as Mr. Big's 1991 breakthrough, *Lean Into It*, but absolutely featured a few songs that were certainly as good as anything the band had put out up to that point. Too bad MTV and radio would no longer touch them with a one-hundred-foot pole.

"Trapped in Toyland" started that album with a soft piano segment before launching into one of Mr. Big's heaviest and grooviest songs yet. Paul Gilbert's guitar work absolutely smoked, and the combination of Billy Sheehan's bass and Pat Torpey's thunderous beat turned the track into a first-class, storming monster. From there, the tempo shifted down to the steady pulse and melodic beauty of "Take Cover," a spectacular example of terrific songwriting and musicianship that belongs on any Mr. Big best-of compilation.

Another gem was the acoustic ballad, "Goin' Where the Wind Blows." Mr. Big had become known for their power ballads, and this was unconditionally one of their best. "Out of the Underground" and "Dancin' Right into the Flame" were also highlights, the former being a heavy, rumbling rocker with genuine heavy metal moments, while the latter was a delightful, hypnotic-like semi-ballad. The remainder of the album mainly consisted of blues, soul, and rock, with a couple of slower tunes mixed in for good measure. All of the songs were solid, and none of the tracks fell into the "filler" category.

Regretfully, but predictably, the market for Mr. Big in the US had long passed them by in 1996, and the album sold poorly. To this day, *Hey Man* is criminally ignored and/or underrated by the average hair metal fan. Similar to Steelheart, however, Mr. Big did see their popularity continue to grow and surge in Asia where the market generally remained favorable to hair bands, particularly those with a strong penchant for melody and power ballads.

Enuff Z' Nuff released their third album in as many years in 1996, titled *Peach Fuzz*, and the record was similar to their 1994 release *1985* in that it was primarily comprised of previously recorded, unreleased material. Some of the songs harked back to the '80s, while several others were recorded during the 1993 *Animals with Human Intelligence* sessions, only to be left off that record when they were deemed too "pop-oriented" to fit alongside the mostly heavier and darker material that comprised the majority of that album.

Not unsurprisingly, as it was Enuff Z' Nuff, *Peach Fuzz* featured several absolutely perfect power-pop-metal gems that stood up to any of their past best output. I defy anyone not to be enchanted by the ridiculously catchy, Beatles-esque pop melodies in songs like "Let It Go," "Who's Got You Now," "Message of Love," "Make Believe," and "So Long." At the end of the day, that was always the style of songwriting that seemed to suit Enuff Z' Nuff best.

Donnie Vie and Chip Z'Nuff were always exceptionally prolific writers who seemingly had literally hundreds of unreleased songs sitting in their vaults. What was surprising, however, was the particularly high quality of this unheard material. Outside of perhaps Bon Jovi (as we will later see), it seemed no other band had as many simply *great* songs just gathering dust on the shelves, waiting to be unearthed and enjoyed by their fans.

The year 1996 also saw a few other albums of particular note. **Great White** issued *Let It Rock,* which was a return to their hard rock roots after the soft, acoustic approach put forth on 1994's *Sail Away.* The new record was somewhat bluesier than their traditional hair metal past, although, in truth, the blues were always an integral component present on all Great White records. *Let It Rock* was solid, but, unfortunately, didn't feature any big, anthem-like tracks similar to prior Great White hits like "Once Bitten, Twice Shy," "Call It Rock N' Roll," or "Big Goodbye." Lead singer Jack Russel also released his very respectable first solo album, *Shelter Me,* later in the year.

Electric Boys had parted ways after the lack of commercial response to their 1994 release, *Freewheelin',* and by 1996, lead singer and principal songwriter Conny Bloom had put together an all-new band under the moniker **Conny Bloom's Titanic Truth,** with whom he recorded a fresh album simply titled *Titanic Truth.* The nomenclature was in reference to the band's feeling that they wrote and played straight from the heart, i.e., their "big truth."

The songs' style was very much akin to Electric Boys: funky, blues-based hard rock, with perhaps a little less funk and a little more '70s rock (but still with heaps of soul). Highlights included "She's So Inventive" and "Good Time Comin'." The album was (is) hard to find, but any fans of Electric Boys would be well served to track it down.

Ex-Ratt singer **Stephen Pearcy** had kept plenty busy following Ratt's breakup in 1991, releasing two albums with **Arcade** between 1993 and 1994, one with new band **Vicious Delite** in 1995, and forming yet another new band (**Vertex**) who issued their debut record in 1996. However, unlike Arcade and Vicious Delite, which were primarily sleaze-metal similar in vein to Ratt, Vertex was a foray into industrial/techno metal. The style was not far removed from what acts like Ministry were doing at the time.

The self-titled release wasn't very popular with Pearcy's hair metal fanbase, at least with those who knew it even existed; the internet had yet to fully bloom in 1996, and without major record label promotion most releases like *Vertex* simply just fell by the wayside, going completely unnoticed.

The album was set forth ambitiously as a concept record featuring reoccurring themes and characters among the lyrics, but overall it was just a lot of noise in places and lacked the coherent song structure to appeal to wider audiences of hard rock. Still, "One Like a Son" (the only track released as a single) was uniquely impressive and remains in frequent playlist rotation for me to this day.

Lastly, in 1996, there was new activity (and drama) in the **Van Halen** camp. Sammy Hagar had split from the group back in May, but Van Halen continued working on the "best of" compilation they had been developing. In a perfunctory move, David Lee Roth was notified of the impending album by Warner Bros., as the record was planned to include songs from his tenure in the band.

In a surprising turn of events, Roth unexpectedly reached out to Eddie Van Halen (for the first time in years) to discuss what tracks should be included on the album. Remarkably, the conversation went surprisingly well and led to the former bandmates putting aside their past differences and agreeing to record a couple of brand-new songs for the compilation.

The fresh "Me Wise Magic" and "Can't Get This Stuff No More" represented the first new Van Halen songs to feature David Lee Roth since 1983. While the tunes weren't particularly outstanding, they each gloriously contained elements and traces of the magic that was once the mighty Van Halen during the late '70s and early '80s.

Van Halen, including Roth, were invited to appear and present an award at the 1996 MTV Video Music Awards in September, which they agreed to do to help promote *Best Of - Volume 1*, which contained eight songs previously done with Roth, seven with Hagar, and the two new tracks.

When the band was brought out on stage together to present Beck with the award for Best Male Video, the crowd went absolutely *crazy*. It was the first public appearance by the original four members of Van Halen in over eleven years and fueled widespread speculation of a reunion.

However, the Van Halen brothers later insisted no such reunion had been agreed upon, and in fact, unbeknownst to Roth, they were actively auditioning other singers at the time in an attempt to fill Hagar's vacated slot. As it turned out, any chance that might have actually existed for a homecoming with Roth was quickly squashed on the spot, as tensions immediately surfaced between Eddie and Dave the moment they stepped on stage.

As Roth would state the following year, in his autobiography, *Crazy from the Heat*, "We walk out on stage and the place goes ballistic, nuclear, off the map. Well, I see those smiles, so I go to work. It's not something I think about. For me, this is natural, this is freewheeling, and, of course, I interjected a few things besides the plain old banal libretto that's being read on a cue card."

In summary, it was classic "Dave being Dave," a situation that had largely contributed to the band's breakup in the first place. The introverted Van Halen brothers were more interested in simply presenting the award with little fanfare, and Eddie was visibly upset with Roth's relished grandstanding. The exasperated guitarist was clearly irritated, visibly seen backing away from the podium in frustration while putting his head down. Eddie would later become further perturbed as Roth was hip-swiveling and playing to the crowd during Beck's acceptance speech.

Hostilities continued once the band arrived backstage to meet the press, with Roth objecting to Eddie's negative comments about his impending hip replacement (stemming from the wear and tear of jumping around concert stages for close to two decades) rather than milking the positivity of the moment. The two came alarmingly close to blows, and just like that, the very short-lived reunion with Roth was abruptly extinguished, much to the great dismay of fans everywhere.

Roth would later release a statement apologizing to fans and the media, stating he was duped into the "publicity stunt" by the Van Halen camp, while the brothers insisted they had been fully upfront with Roth never making any promises to him with regard to a reunion. In other words, it was just an average day in the melodramatic life that was Van Halen. All the attention did help send *Best Of - Volume I* to the No. 1 position on the Billboard Albums chart, however, so I guess there was that, for whatever it was worth.

Other noteworthy albums released in 1996: FireHouse *(Good Acoustics)*, Kip Winger *(This Conversation Seems Like a Dream)*, Bone Machine *(Disappearing Inc.)*

At the end of the day, much like year before it, 1996 was relatively sparse on new material from hair bands, and several of the albums that did see the light failed to sound much like hair metal at all (not to say there wasn't any good stuff among the bunch, as the records from Def Leppard and Steelheart demonstrated, among others).

Around this time, even rock bands outside of the hair metal category, such as Metallica and Megadeth (heavy metal, thrash), were putting out records that seemingly betrayed their roots and succumbed to the new alternative sounds of the times (Metallica with *Load* in 1996, Megadeth with *Cryptic Writings* in 1997). Suffice it to say, if the average hair metal fan was "bummed" or "disappointed" when they heard *Belly to Belly* from Warrant, the average heavy metal fan was full-bore *outraged* upon listening to Metallica's grungy *Load.* Heck, even Rob Halford of the mighty Judas Priest, the "Metal God" himself, was blasphemously putting out industrial-sounding alternative records in the mid-'90s (reference his work with the bands Two and Fight).

Such were the times it would seem. Grunge was at its peak, and all forms of hair metal were about as far down in the dumps as they could go, according to popular sentiment. There would be some small signs of light emerging over the next couple of years, but for the most part, fans would have to continue holding on a little while longer before things would finally start to turn in a more favorable direction, as we will soon see.

Best Albums 1996

1. Def Leppard – *Slang*
2. Steelheart – *Wait*
3. Enuff Z'Nuff – *Peach Fuzz*
4. Mr. Big – *Hey Man*
5. Nelson – *Imaginator*

Chapter 19
Don't Fade Away
(1997)

Hair metal continued to suffer under a cloud of intense, widespread commercial distaste in 1997, and several prominent artists of the genre continued the trend of releasing new music distanced from the sound of their hair metal roots while attempting to incorporate elements of the latest alternative landscape.

That's not to say all of these albums were of poor quality (although many certainly left hair metal fans scratching their heads), as some of the change clearly succeeded in producing strong, if not different, results. That said, other new releases were indeed less impressive. And of course, some bands thankfully did their best to stick closer to home and continued to crank out songs as it if the '80s had never ended. God bless them. For the most part, though, hair metal was still buried deep underground in 1997, although we will see that wouldn't remain the situation for much longer.

David Coverdale had disbanded **Whitesnake** back in 1993 after becoming disillusioned with the band's late '80s evolution to full-blown hair metal following its late '70s and early '80s blues-based, hard rock beginnings. Coverdale had reformed Whitesnake for a greatest hits album and tour in the mid-'90s following the lack of commercial success associated with his pairing with Jimmy Page, but his desire to get back to his roots remained.

In 1997 Coverdale again paired up with Adrian Vandenberg (who co-wrote *Slip of the Tongue*) to issue the new record, *Restless Heart.* The album was intended to be a "solo" release for Coverdale, but the record company insisted it be released under the Whitesnake moniker to assist with sales.

Restless Heart was a faithful and sparkling return to the original Whitesnake blues-rock sound prior to the *1987* album and *Slip of the Tongue*. Amazingly, though, the market for bands like Whitesnake, groups that had sold multiple millions of albums not long before, had soured so much in the US that the new album was limited to release in Europe and Asia only. (To this day in 2019, *Restless Heart* has still never received a US release.)

Right away, it was clear *Restless Heart* had precious little in common with albums like *Whitesnake '87*. "Don't Fade Away" opened the set as a soft and introspective mid-tempo blues ballad, with Coverdale singing multiple octaves lower than when Whitesnake was last heard eight years earlier. It was an amazing song and a truly triumphant piece of songwriting. "All in the Name of Love" followed as a wonderfully stripped-down, pop-soul number with an infectious chorus. It wasn't until the third track, "Restless Heart," that any signs of hard rock life were found, but even there it was more the raw Whitesnake from 1982's *Saints & Sinners* versus the polished hair metal version of the band during the late '80s and early '90s.

"Too Many Tears" was a perfect pop ballad that was released as the album's first single, and the record also featured a few epic, blues-based, slower rockers like the intense "Cryin'," beautiful "Can't Go On," and impassioned "Stay with Me." Coverdale's vocals were exceptional given a chance to shine in a more natural light versus the high-pitched screams that proliferated *Slip of the Tongue*. There wasn't a bad song on the album and the performances were beyond stellar.

Casual Whitesnake observers who never knew the band existed outside of the *1987* album (which was *many* US fans) might have been caught by surprise with the approach put forth on *Restless Heart* (had they heard it, which practically none did), but for longtime Whitesnake diehards, the organic, laid-back style was a welcomed return to form. As a fan of both versions of the band, I have a great appreciation for *Restless Heart* as a tremendous blues-rock masterpiece. It's a genuine shame the record wasn't even given a chance in the US.

Whitesnake proceeded to embark on a tour of Asia to support the album, during which they recorded a brilliant unplugged show in Japan that would later be released in 1998, titled *Starkers In Tokyo*. Any fan of Coverdale and Whitesnake would be wise to get their hands on that scintillating performance.

Toward the end of 1997, Coverdale once again folded up Whitesnake and took another break from the music business, one that would last five years until 2002, when Whitesnake would reform yet again to celebrate its twenty-fifth anniversary.

Another significant hair metal name going in a different direction in 1997 was **Jon Bon Jovi**. In between records with his namesake band, Jon spent much of his time during the '90s studying the art of writing songs for movie soundtracks and pursuing film and television roles, all the while actively taking acting lessons in his spare time to improve upon his burgeoning craft.

In 1996 Jon finally landed his first leading part in the film *The Leading Man* (he had a brief cameo in 1990's *Young Guns II*). The movie was filmed in London which presented him the rare opportunity for some needed "alone" time, during which he wrote a new set of songs to serve as the core of his second solo album, *Destination Anywhere*. The record would be combined with a short, dramatic, contemporary film noir of the same name, starring Jon alongside the likes of mega-stars Demi Moore, Kevin Bacon, and Whoopi Goldberg.

To help shape the songs, Jon worked with Dave Stewart of the Eurythmics after the two first met at a party hosted by Moore. The Bon Jovi frontman wanted to use the occasion to branch out in new directions while employing the motto "nothing's sacred," stating that he and Stewart were ready to "take a leap into the unknown."

The resulting album was indeed very different from Jon's historical output, comprised of dark, slow, emotional ballads combined with British-pop-oriented songs that incorporated modern elements such as electronica and '90s-style guitar tones.

Lead track "Queen of New Orleans" found Jon singing in a low-key, monotone vocal that most listeners wouldn't have even identified as him had they not been aware. Still, it was a superbly catchy tune that showed great promise for what was to follow. "Janie, Don't Take Your Love to Town" saw Jon return to a more recognizable vocal, and the pop-song was perhaps the album's highlight as a masterful, stripped-back ode to his character-wife in the film.

"Midnight in Chelsea" continued the British-pop approach, featuring bona fide dance beats along with yet another irresistible chorus. Among the slower and more somber offerings, standouts included the emotional "Staring at Your Window with a Suitcase in My Hand" and the earnest "Every Word Was a Piece of My Heart," while "It's Just Me" served up a dark, haunting expression.

The album's title track, "Destination Anywhere," however, was more upbeat, with Jon singing about the unique nature of finally finding himself in a situation where he was out on his own. As he stated regarding the song's basis, "Anywhere you stopped, that's where you'd lay down at night and sleep, and that's where you met people and saw things off the beaten path. There was no arena, there was no airport and none of the trappings of life in a rock band. I wanted to capture that in the song."

The record concluded with the grim "August 7, 4:15," which Jon wrote out of distress in response to the tragic, mysterious death of his manager's six-year-old daughter (unsolved to this day).

Destination Anywhere the movie was also based on a dark set of dramatic circumstances, telling the grim story of an estranged couple struggling to overcome life's challenges after the death of their young child. The pair find themselves in a perplexing situation, however, when an abandoned baby is found that subsequently requires them to reassess their embattled relationship. As discussed, the '90s definitely were definitely *not* the '80s—fun was out and real-life affliction was in, not only in music but seemingly all aspects of popular culture.

Both the movie and soundtrack were released on June 17, 1997, with the album achieving only moderate success in the US but impressive results in the UK, where it hit No. 2 on the Albums chart. The US was in full anti-everything hair metal mode, and radio wanted very little to do with a solo record from a name like Jon Bon Jovi. "We played the single for what they call Modern Rock stations in the States," Jon said, "they go, 'Man, we love this! Who is it?' You tell them. (pulls face) 'Can't play it.'"

Nevertheless, *Destination Anywhere* would up selling two million copies worldwide and stood as a mostly great set of songs (at least half of them), even if they had little in common with Jon's hair metal past. Much like Def Leppard's *Slang* the year before, the album was perhaps the lone black sheep in the Bon Jovi catalog (at the time), but that didn't mean it wasn't worthy of its place.

When we last saw **Mötley Crüe** in 1994, they had released the ultra-heavy and very different-sounding *Mötley Crüe* album with new singer John Corabi. Regretfully, the record was met with great dislike by their average fan and great indifference by everyone else. Times were so tough for the Crüe they were forced to cancel their tour midway through due to soft ticket sales. It was a violent crash for a band that just a few years earlier was legitimately on top of the rock 'n' roll world with their 1989 No. 1 album *Dr. Feelgood* and uber-successful *Decade of Decadence* compilation in 1991.

Mötley Crüe heavy-handedly responded to their difficulties by thoroughly cleaning house, firing nearly every single person associated with the group, managers, accountants, producers, lawyers—*everyone.* Their record label begged them to consider reuniting with Vince Neil, but the band stubbornly and steadfastly refused.

When Mötley finally got back together ready to right the ship and work on a new album in 1995, Nikki Sixx and Tommy Lee perhaps foolishly decided to produce the record themselves. While they did bring in producer Scott Humphrey to assist, he would serve more as a bystander (or enabler of disjointed chaos) rather than the taskmaster that was former producer Bob Rock, an unfortunate circumstance as Mötley Crüe were in *desperate* need of structure, at the time.

In typical Crüe self-destruction-mode (yet again), Sixx and Lee were so convinced the failure of *Mötley Crüe* was clearly everyone else's fault that this time around, the band members would handle everything on their own. The problem was, they were way too schizophrenic in terms of the style they were seeking to make good sense of anything.

The new music was radically unlike either the 1994 *Mötley Crüe* album or anything the band had put out before that. Mostly, it was just dreadfully incoherent and disjointed. According to Sixx, the album initially started to move in the direction of "some sort of electro-grunge style," whatever the hell that was supposed to mean.

Humphrey didn't help matters any, routinely (and rudely) discarding any input or playing from guitarist Mick Mars and instead leaning on Corabi for the few guitar parts he did want (prior to running them through distortion synthesizers and computer effects to blur their impact). The result was night-and-day versus the formidable tone of Mars' menacing riffs that had blazed throughout *Shout at the Devil* nearly fifteen years earlier. If the 1994 *Mötley Crüe* record was out in left field for the band, the new material was out of the ballpark entirely.

Meanwhile, a suddenly despondent Corabi endured constant criticism while struggling to pinpoint exactly what the band was looking for, not that they knew themselves. As he related, "Nikki would jump on the intercom and say, 'Crab, I'm kind of thinking of an old Bowie, Sisters of Mercy kind of vibe.' Then Scott would hit the button and add, 'But with a little Cheap Trick, Nine Inch Nails kind of thing.' Finally, Tommy would chime in, 'Yeah, but make it lush like Oasis, and oh yeah, dude, I forgot that the track has gotta be heavy, like Pantera.'" Even Humphrey admitted, "Nikki wanted to be Nine Inch Nails one day and U2's *Zooropa* the next." Unlike the euphoria associated with their first album together, this time around, Corabi was miserable.

As the band continued to flounder with a messy mix of alternative, grunge, punk, techno, industrial, and several other styles mixed in for seemingly good measure, the record label upped its insistence that Vince Neil had to be brought back if Mötley Crüe wanted to have any chance at success moving forward. Sixx and Lee were still firmly against the idea, but reluctantly agreed to a meeting with their former singer that contentiously included no fewer than a dozen lawyers on each side of the table. Sixx, being the obnoxious punk that he was, of course, showed up wearing a T-shirt with big block lettering, simply spelling "JOHN."

While there was clearly no love lost between the two parties, at the end of the day, their management somehow convinced the band they were better off together versus apart, and Neil was reluctantly brought back into the fold as a contract singer. Given the challenges Corabi was having, he was immediately allayed but also understandably upset. "I was totally, totally relieved, but devastated at the same time," he recalled. There was interesting initial talk of retaining Corabi in the group as a rhythm guitar player only, but over time the idea quickly fizzled out and was tossed aside.

From the record company's view, having Neil back in the fold presented the illusion that everything in the Mötley's muddled camp would now come back together seamlessly and fit perfectly in its rightful place. But in reality, nothing was farther from the truth. The songs weren't written in Neil's singing style, and the music was a messy, far cry from the gloried sound of the band's past. Further, there was still no clear, overarching direction to be discerned. From Neil's perspective, he wanted nothing to do with it. He would later state, "I hate that record. I didn't want to do those songs. I didn't want to be there. I probably quit five more times while we were recording. It was a tough record to make."

On January 7, 1997, six months before the album was released, the reunited Mötley Crüe made a much-anticipated reunion appearance at the American Music Awards, strangely performing a sped-up, revamped, industrial-sounding version of their earlier hit, "Shout at the Devil" (in actuality, it was fairly clear the band was miming to a pre-recorded track, for reasons unknown). I remember waiting for that night and watching that performance with anxious, bated breath. As much as I loved the 1994 *Mötley Crüe* album with Corabi, there wasn't much that was more exciting than the thought of a reunited Mötley Crüe cranking out another *Dr. Feelgood.* Little did I know, that was definitely *not* going to be the case.

The album was finally completed in June 1997, with Neil's vocals added as best he could, and titled *Generation Swine.* I can clearly recall my eager trip to the local record store the day it was released. It was common practice back in the day for music outlets to prominently display high-profile new releases in the racks at the very front counter. But as it was 1997, with hair metal so far out of fashion, I not only failed to find the album up front but was unable to find it *anywhere.* Eventually, and with much prodding, the irritated young clerk found an opened box of them sitting with little fanfare in the store's back corner. He had never heard of Mötley Crüe and figured the album "wasn't important." Alas; stupid grunge.

Anyway, as I excitedly popped the compact disc into my car stereo while sitting in the parking lot, I was greeted with . . . well . . . I wasn't exactly sure. The only thing of which I was certain was that it *definitely* was not *Dr. Feelgood,* or even *Girls, Girls, Girls.* An introduction of grungy, electronic guitar(?) sounds were quickly met with vocals by—Nikki Sixx? For some reason, Sixx chose to sing (mumble) the opening verses to "Find Myself." Now, to be clear, I am a big fan of Nikki's, but objectively, he's not a great singer. Neil's familiar voice finally appeared on the song's chorus, but by that time, it was already all too clear that *Generation Swine* was not going to be the Mötley Crüe fans had come to love. The 1994 album wasn't either, but at least that record was *good.*

The entire *Generation Swine* album was a mess of electronic-alternative-punk computerized sounds. And not the kind that "work." Neil's vocals were predictably strained and seemed out of place (at best), as many of the songs were primarily written for Corabi. Several tracks such as "Flush" and "Confessions" were droningly grungy, and boring at that.

The title track, "Generation Swine," was intended to be a marriage of punk and hard rock, I guess, but I am not sure it quite achieved either.

Vocals on "Beauty" were stupidly handled by Tommy Lee, of all people, a lifeless track written in an excessively low key and featuring synthesized drum beats (for the record, Lee can't sing any better than Sixx). Lee also contributed abysmal lead vocals to the pitifully weak piano ballad "Brandon," which he wrote for his son. Nikki then took another turn at the mic for the brief, atmospheric "Rocketship," which just came off as bland. Meanwhile, "Glitter" was a poor attempt at a ballad with downright embarrassing lyrics, while "Anybody Out There" was overly punk, and "A Rat Like Me" just failed to hit the mark despite some promising undercurrents.

The alternative-sounding "Afraid" was released as the album's first single but failed to appeal to most Crüe fans, lacking any semblance of the rock guitars or bite of their previous work. The only semblance of anything that even remotely sparked some interest on the album was the verse structures to "Let It Prey," which were nasty enough to get your attention while backed by computerized but snarling guitar riffs. Unfortunately, the song then devolved into a droning, dull chorus. Corabi's powerful screams were clearly present on the track although the band refused to recognize this for some reason, instead claiming the vocals came from Lee. Corabi was only credited with two writing credits on the album, although he claimed contributions to at least 80 percent of the material.

Ironically, the record's only real bright spot was the industrial high-speed remake applied to "Shout at the Devil," although most would probably say it was in poor taste versus the classic, original version.

At the end of the day, *Generation Swine* just didn't have very much to offer for fans of Mötley Crüe, or perhaps fans of any kind of music, for that matter. It may sound overly harsh, but *Generation Swine* was simply a bad record and a failed attempt at trying to keep Mötley Crüe "relevant." Fans were clearly interested in the reunion with Neil, as the album initially debuted at No. 4 on the Billboard Albums chart, but once heard, it fell all the way to No. 30 the week after, and eventual sales were altogether poor.

Mötley Crüe, once undisputable titans of hair metal and hard rock during the '80s, just couldn't seem to catch a break in the '90s.

Faster Pussycat had broken up back in 1993, but in 1997 ex-lead singer Taime Downe resurfaced to form **The Newlydeads** with ex-Bang Tango bassist Kyle Kyle. The pairing's self-titled debut album was almost a mirror image of the industrial, electronic style employed by Nine Inch Nails. You might be thinking, "oh no, here we go again," similar to *Generation Swine*, but *The Newlydeads* record actually worked quite well for what it was. Granted, it wasn't hair metal, but Downe's unique vocal styling fit the material perfectly and the music was filled with catchy, electronic hooks supplemented with deep, heavy guitar riffs. Songs like "Submission," "In Denial," "Skin Tight Skin," and "Free Weapons" simply smoked, no matter the style or genre.

While L.A. Guns sans **Phil Lewis** were off doing the *American Hardcore* album, Lewis himself was busy forming a new band called **Popsmear**, who released their debut, *Filthy Lucre*, in 1997. The album was a slightly more pop-oriented version of a sound not entirely dissimilar to L.A. Guns and was a surprisingly fun listen in places, featuring the hot rockers "Outta Control" and "Brand New Deal" alongside more mellow but still stylish tracks such as "Baby I Want" and "Ladbroke Groove." Lewis' terrific vocals were a particular highlight.

Slaughter represented another bright spot for hair metal fans in 1997, refusing to bow to or be influenced by any of the '90s alternative trends on their fourth studio album, *Revolution*. The new record was more of a return to the band's original sound versus the darker and heavier *Fear No Evil* in 1995 but was draped in many places with a cool "retro-rock" groove that was saturated across song structure, sound, and production.

Ironically, the album started off with the one song definitely unlike anything Slaughter had done before. "American Pie" was a mid-tempo, '70s-inspired ode to "peace, love and flower power," very reminiscent of Marc Bolan and T-Rex. The song featured Mark Slaughter singing in an unusually low key; you would have never known it was Slaughter if you didn't look. The tune worked very well and was one of the record's highlights.

"Heaven It Cries" was an epic, slow-paced grinder that packed a massive wallop and featured a return to traditional Slaughter-sounding vocals, while "Tongue N' Groove" was 100 percent hair metal. Meanwhile, "Revolution" and "I'm Gone" were solid hard and heavy rockers, and "You're My Everything" was a light and pleasant pop-metal tune similar to the terrific "Streets of Broken Hearts" from Slaughter's 1992 album, *The Wild Life.*

Adding a little diversity, "Heat of the Moment" was a sensual, atmospheric pulse-pounder, and keeping with the retro-theme running throughout many parts of the album, Slaughter even included a faithful rendition of Joe Walsh's "Rocky Mountain Way." Of course, *Revolution* also featured a couple of ballads that were fine enough as well, "Can We Find a Way" and "Hard to Say Goodbye."

The record closed with the Eastern-influenced, psychedelic sounding "Ad-Majorem-Dei-Gloriam," which was originally intended as the opening section for "Heaven It Cries." During dark times for hair metal, Slaughter's *Revolution* was a fun, refreshing ride.

Danger Danger offered a further breath of fresh air, representing a slim sliver of hope that hair metal just *might* be starting to poke its head up from the ashes. Coming off the very grungy *Dawn* album in 1995, Danger Danger (still with new singer Paul Laine) delightfully enlisted guest contributions from original band members Andy Timmons and Kasey Smith and issued the appropriately titled *Four the Hard Way* in 1997. In many places, the album was a much-welcomed return to Danger

Danger's classic hair metal sound.

To begin, the new record featured four re-recorded songs from the unreleased (at the time) *Cockroach* album. All written back in hair metal's heyday, the tunes comprised several of *Four the Hard Way*'s high points. "Still Kickin'" rocked as hard as anything, "Sick Little Twisted Mind" was a bit more modern but still slammed, "Goin' Goin' Gone" was traditional hair metal, and "Afraid of Love" harked back to the grandiose power ballads of the '80s. Outside of that, however, the newer songs were mostly classic pop-metal as well, including the gloriously catchy "Heartbreak Suicide." The album even included a reimaged version of the band's 1991 hit, "Comin' Home."

While I still preferred the classic vocals of Ted Poley over the gruffer-sounding Laine, the latter admittedly had a powerful voice and impressive range that suited the songs just fine. *Four the Hard Way* was a triumphant return of uplifting and energetic sounds consistent with the Danger Danger hair metal fans had grown to know and love.

Ratt also gave fans a reason to hope and be thankful in 1997. The original five band members had discussed a possible reunion album back in 1996, but rhythm guitarist Robbin Crosby's substance addictions, regretfully, left him in no shape to participate, and bassist Juan Croucier wound up opting out as well. Ratt proceeded to bring aboard Robbie Crane (formerly of Vince Neil's solo band) and, in the end, chose to move forward as a four-piece for their 1997 reunion tour, with singer Stephen Pearcy occasionally filling in on rhythm guitar. To support the tour, Ratt released a new compilation album, titled *Collage,* in July.

Collage was a scattered collection of re-recorded songs from the early Mickey Ratt version of the band, unreleased B-sides, and other alternate recordings. The songs, unfortunately, weren't overly impressive (after all, they were left behind for a reason), but it was certainly a great sign to have new material from Ratt in any capacity, and fans proudly came out in good numbers to support the band on their club tour.

Enuff Z' Nuff continued their trend of independently releasing new material seemingly every year, issuing their seventh studio album in 1997, simply titled, *Seven*. The record was originally recorded in 1994, intended to form one half of a double-album to be released in Asia (a vision that never came to fruition), while the other half of the tracks eventually emerged as the *Tweaked* album in 1996. Instead, the former half saw a limited independent release in Japan, branded as "Chip & Donnie" with a title of *Brothers*, and was then rebranded with a couple of bonus tracks for the US-release as *Seven* in 1997.

Seven was a more acoustic, pop-oriented album versus the heavier and darker themed *Tweaked* (originally designed to be contrasting companion pieces). The album had a definite "feel" running throughout that was primarily laid back, breezy, and overtly somber in many places. Still, it was a fantastic set of songs composed with the beautiful structures that seemingly only Vie and Z'Nuff were capable of producing.

Many tracks focused on relationship challenges but nevertheless featured bouncy, acoustic guitars and wonderfully uplifting melodies. Among these were the fantastic "Wheels," "Still Have Tonight," and "It's No Good." Other songs were more straightforward bluesy numbers or Beatles-esque tunes, including "5 Smiles Away," "Clown on the Town," "You and I," and "For You Girl." *Seven* even included a terrific cover of John Lennon's classic "Jealous Guy," featuring fabulous vocals from Vie.

Seven was optimally digested straight through from top to bottom in order to best facilitate its serene mood and tranquil atmosphere. The theme was quite different than the overly pop, cheery orientation found on many of Enuff Z' Nuff's previous releases, but *Seven* was a terrific album just the same.

Nelson also continued to take advantage of the ability to release independent albums with their new record, *The Silence Is Broken*. The album was, for the most part, a more uplifting affair versus the darker *Imaginator*, and the songs were a mix of newer material and finished versions of demos cut in prior years.

The twin brothers were most proud of opening track "Ghostdance," an American Indian-pride rocker that steadily galloped along. Nelson stated the song was the "whole reason for doing the album in the first place."

While there was admittedly some "filler" on the record, there were also a few gems mixed in. "Say It Isn't So" was classic Nelson pop-rock, "What About Me" was a beautiful tear-jerker, and the title track "The Silence Is Broken" was a moody, epic burner including some impressive guitar work from Gunnar Nelson. The album also included the jovial "Why Oh Why," which was seemingly Nelson's tribute to the Beatles.

Overall, *The Silence Is Broken* was a little inconsistent, but the platter was enjoyable for its grand production, some legitimately fun songs mixed in with a few more serious tracks, and, of course, a couple of classic Nelson ballads.

Ex-Kix frontman **Steve Whiteman** found himself teaching vocal technique and giving singing lessons in 1996 after Kix had pretty much hit the end of the road with their 1995 release, *Show Business*. Still, Whiteman had a bunch of Kix demos lying around in addition to some new songs he had written with Shea Quinn of The Sharks fame. Anxious to get going again, he put together the new band **Funny Money** in 1996, and the group then released their self-titled debut album in 1997.

The good news for Kix fans was that Funny Money basically took over exactly where Kix left off, and the new album could have easily been the next Kix record in terms of style and sound. Particularly given Whiteman's vocals, the average fan would have indeed been hard-pressed to tell the difference. *Funny Money* was thankfully a straightforward, good-time, party record. Similar to Kix, the songs were upbeat, melodic, and even pop-oriented in some places versus the darker and heavier styles many hair bands had evolved to during the '90s.

The high energy "Off My Rocker" launched the raucous affair alongside several other spirited tracks such as "Boogie Man," "Can't Take the Heat," and "Pick Me Up." That said, the real standouts were perhaps the more melodic, mid-tempo masterpieces "Baby Blues" and "For Keeps." *Funny Money* was a real treat and another great sign that while hair metal may have been down, it was far from out.

Heavyweights **Aerosmith** were also busy preparing a new album in the mid-'90s after the enormous success of their comeback trilogy, 1987's *Permanent Vacation*, 1989's *Pump*, and 1993's *Get a Grip*, a grouping of records that sold more than twenty million units combined while producing a staggering eleven Top 40 hit singles. However, the band would find it would not be so easy with what would become the twelfth studio album of their career.

To start, the band members spent some needed time off with their families prior to Steven Tyler and Joe Perry reconvening in Miami to begin writing sessions for the new record in 1996. They initially chose to work with producer/songwriter Glen Ballard, who was coming off his blockbuster success with Alanis Morissette's *Jagged Little Pill*, which turned into one of the biggest selling albums of all-time. Aerosmith had also teamed up with other longtime collaborators such as Desmond Child during these initial sessions, and blueprints were laid down for several tracks that would eventually find their way onto the new album.

However, when the rest of the band assembled together in Miami to further the process, it was clear all was not right with drummer Joey Kramer who was suffering from a deep depression related to many issues that had built up over the years, not the least of which was the recent loss of his father. Kramer soon traveled home, and Aerosmith brought in a session drummer to lay down his tracks, but without their true backbone, the band just didn't sound the same.

On top of that, Columbia Records was less than thrilled when

Aerosmith finally presented the initial demos, feeling that Ballard had over-produced the material and robbed the band of its raw energy. In truth, Aerosmith weren't exactly excited about the results either.

Attempting to right the ship, the group first fired longstanding manager Tim Collins, who they felt was contributing to troublesome tensions among the band members. They also parted ways with Ballard in favor of new producer Kevin Shirley, who was known as "The Caveman" for his stripped-back, basic approach—the exact elixir Aerosmith had been seeking. The band then packed up and moved from Miami to New York, where Kramer was now well enough to join them, and completely started over from scratch with the recordings.

The album was eventually finished and released in early 1997, with the title *Nine Lives* reflecting both the struggles the band underwent during its construction and the ups-and-downs that had followed them throughout their long career. The album delightfully went straight to No. 1 on the Billboard Albums chart, but critical reviews were mixed, a feeling I also shared, personally.

On the plus side, there were solid rock songs like "Nine Lives," "Something's Gotta Give," and "Crash." There was also the heavy and cool Middle Eastern-inspired "Taste of India," which featured a unique sarangi performance by Indian musician Ramesh Mishra.

That said, I wasn't an overly big admirer of the album's production, which just seemed to be lacking a little in clarity and "oomph." Also on the downside, *Nine Lives* featured no fewer than four ballads, no doubt an attempt to extend the band's commercial string of success with such songs, and I was undoubtedly not the only fan who had grown tired of the Aerosmith's over-reliance on bland, sappy compositions. The hit singles "Falling in Love (Is Hard on the Knees)" and "Pink" didn't do much for me either, clearly influenced by Ballard and geared toward a generic, radio-friendly pop format.

While *Nine Lives* could have been considered a commercial success, shifting over two million units, the sales were a disappointment to both the record company and the band, particularly when viewed in comparison to their recent past. Still, the album had a long chart life and garnered hit singles on both MTV and radio during a time when Aerosmith's type of hard rock was still primarily out of fashion (I guess it helped that the singles weren't exactly "hard rock"). "Pink" even won the band their fourth Grammy Award in the Best Rock Performance category.

Aerosmith would embark on a massive worldwide tour in support of *Nine Lives* that was initially intended to span only fifteen months, but wound up extended to more than two years to capitalize on the monumental chart-topping success of Aerosmith's contribution to the 1998 *Armageddon* movie soundtrack, the Diane Warren-penned "I Don't Want to Miss a Thing." Yet another mushy ballad, the song was and still is, ironically, Aerosmith's only No. 1 single, a chart position it occupied for four consecutive weeks in the US and much longer in many other countries.

After splitting with Van Halen in 1996, **Sammy Hagar** wasted no time releasing a new solo album less than a year later on May 20, 1997, titled *Marching to Mars*. Hagar enlisted the help of several old friends to make guest appearances on the record, including Slash, Grateful Dead drummer Mickey Hart, his former Montrose bandmates, and funk hero Boosty Collins.

The new album was undoubtedly a classy release with several quality songs, but unfortunately, lacked the strength and power of his material with Van Halen, overall. The album's high point was the first track and single, "Little White Lie" (lyrically, perhaps a not-so-subtle shot at his former bandmates). The song kicked off acoustically with a bluesy groove before slowly adding instrumentation and simmering to a boiling point, finally exploding into a full rock anthem featuring impressive guitar work from Slash.

The remainder of the record was solid, if not spectacular, with other noteworthy inclusions "Both Sides Now," "On the Other Hand," and "Amnesty Is Granted." The album received rave critical reviews and served to successfully relaunch Hagar's solo career.

Lastly, there was one small but perhaps important event of symbolism for hair metal in 1997. Ever since 1992, hair metal had clearly been on the downslope with bands mostly just trying to hang on, or in other cases attempting to change their sound to better fit the times. The landscape certainly didn't invite or support any *new* hair bands.

However, in 1997, strictly against the headwinds of the music industry, four young guys from New Jersey formed a band called **Jester** and independently released the hair metal-sounding album *Tales from the Boogie Man*. I highly doubt the majority of even the most dedicated hair metal fans ever heard of it; if you have, my hats off to you—even better if you own it.

Despite some unavoidable modern influences, *Tales from the Boogie Man* was the first notable taste of new-blood hair metal in many years. Indeed, Jester managed to emulate fellow New Jersey bands such as early Skid Row and Bon Jovi to a great extent, and for a small-budget, independent release, the production and quality of the album was superb.

The title track was a fantastic hard rock, pop-metal anthem, and while there were other songs in that vein as well, the album truly shined with the rootsy "Nothing Special," the wistful "Let It Go" and the sparkling power ballads "All Out of Tears" and "Are You Listening." It sounds like a cliché, but there is absolutely no doubt *Tales from the Boogie Man* would have been a Platinum seller had it been released in 1990.

The album admittedly went unnoticed by almost all, but it was an important underground signal that hair metal's lifeline was perhaps finally ready to once again sprout back up. Kids who grew up loving that style of music were now coming of age where they were ready to assume the mantle. And of course, many original hair metal bands were still adamant about not being left for dead just yet.

The genre wasn't out of the woods, far from it, but Jester's *Tales from the Boogie Man* was an encouraging and welcomed sign.

Best Albums 1997

1. Whitesnake – *Restless Heart*
2. Slaughter – *Revolution*
3. Jon Bon Jovi – *Destination Anywhere*
3. Funny Money – *Funny Money*
4. Enuff Z'Nuff – *Seven*
5. Jester – *Tales from the Boogie Man*

Chapter 20
Hard Times Come Easy
(1998)

The year 1998 was a relatively confounding time for hair metal, primarily marked by a slew of new albums that (mostly) failed to hit the mark, including a large contingent of solo records and side-projects from hair band alumni who were desperately trying to find solid ground in the wake of their genre's deconstruction.

Aside from the mediocre material, though, an undeniable spark was lurking beneath the ashes that, for the first time in a long time, put forth clear, discernable indicators that the genre was indeed showing potential signs of resuscitation. And of course, there were still small pockets of great new music to be found sprinkled in, if you knew where to look.

In an encouraging sign right out of the gate, legendary A&R executive John Kalodner took charge of Sony's newly formed offshoot label, Portrait, and reached out to the recently reunited **Ratt** and **Cinderella,** offering them a prized second chance to record with a major label. It was undoubtedly a harbinger of good things to come. Renewed, both bands promptly hit the touring circuit with much success while at the same time preparing fresh albums planned for release the following year. Kalodner also managed to hook **Great White** as well, a group that would also drop a new record with Sony in 1999.

🤘

Mötley Crüe perhaps finally realized the error of their ways that had been put forth on the ill-advised *Generation Swine*, and in 1998 recorded a couple of new tracks ("Bitter Pill" and "Enslaved") for a greatest hits compilation that were thankfully much more in the style of *Dr. Feelgood* versus anything else the band had done during the ten years since. I was so happy to seemingly have "my" Mötley Crüe back (in part), I distinctly recall playing those two songs over and over until I had driven everyone around me thoroughly crazy.

The compilation's overall tracklist was actually rather agreeable aside from the ridiculous inclusion of "Glitter" from *Generation Swine*; swap that out for the unforgivable omission of "Live Wire" and the album would have been much improved. Still, *Greatest Hits* came in at No. 20 on the Billboard Albums chart and eventually went Gold.

Of course, with Mötley Crüe, there was always drama, and most of the commotion de-jour revolved around drummer Tommy Lee. In 1998, just after recording his drum tracks for "Bitter Pill" and "Enslaved," Lee submitted to serving six months in jail after pleading no contest to assault of his wife at the time, Playboy centerfold and actress Pamela Anderson. This was on top of his recent universal notoriety stemming from the unsolicited leak of the couple's pornographic sex tape in 1995.

Mötley's tour to support the new album was timed to start directly following Lee's release from prison; however, upon his discharge, Lee surprisingly was no longer interested in being a part of the band he had helped form nearly twenty years ago. In truth, he had lost interest in both Mötley Crüe and the entire hair metal style of music right after the *Generation Swine* album, if not earlier. Further, Lee had never been thrilled with the decision to bring Vince Neil back into the band in 1996 and wanted nothing more than to entirely disassociate with all things Mötley Crüe. Lee agreed to participate in the Greatest Hits Tour "for the fans," as he stated, but was noticeably and uncomfortably disinterested and disengaged during press conferences for the upcoming trek.

Lee would not last long, however, as a physical altercation between him and Neil erupted while on tour turning into the proverbial straw that broke the camel's back. Lee officially quit Mötley Crüe in 1999. "All we got was a call from his attorney saying he wasn't coming back," recalled Neil. "He wasn't into rock 'n' roll anymore. He even said that rock is dead." Lee would then go on to form the rap-rock band Methods of Mayhem, collaborating with the likes of Snoop Dog, TiLo, Lil' Kim, Fred Durst, and Mix Master Mike.

Meanwhile, the remaining members of Mötley Crüe had become exceedingly disenchanted and frustrated with their label (Elektra Records) and sought freedom from any remaining contractual obligations in addition to rights over their own music masters, an arrangement that was basically unheard of in the industry. Naturally, the band members intentionally made giant pains-in-the-asses of themselves (which surely did not take too much effort) until Elektra eventually relented and agreed to release Mötley's music catalog back to them in return for just getting the band off its label and out of its face. It was never a dull moment in the world of Mötley Crüe.

Skid Row's own 1998 greatest hits compilation, titled *Forty Seasons: The Best of Skid Row*, also merited special mention if only for the inclusion of an unreleased track dating all the way to recording sessions for the band's first album a decade earlier, "Forever."

Skid Row enthusiasts didn't have much to celebrate in the late '90s, with the band's last recorded output (1995's *Subhuman Race*) distinctly distanced from the sound of their heyday and the group breaking up following the firing of the temperamental Sebastian Bach in 1996. To fans' surprise delight, though, hearing "Forever" was akin to unearthing long-lost treasure, with the terrific song perfectly encapsulating everything Skid Row represented back in the glory days of 1989, a time that was fewer than ten years before but felt like more like a lifetime after all the hardship and adversity hair metal had endured over the past six years.

"Forever" could have undoubtedly been a hit single had it found its way onto Skid Row's self-titled debut, and along with Mötley Crüe's "Bitter Pill," represented one of the best new songs hair metal fans would have the pleasure of hearing in 1998.

Also of interest on *Forty Seasons . . .* was that each of the five songs representing *Subhuman Race* was presented in different formats (remixes, demos, and live recordings) from their native state, as conceivably Skid Row acknowledged the album's original production wasn't quite up to par. Unfortunately, however, the alternate versions did little to improve upon the originals.

Another big name to resurface in 1998 was none other than the mighty **Van Halen**. Following their split with Sammy Hagar in early 1996 and the failed reunion fiasco with David Lee Roth at the MTV Video Music Awards later that same year, Van Halen was determined to carry forward and spent much of 1997 searching for a new singer in hopes that the third time would finally be the charm.

In a somewhat surprising move, the band would eventually select none other than Gary Cherone from Extreme, who were on hiatus following the disappointing commercial reception to 1995's *Waiting for the Punchline*. Rather than deciding to first head out on tour and establish a little chemistry together, the new lineup instead chose to go directly into the studio, and on March 17, 1998, came out with the band's eleventh album, fittingly titled *Van Halen III*. Unfortunately, it was the first Van Halen record ever truly to disappoint.

Much can be said about the fact that maybe Cherone wasn't the right fit for the band, but at the end of the day, Cherone wasn't really the problem; the real ill was that the songs simply weren't there. The songwriting process on earlier Van Halen records, particularly those with Sammy Hagar, typically involved Eddie coming up with a riff or musical idea followed by Hagar or Roth developing a melody and song structure to match. With the new lineup, however, Cherone was relegated to merely taking direction in too many places, and left to fully flesh the songs out on his own, Eddie simply fell flat.

Van Halen III had some cool riffs here and there, for sure, but with seemingly no one capable at the steering wheel (new producer Mike Post was also a poor fit), the quick-hitting, pop-sensibility of past Van Halen was missing in action. Most of the songs were either too messy, too dull, too experimental, or just too long and rambling (often a combination of all of the above). Indeed, *Van Halen III* tediously clocked in at a whopping sixty-five minutes, with no song fewer than five minutes in length. Van Halen's first two albums *combined* didn't run that long.

Tracks like the acoustic ballad "Josephina" and the strange, spacey, eight-minute "Once" were simply too far removed from the band's traditional palate to find favor with longtime fans. Other misses included the long, dreary "Year to the Day" and the horrendous debut of Eddie on lead vocals for "How Many Say I."

In reality, *none* of the tunes really hit the mark with the possible exception of the first single, "Without You," which, while containing some decent elements, still suffered from an uneven song structure, poor editing, and Cherone singing in a register and style too similar to Hagar to truly suit him. The album's few attempts at "rock" songs regrettably lacked any real punch or melody to result in anything exciting or memorable. Both "Fire in the Hole" and "Dirty Water Dog" contained spots where it felt like they might have had a little tooth to them, but in the end, the songs blandly wound up going nowhere.

Further contributing to the misstep, the band completely passed on including any high-harmony background vocals from bass player Michael Anthony, an essential staple of classic Van Halen and perhaps as much a part of their sound as Eddie's guitar. In fact, aside from an insular three songs, Anthony didn't even *play* on the album, with Eddie bizarrely choosing to record the bass parts himself.

Van Halen III resonated poorly with fans and was the first Van Halen album to sell fewer than one million copies. Granted, the fanbase was already in rather poor spirits given the disappointment they felt after being teased with the failed Roth reunion. Either way, though, the material on *Van Halen III* just wasn't going to cut it. Many fans even chose to dismiss the album outright given the presence of Cherone, knowing him only as the "More Than Words-guy" and blindly deeming the singer a poor choice for the hallowed, revered, rock-oriented Van Halen.

The band toured the record with Cherone to some moderate success, however, as audiences *were* pleased to hear many Roth-era songs dusted off for the first time in years after being mothballed during Hagar's stint with the group, but the tour failed to live up to expectations overall. I saw Van Halen during that time myself and the show was admittedly a letdown, not only featuring far too many subpar selections from *Van Halen III* but somehow feeling just not quite right with Cherone singing the Hagar and Roth material (although I was/am a big fan of Cherone outside of Van Halen, and he is objectively an extremely talented vocalist).

After the tour's conclusion, Van Halen got reasonably far along writing a second album with Cherone prior to eventually parting ways in 1999. Similar to Mötley Crüe's ousting of John Corabi and reunion with Vince Neil, record company pressure played a significant role in the change. Unlike Van Halen's split with Roth and Hagar, however, the break-up with Cherone was amicable and all parties remained on good terms.

Meanwhile, on the other side of the original Van Halen camp, perhaps buoyed by his brief "reunion" with the band, **David Lee Roth** stormed back to his hard rock roots in 1998 after the stylistic diversion that was 1994's *Your Filthy Little Mouth* and Roth's foray into performing as a Vegas lounge act during the years after.

Roth assembled a fresh new band featuring a couple of young hotshots on guitar, one of whom was John Lowery, who would later adopt the moniker John 5 and go on to stardom supporting the likes of Marilyn Manson and Rob Zombie. To emphasize his focus on the band as a whole, Roth elected to issue the new album not as a solo record but rather under the simple nomenclature **The DLR Band**.

As much as it was terrific to see Diamond Dave back in his element, a picture we hadn't fully seen since the early '90s, the new album, regrettably, left a little to be desired. For starters, in the absence of record label support, the independent release carried a relatively low budget, and the results, unfortunately, reflected the price of admission in many places. The overall production was minimalistic, and the thin sound lacked the requisite oomph and punch the music so desperately needed to fully come alive. Further, most of the songs were recorded live in only one or two takes, at most. Indeed, the entire recording process took a sparse ten days. While there was something to be admired about trying to capture the raw energy of the moment (a-la early Van Halen), the tunes clearly could have benefitted from a little more polish. Roth's voice was also beginning to show signs of age and came across as a little strained and worse for wear in certain places.

DRL Band just seemed like a wasted opportunity, in my view. Clearly (and thankfully), Roth was going for an early *Van Halen I* or *II* type of sound, and while he admittedly got close in some respects, the album just failed to spark overall, falling short of what could have possibly been a great record had it been fleshed out a little further and fully developed. Still, the effort was a welcomed attempt at a return to form (particularly in the aftermath of *Your Filthy Little Mouth*), and it was good to see "Dave being Dave" in all his glory, once again. Lowery's guitar playing was a highlight, and songs like "Slam Dunk!," "King of the Hill," "Relentless," and "Lose the Dress (Keep the Shoes)" were admittedly good fun. And hey, at least it wasn't *Van Halen III*.

FireHouse had released *3* in 1995 and the acoustic album *Good Acoustics* in 1996, both to little fanfare in the US but with much acclaim and sales success overseas, specifically in Asia. The band capitalized on this foreign achievement by performing sold-out shows throughout 1997 across Japan, Thailand, Malaysia, Philippines, India, and Singapore, including an unprecedented twenty-five-city, sold-out tour of Indonesia.

As 1998 rolled around, FireHouse requested a release from their US record contract due to lack of support and promotion, and the label was only too happy to oblige, ignoring the band's overseas accomplishments while concluding there was no longer any market for hair metal in the US.

FireHouse proceeded to sign with Pony Canyon Records in Japan and released their fifth album, *Category 5*, in October 1998. Outside of the US many hair bands managed to hold onto portions of their international fanbase in the mid-to-late '90s, but it was important to recognize that these overseas markets had generally grown to appreciate the *lighter* side of hair metal versus the genre's heavier segments such as Skid Row's *Slave to the Grind.* Particularly in Asia, it was the ballads, acoustic tracks, or otherwise overly melodic, pop-based songs that found the most success.

FireHouse was well aware of their clientele and specifically wrote *Category 5* with that understanding in mind, similar to the approach employed by Steelheart on 1996's *Wait.* Indeed, *Category 5* featured a much softer and experimental feel versus the band's earlier hard rock stylings.

The majority of the album's songs were either mid-paced pop-rock, big ballads, or just generally lighter fare. If *Category 5* was accepted for the type of album it was fashioned as, versus mourned for its lack of hard rock or pop-metal, it really did have some fine moments. "Acid Rain," for example, was impossibly catchy and delivered a well-crafted song structure. Incidentally, I was present at the FireHouse concert where they filmed the music video for that song; the band played it three consecutive times to ensure they had ample footage, and as such, the tune seems to be forever etched into my brain.

Back to the album, though, other enjoyable moments included "Bringing Me Down," "The Nights Were Young," and "If It Changes," all solid pop numbers even if failing to make a hard rock imprint or fully rising to the level of the band's past output (particularly their 1990 debut). Unfortunately, though, many of the record's remaining songs came off a little bland, boring, or monotonous for my taste.

Still, *Category 5* was a considerable success in Asia and enabled FireHouse to tour heavily in that region throughout both 1998 and 1999. The band also toured in the US during that time as well, earning a spot on the inaugural "Rock Never Stops Tour" featuring fellow hair bands Slaughter and Quiet Riot, as the demand for domestic hair metal continued to show small, encouraging signs of life once again.

🤘

The hair band with the absolute *biggest* Asian fanbase in the '90s, however, was undoubtedly **Mr. Big**. As the Asian market tended to gravitate to hair bands with huge ballads, Mr. Big managed to capture the region's heart with softies such as "To Be with You," "Just Take My Heart," "Promise Her the Moon," "Wild World," and "Goin' Where the Wind Blows." It was not a coincidence then, that bands like Steelheart and FireHouse, who were also experiencing ample success in Asia, also had massive hit ballads to their name as well, including "I'll Never Let You Go" and "Love of a Lifetime," respectively.

Mr. Big had released the impressive *Hey Man* album in 1996, but the record was unfortunately met with poor domestic sales results in the face of grunge. Meanwhile, internal tensions had arisen within the band and guitarist **Paul Gilbert** had grown tired of the constant bickering between singer Eric Martin and bassist Billy Sheehan. Finally fed up, Gilbert decided to part ways with Mr. Big in 1997 to pursue a solo career, which he focused on the Japanese market where he was quite literally revered as a "guitar god" (which wasn't far from the actual truth).

Gilbert's first solo album, *King of Clubs*, was initially released exclusively in Japan, in 1998. In a surprising move, Gilbert not only handled all songwriting, guitars, and bass, but also took on the daunting task of lead vocals. While his voice wasn't as powerful or polished as Martin's, it was more than adequate and actually quite capable in its own right. The style of the album was strictly simple, harmonious pop tracks layered up against Gilbert's amazing, intricate guitar stylings, which gave the record a pop-metal-light type of feel.

King of Clubs was a fabulous set of songs, all featuring superb hooks and ultra-catchy melodies intertwined with blazing guitar solos and highly developed fretwork. High points included the pop-masterpieces

"Champagne," "Vinyl," and "Girls Who Can Read Your Mind." Particularly impressive was Gilbert's guitar work on the frantic "Bumblebee" and his remarkable (but liberal) take on Johann Sebastian Bach's classic Irish dance-tune, "The Jig." (Gilbert is easily one of my absolute *favorite* guitarists.)

The album ended in dramatic fashion with the nearly twenty-minute instrumental "Jam," upon which Gilbert's ex-Racer X bandmates joined him for a sizzling, no-holds-barred shred-session. As much as I hated to see Gilbert split with Mr. Big, *King of Clubs* was a thoroughly enjoyable surprise and the definitive album of the year, in my view.

🤘

After **L.A. Guns** flopped big-time with their 1996 *American Hardcore* record, new singer Chris Van Dahl was promptly shown the door, and the band welcomed aboard third vocalist Ralph Saenz, who up until that point was best known for his perfectly on-point imitation of David Lee Roth in his popular Van Halen cover band, Atomic Punks.

The new lineup released an EP titled *Wasted* that was a little closer to the original L.A. Guns sound than *American Hardcore* but mostly forgettable overall. The problem wasn't Saenz's vocals, but rather simply a lack of decent songs. Nevertheless, Saenz was dismissed from the band in short order. While he wouldn't return to L.A. Guns, we will see that Saenz would wind up playing a *major* role for hair metal in the new millennium (more to come).

🤘

Glam kings **Pretty Boy Floyd** had broken up in the early '90s after the grunge wave quickly swept away any momentum the band had built with their 1989 hair metal classic, *Leather Boyz with Electric Toyz*. Thankfully, though, the group reformed in 1998 and released a five-song EP unequivocally titled *A Tale of Sex, Designer Drugs, and the Death of Rock n' Roll*. Unlike L.A. Guns' EP *Wasted*, however, the short set of songs offered up on the new PBF record were super-catchy, and it was a joy to see singer Steve Summers and guitarist Kristy Majors (this time with new addition Keri Kelli on board as well) back in action.

"Shut Up" was irresistibly dark and nasty, while "Junkie Girl" was splendidly pop-based with a riff and chorus that were almost impossible to forget. Meanwhile, "Everybody Needs a Hero" was a catchy cover previously put forth by Kelli's former band Big Bang Babies, and "Do You Love Me" was pure pop-metal delight. The rocking "Good Girl Gone Bad" rounded out the short record in classic PBF style.

By the late '90s, **Nelson** had become exceedingly disillusioned with the hair metal/L.A. Sunset Strip scene (or what was left of it) and decided to pack it up and take a chance on the classic music town of Nashville, Tennessee, where the brothers found they fit right in among a trove of talented songwriters. Taking up permanent residence in their new haunt, Matthew and Gunnar quickly made several local contacts and, surprisingly, wound up signing with none other than major label Warner Records to record their first "country" album. (At the time, Shania Twain and Garth Brooks were all the rage on radio.)

Halfway through recording, however, the record company suddenly took an about-face and abruptly pulled the plug on the promising project. Nelson reflected, "We made half the album and were taken out to dinner by the head of marketing at Warner. Halfway into the appetizers, he said, 'I have you here because I'm going to be dropping you from the label.' We thought it was a joke. We said, 'Did you not like the music?' He said, 'I haven't heard a note. But nobody would think it was real, so we're dropping you.'" Such was not only the stigma of all things hair metal, but also the band's luck it would seem—the scene being all too familiar and somewhat reminiscent of when Nelson had first presented their *Imaginator* album back in 1993.

Still, no strangers to adversity, the brothers soldiered on and completed the record, titling it *Brother Harmony* under the moniker The Nelsons, and self-releasing a limited pressing under their own independent label. With no promotion or advertising behind it, however, the album went completely unnoticed outside of the band's most hardcore fans.

As far as the music itself? Put it this way: if you liked country music, *Brother Harmony* was great; if you were looking for pop-metal, it was probably best avoided. Either way, "Try My Love" and "One of the Things About You" are two of the catchiest songs you could hope to hear, and I absolutely defy anyone who has ever lost a loved one to listen to the insanely beautiful "Just Once More" and not shed a few tears. The album is easily worth picking up for that song alone, but beware, used copies of the rare record currently sell for upwards of $150 on sites like eBay in 2019. Genre aside, the Nelson brother's talent and penchant for writing high-quality songs were without question.

Lastly, 1998 featured several albums by ex-hair band alumni who had bravely branched out to either side projects or solo albums of their own. Sadly, most of these releases offered little in the way of similarity to hair metal, but most of these artists were understandably seeking something different given the genre that had spawned their former success was so far down and out, removed from the social graces.

Ex-White Lion singer **Mike Tramp** had moved on from the defunct Freak of Nature and released his first solo album, *Capricorn*, which was much more pop and stripped-down than either of his prior two bands. It was an honest and sincere effort with a few bright spots but, regretfully, failed to make a lasting impression.

Ex-L.A. Guns singer **Phil Lewis** had similarly progressed away from Filthy Lucre, the initial band he had formed upon leaving his original outfit, and put forth his first solo album, *More Purple Than Black* (also released as *El Niño*). The record was decidedly more varied and eclectic versus anything Lewis had done before but did feature the very cool "No Sell Out," which alternated between soft, slow, groovy sections and raucous rock parts more akin to heavy metal.

After **The Quireboys** split up back in 1993, lead singer **Spike** had busied himself with several different projects, including a fun album he recorded with Dogs D'Amour frontman Tyla in 1996, titled *Flagrantly Yours*, issued under the artist name Spike and Tyla's Hot Knives. In 1998, however, Spike dropped his long-awaited first solo release, titled *Blue Eyed Soul.* It was a very bluesy, soulful affair featuring several slow, heartfelt numbers delivered only as Spike's emotive, raspy voice could.

Bon Jovi guitarist **Richie Sambora** released his second solo record, *Undiscovered Soul*, on February 23, 1998. Unlike the *ultra*-bluesy set of songs that comprised Sambora's first solo album (1991's *Stranger in This Town*), this time around the talented guitarist aimed mostly for a commercial, pop-oriented approach and delivered a set of songs of which half could have easily been mistaken for a John Cougar Mellencamp album, with the remainder being blues-based ballads. Among the songs in the former camp, "Made in America" and the wonderful "Hard Times Come Easy" were standouts.

A couple of ex-Guns N' Roses guitarists also released individual new solo albums as well: **Izzy Stradlin**'s *117 Degrees* and **Gilby Clarke**'s *Rubber.* Both records stayed true to the artists' previous visions, but, unfortunately, were primarily filled with material that managed to underwhelm overall.

Ex-Tuff singer **Stevie Rachelle** issued the very minimalistic and organic *Who the Hell Am I*, which was *nothing* like Tuff's hair metal past but still managed to contain a few highlights, including the wistfully poppy and nostalgic "Harbor Valley" and an enjoyable cover of Andy Kim's 1974 hit single, "Rock Me Gently."

John Corabi had moved on from Mötley Crüe after just one album, dismissed from the band in 1997 to support the return of Vince Neil for *Generation Swine.* Corabi then proceeded to hook up with guitarist Bruce Kulick, who found himself in a similar situation being ousted from Kiss when they decided to reunite with their original lineup in 1997.

Together, Corabi and Kulick formed the band **Union** and released their self-titled debut in 1998. The album was a solid slice of rock, although it was a little too grungy in several places for my overall liking. Happy exceptions to that were the peppy "Love (I Don't Need It Anymore)," the similar-to-Led Zeppelin "Let It Flow," the *exactly*-like-Led Zeppelin "October Morning Wind," and the absolutely beautiful ballad "Robin's Song." *Union* was received to generally favorable critical reviews.

In 1996, ex-Skid Row frontman **Sebastian Bach** formed **The Last Hard Men** with The Frogs' guitarist Jimmy Flemion, The Breeders' guitarist Kelley Deal, and Smashing Pumpkins' drummer Jimmy Chamberlin. The group proceeded to put together a self-titled album for Skid Row's former label Atlantic Records, who, of course, decided not to release it. The record was eventually issued with a limited run of only one thousand pressings on the underground label Nice Records; however, even that small amount proved to be significantly in excess versus the demand the album would generate.

The Last Hard Men was, as Bach would later put it, "an experiment to see if heavy metal could successfully merge with alternative rock." Bach would then go on to emphatically answer that question with a resounding "NO!" The album was a bizarre mix of sounds and styles, almost entirely on the "alternative" side of the fence versus hard rock. Aside from the vicious single "Sleep," which actually rocked quite hard and was not entirely dissimilar from Skid Row, the record contained absolutely *nothing* even remotely accessible for hair metal fans. The less said about *The Last Hard Men*, the better—trust me.

Lastly, perhaps the biggest hair metal name associated with a solo album in 1998 was Poison singer **Bret Michaels**. Michaels teamed up with actor Charlie Sheen to write and direct the independent film *A Letter from Death Row*, and Michaels would go on to star in the movie alongside both Sheen and his father, Martin.

The psychological thriller focused on a man (Michaels) sentenced to death for a crime he didn't commit. Michaels famously shaved his head for the role, a move that would have been inconceivable back in the '80s. The movie itself didn't make much noise, but it was the soundtrack

Michaels recorded for it that was of greater interest to hair metal fans.

A Letter from Death Row was a much more stripped-down affair than any Poison record and contained several tracks that were very movie-specific only. However, the album did include a couple of noteworthy songs in "Party Rock Band" and "Times Like These." The former was a basic but catchy punk-rock track with lyrics that saw Michaels poking fun at both the hair metal genre and himself while lamenting his career's downtrodden state, but at the end of the day "not giving a damn, because I sing for my party rock band."

The real noteworthy aspect of "Party Rock Band," however, was the guest appearance by Michael's estranged former bandmate C.C. DeVille, who agreed to play guitar on the song. The occasion marked the first time Michaels and DeVille had worked together since 1991 and gave fans high hopes for a possible formal reunion with Poison at some point in the future.

"Times Like These," meanwhile, was a mostly acoustic, southern-flavored, pop-rock song that held a pleasant melody alongside emotionally nostalgic lyrics. Aside from that, though, the album was plainly disappointing for fans who picked it up expecting to hear anything even remotely similar to Poison.

Other noteworthy albums released in 1998: Freak of Nature *(Outcasts)*, Erotic Suicide *(Perseverance)*

The year 1998 was unquestionably a lean time for hair metal fans and perhaps represented the genre's true nadir. At the end of the day, the majority of new music released either underwhelmed or flat out missed the mark, while the overwhelming mass public continued to foster great disdain and ridicule for all things hair metal. Still, Cinderella and Ratt reuniting and hitting the touring circuit with plans for new records in 1999 was an encouraging sign, as was Mötley Crüe finally putting together a couple of tracks that sounded closer to a natural offshoot of *Dr. Feelgood.*

But even if the output from a lot of hair metal artists proved to be quite distanced from their glory days, at least they hadn't completely folded up shop; no one could have blamed them if they had given the vicious backlash against hair metal in the mid-to-late '90s. But as they say, it is always darkest just before the dawn, and as it turned out, a hair metal resurrection of sorts was just around the corner . . .

Best Albums 1998

1. Paul Gilbert – *King of Clubs*
2. Pretty Boy Floyd – *A Tale of Sex, Designer Drugs, and the Death of Rock n' Roll*

V

Resurrection

1999 – 2001

Chapter 21
Back in Your Face
(1999-2001)

As the turn of the century came about, hair metal was at long last ready to emerge from the ashes and joyously wake back to life. Grunge, finally, had just about run its course and was thankfully on the way out. The new commercially popular music "fads" emerging in its place were tagged as "nu-metal" and "rap-rock." These mash-up styles fused hard rock and metal guitar riffs alongside alternative/grunge elements, hip hop, and rap vocals. Leading the way with this new approach were bands like Korn, Limp Bizkit, Kid Rock, Linkin Park, and Disturbed.

Granted, these new styles weren't exactly in the immediate hair metal family, but they were undoubtedly much closer relatives than the black sheep that was grunge. For starters, the music possessed a renewed sense of energy and passion. Whereas bands like Pearl Jam and Stone Temple Pilots may have been content to depressingly drone along, Korn and Limp Bizkit were clearly aggressive and agitated. Kid Rock, meanwhile, was distinctly focused on intensity, excess, partying, and spectacle, all traits that decidedly held common belief systems with hair metal. Indeed, after first meeting Kid Rock and coming away thoroughly impressed with his high-energy show and captivating performance, Sebastian Bach's manager reached out to him and excitedly exclaimed, "Sebastian, you have to meet this Kid Rock guy—He's YOU"!

And at the very least, rap-rock and nu-metal often featured heavy metal guitar riffs, even if they were still down-tuned and not exactly centered on the blazing fretwork of the '80s.

From a distinctly hair metal standpoint, however, it appeared people were finally ready to embrace nostalgia and renew their vows, so to speak. As the '90s drew to a close, the general population seemed poised to usher back in a culture of optimism while placing a higher priority back on merriment, and it made sense that music and fashion preferences would follow along in lockstep. The economy was flourishing, the dot-com bubble was growing, and many people looked as if they were once again ready to have "Nothing But a Good Time."

As this sentiment came to rise, hair metal bands, in turn, were quick to respond. Myriad artists and groups who had been forced to disband in the '90s welcomed the opportunity to reunite, and other bands who had shifted away from their musical roots gladly returned to the '80s hair metal sound of their gloried past.

There were a ton of new hair metal albums released during this time, and while not all were "home-runs" or records that fully lived up to the peak albums of the late '80s and early '90s, the point was simply the return of the long-lost sound of good-times, pop-metal, and party rock.

In the '90s, it perpetually appeared we couldn't seem to get away from hair bands that were "changing their style" or becoming darker, bluesier, heavier, more stripped-back, alternative—you name it. But starting around 1999, it was a wonderfully welcomed breath of fresh air to witness the music turning back to the more festive times of days gone by.

Don't get me wrong; hair metal albums weren't suddenly going to go back to effortlessly selling multiple millions of copies—those levels of success were clearly left in the past. But the resurrection of sorts was more than enough to slowly push the music back into "healthy" mode, which was a minor miracle in and of itself considering just how far the genre had fallen during the '90s.

Aside from new albums, however, the touring circuit was really where most of hair metal's true revival was felt. Throngs of fans were all too happy to fill up amphitheaters, attempting to relive parts of their youth and eager to witness the immensely popular "package tours" that developed, as hair bands recognized they could combine their efforts onto the same bill to draw larger crowds. The VH1 Rock Never Stops Tour, for example, initially launched in 1998 and continued strong for years after, featuring bands like Warrant, FireHouse, Slaughter, L.A. Guns, and Quiet Riot. Other tours saw groups like Poison, Cinderella, and Great White merging forces, while bigger acts like Bon Jovi and Mötley Crüe went back to selling out arenas on their own.

Other commercial avenues were also quick to jump on the bandwagon and support the shifting tide. Record labels began to proliferate greatest hits albums and other compilations such as the Monster Ballads series, which focused on the big power ballads from the hair metal era and saw its first volume sell more than one million copies. In other areas the rebirth showed in different ways, such as the welcomed 1999 reintroduction of the L.A. heavy metal radio station KNAC, which had been off the air and silent since the rise of grunge. VH1 also began to produce popular TV segments titled *Behind the Music*, primarily focused on the sensational rise and fall of prominent '80s hair bands. This widespread television exposure, along with the introduction and pervasive expansion of the internet, played a crucial role in spreading needed awareness to hair metal music, both past and present.

The moment had finally come: after almost a full decade spent mostly submerged in the dark, it was time for the hair metal monster to rise again.

Def Leppard was one of the first bands to be featured on VH1's *Behind the Music* in 1998, and airings of the episode produced some of the series all-time highest ratings. As Def Leppard slowly crept back into the public consciousness, the band was at a crossroad regarding its future direction, particularly in the light of the commercially disappointing, alternative-sounding 1996 *Slang* record.

A quick survey of both the industry and their fans, however, yielded a clear, definitive answer: what was needed, plainly, was a new album that sounded like *classic* Def Leppard. And with the creative foray that was *Slang* out of their system, the band was only too happy to oblige.

On June 8, 1999, Def Leppard released their seventh studio album, suitably titled *Euphoria.* And, by in large, it was indeed a return to the delightfully bombastic, happy-go-lucky, pop-metal of their *Pyromania, Hysteria,* and *Adrenalize* heydays.

The high-energy, spirited opener "Demolition Man" triumphantly set the tone with its first lyric right out of the gate: "Let Me Loose, I Just Got Back!" The song was a peppy, guitar-driven rocker that fully harked back to the *Adrenalize* era, where it would have been right at home on that record.

The second track and first single "Promises" was the album's real gem, though. An ultra-melodic, pop-metal anthem, the song was somewhat derivative of earlier hits like "Photograph," but who could complain when the tune was so fantastic? The track was instantly one of the best in the Def Leppard catalog, and in a sign that hair metal was indeed ready to re-enter the commercial arena, "Promises" went all the way to No. 1 on the US Mainstream Rock chart and stayed there for three consecutive weeks!

Euphoria's third track continued the hair metal assault with a catchy, T-Rex-like rocker, appropriated titled "Back in Your Face," where Elliot clearly laid down the law of the new landscape:

I'm back in your face like I've never been away
I'm back in your face and it's where I'm gonna stay

Other album highlights included the feisty and upbeat "21st Century Sha La La La Girl," the light, atmospheric ballad "To Be Alive," and "Guilty," which shared quite a few similarities with the beloved "Animal" from *Hysteria.*

Euphoria was indeed a welcomed return to Def Leppard's late '80s and early '90s flair, a big-sounding, cheery, pop-metal record inclusive of the massive production techniques that marked the band's output prior to *Slang.* Heck, even the album's title paid tribute to the past, ending in "-ia" similar to *Pyromania* and *Hysteria.* And while *Euphoria* unquestionably couldn't compete with those classic albums, it was at least in the same ballpark as *Adrenalize*, and for the casual fan, a much-welcomed return to form versus *Slang.* Still, as lead singer Joe Elliott noted, "Back in 1996, I don't think we could have made *Euphoria*; we would have been laughed off the face of the planet."

Still, despite the welcomed bounce back to prior sonics and the substantial success of "Promises," *Euphoria* was simply not going to duplicate the sales performance of *Adrenalize.* It was fantastic to witness hair metal's revival in many ways, but some things, such as easily attainable multi-Platinum records, were clearly not destined to return, particularly with the advent of nu-metal and the teen pop acts and boy bands that were dominating the landscape around that time.

That said, *Euphoria* did climb to an impressive No. 11 position on the Billboard Albums chart, sold more than five hundred thousand copies, and generated Def Leppard's first No. 1 single ("Promises") on the Mainstream Rock chart since "Stand Up (Kick Love into Motion)" in 1992. The album also served to launch an immensely successful two-year tour for the band that spanned twelve different countries.

Yes, Def Leppard and hair metal were undeniably and happily "back in our face."

Another hair metal legend aiming for a return to their classic sound was none other than **Mötley Crüe**. The Crüe had suffered through a categorically miserable run during the '90. They first suffered the breakup with Vince Neil at the height of their fame in 1992 before proceeding to put forth the commercially disastrous (but critically amazing) *Mötley Crüe* album with John Corabi in 1994. The band then acrimoniously reunited with Neil for the horrendous, alternative-sounding *Generation Swine* in 1997. Finally, they watched Tommy Lee quit the group in 1999, claiming his heart just wasn't into rock 'n' roll anymore. Good grief.

Given the extreme lack of success Mötley Crüe had while going in different musical directions during the '90s, combined with the more favorable climate that was seemingly emerging for the classic hair metal sound, Nikki Sixx decided it was finally time to get back to the Crüe's roots in 2000, determined to at long last, as he put it, "make the album that *should* have been the successor to Dr. Feelgood."

As far as a replacement for the missing Lee, the band brought aboard Neil's longtime friend, Randy Castillo, who had spent the previous ten years drumming in Ozzy Osbourne's solo band.

Mötley Crüe finally issued their eighth studio album, *New Tattoo*, on July 11, 2000. But was the record truly a return to the Crüe's classic sound and a worthy successor to *Dr. Feelgood*? Well, the answer was both yes and no, unfortunately.

On the plus side, *New Tattoo* was clearly a straightforward, rock 'n' roll, hair metal album. There was none of the serious hard and heavy style embodied on 1994's *Mötley Crüe* nor the grunge-alternative-whatever-the-hell 1997's *Generation Swine* was supposed to be. The songs were gloriously sleazy, slick, guitar-based metal, focused on Mötley's Crüe's bread-and-butter: partying, girls, and good times.

On the downside, something just seemed to be missing, with the album, regretfully, coming off as somewhat uninspired and lifeless, a far cry indeed from the powerhouse energy and wallop of *Dr. Feelgood or Shout at the Devil.* It was hard to pinpoint exactly what was lacking, but several quandaries were quickly apparent. First off, Castillo, while undoubtedly a competent technical drummer, just couldn't replace the bombastic sound, style, and thunder consistently provided by Lee. Second, the production of the album was thin and tinny, with the guitars possessing little layering or aggressive impact. And perhaps most of all, the majority of songs sadly fell into the insipid categories of "dull" or "average," with no real standouts to even remotely compete with the best seven or eight tracks on *Dr. Feelgood.*

Granted, none of the songs were flat-out *awful* as was the case with *Generation Swine*, but none of them would probably appear on a Mötley Crüe greatest hits album, either. Some of the tunes seemed to have a decent enough basis that they might have turned into something more impressive with a little more fleshing out, better production, and Lee's drumming, but that wasn't the case, unfortunately. Among those that showed promise and did succeed in offering some degree of fun were "Hell on High Heels" (the album's brightest spot and first single), "Treat Me Like the Dog I Am," "Punched in the Teeth By Love," and "1st Band on the Moon."

All that said, however, at the time, it was simply just an overwhelmingly gratifying pleasure to hear Mötley Crüe trying to be their loud, raucous, sleazy selves again, although the integral Lee was sorely missed. It was great to have the band back on the right track again with *New Tattoo*, even if the train wasn't rolling at full steam. The album suffered from soft sales overall but did manage to hit No. 41 on the Billboard Albums chart, and "Hell on High Heels" went all the way to No. 13 on the Mainstream Rock chart.

By this time, Mötley Crüe had successfully secured full ownership of both their music catalog and publishing rights and proceeded to form their own label, Mötley Records. The band then went about reissuing all their past albums in remastered format, each including several tantalizing bonus tracks. There was also a cool album of rarities and B-sides, titled *Supersonic and Demonic Relics*. All the discs were issued under the Crucial Crüe Albums moniker and were a special treat for longstanding fans.

On a sadder note, just before the tour for *New Tattoo*, Castillo fell ill with a duodenal ulcer that would eventually be revealed as cancer. With Castillo unable to tour as a result, Mötley Crüe oddly recruited alternative-band Hole drummer Samantha Maloney to take his place behind the kit. Maloney could no doubt pound the drums, but still, she was a strange choice. Tragically, Castillo would pass away from the illness two years later.

But at least Mötley Crüe seemed to be moving in the right direction again. Perhaps *New Tattoo*'s liner notes best expressed the overall sentiment of Mötley's shift back to hair metal:

"I PROMISE YOU THIS: One day you'll walk into the tattoo shop of life and say 'I'm back. I'm ready for my new tattoo. And her name is rock n' roll. Now it's time to make it permanent.' You will have been thru all the temporary fifteen minutes of flash. That you've been being served fast food music and disposable heroes so long you've somehow forgotten what it real and what is not. And you know what the man behind the counter will say? 'WE KNEW YOU'D BE BACK'— Mötley Crüe."

🤘

The biggest and most successful comeback for the genre, however, was naturally **Bon Jovi**, the band that had first broken hair metal's commercial doors off the hinges fourteen years earlier with their 1986 breakthrough album, *Slippery When Wet.*

Bon Jovi had been on an informal hiatus since the band issued the dark and somber *These Days* album in 1995. During the downtime, both Jon Bon Jovi and Richie Sambora filled the gap with their second solo albums, while Jon also continued to pursue his acting career.

By the time 1999 rolled around, Jon had already begun work on what was to be his third solo album (tentatively titled *Sex Sells*) when discussions suddenly started up again with regard to potentially resurrecting Bon Jovi. The band was admittedly unsure about the proposition at first, particularly given the uncertainty of where they would take the material after so much time and change had passed, but after much debate and deliberation, the group eventually decided to give it a go.

The first step was to choose a producer, but early plans to work with Bob Rock (who produced 1992's *Keep The Faith*) fell through, and later attempts to get Bruce Fairbairn (1986's *Slippery When Wet* and 1988's *New Jersey*) were dashed when Fairbairn unexpectedly and tragically passed away on May 17, 1999.

On the recommendation of A&R legend John Kalodner, Bon Jovi wound up going with the up-and-coming Luke Ebbin, who would prove a valuable asset to the new album with the band focused (as always) on ensuring the songs would be contemporary and commercial enough to garner acceptance on Top 40 radio. Ebbin brought an approach that allowed the group to still sound like themselves, but also added a necessary element of modern arrangement and technique.

The resulting album was titled *Crush*, and it was an emphatic victory for both Bon Jovi and hair metal in aggregate. The new material was an enjoyable return to the more inspiring, hopeful, pop-metal the band had been known for during the '80s (versus the largely solemn, dreary affair that was 1995's *These Days*). First track and lead single "It's My Life" roared out of the gate, representing a rock anthem virtually just as big as any in the Bon Jovi catalog. Co-written with pop song-master Max Martin, the tune featured Sambora on a voice-box similar to "Livin' on a Prayer" and even contained a resolute reference to that song's famous characters, Tommy and Gina:

This is for the ones who stood their ground
It's for Tommy and Gina, who never backed down

"It's My Life" offered a colossal chorus and an uplifting message, and the song hit on multiple international charts while also earning a Grammy Award nomination for Best Rock Performance. *Crush* correspondingly received a nomination for Best Rock Album, the first Bon Jovi album to be honored as such. Moreover, "It's My Life" was the third best-selling single *worldwide* in 2000!

Other album highlights included the wonderful storytelling of pop-rocker "Just Older" (brought to the band from Jon's abandoned *Sex Sells* sessions), the hauntingly beautiful "Mystery Train," the enjoyable, catchy, pop-metal "Captain Crash & The Beauty Queen From Mars," and the undeniably epic "Next 100 Years," which bore similarities to the Bon Jovi classic "Blood on Blood" and featured one of the most impressive, blazing guitar solos Richie Sambora had ever laid down to tape.

Crush, of course, also featured three traditional power ballads, two of which were mostly average, but the heartfelt "Thank You for Loving Me" came closer to hitting the mark. The album concluded with the raucous and energetic rocker, "One Wild Night."

Crush was an incredible comeback for Bon Jovi that once again saw them rise to the top of the mountain. The album broke the Top 10 in the US and hit No. 1 in many regions throughout Europe and Asia while selling an astonishing eleven million copies worldwide. More importantly, it gave Bon Jovi a new lease on life while introducing them to an entirely new generation of adoring admirers. *Crush* was a resounding triumph along hair metal's comeback trail and a joyous treat for fans of the genre who had gone without for so long.

The good news just kept coming, with hair metal kings **Poison** also experiencing a refreshing rebirth and renewed commercial viability as the '90s transitioned to the '00s.

Before any of that could happen, however, Poison needed to get back together with estranged guitarist C.C. DeVille, who had been ousted from the group back in 1991. Conversations were held and burned bridges rebuilt, and with fences mended and the band ceremoniously reassembled (let's face it, Poison could never *really* be Poison without DeVille), the reunited self-appointed Glam Slam Kings of Noise hit the road in the summer of 1999 for an enormously successful Greatest Hits Reunion tour. The shows routinely drew more than fifteen thousand ecstatic fans at each stop along the way, all of them thrilled to see the reunified rockers back doing what they do best and party along with the colossal glam metal celebration that comprised Poison's extravagant live show.

With demand for Poison suddenly on the rise again, other commercial avenues were quick to jump back on the train, similar to what was happening with Def Leppard at the time. The Poison special on VH1's *Behind the Music* achieved substantial ratings, and Capitol Records even stood up and took notice, finally releasing the long-shelved 1995 album *Crack A Smile* that Poison had recorded with guitarist Blues Saraceno.

The album was officially issued as *Crack a Smile . . . And More!* on March 14, 2000, featuring the original unreleased record plus eight bonus tracks (demos and live recordings). The added content was tacked on to compete primarily with the high demand for bootleg copies that had been floating around ever since the album got mothballed back in the mid-'90s.

As it turned out, *Crack a Smile* was worth the wait, an enjoyable set of entertaining party tunes that, style-wise, fell somewhere in between *Flesh & Blood* and *Native Tongue.* The songs didn't necessarily possess the full youth, energy, or sparkle associated with *Open Up and Say... Ahh!* but were a welcomed breath of fresh air nevertheless versus the dark, serious, and overly bluesy *Native Tongue.* Saraceno's style wasn't as colorful as DeVille's (realistically, who's was?), but it was certainly more rooted in hair metal than Kotzen's approach on *Native Tongue* while still merging the best of both worlds as the situation called for on each track.

Two of the album's better songs had already been extracted and featured as new bonus tracks on the *Poison's Greatest Hits* record Capitol had issued in 1996, "Sexual Thing" and "Lay Your Body Down." The former was a raunchy, upbeat rocker while the latter was a beautiful, bluesy power ballad. Other highlights on the album included the harmonica-driven, pop-metal opener "Best Thing You Ever Had," the pulsing, "Mr. Smiley," and the juvenile (but fun) "Shut Up, Let's Make Love."

Poison took advantage of their newfound momentum to issue yet another new album the very same year, titled *Power to the People.* The record was comprised mainly of twelve live recordings taken from Poison's popular 1999 reunion tour, but was perhaps more notable for the inclusion of five new studio songs, representing the first new material to be recorded with C.C. DeVille since the four supplemental tracks placed on Poison's first live album, *Swallow This Live*, in 1991.

While it was fantastic to see the band putting out fresh music with DeVille again, the new songs, unfortunately, left a little to be desired. Opener "Power to the People" was undoubtedly lively enough, but was a little too heavy versus classic Poison and featured Michaels singing in an almost monotone, rap-like nature (seemingly in an attempt to align with the nu-metal sound of the day). Still, you couldn't argue with the song's aggression as Michaels had begged the band to write something that would allow them to open their live set with an explosion of raw energy.

"Can't Bring Me Down," however, was lighter and more pop-oriented, with the band seeking to get back to penning genuinely uplifting material, but the sound unfavorably came off more like Blink-182 than Poison. "The Last Song" was the obligatory power ballad, but it failed to come across as anything greater than average, at most. "Strange" was an unconventional highlight and an objectively good song, but was again devoid of the classic Poison sound, with the mid-tempo, mostly acoustic track perhaps fitting better on a country album.

And lastly, there was the reunited band's concession to DeVille, allowing him to sing lead vocals on the final new track, the punk-based "I Hate Every Bone In Your Body But Mine." Let's just say that DeVille's high-pitched, nasally, auto-tuned vocals could, at best, be described only as an acquired taste.

Poison may have missed the mark with the new material, but fans were so thrilled to have the group back together again and touring that they could hardly be bothered to notice. With two new albums released in 2000, Poison again hit the road in the summer that year to make it back-to-back touring triumphs.

Poison then kept the ball rolling by releasing yet another new single, "Rockstar," in May 2001, as a preview of the full new studio album they were in the process of recording at the time (what would eventually become 2002's *Hollyweird*). The band then went back out on tour yet again with Warrant, Quiet Riot, and Enuff Z' Nuff on the wildly successful Glam Slam Metal Jam trek.

Poison wasn't the only hair metal band to see one of their long-lost '90s albums finally see the light of day in the early '00s, however. **Danger Danger** had recorded their third album, *Cockroach*, in 1993, only to see it placed in indeterminate limbo after fired singer Ted Poley took legal action to block the record's release after the band hired Paul Laine to replace Poley's vocals. At the time, in the wake of grunge, Epic Records was all too happy to cut its losses and forget the album even existed.

While a few songs from *Cockroach* managed to make their way onto Dander Danger's *Four the Hard Way* in re-recorded form with Paul Laine in 1997, the original release sat dormant on the shelf until 2001, a full eight years after it was originally completed. With the demand for hair metal back in vogue in the early '00s, however, Epic worked with all involved parties to dismiss the lawsuits and proceeded to issue the album as a unique two-CD set, one disc containing the songs originally recorded by Ted Poley in 1993, and another with the re-recorded vocals provided by Laine in 1994. It was an unconventional approach but a special delight for fans.

As it turned out, *Cockroach* proved to be one of the Danger Danger's finest moments. The album was a perfect representation of what hair metal had evolved to in the very early '90s': fun, pop-metal party tunes with an edge of heaviness to them. Songs like the hard-rockers "Still Kickin'" and "Don't Pull the Plug," along with the pop-metal oriented "Good Time" and the ballads "Afraid of Love" and "Don't Break My Heart Again" were a hair metal fan's dream. Also, enthusiasts were finally able to hear the studio version of what had become a favorite Danger Danger concert staple, the superbly catchy and upbeat "Shot O' Love."

It was also of great interest to compare the vocal differences between Poley and Laine. Laine's vocals were more gruff and edgy versus the smooth, clean stylings offered by Poley, but both versions were formidable in the own unique way. Some tracks admittedly fit one singer better than the other, but you really couldn't go wrong with either. For me, personally, I preferred the Poley version, feeling it better represented the classic Danger Danger sound, but admittedly enjoyed both of the albums to a high degree.

Danger Danger continued to forge ahead, creating new material with Laine at the time as well. The band issued *The Return of the Great Gildersleeves* in 2000 (named after the famous New York Music Club), an album that bridged the gap between classic hair metal and the more alternative sounds of the '90s. Highlights included the pop-metal "Dead, Drunk and Wasted" and the light, airy and acoustic "My Cherry."

Hair metal mavens L.A. Guns were also busy with an overflowing flurry of activity between 1999 and 2001. The band's recently rotating door of singers continued to turn as the group's third vocalist, Ralph Saenz, was promptly dismissed after the 1988 *Wasted* EP. L.A. Guns then added ex-Love/Hate frontman Jizzy Pearl and released the new album, *Shrinking Violet*, on June 1, 1999. Unfortunately, the record was no better than average, absent of any real standout songs while lacking the polish and production to legitimately compete with the band's classic back-catalog.

Pearl's vocals were assuredly technically proficient but just didn't seem to adequately match the L.A. Guns style to which fans had become accustomed. The heavy rocker "I'll Be There" was probably the album's lone highlight. L.A. Guns toured alongside Poison at the time with Pearl on vocals, but he clearly wasn't the best fit to represent the band's earlier work.

As it became apparent that hair metal was making a comeback of sorts, L.A. Guns quickly took advantage of the opportunity and reformed their "classic" lineup in the summer of 1999, including estranged singer Phil Lewis. The reunited L.A. Guns speedily put together another new album, titled *Greatest Hits and Black Beauties*, which featured re-recordings of their past hits (done in a slightly more modernized style) alongside a few new tracks as well. The band then hit the road yet again, during which time they assembled the live album *A Night on the Strip*, released in 2001.

Never fully pleased with the original production on their 1989 classic, *Cocked and Loaded*, L.A. Guns also re-recorded that album in 2000, issuing it under the moniker *Cocked & Re-Loaded: Millennium Edition* (although I personally did not find that it improved any on the original version).

The band proceeded to change out a couple of other members, but the original core of singer Phil Lewis and guitarist Tracii Guns remained committed and partnered together to produce L.A. Guns' true comeback album, *Man in the Moon*, in 2001. It was the first record of all-new material to feature Lewis and Guns since 1994's *Vicious Circle*.

Lewis was pleased to work together with Guns anew, with the latter once again open to incorporating melody into the songs versus simply focusing on the heavy riffage that dominated 1996's *American Hardcore*. Nowhere did this shine through more than on the pleasant-sounding "Beautiful," an ultra-melodic, pop-based tune with super-catchy harmonies. Mostly, though, the new material rocked relatively hard in the vein of traditional L.A. Guns sleaze metal, particularly on the romping title track. The dramatic "Don't Call Me Crazy" served as the record's epic, heavy ballad.

That said, *Man in the Moon* was clearly a step down from the band's late '80s and early '90s works. It was evident L.A. Guns were trying to drive back to their roots (the riff on "Spider's Web" was *very* similar to "Never Enough," for example), but the record simply fell short of the songwriting, production and overall energy of classic albums like *Cocked & Loaded*.

Still, as with Poison, Mötley Crüe, Def Leppard, and several other hair bands at the time, it was just a pleasure to see Lewis and Guns back together again, actively touring and churning out new material that was at least a solid attempt at evoking their classic hair metal past.

Meanwhile, **Ratt** was busy thinking along the same lines of L.A. Guns, with mostly comparable results. The group had reunited for a successful tour and the compilation album *Collage* back in 1997, and by 1998 had managed to secure a global record deal with A&R-king John Kalodner's new Sony offshoot label, Portrait Records.

In 1999, Ratt issued their sixth studio album, simply titled *Ratt* (often referred to as the *1999* album). Similar to L.A. Guns, it was *fantastic* to have a new Ratt album, as it had seemed the group (along with many of their hair band contemporaries) had possibly been put down for good in the mid-'90s, but, unfortunately, the fresh material just couldn't hold a candle to the band's earlier work.

Part of the challenge was Kalodner's insistence that the songs were written in an overly commercial direction to theoretically position them for success on radio. To this extent, the band members were forced to work with outside writers who specialized in delivering the specific style he was seeking. The result was a set of songs that, while plainly deriving themselves from the hair metal template, turned out mostly toothless and generic, overall. The general blues-based, pop/rock sound was clearly more routine in comparison to the energetic and pounding sleaze metal of Ratt's past.

"Dead Reckoning" and "Luv Sick" were moderately appealing and the best the album had to offer, but it wasn't near enough to salvage the set, with *Ratt* failing to generate any meaningful sales and leaving fans generally disappointed. The band members admittedly weren't entirely pleased with the songs themselves, but seeing as Ratt was likely label-less without Kalodner, the group understandably felt obligated to follow his direction.

That said, Ratt did, however, continue successfully touring to a legion of reinvigorated fans, all of whom were seemingly more than elated to watch the band perform its immensely popular back-catalog at packed shows all across America.

At the same time, Kalodner had also signed new record deals with both Great White and Cinderella. **Great White** took the opportunity to release their ninth studio album, *Can't Get There from Here*, in 1999. Unlike 1996's darker *Let It Rock*, the new material was noticeably lighter and more inspiring in style, delivering a set of songs perfectly consistent with the type of music the band had been churning out in the early '90s.

The album even managed to feature a hit single, as "Rolling Stoned" was a fantastic rock anthem that ascended all the way to the No. 8 position on the Billboard Mainstream Rock chart. Other highlights included the Irish-flavored, acoustic "In the Tradition" and the mid-tempo, southern styled "Freedom Song."

Great White supported the album by touring on a popular package bill that included fellow hair metal contemporaries Poison, Ratt, and L.A. Guns.

Cinderella, meanwhile, had recently come off hiatus to promote their new greatest hits album, *Once Upon A . . .*, in 1997. Lead singer Tom Kiefer was still struggling to fully recuperate from his long-running challenges with vocal cord paralysis but had recovered well enough to tour (on most occasions) with the help of proper physical therapy protocols. Stemming from these concerts, the band released the fantastic live album *Live at the Key Club* in 1999. I recall seeing Cinderella on that tour in 1998 and distinctly remember being astounded at how tight and terrific both Keifer and the band sounded.

Keifer himself had moved to Nashville by that time and begun initial writings for a fresh slate of Cinderella songs to be issued by Kalodner's label in 2000. Regrettably, however, Sony was less than pleased with the sales results associated with the Great White and Ratt records, and Cinderella's recording contract was canceled before the new album could begin in earnest. The resulting litigation put a disappointing hold on any new material from Cinderella that would, unfortunately, last for many years.

On the plus side, however, the band continued to tour to an enthusiastic response in 2000 and 2001, playing alongside fellow hair bands Poison, Ratt, Quiet Riot, FireHouse, and others.

Hair metal legends **Warrant** were also busy taking a page from the L.A. Guns playbook, re-recording a portion of their earlier material for Cleopatra Deadline Records, the label behind the, at the time, seemingly endless wave of new albums offering fresh takes on hair bands' old hits.

Warrant's contribution in this area was the appropriately titled *Greatest & Latest.*

Issued in 1999, the album mostly featured re-recordings that were generally less impressive than the originals (although the raw, stripped-back, rehearsal session of "I Saw Red" added some beautiful elements), but also included three tantalizing, new studio tracks. While the latest songs didn't necessarily stand up against the best of the band's early output, they were at least very refreshingly *not* grunge or alternative, as was the material on Warrant's mid-'90s albums (*Ultraphobic* and *Belly to Belly Vol. 1*).

In reality, the new tunes were actually pretty decent, with "The Jones" being straight-up pop-metal, "Southern Comfort" a bluesy, mid-tempo, "southern" ditty, and "Bad Tattoo" a groovy rocker that would have been right at home on 1993's *Dog Eat Dog* album. Lead singer Jani Lane sounded great on each of the tracks.

Warrant underwent a couple of lineup changes during that time, but the core of Lane, rhythm guitarist Erik Turner, and bassist Jerry Dixon remained intact, and, in between touring, Warrant issued another album in 2001, this time a cover-songs record again featuring two new studio tunes. It was aptly titled *Under the Influence*, inclusive of a carefully chosen group of songs from artists who had contributed to the shaping and development of the band's sound back when the members were first coming into their own as musicians.

Among those covered were Aerosmith, Queen, David Bowie, Cheap Trick, AC/DC, Thin Lizzy, Nazareth, and Hanoi Rocks; in other words, a standard "who's who" of bands that first helped sculpt hair metal's statue during the early-to-mid-'80s.

The new tracks included "Subhuman," which had a good groove but unfortunately shared a lot in common with Warrant's *Ultraphobic* album, and "Face," which was further inspired but again might have felt a little too alternative for fans who desired something more traditional along the lines of "Down Boys."

Warrant would go on to tour with Poison on the famous Glam Slam Metal Tour in 2001.

Speaking of re-recordings, **Pretty Boy Floyd** also got in on the action with Cleopatra records and in 1999 released the album *Porn Stars*, which featured six remade tracks from their 1989 debut *Leather Boyz with Electric Toyz* along with fresh takes on several older songs previously laid down only in demo form.

The result was a terrific treat for longtime fans, with the new *Leather Boyz . . .* performances sounding fantastic and the formerly unheard tunes generally just as high in quality as those that had made the first album's final cut. Among the excellent "new" tunes were the glam/hair metal classics "Shy Diane," "Saturday Nite," "Summer Luv," and "Restless." Suffice it to say, it was *magnificent* to have Pretty Boy Floyd back in action.

Lead singer Steve Summers also remained busy outside of the PBF, as he was among those contributing lead vocals to two albums generated by the new glam rock super-group, **Shameless**.

Shameless was first formed in 1989 by German songwriter and bassist Alexx Michael, but despite some local success, a couple of mostly lean years forced the band to rather quickly fold up shop in 1991. Michaels was a huge fan of hair metal, however, and relaunched Shameless in 1999 as an homage to all things '80s rock. He went about recruiting a cast of hair metal all-stars to perform on a new album, including Summers, Stevie Rachelle (Tuff), Bruce Kulick and Eric Singer (Kiss), Tracii Guns (L.A. Guns), and Brian Tichy (Billy Idol's band).

The resulting record was titled *Backstreet Anthems*, and the music was very much in the same vein as Pretty Boy Floyd, making Summers the perfect fit as the primary vocalist for the catchy, good-times, pop-metal, raunchy rock 'n' roll.

The album established a cult following of fans eager for the return of the '80s glam rock sound, and Shameless successfully issued the excellent follow-up album, *Queen for A Day*, in 2001. The new record featured many of the same faces but also included guest appearances from Keri Kelli

(PBF), Gilby Clarke (Guns N' Roses), and Jani Lane (Warrant). The sophomore album was even better than the band's debut, featuring one classic sleaze/glam metal track after another. The impeccable lead track, "Shock the World," was originally written by Aeriel Stiles in the late '80s, Pretty Boy Floy's first guitarist and the band's primary songwriter prior to leaving the group just before they landed their first record deal in 1988.

But it was the second track, "Queen for a Day," that really sparkled as an instant classic, perhaps as good or better as anything the glam metal scene had produced before. It was basic, upbeat, super-catchy hair metal, plain and simple. Other highlights included the rockers "Steal the Girlz," "I'm So Good," and "You Can't Stop Me," the amazing power ballad "Far Away," and the stunningly beautiful cover of Kiss' "Tomorrow." Again, Steve Summers shined as *the* voice of glam metal.

For fans of the glam rock genre, Shameless was a marvelous gift to be treasured.

Nelson also desired a return to their roots and sprung back from their 1998 "country" album to release the pop-rock masterpiece, *Life*, in 1999. The new songs were unabashedly pop-metal-lite and featured some of the most catchy, melodic tunes in Nelson's catalog, including the infectious "A Girl Like That," irresistible "I Would If You Want Me To," ultra-pop "Life" (first written by the brother's father, Ricky Nelson, in 1970) and perfectly charming "She Said She'd Be Mine."

Ex-Skid Row singer **Sebastian Bach** was also intent on flying the hair metal flag high in 1999, putting together a new solo band and playing sold-out shows across the US for rabid groups of fans who couldn't seem to get enough of his high-energy, charismatic performances chock full of Skid Row's best material from the late '80s and early '90s. I saw Bach on more than one of these occasions, and, at the time, he was indeed a force with which to be reckoned, consistently belting out intense, powerful sets of Skid Row's heavy metal rock songs.

To properly commemorate those incredible concerts, Bach issued his debut solo album, *Bring 'Em Bach Alive!*, in 1999. The record primarily featured stage performances of Skid Row material, but also included a beautiful, absolutely striking, live version of "The Most Powerful Man in the World" from Bach's failed *The Last Hard Men* experiment in the mid-'90s. The album also contained five recent studio tracks Bach recorded with his solo band.

Most of the new songs were primarily in the same vein as the *Subhuman Race* album, with "Rock 'N Roll," "Done Bleeding," and Counterpunch" all presenting as mid-paced grinders with massive guitar riffs and a slightly sludgier tone versus the more harmonious sensibilities of early Skid Row. The exception to this was the melodic, mostly acoustic "Superjerk, Superstar, Supertears."

In the year 2000, Bach began performing on Broadway, making his debut with the title role in *Jekyll & Hyde*, going on to appear as Riff Raff in the *Rocky Horror Show* in 2001, and playing the lead part in *Jesus Christ Superstar* in 2002. His immense vocal talent and commanding stage presence made him a playhouse star, a perfect (if unexpected) fit for Broadway's inspired, dramatic performances.

Another ex-hair band lead singer to shine in 2001 was **Mike Tramp**, formerly of White Lion. Tramp had issued his first solo album, *Capricorn*, in 1997, and while it was a solid record, it failed to generate a resounding overall impact. Tramp's sophomore release, however, *Recovering the Wasted Years* (issued on New Year's Eve, 2001), was truly something extraordinary.

The style of the new album shared little in common with either the hair metal mold of White Lion or the dark, aggressive hard rock of Tramp's Freak of Nature. The songs were rather much more organic and natural, not entirely dissimilar from a Don Henley-type of approach, with, naturally, a tad more rock 'n' roll.

The sophisticated production and lush orchestration were among the record's strengths, with loads of layers, hooks, and harmonies to be found in every crack and corner. The lyrical themes revolved around contemplative thought, reflection, nostalgia, existential choices, and the journey of life in general. While Tramp certainly hit on some dark topics, the overwhelming premise of the album remained uplifting and optimistic. *Recovering the Wasted Years* and the songs within took the listener on quite an emotional journey, all the while delivering peppy arrangements and fantastic songwriting.

Lead track "Falling Down" was a perfect microcosm of the album, opening slowly with a single lonely organ, followed by the deliberate addition of bright, atmospheric orchestration, then building to the point where the song settled contentedly into an inspired melody with somber and thoughtful lyrics, all along remaining heartening in nature.

"If It Ain't Gonna Rock" was another highlight, comprised of dark, passive, verses layered up against a happy, pop-based chorus aspiring to convey to the listener that which is truly important in life. Similar themes emerged in the contemplative but beautifully spirited "Endless Highway," optimistic "Always Tomorrow," and the nostalgic "Do It All Over," where Tramp acknowledged the many mistakes he made along the road but concluded that, without them, his life might not have turned out to be such an amazing journey.

The pop-based songs all contained a solid backbone of rock 'n' roll styling, even if it was much more constrained versus Tramp's hair metal past. The grooving "Don't Take My Rock 'N' Roll" was one of the more raucous tracks, while still containing very personal and serious-minded lyrics.

To best absorb the album's overall messaging, *Recovering the Wasted Years* was best appreciated via an uninterrupted spin from start to finish, an approach that was well supported by the wonderful musical flow of the song sequencing. Unlike the often party-natured theme of traditional hair metal albums, if you listened carefully, *Recovering the Wasted Years* truly forced you to consider some of life's deeper tenets.

That said, the record certainly had to fit your mood. While it was undoubtedly an accomplished effort, there are unquestionably times when you simply need to mindlessly rock out to more straightforward fare such "You Give Love a Bad Name" (not to take anything away from that song; I like to think there is a time and a place for both). But either way, there was no denying the brilliance of *Recovering the Wasted Years*, an irrefutable victory and marked achievement for Mike Tramp, an individual who had come a very long way, indeed, since occupying a spot on the top of hair metal's mountain back in 1988.

🤘

Another band had been through quite a roller coaster ride by the time the late '90s rolled around was **Mr. Big**. The group was on top of the world with "To Be with You" in 1992, but their 1996 *Hey Man* album suffered from poor sales in the wake of grunge, and tensions emerged within the group that eventually led to guitarist Paul Gilbert departing for a solo career in 1997. Mr. Big temporarily broke up following Gilbert's exit but spontaneously decided to give it a go again with the genre's resurgence in 1999, bringing aboard guitarist Richie Kotzen to fill the vacated guitar slot.

Reminiscent of when Kotzen briefly teamed up Poison in the early '90s, he was a more than capable guitar player, but his ultra-bluesy style proved almost as far removed from Gilbert as it had been from C.C. DeVille. Kotzen's effect on Mr. Big's music was similar as well, with the band's new album *Get Over It* being saturated by a blanket of blues. It wasn't quite on the same level Poison experienced with *Native Tongue,* but it was enough to cause the songs to sound like a completely different animal versus the group's previous work.

Of course, Eric Martin's vocals still indisputably defined the album as Mr. Big, but unfortunately, this time around, the record lacked any real standout songs successfully merging the soulful vocals and bluesy guitars with melodic hooks and catchy choruses. The lone exception was perhaps the excellent acoustic ballad "Superfantastic," which would have undoubtedly been a considerable hit had it been released ten years earlier.

In response to the album's soft reaction from fans, Mr. Big proceeded to go in a different direction on their second album with Kotzen, 2001's *Actual Size*. This time, the record was dominated by overly light, pop, and commercial songs that, while certainly great tunes, were missing any of the real bite or intensity associated with Mr. Big's '80s or early '90s output.

The change in style went over particularly poorly with bassist Billy Sheehan, who strenuously objected to the shift away from harder-edged rock 'n' roll. Indeed, Sheehan ultimately backed away from the process (he is only given writing credits on two songs on *Actual Size*), and the tensions between Martin and himself that had initially contributed to Gilbert's departure in 1997 grew markedly worse.

Unlike *Get Over It*, however, many of the songs on *Actual Size* were actually quite good if accepted for their inherent pop-based nature, with most being masterful displays of how to write an upbeat, catchy, pop-rock tune. Highlights included "Wake Up," "One World Away," "How Did I Give Myself Away," the gentle ballad "Arrow," and the hit single "Shine," which went all the way to No. 1 in Japan (the overall album hit No. 3).

Sheehan's objections, however, proved to be a dividing force and served to exacerbate his deteriorating relationship with Martin. "Watch the video for the 'Shine,'' Martin said, stating evidence that Sheehan was "an unhappy rock 'n' roll guy." "He hated that song," Martin stated, "a couple of times I'd ask, 'Are you mad at me?' and he'd say, 'No, I just don't like what we're doing.'"

Martin and drummer Pat Torpey eventually decided they could no longer move forward with Sheehan in tow, but Kotzen felt considerably less sure about the prospect of parting with the ultra-talented bassist. Unable to get everyone on the same page, Mr. Big decided to conduct one final farewell tour in 2002 before breaking up and going their separate ways. The split would turn out to be more of a hiatus, however, as thankfully, the band amicably and successfully reunited with all four original members (including Gilbert) ten years later, in 2009.

Speaking of Gilbert, he was plenty busy on his own, also releasing two new albums (solo) between 1999 and 2001. The new records, titled *Flying Dog* (2000) and *Alligator Farm* (2001), picked up perfectly from where the brilliant *King of Clubs* left off in 1998, masterfully blending super-catchy pop melodies with alternatingly harmonious and shredding guitar riffs. Both albums broke the Top 25 on the Japan Oricon Album Chart.

Neither record included any weak spots, but favorites included the poppy tracks "Get It," "Be My Wife," and "Individually Twisted," blazing rockers "Heavy Disco Trip" and "Down to Mexico," and softer semi-ballads "Kate Is A Star," and "Rosalinda Told Me."

Back in the US, the legendary Boston-based **Aerosmith** were enjoying their new steady-state as renewed superstars following the humongous success of their 1998 single, "I Don't Want to Miss a Thing." The band's elongated tour to support both the smash hit and their 1997 *Nine Lives* album lasted well into 1999, seeing Aerosmith successfully endear themselves to an entirely new generation of fans on top of their existing hardcore '70s fanbase, which ironically was none too pleased with the group's recent direction.

Aerosmith were seemingly everywhere between 1999 and 2001, getting their own roller coaster at Walt Disney World, joining Kid Rock for a prestigious performance at the MTV Video Music Awards, going out on their mammoth Girls of Summer Tour, contributing new music to the *Charlie's Angels* soundtrack, and performing at the Super Bowl XXXV halftime show in 2001 (duetting alongside pop mega-stars of the time 'N Sync and Britney Spears on the band's 1975 hit, "Walk This Way").

Somewhere in between all the madness, the band somehow found time to record their thirteenth studio album, *Just Push Play*, released on March 6, 2001. Driven by the Top 10 single "Jaded," the record was a sizable commercial success, debuting at No. 2 on the Billboard Albums chart and quickly going Platinum. But while newer Aerosmith devotees happily ate up the fresh material, longtime fans were less than thrilled.

Just Push Play contained few hints of the raw Aerosmith rock 'n' roll sound of the '70s, nor did it even have much in common with the band's more hair metal-styled output during the '80s. The album was viewed as exceedingly commercial and pop in certain places while overtly pandering to the latest trends in others.

Lead single "Jaded" (written by Marti Frederiksen and Steven Tyler, with lyrics in reference to Tyler's daughter, Liv) was lushly melodic and pop-based, but, unfortunately, more in a "sell-out" way versus a good way. Ballads like "Fly Away from Here" had simply been done to death by the band already and were obvious attempts to simply score radio success. Meanwhile, the title track, "Just Push Play," (while admittedly catchy) included off-putting rapping, hip-hop synthesizers, and unwelcomed street beats. Even "Outta Your Head," one of the only songs on the album to possess any real "bite," featured its own rap-metal styling similar to the popular nu-metal and rap-rock trends of the day. Other songs were unsatisfyingly just dull.

Nevertheless, the general public lapped it up (largely on the strength of "Jaded"), and the album was nominated for three Grammy Awards, including Best Rock Album, Best Rock Performance ("Jaded") and Best Music Video ("Fly Away from Here").

It was admittedly fortuitous to have a hair band so prominent in the commercial spotlight again, but you had to honestly question whether Aerosmith could truly even be considered a part of that genre anymore (acknowledging that they were never a perfect fit in the first place). Not that the band lost any sleep over such a potential ousting, though, particularly while they were busy enjoying their monumental success.

One band that fans thankfully didn't have to worry about regarding the undesirable proposition of shifting away from their hair metal roots was **Slaughter**. The group released the groovy *Revolution* album in 1997, but, regretfully, heartbreaking tragedy struck soon after on February 5, 1998, when guitarist Tim Kelly was killed after his car collided with a jackknifed tractor-trailer in the Arizona desert. The distressed band was in deep mourning but vowed to carry on in Kelly's name, knowing the last thing he would've wanted was for the group to break up.

Slaughter hired ex-Left For Dead guitarist Jeff Blando and released their fifth studio album, *Back To Reality*, in 1999. Not to take anything away from Kelly, who was a fantastic musician, but Blando's electric style of play just seemed to light a fresh fire under the new material, and songs like "All Fired Up," "Take Me Away," and "Trailer Park Boogie" were some of the heaviest and most intense rock songs in Slaughter's catalog. Not only on record but also in concert, at the time, it certainly seemed as though the band was firing on all cylinders with a poignantly high burst of energy.

Back to Reality was balanced with other more measured styles as well, such as the terrific power ballad "Love Is Forever," more traditional hair metal-sounding "Dangerous," swinging "Bad Groove," spacey, epic "Headin' For a Dream" and melodic "Nothin' Left to Lose." It was a marvelous set of songs and a terrific comeback for the band.

Like many of their contemporaries, Slaughter took advantage of the renewed interest in hair metal and successfully joined up with many of the package tours of the day, including the 1999 Rock Never Stops Tour with Ted Nugent and Night Ranger, the 2000 Poison, Cinderella, Dokken & Slaughter Tour, and 2001's Voices Of Metal Tour with Vince Neil, Ratt, and Vixen.

🤘

Another '80s hair metal legend still carrying the torch in the new millennium was ex-Guns N' Roses guitarist, **Slash**. In 1995 Slash formed his side-project Slash's Snakepit and released the rather average *It's Five O'Clock Somewhere* album. He eventually exited GN'R in 1996, touring with his blues-rock cover band Slash's Blues Ball up until 1999, at which time the determine guitarist decided to reform Slash's Snakepit and give the group another go.

The latest lineup included Ryan Roxie (Alice Cooper Band) on rhythm guitar and the somewhat-unknown new singer, Rod Jackson. The group proceeded to record a fresh album titled *Ain't Life Grand*, released on October 10, 2000. Happily, this time around (unlike with *It's Five O'Clock Somewhere)*, the songs were muscular and powerful, driven by Slash's dominant guitar riffs and the formidable strength of Jackson's pipes. Jackson didn't necessarily possess the wide range of Axl Rose, but his delivery was strong and brawny, adding a weight and intensity to the tunes that packed a heavy punch. Keri Kelli, a veteran of many bands who was added to the group's touring lineup to replace Roxie, claimed Snakepit was the "most powerful" unit in which he ever played.

The songs were a massive load of meaty, straightforward, hard and heavy rock 'n' roll, with multiple layers of Slash's guitar everywhere you turned. The impressive set contained the barn burners "Been There Lately," "Mean Bone," "Life's Sweet Drug," and "Landslide," as well as the driving "Serial Killer." The album also featured the striking, jazz-blues title track "Ain't Life Grand," heavy metal "Speed Parade," and even the moving power ballad "Back to the Moment."

For whatever reason, however, *Ain't Life Grand* failed to generate significant commercial success, likely due to a set of songs that were simply too heavy and aggressive for radio at the time. Still, the album was a fun slice of intense, unfettered, hard rock heaven. Slash and his band proceeded to embark on a worldwide tour in support of AC/DC in the summer of 2000, and successfully headlined their own theater tour thereafter.

Perhaps the very best hard rock album in the early '00s came from an unanticipated collaboration between ex-Bang Tango singer Joe Lesté and ex-Bulletboys guitarist DJ Ashba. Looking to put together a fresh new band, the pair hooked up with bassist Kenny Kweens and session players Anthony Focx and Glen Sobel to fill out rhythm guitar and drums. Initially going under the name Hellstar, the group wound up opening a few dates for Kiss and were then surprisingly signed to major label Warner

Bros. in 2001 to record an album. This was a *fantastic* sign for hair metal—it was one thing for the classic bands of the genre to be making comebacks, but it was another thing entirely for major labels to be signing *new* hair metal-based bands, something that would have been entirely out of the question between 1993 and 1998.

Hellstar was renamed **Beautiful Creatures**, and the group released their self-titled debut on August 14, 2001. And what a monster of a record it was. Similar to *Ain't Life Grand*, *Beautiful Creatures* was a take-no-prisoners, full-on hard rock and heavy metal assault. The dual guitar attack supplied by Ashba and Focx was brought forth with ferocious intensity, including guitar solos that harked back to the '80s in terms of sound and style. Lesté's vocals, meanwhile, fit the material perfectly, with his signature growl and menacing screech adding to the album's vigor.

While *Beautiful Creatures* clearly had its roots in hair metal, the record also possessed many of the more modern-sounding styles of the late '90s, and even a few grunge tinges in certain places (primarily on the tracks "Wish" and "Blacklist"). But none of those departures could take away from the pure, adrenalized blast of hard rock that screamed out from your speakers.

Upon first hearing the album, I remember thinking, I hadn't really heard that level of raw energy and intensity layered up against melodic structures and big choruses since, maybe . . . *Appetite for Destruction*? Really? And apparently, I wasn't the only one to arrive at that comparison, with critical reviews observing a similar resemblance. *Exclaim!* journalist Craig Daniels stated, "Opening song, '1 A.M.' could easily be mistaken for vintage GN'R," and *PopMatters*' Andrew Ellis described Beautiful Creatures as "attempting to merge the aggression, street sass and sound of the incomparable *Appetite for Destruction* with the modern leanings of the contemporary rock scene."

Almost every track was a high-energy, thorough beating of pumping guitar riffs, pounding drums, and Lesté's killer vocals. It was indeed music to my ears, particularly after so many years awash with mostly mediocrity in the mid-'90s. It was hard to isolate specific highlights given the album's consistency, but particular standouts included "1 A.M," first single "Wasted," "Step Back," "Ride," "Kickin' for Days," "Goin' Off," and the AC/DC-like "I Got It All." Also outstanding was the lighter and partially acoustic track, "New Orleans."

As if to call attention to the album's glam metal roots, the first one hundred pressings featured a sparkling, embossed, silver compact disc insert reminiscent of an earlier time, when an integral part of the music was the flash and style that surrounded it.

Beautiful Creatures achieved the No. 29 position on the Billboard Top Heatseekers chart while "Wasted" went to No. 27 on the Mainstream Rock chart, and the band received the honor of being added to the 2001 Ozzfest lineup. Beautiful Creatures were even granted the opportunity to perform on HBO's *Reverb TV*, filmed in New York City, in October 2001.

Warner Bros. certainly couldn't be accused of failing to promote the band, but at the end of the day the merger between Time Warner and AOL caused enough of a record label shake-up to result in the album falling through the cracks, and a disappointing level of overall sales was just enough to prompt Beautiful Creatures from being disappointingly dropped from the label.

Still, none of that took away from the fact that *Beautiful Creatures* was one kick-ass slice of fierce, hard rock ecstasy.

The hair metal resurrection at the turn of the century was marked by many other reunions as well, as hair bands were more than happy to get the party started again having waited out the long, dreary drought that was the '90s.

The remaining members of **Skid Row** had formed the alternative-sounding Ozone Monday following Sebastian Bach's departure in late 1996, but in 1999 decided to reform Skid Row with new singer Johnny Solinger and ex-Saigon Kick drummer Phil Varone. While Solinger was clearly not Bach (who could be?), he managed to do the Skid Row material justice as best possible, and the band successfully toured with Kiss, Poison, and Vince Neil, in addition to headlining their own club shows. I saw Skid Row in a small bar during that time, and while Bach was sorely missed, I remember simply being thrilled to once again hear the band hammer out their powerful, classic catalog.

After first breaking up in 1993 during the advent of grunge, **The Quireboys** had reassembled for a few one-off shows during the mid-'90s, but in 2001, frontman Spike and guitarist Guy Griffin officially put the band back together with a new lineup and released the terrific comeback album *This Is Rock 'n' Roll*, featuring classic tunes such as the title track, "Six Degrees," "C'Mon," "Coldharbour Lane," and "Turn Away."

Tesla also reunited in 2000, five years after their initial separation in the mid-'90s. The individual band members had busied themselves with side projects during the group's downtime, including the Bar 7 band featuring singer Jeff Keith and guitarist Tommy Skeoch, but Tesla formerly getting back together again was a heavenly sight for hair metal fans, with the band playing an emotional sold-out reunion show at Sacramento's ARCO Arena on October 25, 2000. Tesla would then go on to release the double-live album, *Replugged Live*, featuring performances from their successful 2001 reunion tour.

Faster Pussycat split up in 1993, but lead singer Taime Downe forged ahead with his industrial-sounding band, The Newlydeads, during the late '90s. In 2001, however, Downe reformed Faster Pussycat with original guitarists Brent Muscat and Greg Steele, alongside his former Newlydeads bandmates Xristian Simon (guitar), Danny Nordahl (bass), and Chad Stewart (drums).

A new album titled *Between the Valley of the Ultra Pussy* was quickly released featuring industrial, electronic-rock remixes of Faster Pussycat's classic tracks, similar in style to the Newlydeads material. Traditional hair metal fans weren't necessarily thrilled with the peculiar change, but all was forgiven when Faster Pussycat proceeded to embark on a popular reunion tour that saw them playing their earlier material in (mostly) its traditional format.

Britny Fox also got back together in 2000 after nine years of inactivity, with the same lineup that generated 1991's *Bite Down Hard*, featuring Tommy Paris on lead vocals. The band successfully toured during 2000 and 2001, then began work on a new album that would eventually see the light of day in 2003 (*Springhead Motorshark*).

Even **Quiet Riot**, who were perhaps the very first to successfully launch hair metal into the mainstream commercial consciousness with their hit single, "Cum On Feel the Noize," sixteen years earlier, got back on the scene, reuniting with singer Kevin DuBrow after nearly a ten-year absence. In 1999 Quiet Riot released the new, aptly titled album *Alive and Well* via Cleopatra Records, featuring eight new songs alongside re-recorded versions of six of the band's most well-known hits.

The new tracks were classic Quiet Riot in the traditional hair metal vein and were actually quite good aside from lacking production values (likely due to Cleopatra's limited budget). "Don't Know What I Want," "Angry," "Alive and Well," and "The Ritual" were particularly potent, with DuBrow's commanding, snarling vocals seemingly having not lost a step since the mid-'80s. As for the re-recordings, they were thankfully faithful renditions that even managed to add little welcomed beef and bottom-end that had been missing from the originals.

The overwhelmingly strong response to Quiet Riot on tour afterward spurred the band to quickly issue the follow-up record, *Guilty Pleasures*, in 2001, this time featuring all-new material throughout. It was again vintage Quiet Riot, full of fun, brawny hair metal anthems, including the splendid rockers "Vicious Circle," "Feel the Pain," "Rock The House," and "Feed the Machine." Listening to the latest songs, it felt gloriously as if the band had taken a time machine straight back to 1983.

The burgeoning nostalgia for hair metal circa 1999-2001 was evident everywhere you looked, even on the big screen, as evidenced by the 2001 film *Rock Star*, starring Mark Wahlberg and Jennifer Aniston. The movie was loosely based on the non-fictional events surrounding Judas Priest's replacement of original singer Rob Halford with the unknown Tim "Ripper" Owens, plucked from a local tribute band.

The film pleasantly succeeded in doing a relatively spot-on job depicting the sensational aspects of hair metal life in the late '80s and early '90s. The movie's fictional band, Steel Dragon, was actually mimicked by a real-life persona group featuring lead singers Miljenko Matijevic (Steelheart) and Jeff Scott Soto (Yngwie Malmsteen) alongside guitarists Zakk Wylde (Ozzy Osbourne) and Jeff Pilson (Dokken). The "band" contributed five new songs to the film's soundtrack, which was rounded out by (mostly) other classic Hair Metal-era anthems (Mötley Crüe, Bon Jovi, Kiss, and others).

The new Steel Dragon songs were intentionally shaped to sound as if they were crafted at the peak of hair metal dominance between 1986 and 1991, and the results were a magnificently authentic triumph. "Blood Pollution" was possibly as good as anything the genre had ever produced, featuring stunning vocals from Matijevic, and "Stand Up" (written specifically for the movie by Sammy Hagar) was a classic arena-rock anthem.

Also included was a bombastic, hair metal reimaging of the formerly restrained Steelheart track "We All Die Young," which had made its initial appearance on the 1996 *Wait* album. Featuring yet another astounding performance by Matijevic, the Steel Dragon version is one of my favorite songs—*ever*. The scene where the film's main character auditions for Steel Dragon with the track's opening verses never fails to give me goosebumps.

Several other bands experienced a revitalization moving into the new millennium as well, among them **Enuff Z'Nuff**, who toured on the Glam Slam Metal Jam Tour and managed to release two more-than-solid new albums, *Paraphernalia* in 1999 and *10* in 2000. Make sure not to miss the excellent "Believe in Love" from the former, and the splendid "There Goes My Heart" from the latter.

But it wasn't *just* traditional hair bands that were returning to their

'80s rock 'n' roll roots. Even **Rob Halford**, the revered "Metal God" himself, who, after leaving Judas Priest, experimented with the grungy, industrial-electronic bands Two and Fight in the mid-'90s, happily found the way back to his true calling with the tremendous *Resurrection* album in 2000. On the record's screaming title track, an enlightened Halford belted out the pertinent lyric, "I tried to look too far ahead—and saw the road go to my past instead"!

Even newer hair bands like **Jester** were clamoring for the glory days of hair metal past, evidenced on songs like the spirited "Radio" from their 1999 sophomore release, *Digitalia*, where the band lamented the depressing state of '90s-radio and shouted lyrics such as "Take me back to where I wanna' be—before we crashed 'round 1993!"

Heck, even the majestic **Whitesnake** was once again active and busy in late 2001, as David Coverdale was preparing to reform the band for its spectacular, legendary 2002 Twenty-Fifth-Anniversary Tour.

Other noteworthy albums released between 1999 and 2001: Heavens Edge (*Some Other Place Some Other Time*), Sammy Hagar (*Ten 13*), Sammy Hagar (*Red Voodoo*), The Newlydeads (*Dead End*), Melodica (*Lovemetal*), Conny Bloom (*Psychonaut*), FireHouse (*O2*), David Coverdale (*Into The Light*), Melodica (*Long Way from Home*), Funny Money *(Back Again)*, Bang Gang *(Vanity Kills)*, Union *(The Blue Room)*, Izzy Stradlin *(River)*, Stevie Rachelle *(Since Sixty Six)*

The period time between 1999 and 2001 was a magical time for hair metal fans, with many of their favorite bands gloriously resurrected from the near-death experience that was the '90s, and once again freshly visible from both a touring and new music standpoint. Even if all of the latest albums didn't necessarily live up to the classic records of the genre's glory days between 1986 and 1991, at least there *was* new hair metal music to be enjoyed, and a good amount of it was more than worthy of the audience's attention.

Although the records no longer automatically shifted multiple millions of copies (Bon Jovi, notwithstanding), that level of commercial success wasn't necessarily a requirement, as long as bands were able to sell just enough albums (and increasingly more important, concert tickets) to continue sustaining a viable musical existence.

Outside of the music, though, the shifting tide was also apparent from a cultural standpoint. In the mid-'90s, you risked being burnt at the stake for even the mere suggestion that '80s hair metal might've had a *hint* of a redeeming quality. But as the '90s turned to the '00s, more people began to nostalgically appreciate the era for its ability to foster a carefree good time and refreshingly provide catchy, energetic, upbeat rock 'n' roll.

The activity and rebirthing phenomenon that occurred during this time succeeded in establishing a stable, robust platform from which hair bands, both new and old, would successfully operate from for the next twenty years, as of this writing.

As for me? How did I celebrate hair metal's glorious resurrection? I traveled to Las Vegas with a few friends for New Year's Eve 1999, to rock in the new century at a small, raucous club in Sin City, partying to a cherished concert bill of Pretty Boy Floyd, Sofa Kings (Tesla), Slaughter, and Warrant. Needless to say, the new millennium was ushered forth in a most glorious hair metal fashion, naturally.

Best Albums 1999-2001

1. Beautiful Creatures – *Beautiful Creatures (Top 25 in Genre!)*
2. Mike Tramp – *Recovering the Wasted Years (Top 25 in Genre!)*
3. Bon Jovi – *Crush*
4. Pretty Boy Floyd – *Porn Stars*
5. Halford – *Resurrection*
6. Danger Danger – *Cockroach*
7. Slaughter – *Back to Reality*
8. Shameless – *Queen 4 A Day*
9. Slash's Snakepit – *Ain't Life Grand*
10. Def Leppard – *Euphoria*

11. Poison – *Crack A Smile . . . And More*
12. Paul Gilbert – *Flying Dog*
13. Nelson – *Life*
14. Enuff Z'Nuff – *10*
15. Sebastian Bach – *Bring 'Em Bach Alive!*
16. The Quireboys – *This Is Rock 'n' Roll*

VI
Hair Metal in the New Millennium

2002 – 2019

Chapter 22

Cry Tough

(2002-2019)

Prelude

For rock 'n' roll bands originating in the '80s, hair metal in the new millennium enjoyed a considerably more welcoming atmosphere versus the harsh inhospitality of the '90s, but it wasn't exactly a full-blown return to the glory days, either. Hair bands were fortunate to maintain a large enough fanbase to continue making new albums and touring, but the boundless funding and extravagant lifestyles were mostly things of the past, or at least limited to a much smaller scale.

The genre as a whole existed in more of a "steady-state" (at least commercially) from 2002 through 2019 versus the intense roller coaster ride of the decades prior, but deeper down there was still ample drama at the individual band level depending on the specific trials and tribulations each artist was or wasn't going through at the time.

One of the most significant challenges as the '00s progressed was the simple fact that just *existing* in a rock band at age forty or fifty was an entirely different proposition versus when band members were twenty-five-year-old kids with a mission to simply to rock 'n' roll all night and party every day. Too often, "life" simply gets in the way. Musicians mature, have families, require a steady source of income, expand their horizons, move to different geographies, encounter health challenges, and everything else that comes along with "growing up."

It was one thing to be blissfully young and happily residing in a rundown apartment with your bandmates, partying every night, writing songs, and heading out each year on tour with the substantial financial backing of major record labels. But maintaining a healthy and successful band dynamic, producing new music, and continuing to pull off a touring schedule nearly thirty years later, as personalities naturally evolve and life "happens"? That's decidedly a far trickier landscape to navigate.

To this extent many hair bands went through changing lineups in the new millennium, cycling through revolving doors of different musicians coming and going, with most, unfortunately, retaining only portions of the original groups dating back to their '80s heyday. In a few extreme instances, there were even two different versions of the same band on tour using a shared moniker, with various members splitting off in their individual directions while still claiming sole ownership of the band's name. This seemingly absurd scenario applied at different times to Ratt, L.A. Guns, Great White, and others.

As silly as it may have appeared, though, the artists were simply trying to make a living while playing music with like-minded individuals with whom they could get along; to a certain extent you really couldn't fault them. As much as fans yearn for the "original" lineups, personalities change, priorities shift, and it's just not always practical to stay together. Still, thankfully, some bands did manage to remain fully intact during this time, among them Def Leppard, Mötley Crüe, Poison, and Aerosmith, just to name a few.

Despite the turmoil and turnover, however, many hair bands happily soldiered on into the new century just grateful for the opportunity to continue doing what they love making and playing music, or at least thankful to be able to earn a modest living.

Another momentous change centered on the advent of the internet as it related to digital file sharing and music streaming services. Starting with Napster in the early '00s and evolving to a point where music was widely shared for "free" across peer-to-peer download sites, the physical form of music and the compact disc marched toward a slow, painful death, becoming almost extinct as of this writing (although it should be noted that vinyl has managed to stage a small comeback among older fans and self-proclaimed audiophiles).

With the significant shift toward digital music, primarily distributed without adequate compensation to the artists (either via "stealing" over the internet or lower-reimbursing subscription streaming services), the creation of new albums, particularly by older, more established bands, took on a new light. Whereas once new music was a primary source of income for hair bands, suddenly there was now little (if any) money to be made from it. Back in the '80s, you had to sell at least five hundred thousand copies of an album to be considered even remotely successful, bands today consider it a victory if they move even ten thousand.

On the positive side, the continual evolution of technology has made it far easier and more cost-efficient than ever to create a record, particularly after 2010. While expenses traditionally ran in the area of several hundred thousand dollars for bands to convene in a proper studio and record an album, today, the same process can amazingly be accomplished at a fraction of that cost primarily on people's phones while in the comfort of their homes, on tour buses, or practically anywhere else, for that matter. To this degree, some bands now record entire records without ever getting in the same room together, simply passing files back and forth over the internet. This computerization may certainly make putting out an album more convenient, but I'm not sure it always results in a high-quality product.

While this progression of technology was beneficial in enabling artists to continue making music despite the lower levels of income it generated (if an artist is lucky, they can break even), the end result was still, inevitably, much fewer new albums versus the past, mainly as it applied to legacy artists. The typical cycle in the late '80s was primarily: record an album, tour for a year in support of said album, take a couple of weeks off, get back in the studio for a few months to record a new record, go back out on tour—rinse and repeat. In the new millennium, however, many hair bands often go several years between new releases, sometimes even longer.

With the decline in physical album sales, concert touring became the primary source of income for these aging music groups. And to an extent, the nature of these performances further served to heighten the disincentive to produce new music, especially for the incumbent, legacy hair bands. For artists just starting out, the creation of new music is essential, as without it, there is no commercial hook enticing people to attend their concerts. But for older hair bands, the *average* audience member is, regretfully, not particularly interested in "new" music.

Most of the fans attending these shows have reached middle age (surprisingly not all, though), and their primary goal is to simply enjoy a little nostalgia while listening to the songs that defined their youth as they attempt to briefly relive a small part of their "good old days." It is generally acknowledged that the worst nine words a band can utter during a performance are, "now we are going to play a new song." For the casual fan, it's an instant invitation to disengage, take a seat, check their phone, or make a beer or bathroom run. Very sad, but very true.

Often, hair bands would love nothing more than to incorporate some fresh material into their set, but, realistically, they would do so at the risk of disappointing at least 85 percent of the audience. Especially with the trend toward concert "packages" featuring multiple acts on the same bill, where limited time slots force artists to leave out what would most likely be a fan favorite should they attempt to squeeze in a new song—not smart perhaps.

The unfortunate thing, however, is that the smaller percentage of "true" fans and more devoted followers (likely almost all who are reading this) would generally love nothing more than to hear newer and/or rarer "deep tracks" worked into the setlists. Personally, I have recently stopped attending Poison concerts, as the band has been playing basically the exact same setlist for the past fifteen years (give or take a song or two). It has simply become a little stale. It's a shame too, because Poison throws one hell of a party—trust me.

So, not only has making albums generally become a non-money-making proposition, but bands tend to find it difficult to successfully integrate any new material they do produce into their live shows.

And while this works just fine for some acts that aren't necessarily in a particularly creative place any longer and are more than happy to simply deliver the nostalgic "hits" package, most hair bands thankfully do still make new music, even if it's not as frequent as in their past. Many artists simply feel the need to create, as they are, in fact, *artists*. Creating music is in their lifeblood and serves as an essential ingredient to avoid stagnation and facilitate continued evolution as both musicians and performers.

But even the way new music is brought to market began to change as the new millennium progressed. Younger acts, especially, were still mainly dependent on fresh output as a drawing card for their shows, but the concept of a full "album" unfortunately began to lose steam. Particularly with genres like pop and hip-hop, albums were increasingly passed over in favor of more frequent, one-off "singles." The idea was to keep new product flowing more regularly (if in smaller batches), while also acknowledging that a large portion of the audience for these formats seemingly no longer had either the attention span or desire to digest a full ten or twelve-song record anymore. Sadly, for casual fans, music was becoming disposable.

There is a similar groundswell for rock music's format to follow in kind, but luckily it hasn't taken majority hold just yet, as of 2019. It's disappointing enough that the physical form of music has mostly passed by, as there was great joy in holding a hair metal album in your hand, looking at the pictures, reading through the liner notes, and experiencing the full "package." In my view, forgoing albums in totality would represent another disappointing step backward.

While singles may represent the "hits" per se, it was the complete record that often took the listener on a broader and more fulfilling journey. It would be a shame to have been robbed of the deeper album tracks that often gave the overarching music experience a sense of context and depth. For me, the singles from Bon Jovi's *New Jersey* wouldn't necessarily be as meaningful without adjacent album tracks like "Ride Cowboy Ride" and 'Stick to Your Guns," which would never exist in a landscape that only catered to the "hits."

Thankfully though, hair metal fans don't have to worry too much about all that just yet, as for the most part, despite all the challenges and changes post 2001, there is still ample new music to be enjoyed and seemingly always an opportunity to catch several of their favorite acts out on the touring circuit. Believe it or not, some of the tours and music releases are even bigger and better than ever! Guns N' Roses' Not in this Lifetime Tour that ran from 2016 through 2019 was the third highest-grossing tour of *all-time*, and acts like Def Leppard, Winger, Trixter, Whitesnake, and Pretty Boy Floyd have all recently issued new albums that rank in the upper tier of their catalogs (not to mention the fantastic offerings from countless *new* hair metal bands, who we will cover a little while later).

Hair metal in the new millennium may not fully encompass the glamorous lifestyle it reflected during the '80s, and the quantity and quality of the music may ebb and flow a bit, but the genre unquestionably remains alive and well. There are even legitimate signs indicating hair metal is getting stronger with each passing year. Some say that "rock is dead," and while the beloved format may, admittedly, reside in the commercial rearview mirror compared to popular styles such as hip-hop, pop and country, clearly, and thankfully, nothing could be farther from the truth.

Chapter 23

Let It Play

(2002-2019)

'80s Legacy Artists

Hair metal's story from 1981 to 2001 was an overarching arc that bands generally rode up, down, and then back up again together in tandem, with situational exceptions, of course. During the decades that followed, however, the genre operated mostly status-quo, with peaks and valleys occurring at different times depending on each band's specific situation. To this end, we will (briefly) cover 2002 through 2019 not annually, but rather at the artist level, starting with the more prominent groups whose hair metal origins traced back to the '80s.

Mötley Crüe

It is perhaps fitting then to start with Mötley Crüe, the band that played possibly the singular primary role in launching the entire hair metal genre at its onset.

In late 2001 the Crüe went on hiatus after releasing their famous autobiography, *The Dirt*, and touring to support 2000's *New Tattoo* album. From that time up until late 2005, both Nikki Sixx and Tommy Lee (who had been out of the band since 1999) dabbled in side-projects (Sixx with Brides of Destruction, and Lee with rap-rock group Methods of Mayhem and solo) while Mick Mars' struggled against his crippling ankylosing spondylitis illness to the point of nearly dying in recluse.

In late 2004, however, Lee reluctantly returned to the group, Mars was resurrected off the scrap heap back to operating condition, and Mötley Crüe embarked on their celebrated 2005 Carnival of Sins reunion tour while releasing a fresh greatest hits compilation, *Red, White & Crüe.* The new album featuring three new studio tracks, the first of which, "If I Die Tomorrow" (an unused leftover from the band Simple Plan), received decent critical acclaim, but in my view was relatively bland and weak. I much preferred the pounding "Sick Luv Song," which was the meanest, nastiest, best thing I had heard from the Crüe since "Primal Scream" sixteen years earlier.

Mötley Crüe continued with successful tours in both 2006 and 2007 before releasing what would be their final full studio album, *Saints of Los Angeles*, in 2008. The record was originally intended as a companion soundtrack for the movie adaptation of *The Dirt*, with each song loosely reflecting one of the book's chapters, but the title was eventually revised due to the film consistently getting bogged down in numerous delays.

Saints of Los Angeles was actually a pretty decent album and closer to *Dr. Feelgood* than anything the band had done since that time (although still not in the same league). At least the sound was big and beefy, rectifying one of the primary issues with 2000's *New Tattoo.* Still, the material likely suffered from the relative lack of input from Lee and Mars, as Sixx co-wrote most of the record with his side-project Sixx A.M. bandmates and songwriter Marti Frederiksen.

The album did include the gem that was its bombastic title track, which could legitimately and proudly stand alongside some of the Crüe's best past output. "Saints of Los Angeles" was even nominated for a Grammy Award in the Best Hard Rock Performance category. Other album highlights included the stomping "Face Down in the Dirt" and the melodic, nostalgic "Down at the Whiskey."

Mötley Crüe continued to perform annually up until 2014, at which time the band announced they would embark on one last tour prior to "retiring" the group at the end of 2015. Mötley Crüe wanted to ensure they went out as close to on top of their game as possible as opposed to slowly deteriorating over time. As Sixx stated, “rock ‘n’ roll doesn’t age well.”

Further, to protect the band’s legacy and guarantee Mötley Crüe couldn’t continue with partial membership afterward, as many other hair bands often did, the group signed a binding “cessation of touring agreement,” preventing any of them from touring under the name Mötley Crüe after 2015. The Crüe would go out just as they came in, it appeared—on their own terms and under their own rules.

The band’s highly emotional last show was appropriately staged on their home turf in Los Angeles on New Year’s Eve 2015.

Three years later, in 2018, the film adaptation of *The Dirt* finally picked up steam, and a re-energized Mötley Crüe got back together in the studio to record four new tracks for yet another greatest hits album to coincide with the movie’s release. The film finally received its long-awaited premiere (along with the soundtrack release) on March 22, 2019, the former being a Netflix exclusive.

The movie was predictably met with amazing fan reviews and harsh critical reviews, as anything related to Mötley Crüe apparently couldn’t come to fruition any other way. Other than being burdened with the impossible task of doing any sort of justice to the band’s incredible, outrageous career in a way-to-short 108 minutes, I felt the movie was quite enjoyable. As for the new studio tracks, it was great to have them, but only "The Dirt (Est. 1981)" featured any real spark. “Ride With the Devil” and “Crash and Burn” were little more than average, while the band’s cover version of Madonna’s “Like a Virgin” may have seemed to Sixx like it just *had* to work since it was such a ridiculous idea, but to me—just *no*.

Still, the soundtrack went to No. 1 on the iTunes Albums chart and No. 3 on the Billboard Albums chart, while *The Dirt*, in book format, returned to the New York Times Best Seller list. Mötley Crüe, once more against the odds, somewhat naturally, found themselves in the spotlight yet again.

Mötley Crüe remains open to promoting the band in the future, but will they ever perform together again? Perhaps a one-off for something grand, such as a Rock and Roll Hall of Fame induction ceremony? The band members seem committed to their cessation contract, but with Mötley Crüe, there is perhaps only one thing you can ever be sure of, and that's that anything can, and often does, happen.

Guns N' Roses

Duff McKagan was the group's final original member (other than Axl Rose) to exit the embattled Guns N' Roses in 1997, leaving Rose as the proverbial last man standing. For the next ten years, Rose set forth on an odyssey unlike any other, attempting to reshape the band in whatever image he saw fit while toiling away on a follow-up to the *Use Your Illusion* albums that had been in the works dating all the way back to 1994.

The new album, and specifically the making of it, would legitimately go down as one of the most infamous sagas the music industry had ever seen—an entire text could easily be written on the topic. The record was plagued with more delays, reconfigurations, re-recordings, lineup changes, and management turnover (not to mention every other form of havoc and disruption you could possibly imagine) than any other album in history.

Over its outlandish fourteen years in the making, the record became a rumor-mongered white whale; every year, it was "sure to be released," but it would never happen. Myriad different producers, mixers, and musicians came and went among countless rumors and music leaks. Never was the recording of an album so steeped in folly and absurdity. The *only* thing that stayed constant was the record's title, which was cemented as far back as 1999: *Chinese Democracy*.

That same year, Rose and his freshly hired hands did manage to briefly pop up above ground, placing a new song on the *End of Days* movie soundtrack—the bizarre, industrial-sounding "Oh My God." The revamped GN'R then played their much-awaited first concerts in 2001 and continued with sporadic tours and live appearances over the years that followed, all with varying degrees of success and failure, along with, of course, ever-present drama and controversy.

Ultimately, at long last, the most anticipated album in rock music history was finally released on November 23, 2008, distributed exclusively by big-box electronics outlet Best Buy. In the end, production costs for the record tallied an outrageous thirteen million dollars, making it by far the most expensive album ever made. Outside of the madness that was the record's creation, however, the real question was whether *Chinese Democracy*, after fourteen years in the making, would manage to live up to the larger-than-life expectations that accompanied its long, tortured journey.

The short answer, for most, was a resounding "no," although, in reality, there was no way it possibly could've given all that had transpired during its creation. Expectations aside, from my view, the album was overtly an overzealous, disjointed mess. *Chinese Democracy* sounded a lot like its indulgent production process: a mix of far too many different styles, musicians, and pieced-together performances surrounded by an overblown, excessively technical production. The fact that Rose included no fewer than four new grandiose attempts at another "Estranged" didn't help matters.

To be fair, several of the songs had various pieces and parts that were promising, such as the pop-based "Better," techno-flavored "Shackler's Revenge," power ballad "Street of Dreams," and beautiful, piano-driven "This I Love." But, at the end of the day, there was simply too much inconsistency and dissonance to really allow any of the tunes to work.

Sales of *Chinese Democracy* were limited to an extremely disappointing 2.6 million copies worldwide, and the album was generally considered a monumental flop. That said, I have also met a few hair metal fans who consider it brilliant, so to each his own, I guess.

Guns N' Roses often spoke of plans to release a quick follow-up album(s), as, allegedly, there were up to three or four records of unused material remaining in various states of readiness sitting in the can, but of course, nothing ever materialized or surfaced.

The former members of GN'R also kept busy during those years with assorted solo albums and side-projects, the most notable of which was Velvet Revolver, featuring Slash, Duff McKagan, and Matt Sorum. The group put out two albums to much critical acclaim and commercial success, but personally, I could never quite get into the alternative vocal stylings of lead singer Scott Weiland (ex-Stone Temple Pilots).

The real question that persisted was whether the world would ever see the much-coveted reunion of Guns N' Roses' classic lineup. Both Rose and Slash were adamant in multiple interviews circa 2009-2012 that it would *never* happen, with Slash going so far as to say, "what's clear is that one of the two of us (Slash, Axl) will die before a reunion, and however sad, ugly or unfortunate anyone views it, it is how it is."

Not even Guns N' Roses induction into the Rock and Roll Hall of Fame in 2012 could bring them back together, with Rose and Izzy Stradlin no-showing while other GN'R members performed with Myles Kennedy (from Slash's solo band) stepping in on vocals.

And then, finally, in late 2015, rampant imprecise rumors suddenly abounded of a "reunited" Guns N' Roses headlining the Coachella festival in January 2016. With Hell supposedly freezing over, the show miraculously brought Slash, Rose, and McKagan back together again on the same stage for the first time in twenty-three years (regrettably without Izzy Stradlin or Steve Adler, though).

A full reunion tour was planned, and after a magical warm-up show as the famous Troubadour in Los Angeles on April 1, 2016, the partially reformed Guns N' Roses launched the aptly titled Not in this Lifetime Tour, which, with Rose on his newfound best behavior, would run a massive forty-two months while selling out arenas and stadiums across the globe and eventually grossing over $580 million, making it the third highest-grossing tour of all-time in any genre.

In the back half of 2016, between legs of the GN'R tour, Rose somewhat shockingly filled in for AC/DC's suddenly hearing-impaired lead singer Brian Johnson, quite capably performing twenty-three incredible concerts to finish out the band's Rock or Bust Tour.

Guns N' Roses proceeded to release a deluxe box set edition of *Appetite for Destruction* in 2018 that was nominated for a Grammy Award, but thoughts now in 2019 focus on whether fans will ever be lucky enough to see any newly recorded material from the reunited band. Only time will tell it would seem, as the future of the one-time "most dangerous band in the world" appears as up for grabs as ever.

Def Leppard

Def Leppard managed to stay plenty busy between 2002 and 2019, consistently touring to faithful fans while releasing four new studio albums. The band followed up 1999's return-to-style *Euphoria* record with a left turn in 2002, issuing the very light and pop-oriented *X* album. While fans of the Def Leppard's harder-edged rock sound were left disappointed, *X* was a superb collection of finely-crafted pop-rock songs, assuming they could be accepted as such. Highlights included "Now," "You're So Beautiful," "Torn to Shreds," "Four Letter Word," and the ballad "Long, Long Way to Go."

Def Leppard then released the well-performed but underwhelming covers album, *Yeah!*, in 2006, then managed to get a little closer back to their roots in 2008 with the varied and somewhat inconsistent *Songs from the Sparkle Lounge*, named after the bright, spirited area the band would set up backstage to write new songs while touring. The record featured an assorted mix of styles from the group's past, including the grungy "Go" (which would have been right at home on 1996's *Slang*), the '70s-styled "C'Mon C'Mon" (a-la *Yeah!*), pop-oriented "Tomorrow" (*X*), and hair metal-natured "Nine Lives" (akin to *Euphoria*). The album also featured the charming, Queen-inspired ballad, "Love." *Songs from the Sparkle Lounge* had its moments but is probably my least favorite album from the band, overall.

Def Leppard did, however, manage a wonderful return-to-form in 2015 with their eleventh studio album, simply titled *Def Leppard*. While still a diverse effort, the tracks flowed together well and represented some of the band's best songwriting since *Adrenalize*. Lead single "Let's Go" brazenly borrowed from "Pour Some Sugar on Me" but did so in fine fashion, while "Dangerous" was classic Def Leppard pop-metal and perhaps the album's standout moment. Other highlights included the semi-ballad "We Belong," energetic "All Time High," and the beautiful "Last Dance," penned by bassist Rick Savage. The record peaked at No. 10 on the Billboard Albums chart.

As of this writing in 2019, Def Leppard were out rocking audiences around the globe on their latest, highly successful world tour.

Bon Jovi

Another band that has kept very busy in the new millennium is the legendary Bon Jovi, although the group's musical output has, regrettably, consistently moved further and further away from their hair metal roots. That said, the band has unquestionably sustained the highest commercial profile and success level of any '80s rock act, maintaining a near-constant album-tour-album cycle with multi-Platinum records and world tours that have consistently ranked among the top three highest-grossing concert events each year.

After Bon Jovi played a central role ushering in hair metal's resurrection in 2000 with their fantastic *Crush* album and the massive hit single "It's My Life," the band released their follow-up, *Bounce*, in 2002, and despite falling short of *Crush*'s overall magic, the record was mostly a worthy successor. The single "Everyday" came close to matching "It's My Life," while "Undivided" was a crushing rocker inspired by the tragic events of the September 11, 2001 terrorist attacks. Meanwhile, "You Had Me from Hello" was a superbly beautiful ballad that ranked among Bon Jovi's best.

This Left Feels Right followed in 2003, featuring revised and re-recorded versions of earlier Bon Jovi hits. Without going into too much detail, it may have felt "right" for the band, but generally felt all wrong to fans.

Bon Jovi would make it up to their followers in spades, however, with their amazing 2004 box set, *100,000,000 Bon Jovi Fans Can't Be Wrong*. The package was simply magnificent, featuring four compact discs filled with over fifty previously unreleased and rare tracks spanning the band's sweeping career. I can't say enough about the quality of the records, as it was shocking just how many songs the band had left behind that were just as good if not better than much of what had made their final albums. Adding to that, the sound quality of the "demos" was fantastic, being practically indeterminate in many instances from full and proper studio productions.

I could easily spend thirty pages dissecting the box set's massive amount of content, but for the purposes of brevity, suffice it to say the package is flat-out a must-own for all Bon Jovi fans. Be sure not to miss standouts such as "The Radio Saved My Life Tonight," "Miss Fourth of July," "Maybe Someday," "Last Chance Train," "Starting All Over Again," "Open All Night," "I Get a Rush," and the long-sought formal release of "Edge of a Broken Heart," one of Bon Jovi's absolute best songs that was unfathomably left on the cutting room floor during the *Slippery When Wet* sessions.

Bon Jovi then released the fresh new album *Have a Nice Day* in 2005 and the record was yet again another massive success, moving over six million copies worldwide on the backs of the rock-based hit single title track and the pop-oriented "Who Says You Can't Go Home," which Bon Jovi also recorded as a duet with country singer Jennifer Nettles of Sugarland. The country-version hit No. 1 on Billboard's Country chart and won the pairing a Grammy Award. Personally, however, outside of the semi-ballad "Welcome to Wherever You Are," I was not a big fan of the album, finding it far too generic and uninspired for my taste. Ironically, two of the record's best songs, in my view, "Dirty Little Secret" and "Unbreakable," were left off the US release and included only as bonus tracks on overseas editions of the album.

In an even further departure from their former hair metal sound (likely spurred by the success of "Who Says You Can't Go Home"), in 2007, Bon Jovi released their first official "country" album, titled *Lost Highway*. In short, if you like country music mixed with a little rock, then you'll probably dig it, but if it is hair metal you seek (or anything close to that), best to look elsewhere. Naturally, though, the album was a smash hit commercially. Highlights included "Lost Highway" and "Whole Lotta

Leavin'."

Bon Jovi released four additional studio albums between 2009 and 2016, each basically the same style, featuring a fairly generic, radio-friendly, modern, AOR-type sound. None of them were all that impressive, from my perspective, but there were certainly a few bright spots, such as "When We Were Beautiful" from 2009's *The Circle*, "Pictures of You" from 2013's *What About Now*, "A Teardrop to the Sea" from 2015's hastily put together "contractual obligation album," *Burning Bridges*, and several tracks from the best-of-the-bunch 2016's *This House Is Not for Sale*, including "Living with the Ghost," "Reunion," and "Real Love." All the albums were ultra-successful commercially, however, and the accompanying tour for each sold-out arenas all over the world.

Regretfully, guitarist Richie Sambora split from Bon Jovi in 2013 for reasons that are strangely still unclear to this day. The relationship between Sambora and Jon Bon Jovi still appears amicable, though, and the band briefly reunited in 2017 to perform at their induction into the Rock and Roll Hall of Fame.

It is likely Bon Jovi will continue their massive run of success into the foreseeable future (specifically, Jon Bon Jovi), but unfortunately, those still holding out a sliver of hope for a new album sounding anything even remotely similar to *New Jersey* will likely find themselves considerably disappointed.

Poison

Poison has also remained very active, specifically on the touring circuit, heading out on the road almost every summer and delivering a glam metal party-bash that always proves a huge hit with their fans and scores a considerable level of commercial success. Most unfortunately, however, other than the release of their sixth studio album, *Hollyweird*, in 2002, there has been no new material from the band other than an unnecessary cover-songs album in 2007 along with various band member solo releases and side-projects.

As far as *Hollyweird*, which represented Poison's first full album with

C.C. DeVille back in the band since 1990, even a hardcore Poison fan like myself would have to admit it was mostly an embarrassing disappointment. The album's biggest drawback was likely the muddy, low-budget production, but further to that, the songs simply weren't of high quality, with some of them being not just average but downright *bad* ("Get 'Ya Some," "Stupid, Stoned & Dumb"). And of course, there were two throwaway tracks featuring DeVille on lead vocals.

To the album's credit, "Shooting Star" could have been a great song with better production (it's still a guilty pleasure of mine), and "Hollyweird" featured a solid, crunchy guitar riff, but regrettably, everything else on *Hollyweird* can probably be passed over.

Lead singer Bret Michaels managed to stay supremely busy outside of Poison, overcoming repeated health challenges to star in several seasons of different reality TV shows while also issuing a few solo albums (none of which are essential, however). Much better in quality is the surprisingly good *Devil City Angels* album, generated in 2015 by the side-project supergroup of the same name formed by Poison drummer Rikki Rocket and featuring guitarist Tracii Guns (L.A. Guns), bassist Eric Brittingham (Cinderella), and the wonderfully talented Brandon Gibbs on lead vocals. Make sure to check out "Numb," "I'm Living," and "Back to the Drive" from that album, at a minimum.

While Poison fans are thrilled to party with the band on tour, a new studio album remains the desire of many hardcore supporters. Why exactly has Poison gone seventeen years between albums? Perhaps the band is just too dysfunctional at this point in its career, or maybe the member's creative juices have simply run dry. More likely, it's a result of Michaels prioritizing his solo career, as the other band members have repeatedly expressed interest in new Poison music while repeatedly hinting that Michaels is the hold-up. In his defense, even if Poison did manage to put out a great new record, it's hard to believe sales would recoup costs, and there isn't exactly room for new material in the group's setlist (according to the average fan). The band has admitted their awareness to these points.

On a positive note, Poison has recently hinted a desire to at least put out *one* new single (don't hurt yourselves, guys) to coincide with a rumored package tour tentatively planned for 2020. We shall see. Does the world really *need* a new Poison album? Probably not. Do hair metal fans? Most definitely. Come on fellas—how about just one more for old times' sake? (But please make sure to do it right this time, i.e., *not* like Hollyweird.)

Skid Row

After reforming in 1999 and successfully touring with new singer Johnny Solinger, Skid Row put out their first album without Sebastian Bach in 2003, titled *Thick Skin.* Sollinger's vocals were fine, even better than fine in some places, but the album was an inconsistent platter consisting mostly of grungy, modern/alternative rock sounds sprinkled with some pop and thrash metal in places. Not exactly what Skid Row fans were hoping for. Be sure to check out the awesome title track, though (the record's one saving grace), as it undeniably lays hard rock waste.

The band unfortunately followed *Thick Skin* with the even more disappointing *Revolutions Per Minute* in 2006 ("Shut Up Baby, I Love You" being the only track possibly worth listening to), and the underwhelming EPs *United World Rebellion: Chapter One* and *Rise Of The Damnation Army—United World Rebellion: Chapter Two* in 2013 and 2014, respectively. Despite the subpar material, Skid Row remained a force to be reckoned while on tour during this time, mainly focusing on material from the first two Skid Row albums.

Solinger was fired in 2015, sixteen years after first joining the group, with the band feeling his commitment had grown lacking. Skid Row then brought aboard Tony Harnell from TNT, who was a gifted vocalist but simply a bad match with Skid Row's catalog. Harnell would leave the group within a year.

Skid Row is confident they finally found the right fit, however, hooking up South African-born singer ZP Theart, formerly of the power metal band, DragonForce. As of late 2019, the band was hard at work with Theart finishing up the final installment of their United World Rebellion trilogy, due for release in 2020.

Ex-Skid Row singer Sebastian Bach, meanwhile, kept quite busy on his own. After carrying out stints on Broadway concurrent with a recurring role on the hit TV show, *Gilmore Girls*, in the early-to-mid-'00s, Bach hooked up with songwriter and musician Henning Pauly to contribute vocals to Pauly's concept album, *An Absence of Empathy* (issued under the Frameshift moniker), released in April 2005. Be sure to check out that record's "Just One More" and the epic, Braveheart-inspired "Blade."

Bach issued his first official studio solo album, *Angel Down*, in 2007, and it was a *monster* record. A true heavy metal album with a top-notch band and fantastic production and sound, the platter rocked gloriously hard from start to finish, pausing only to offer brief respite with two beautiful ballads. Bach even managed to somehow coax Axl Rose out of recluse to provide backing vocals for a couple of songs in addition to duetting on a raging cover of Aerosmith's "Back in the Saddle."

Angel Down was almost universally critically acclaimed, but for whatever reason, turned out to be a significant commercial letdown, a situation which left a confused Bach in a decidedly foul mood for months.

Bach would continuously tour, though, and went on to release two follow-up solo albums (2011's *Kicking & Screaming* and 2014's *Give 'Em Hell*); however, neither of release matched the intensity or quality of *Angel Down*, too often veering into more modern rock sounds and production techniques.

Of course, even though he may have lost a vocal step or two versus his power-packed youth, Bach still brings it on stage like few others from the genre and is always a must-see in concert.

From the outside, it would seem the obvious answer to both Skid Row and Sebastian Bach's situations would be to reunite and attempt to recapture some of their prior magic together. But while Bach has repeatedly lobbied for a reunion, the remaining original members of Skid Row couldn't be more violently opposed, firmly believing Bach's personality simply isn't a match for the band-dynamic and relationship they seek.

It really is a shame, though, as Skid Row in their prime were a flat-out juggernaut. Unlike with Guns N' Roses, however, it appears the past will have to remain in the past, in their case.

Cinderella

Cinderella was regretfully unable to complete what would have been their fifth studio album before John Kalodner's Sony Portrait label abruptly folded up shop in 2001. Several years of litigation followed as a result of record label contract disputes that, unfortunately, prevented the band from releasing any new material for quite some time.

Cinderella did stay active, however, touring in both 2005 and 2006 before taking some needed time off while Tom Keifer dealt with a setback to his vocal cords in 2007. Cinderella would hit the road again each year from 2010 up through 2014, but the band remained unsigned as continuing personal issues within the group inhibited any new recording even though their legal troubles were behind them at that point.

As a result of Cinderella's internal strife and Keifer feeling he finally had his vocal cord condition under control (undergoing a three-hour daily regimen of vocal physical therapy while performing), the singer-songwriter finally focused his efforts on his first solo album, *The Way Life Goes*, issued in 2013.

The Way Life Goes was an impressive (if inconsistent) effort that, thankfully, showcased Keifer's voice to be in more than fine form. The album was a stylistically diverse mix of rockers and ballads that would have fit perfectly somewhere between 1990's *Heartbreak Station* and 1994's *Still Climbing*. Highlights included the rockers "Solid Ground" and "It's Not Enough," along with the beautiful sentimental ballad, "Ask Me Yesterday."

Keifer and his newfound solo band then turned their attention to honing the group's performance chops, touring up until 2019 at which time they released their sophomore album, *Rise*. The new platter truly allowed the band to shine, with Keifer again putting in a stunning vocal performance. Unfortunately, the album's production was highly compressed in places, rendering Keifer's vocals buried deep in the mix on the record's heavier tracks. It was truly a shame, as rocking songs like "The Death of Me," "Hype," and "All Amped Up" failed to achieve their full potential as a result. Still, the record was a critical achievement and a strong statement.

As far as Cinderella stands, the band could at best be described as on "extended hiatus" following an incident on the 2014 Monsters of Rock Cruise that saw guitarist Jeff LaBar's continued alcohol struggles put on full display when he basically passed out on stage. The band members made a pact to put the group on hold until their internal issues could be fully resolved, and it doesn't look promising anything will be worked out soon. Cinderella does well to keep their dirty laundry out of the press, but in 2019 Keifer was adamant that Cinderella "is a situation that doesn't work anymore . . . there's been a lot of issues over the course of decades and build-up that is beyond repair; there won't be any reunion."

Cinderella fans will have to be content then with Keifer as a solo artist for the foreseeable future, which is certainly something to be grateful for on its own.

Warrant

Warrant continued to tour during the early '00s, while Jani Lane issued his first solo album in 2002, the largely modern, pop-oriented *Back Down to One*, written with guitarist Keri Kelli. Lane would officially quit Warrant for the second time in 2004, however, following a stint in rehab attempting to address his struggles with depression and alcoholism.

All four original members of Warrant other than Lane then reunited, bringing aboard new singer Jamie St. James (ex-Black N' Blue), and in 2006 put out the band's first album sans Lane, appropriately titled *Born Again*. The new songs were happily rooted in the style of '80s hair metal, but the material sorely missed Lane's songwriting and signature vocal style.

Warrant and Lane attempted to work together again in 2008 to facilitate the band's twentieth-anniversary tour, but sadly, the shows were plagued with challenges as Lane continued to battle his inner demons.

Despite all members' best intentions, the reunion was aborted later that year, and singer Robert Mason (ex-Lynch Mob) was brought on to finish the shows and serve as Warrant's new vocalist.

With Mason on board, outside of a few brief layoffs, Warrant has continued to tour consistently up through 2019 while also releasing two additional new albums, 2011's *Rockaholic* and 2017's *Louder Harder Faster*. The band's live performances are tight and spirited, and Mason is a fine technical vocalist, but there's just something about Warrant's historical catalog that simply can't be done full justice without Lane. The new albums share a similar fate; the songs are solid enough but seem to struggle to get past "average" in the absence of Lane's magic touch.

As far as Lane himself, after his final split from Warrant in 2008, the troubled singer put together a side-project under the name Saints of the Underground featuring Ratt members Bobby Blotzer and Robbie Crane, along with long-term collaborator Keri Kelli. The group then issued the album *Love the Sin, Hate the Sinner*. It was great to hear Jani's voice on a studio project again, but the material was, unfortunately, a little underwhelming.

In 2010, Lane would go on to tour with Great White, ably filling in for singer Jack Russell who was recuperating from surgery at the time. Lane was still struggling with his addictions but objectively did a fantastic job performing the Great White catalog.

And then, suddenly and tragically, on August 11, 2011, Jani Lane was heartbreakingly found dead of alcohol poisoning at a hotel just outside of Los Angeles, CA. He was only forty-seven years old. The only thing found on his person was a mysterious hand-scribbled note that simply read, "I am Jani Lane."

I will never forget getting the call from a friend informing me of the news, as Lane was always one of my very favorite songwriters, singers, and personalities of the hair metal era. I had the pleasure of meeting Jani several times—he was a talented, wonderful, special guy who simply lost his battle with a serious disease.

One thing fans can be hopeful for, though, is to someday see the official release of the songs Lane was working on as part of his long-running Jabberwocky project that dated as far back as 1993. Many demos of varying production quality can be found on the internet, but allegedly there are fully-produced studio versions hiding somewhere that Lane was just about to release prior to his untimely passing. Songs like "Washington Square" and "Private Blue World" are among the finest he ever wrote, in my opinion.

R.I.P. Jani, we look forward to meeting up with you again someday in Rock 'n' Roll Heaven.

Whitesnake

After a five-year layoff dating back to late 1997, David Coverdale once again jumpstarted Whitesnake in 2002 for the band's Twenty-Fifth-Anniversary Tour. Joining the new lineup were guitarists Reb Beach (ex-Winger) and Doug Aldrich (ex-Dio). Whitesnake continued to tour fairly consistently up through 2006, at which point a new double-live album was released titled, *Live: In the Shadow of the Blues*, that also included four new studio tracks, among them the rollicking "Ready To Rock," Whitesnake's first fresh output in over nine years.

Whitesnake would go on to release two additional albums written by the Coverdale and Aldrich pairing, 2008's *Good to Be Bad* and 2011's *Forevermore*. Both records were superb and well-worthy of the Whitesnake name, containing rock songs as heavy as anything the band had done prior, impassioned blues numbers, and of course, classic Whitesnake power ballads. Coverdale's voice had aged relatively well, and the twin-guitar attack of Beach and Aldrich laid down an intense assault of hard rocking riffs. Highlights from those albums included "Best Years," "Call on Me," and "All I Want All I Need" from *Good to Be Bad*, and "Steal Your Heart Away," "All Out of Luck," and "Tell Me How" from *Forevermore*. Both albums were supported by highly successful world tours.

Aldrich amicably parted ways with Whitesnake in 2014, and Coverdale brought aboard famed ex-Night Ranger guitarist Joel Hoekstra to fill the gap. The band then put together *The Purple Album*, a set of beefed-up, re-recorded versions of Deep Purple songs from the David Coverdale-era. A global greatest hits tour followed in 2016.

During 2017 and 2018, Coverdale went about writing the first Whitesnake album to feature both Beach and Hoekstra as new songwriting partners. Going all the way back to 1987, Coverdale had historically only written with one guitarist each time out: John Sykes on 1987's *Whitesnake*, Adrian Vandenberg on *Slip of the Tongue* and *Restless Heart*, and Aldrich on *Good to Be Bad* and *Forevermore*.

The new songwriting team proved a huge success, as 2019's *Flesh & Blood* was perhaps Whitesnake's best album in decades. Combining some of the best elements of *Good to Be Bad*, *Slip of the Tongue,* and even earlier Whitesnake, *Flesh & Blood* was an outstanding set of grooving rockers, bluesy rhythms, and a few lighter tracks mixed in for proper balance. High points include the driving, slide guitar-filled opener "Good to See You Again," hypnotic "Gonna Be Alright," forceful "Hey You (You Make Me Rock)," rocking "Trouble Is Your Middle Name," bluesy and epic "Heart of Stone," and acoustic beauty "After All."

If there was any detractor on the album, it was that Coverdale's vocals were a little low in the mix, perhaps to mask any underlying vocal issues; as of this writing, Coverdale is approaching seventy years of age and has unfortunately struggled mightily with his voice on the Flesh & Blood World Tour. That said, Coverdale seemed to be in mostly fine form on the album, accepting, of course, that he is no longer the high-register, powerhouse barn-blaster he was in his younger days.

How long can Coverdale keep Whitesnake firing on all cylinders (at least on record)? That remains to be seen, but if *Flesh & Blood* is any indicator, I wouldn't count him out just yet.

Van Halen

Van Halen has seemingly been mired in constant drama for the better part of the past forty years, with the two decades following the turn of the century of representing, unfortunately, a particularly heightened level of unrest. Of all the great rock bands from the era, Van Halen (specifically brothers Eddie and Alex) has perhaps treated their legions of devoted fans the worst regarding a lack of communication and consistent, quality output.

Van Halen completely sat out the hair metal resurgence from 1999 through 2001 after parting ways with singer Gary Cherone following the failed *Van Halen III* experiment. There was nothing new from the band for the five years that followed through 2004, outside of constant unsubstantiated on-and-off rumors regarding a potential reunion with Roth. During this time Eddie progressively worked through multiple health challenges, including treatment for oral cancer (which resulted in him losing a third of his tongue) and a difficult separation from his wife of thirty years, Valeri Bertinelli.

On a more positive note, fans were treated to the fascinatingly unique Heavyweight Champs of Rock and Roll Tour in 2002, with ex-Van Halen lead singer David Lee Roth and Sammy Hagar surprisingly teaming up to perform co-headlining sets on the same bill. I attended that special show (of course), and recall it being an absolute blast. Naturally, though, despite Roth and Hagar maintaining separate spaces during the tour, their disparate personalities inevitably clashed, and it was a minor miracle the trek lasted to completion. I remember one of Roth's famous quotes at the time—"Sammy throws a party, I *am* the party"!

In 2004 Van Halen reunited with Hagar for a summer tour and a new, career-spanning, double-album hits compilation titled *The Best of Both Worlds*, featuring alternating tracks from both Roth and Hagar and including three fresh studio tracks with the latter. The new songs were somewhat decent (particularly "It's About Time") but unfortunately failed to live up to the band's best historical output. From an outsider's view, the tour was certainly a commercial success, but on the inside, it was an utter disaster in terms of band relations. Eddie's continued drinking problems created significant challenges, and no one in the band seemed to have any fun during the trek.

Hagar then proceeded to leave Van Halen once again, returning to his solo career and often teaming up with Van Halen bassist Michael Anthony for select performances and tours. The Van Halen brothers, meanwhile, didn't care one-bit for the alliance, and in 2006 formally kicked Anthony out of Van Halen, citing his official replacement as Eddie's son, Wolfgang. In reality, the Van Halen brothers had been trying to marginalize Anthony's role in the band dating as far back to his forced-limited participation on the studio tracks for *The Best of Both Worlds*.

Van Halen received a well-deserved induction into the Rock and Roll Hall of Fame in 2007, although only Hagar and Anthony appeared at the ceremony. Eddie entered rehab during this time amid almost constant rumors of reunion fits-and-starts with Roth. Finally, the last obstacles were cleared later that year, and the much-hyped reunification with Roth was decisively made official.

On September 27, 2007, I attended the very first Van Halen show with David Lee Roth in almost twenty-five years—it was a glorious moment. The tour ran through mid-2008 and was wildly successful, grossing nearly $100 million.

Four years later, in 2012, Van Halen issued their first new studio album since 1998, and first full-length record with Roth in over twenty-seven years. It was also Roth's first freshly recorded output since his 2003 set of mostly cover songs, *Diamond Dave*. The new Van Halen album was aptly titled *A Different Kind of Truth*.

Critical reviews for the record were almost universally positive (it hit No. 2 on the Billboard Albums chart) outside of the strange choice to release what was likely the album's weakest track as the first single, the rather bland "Tattoo." For me, however, the album was more of a mixed bag.

On the plus side, most of the songs and indeed all the musical performances absolutely smoked, with Eddie displaying every bit of guitar-God pyrotechnics you would expect while Alex thunderously pounded away at the drums. No one would be able to accuse Van Halen of going soft. Unfortunately, though, the material was marred in my opinion by an overly loud, muddy, "brick-walled" production atypical of

Van Halen's traditional sharp and well-spaced sound. Further, Roth's vocals clearly weren't what they used to be, although who could blame him at almost sixty years of age with a ton of mileage heaped on top to boot. Perhaps just as important, the music clearly missed Anthony's high-tenor background vocals, which were as much as part of Van Halen's signature sound as anything.

Still, a new Van Halen album was indeed a rare treasure, and most fans viewed it as a magnificent return-to-form, which in many ways it was. Of course, the record did include reworked versions of many demos that harked as far back as the '70s, but it was nothing new for Van Halen to revisit their vaults each time they shaped a new album.

A massive world tour commenced in support of *A Different Kind of Truth* that lasted until mid-2013, followed by the 2015 live album *Tokyo Dome Live in Concert.* After that, though, it's regrettably been pretty much radio silence for Van Halen the past several years. Hagar has seemingly written off any potential for a reunion at this point while keeping busy releasing no fewer than ten albums since 2002, both solo and with his bands The Waboritas, Chickenfoot (featuring Anthony, guitarist-extraordinaire Joe Satriani, and drummer Chad Smith from Red Hot Chili Peppers), and The Circle (Anthony, guitarist Vic Johnson and Jason Bonham on drums).

Hagar's records each have their own flavor, from the Jimmy Buffet-style of his solo/Waboritas albums (check out the 2006 masterpiece *Livin' It Up!*), to the funky, hard rock of Chickenfoot, to the classic rock meat-and-potatoes of 2019's terrific *Space Between* album with The Circle, which went all the way to No. 4 on the Billboard Albums chart. (Have a listen to song "Affirmation" for a fun, welcomed trip back to the sounds of *5150.*)

Roth, on the other hand, seems more than up for another celebrated reunion tour (hopefully this time with Anthony back in the fold), but rumored plans for a summer 2019 stadium trek fizzled out before they could even get off the ground. Disturbingly, somewhat unsubstantiated gossip of poor health for Eddie may be contributing to the inactivity, but to what extent, no one seems to know for sure.

Such is life with Van Halen, it appears, where everything is uncertain, nothing comes easy, and chaos is the coin of the realm. At the end of the day, only one new album in the past twenty years from one of the unquestionably greatest rock bands of all-time is just plain disappointing and a depressing waste of talent. Here's hoping the Van Halen brothers get their act together soon, because the clock is ticking on all of us.

L.A. Guns

Similar to Van Halen, sleaze-metal heroes L.A Guns have been no strangers to drama. The band released the fantastic *Waking the Dead* album in 2002 (be sure not to miss the tracks "Don't Look at Me That Way" and "Waking the Dead") only to see Tracii Guns abruptly jump ship in the middle of the group's subsequent tour with Alice Cooper to focus on his new Brides of Destruction project with Nikki Sixx.

An agitated Phil Lewis chose to move forward with the L.A. Guns name in Tracii's absence, touring and recording with multiple lineups for the next fourteen years. Key albums included 2005's *Tales From The Strip* and 2012's *Hollywood Forever.* Both records were substantial slices of sleazy hair metal but didn't quite live up to L.A. Guns classics like *Cocked & Loaded* or *Vicious Circle.*

Meanwhile, Guns shut down Brides of Destruction in 2006 (Sixx had left in 2004 to facilitate Mötley Crüe's reunion tour) and then proceeded to recruit original L.A. Guns singer Paul Black, who had left the group in 1987 before the band signed their first record deal. Guns and Black headed out on tour using the L.A. Guns moniker while Lewis's version of the group was performing under the same name. Naturally, there was no love lost between the two parties during this time. Guns iteration of the band wound up going through multiple singers over the next several years, including a brief reunion with Jizzy Pearl and even a curious stint with *Rock Star: Supernova* finalist, Dilana.

In 2012, Guns agreed to drop his usage of the L.A. Guns name and issued a blues-rock record under the title Tracii Guns' League of

Gentlemen with Scott Harris on vocals. Guns then moved on to form Devil City Angels with Poison's Rikki Rockett in 2015.

Finally, in the spring of 2016, a reunited Lewis and Guns performed a few select shows together (their first in fourteen years), followed by Lewis disbanding his version of L.A. Guns with Steve Riley to officially join back up with Guns, with the two of them absconding with the band name. Clear as mud, right?

With the core of Lewis and Guns back together at long last, L.A. Guns issued their "comeback" records *The Missing Peace* and *The Devil You Know* in 2017 and 2019, respectively, and the new material was widely praised by longtime fans who were thrilled to see the two erstwhile musicians back together again. I wasn't as much an enthusiast as most, as both records featured very poor production that blemished the songs, but the albums were certainly to be commended for their straightforward musical attack blending sleaze metal with moments that were almost Black Sabbath-ish in style.

L.A Guns continues to be a force performing live, and I will remain hopeful the band moves to a more polished approach on their next album.

Mr. Big

Mr. Big broke up in 2002, mainly due to disagreements between singer Eric Martin and bassist Billy Sheehan over the musical direction of the band's material. The group had already been without original guitarist Paul Gilbert since 1997, with the famous shredder maintaining a busy solo career on his own between 2002 and 2019, releasing a total of twelve albums and handling lead vocals himself on most while other releases were strictly instrumental. Gilbert also paired up with Freddie Mercury sound-a-like Freddie Nelson in 2009 for the special one-off collaboration album *United States* (a personal favorite).

Meanwhile, Martin resumed his own solo career after Mr. Big's breakup, releasing, in his words, the "distorted power-pop" albums *I'm Goin' Sane* in 2002 and *Destroy All Monsters* in 2004. Martin also contributed lyrics and lead vocals to Japanese guitar hero Tak

Matsumoto's heavy and hard rocking 2004 supergroup album, *TMG 1.*

In 2008 a spirited, impromptu one-off performance at the L.A. House of Blues between all Mr. Big members sans Martin went off so well that it soon led to a full-blown Mr. Big reunion with an incredibly successful tour of Asia to celebrate the band's twentieth anniversary. A greatest hits album was also released at this time, including the bright new studio track "Next Time Around," which in terms of style would have fit perfectly on the 1991 *Lean Into It* record.

In 2010, the reunited Mr. Big (including Gilbert) issued their first new album in ten years, titled *What If...*, and it was an amazing comeback across the board. Chock full of shredding guitar and bass with Gilbert and Sheehan working their magic together once again, Martin's voice was in top form (recently honed on his Mr. Vocalist records in Japan), and the songwriting was some of the band's best. Tracks like "American Beauty," "Undertow," "Once Upon a Time," and "Around the World" flat-out smoked, while the classic Mr. Big melodies were present on lighter numbers like "Stranger in My Life," "All the Way Up," and "I Get the Feeling." The Irish-flavored "Nobody Left to Blame" was also a treat.

Mr. Big kept their momentum going with 2014's *. . . The Stories We Could Tell*, which was a little too bluesy to rank as one of my favorites, and 2017's *Defying Gravity*, which was much more to my liking, featuring the bouncy "Defying Gravity," pop-acoustic "Damn I'm in Love Again," and beautiful "Forever and Back."

On a sadder note, drummer Pat Torpey announced in 2014 he had been diagnosed with Parkinson's disease. He was no longer able to play the drums on a full-time basis, but determinedly remained a vital part of the band, contributing his parts to Mr. Big's albums via computer programming. The resilient Torpey would continue to provide percussion while touring as well (with support from fill-in drummer Matt Starr). Tragically, Torpey passed away from complications of the disease on February 7, 2018, at the relatively young age of sixty-four.

Mr. Big's future is uncertain, but Martin has talked of possibly doing one last album and tour as a tribute to Torpey prior to permanently disbanding the group, with the band just not feeling right about continuing in his absence. We will see.

Winger

After disbanding in 1994 in the wake of grunge, Winger rode the hair metal resuscitation of the early '00s by placing the new studio track "On the Inside" (a leftover from *Pull*) on their 2001 Very Best of Winger greatest hits album prior to embarking on a spirited reunion tour with Poison in 2002.

In 2006, Winger released their first new album in thirteen years, simply titled *IV*. The new songs were very much in the "progressive rock" vein sharing little in common with hair metal, but the record was an impressive piece of songwriting, nonetheless. Winger went on to successfully tour the album in nine different countries.

Kip Winger, meanwhile, stayed busy with his parallel solo career, which was even further removed from the classic Winger style, as evidenced by the eclectic, Tantric-like sounds on 2008's *From the Moon to the Sun* and the classical, symphonic 2010 release, *Ghosts*, which supported the popular ballet developed in conjunction. Kip also composed the four-part work *Conversations with Nijinsky* that topped the Billboard Classical chart while being nominated for a Grammy Award for his outstanding efforts on that project.

Winger, as a group, got back to their hard rock roots with their excellent 2009 release, *Karma*, featuring some of the band's heaviest material to date, including the driving "Deal with the Devil" and forceful rockers "Stone Cold Killer," "Come a Little Closer," and "Pull Me Under."

The band then released their sixth studio album, *Better Days Comin'*, in 2014, which was a more diverse and uneven platter in comparison to *Karma* but did include the swaggering "Midnight Driver of a Love Machine" and the beautifully atmospheric "Ever Wonder." The album even hit No. 85 on the Billboard Albums chart.

Winger continues to tour fairly consistently and is currently putting the finishing touches on a new album for 2020, as of this writing.

Tesla

After reuniting in 2000, Tesla went out on the highly successful Rock Never Stops Tour in 2002, and in 2004 released their fifth studio album, *Into the Now*, which was a mostly heavy rock record including the highlights "Into the Now," "Look at Me," and "Got No Glory."

Tesla continued to tour afterward but unfortunately suffered the loss of Tommy Skeoch in 2006, with the guitarist departing the band for personal reasons that included continued challenges with substance abuse.

The band brought aboard the younger Dave Rude to fill the gap and promptly got back to their '70s roots, issuing the double-album collection of classic rock cover songs titled *Reel to Reel Volumes 1 & 2.* Recorded all on analog tape, Tesla did an outstanding job staying faithful to the original recordings and the production mimicked the '70s sound perfectly. The *Reel to Reel* records were loads of fun and included the standouts "Space Truckin'" (Deep Purple), "Walk Away" (The James Gang), "I've Got a Feeling" (The Beatles), "Shooting Star" (Bad Company), and "All the Young Dudes" (Mott The Hoople).

Tesla would then go on to release *Forever More* in 2008, followed by *Simplicity* in 2014, but to me, both albums underwhelmed quite a bit due to their overly stripped-back and raw production approach. The records did kick off successful world tours, however, while also generating a good bit of both critical and commercial success.

After a tour with Def Leppard and REO Speedwagon in 2016, Tesla issued *Mechanical Resonance Live* to celebrate their debut album's thirtieth anniversary and included the new studio bonus track "Save that Goodness," written with and produced by Def Leppard guitarist Phil Collen. The collaboration went so well that Tesla decided to partner with Collen again for the entirety of their 2019 *Shock* album, which mostly produced fantastic results.

Some fans criticized *Shock* for predictably sounding too much like Def Leppard, and the album admittedly featured a few too many ballads, but there was no denying the overall production was a huge step forward from Tesla's recent releases and songs like "You Won't Take Me Alive," "Tastes Like," "Tied to the Tracks," and "Afterlife" were some of the best tunes Tesla had put out in over two decades.

As of this writing, Tesla was out on tour supporting *Shock* and keeping their fanbase happy.

Enuff Z' Nuff

Enuff Z' Nuff released their new album, *Welcome to Blue Island*, in 2002, which was a solid set of tracks featuring the terrific "Sanibel Island" and charming "I've Fallen in Love Again." Following the album, Donnie Vie elected to stop touring with the band to focus on a solo career, although he would temporarily remain a member of Enuff Z' Nuff with regard to future writing and recording. Talented lead guitarist Johnny Monaco took over on vocals, and from my observations, at the time, did a very admirable Vie-like impersonation, all things considered (not that anyone could ever truly replace Vie, who was unquestionably the band's heart and soul).

Vie released his first solo album, appropriately titled *Just Enuff*, in 2003. If it wasn't for the extremely low-budget production (the songs could really be considered just demos), *Just Enuff* might be one of my *all-time* favorite albums (it's cherished even as it is). Nearly every song was wonderfully composed with flowing melodies and ridiculously catchy hooks that even the Beatles would have admired. Additionally, the record included a few stunningly beautiful ballads, including "That's What Love Is," "Wasting Time," and a lovely cover of the Beatles' "Yesterday."

Enuff Z' Nuff then issued an album of previously unreleased material with a few newly recorded songs in 2004, simply titled *?*. The record featured the marvelously melodic "Home Tonight" and the sweet, sentimental "How Are You?."

The band endured the unfortunate passing of drummer Ricky Parent (cancer) in 2007 but continued to tour without Vie up until 2008, at which time the singer decided to rejoin the group once again for their live shows. Enuff Z' Nuff issued their twelfth album, *Dissonance*, in 2009, which Vie to this day states as one of his favorite EZN albums. For me, however, *Dissonance* seemed slightly lacking other than the wistful "Roll Away" and the spirited, energetic cover of the Beatles' "Run for Your Life."

Vie then released solo albums in both 2013 (*Wrapped Around My Middle Finger*) and 2014 (*The White Album*). The latter was an amazing double-disc set that, with (again) better production and a trimming down to ten or twelve of the best songs, could have been truly superb. Vie then split with Enuff Z' Nuff yet again in 2013 (this time in all aspects), and Monaco departed as well during the following year.

Enuff Z' Nuff continued as a three-piece with Chip Z'Nuff taking over vocal duties and released the back-album of rarities *Clowns Lounge* in 2016 and *Diamond Boy* in 2018, the band's first record with no input or performance from Vie. The album might have had the basis for some good songs but clearly suffered from Vie's absence.

Meanwhile, Vie finally managed to bring it all together on his magnificent 2018 release, *Beautiful Things*, which consistently featured some of the most melodic, catchy, and beautiful songwriting of his career combined with a top-notch production job.

It's a shame Donnie and Chip are no longer working together, as combined they were one of the best songwriting teams the pop-rock landscape had ever seen. However, if *Beautiful Things* is indicative of what Vie can accomplish on his own moving forward, and with Z'Nuff carrying the torch out on the road with Enuff Z' Nuff, fans still have plenty for which to be thankful.

Pretty Boy Floyd

The core of Pretty Boy Floyd has always been singer Steve Summers and guitarist Kristy Majors (other than original guitarist and primary songwriter Aeriel Stiles, who left the band before they signed their first record deal). Between 2002 and 2019, however, the combative partners consistently struggled to get along, breaking up and getting back together again multiple times while also working on solo and side-projects. During this time, PBF intermittently issued loads of unreleased demo material from their vaults, in addition to frequently touring with various lineups.

In 2015, however, Summers and Majors finally buried their hatchets hopefully once and for all, recognizing that for Pretty Boy Floyd to thrive, the essential pairing needed to come together and put aside any differences that remained between them. At last, in 2018, after countless delays, PBF issued the new album *Public Enemies*, proclaiming it the "real, *true* follow-up" to 1989's *Leather Boyz with Electric Toyz.*

And in many ways, they were correct, with *Public Enemies* being gloriously akin to taking a time-machine straight back to the age of '80s glam rock. Indeed, many of the album's songs were leftovers from that era (contributed by Stiles), but several were more recently written, as well. Tracks like "High School Queen" and "Girls All over the World" were classic Pretty Boy Floyd, with Summers sounding like he hadn't aged a day in thirty years, while "Feel The Heat" showcased an enjoyable heavier side of the band.

PBF's current contract with Frontiers Records includes one more album, hopefully to be issued in 2020. Personally, I can't wait.

Nelson

Outside of occasional sporadic live performances, Nelson had been mostly quiet during the ten years following the release of *Life* in 1999, but much like Pretty Boy Floyd, they too eventually managed to recapture their glory days in splendid fashion.

The hair metal-loving Frontiers Records approach the twins in 2009 requesting they put together a new album similar in style to 1990's *After the Rain*, and after some thought, the brothers decided they were happy to rise to the challenge. The result was 2010's magnificent throwback-sounding album, *Lightning Strikes Twice*, an appropriate title as it turned out.

The new record was a glorious pop-rock masterpiece bursting with heaps of the catchy hooks, harmonies, and melodies for which Nelson were best known, including the standout tracks "Call Me," "Day By Day," "How Can I Miss You," "When Your Gone," and "Take Me There."

Maybe there wasn't a "mega-hit" as big as "(Can't Live Without Your) Love and Affection," but *Lightning Strikes Twice* was assuredly consistently "great" throughout. A strikingly pleasant surprise for longtime fans, to say the least.

In 2015, Nelson released another new album, *Peace Out*, which the twins stated was the definitive "last rock record" they would ever make, choosing to focus on more of an "Everly Brothers meets The Eagles country rock project" called "Matthey and Gunnar" from that point forward. *Peace Out* very much picked up where *Lightning Strikes Twice* left off, and while it was a terrific album, it couldn't quite match the overall magic of the former record. That said, a few songs were undeniably of equal standing, including "Back in the Day," "I Wanna Stay Home," and "What's Not To Love."

It's disappointing to think there might be no more Nelson rock albums, especially given the quality of their last two releases, but anything the Nelson brothers create is guaranteed to be worthy of a listen, no matter the genre. Hopefully, fans will indeed continue to be treated to future records of any style; as of 2019, there has regrettably been no hint of anything from the Nelson camp for the past few years. We will keep our fingers crossed.

Extreme

Both singer Gary Cherone and guitarist Nuno Bettencourt participated in side-projects or solo efforts in the early '00s before Extreme reunited for a few short tours between 2004 and 2007. In 2008 Extreme issued their first album of new material in over thirteen years, titled *Saudades de Rock* (loosely translates to "Nostalgic Yearnings of Rock" in Portuguese, Bettencourt's native nationality).

The new songs were a natural extension of the style Extreme had evolved to on 1995's *Waiting for the Punchline*, and the album was a worthy effort even if it failed to live up to the glory of *Pornograffitti* or *III Sides to Every Story*. The single "Star" was a highlight, as was the western-styled "Take Us Alive" and the fun-flavored "King of the Ladies." Extreme proceeded to embark on a successful world tour in support of the record that ran well into 2009.

In 2012 the band did a popular string of shows to celebrate the twentieth anniversary of *Pornograffitti*, performing the entire record front-to-back for elated fans of the album. Extreme then continued to tour up through 2019, all the while stating they were intermittently working on a much-delayed new record. Cherone also kept busy with his side-project, Hurtsmile, issuing the Extreme-like *Retro Grenade* album in 2014.

As of this writing, the band was optimistic their next album would see the light of day in 2020. Let's hope so.

Electric Boys

Electric Boys singer/guitarist Conny Bloom and bassist Andy Christell joined up with the legendary glam rock band Hanoi Rocks from 2004 to 2008 before Electric Boys reformed in 2009 and issued their fantastic comeback album, *And Them Boys Done Swang*, in 2011. The new record mostly picked up right where the band left off in 1995, featuring eleven tracks of the funky, '70s-influenced hard rock for which Electric Boys had best been known, including the excellent "My Heart's Not for Sale," "Rollin' Down the Road," "Reeferlord," and "Father Popcorn's Magic Oysters."

The band toured over the following years and released two subsequent albums, 2014's *Starflight United* and 2018's *The Ghost Ward Diaries*, both irrefutably high in quality and consistent with the style of prior output but admittedly a slight step below *And Them Boys Done Swang*, overall. Electric Boys were out on tour as of this writing and thankfully show no signs of slowing down anytime soon.

White Lion

After breaking up in 2003, White Lion (the version with both Mike Tramp and Vito Bratta, which is the *only* version that counts) was one of the few '80s hair bands that never wound up reuniting, as guitar hero

Bratta not only completely dropped out of the music scene after 1994 but seemingly off the entire planet until momentarily surfacing for a rare interview in 2007. The talented and enigmatic Bratta would regrettably never return to music.

Tramp, meanwhile, carved out a pleasing solo career from 2002 through 2019, during which time he also undertook the brief, misguided action of reforming White Lion without Bratta in 2008, resulting in the underwhelming *Return of The Pride* album (although the tour to support the record was an overwhelming success).

Tramp also issued a robust nine solo albums between 2003 and 2019. The first two, 2003's *More to Life Than This* and 2009's *Rock 'n' Roll Circuz* were very similar in style to his 2001 masterpiece, *Recovering the Wasted Years*, and although they didn't quite match that album in aggregate, the records did include several absolutely standout songs, including "Don't Want to Say Goodnight," "Day by Day," "I Won't Let Go," "All of My Life," and "Come On."

The six albums that followed were significantly more low-key, featuring a stripped-back, singer/songwriter style that Tramp insists is the "new Mike Tramp" to which he has evolved and is very comfortable with. Tramp has made clear on multiple recent occasions there will *never* be a White Lion reunion, as although the singer treasures that time immensely, he is no longer that person and prefers to leave the past untarnished.

Tramp can often be found touring and performing alone on stage with just his voice and an acoustic guitar, or a very minimal backing band, at most. Catch his act if you can; it's not White Lion, but it's most certainly still a special night with one of rock 'n' roll's most dedicated true survivors.

Ratt

Similar to Van Halen, Ratt really struggled to get their act together and maintain any type of consistency after the turn of the century, seemingly embroiled in near-constant drama and controversy.

The band's 1997 reunion was short-lived after their 1999 self-titled *Ratt* album bombed, and Pearcy left the group in 2000 to try his hand at a solo career. Then, in 2002, original rhythm guitarist Robbin Crosby tragically passed away from a heroin overdose while suffering from HIV-complications.

Ratt brought ex-Love Hate singer Jizzy Pearl aboard and toured from 2002 through 2006, while Pearcy released two subpar solo albums. The band mostly reunited in 2006 minus bassist Juan Croucier, with the pleasing result of much bigger and successful touring now that Pearcy was back in the fold.

In 2010 Ratt released their first new album in ten years and only their second in two decades, titled *Infestation.* Somewhat surprisingly considering the band's checkered history, the record was actually quite good, with Ratt aiming for a sound more consistent with their classic mid-'80s output, and for the most part, succeeding.

First track "Eat Me Up Alive" was a scorching hair metal rocker in the vein of 1985's "You're in Love," and lead single "Best of Me" was melodically radio-friendly, similar to 1988's "I Want a Woman." The album remarkably even broke the Top 30 on the Billboard Albums chart. A successful world tour followed, but by the end of the year, the band had somewhat expectedly split up once again, driven by conflict and tensions that inevitably began to surface while out on the road.

Yet another reunion was attempted in 2012, this time with Croucier back in the fold, but the endeavor predictably imploded in 2014. Pearcy left the group yet again to release additional solo albums, while Croucier and drummer Bobby Blotzer both proceeded to messily form their own individual versions of Ratt, touring simultaneously under the same moniker. Blotzer's version lasted longer but was eventually halted in 2016 as a result of legal action brought forth by Pearcy, Croucier, and DeMartini.

Finally, in 2018, with the court proceedings behind them, Pearcy and Croucier moved forward with the Ratt name and hit the road with a new lineup that excluded both DeMartini and Blotzer, affectionately referring to themselves as "the new breed of Ratt." What an embarrassing shamble, from fans' point of view. For what it's worth, Pearcy states the latest version of Ratt will be releasing "a couple new songs" in 2020 to correspond with their planned touring schedule. Personally, I'm not holding my breath.

Aerosmith

Aerosmith was commercially on fire at the turn of the century but took an enjoyably less fiscal-oriented approach in 2004, finally getting back to their classic rock roots with the album *Honkin' on Bobo*, which featured cover versions of blues-rock songs from the '50s and '60s. The record was mostly successful, including the enjoyably sizzling "Baby, Please Don't Go" (Big Joe Williams) and the grinding, groovy "You Gotta Move" (Mississippi Fred McDowell).

Aerosmith then embarked on a relentless tour schedule from 2004 to 2012 that, combined with Steven Tyler's brief fixation on a solo career that threatened the band's very existence, repeatedly delayed any attempts to put out any new material.

Aerosmith's fifteenth studio album, *Music from Another Dimension!*, was finally released on November 6, 2012, but, regrettably, it was a significant letdown, featuring no fewer than *six* lame ballads, all sounding like half-hearted attempts to re-write "I Don't Want to Miss a Thing." The rock songs weren't much better, mostly sounding like leftover B-sides; indeed, first single "Legendary Child" was a discarded vestige from the 1991 *Get a Grip* sessions. The funky "Out Go the Lights" was perhaps the only track that stood out among the mass of "average."

More touring ensued over the following seven years (interrupted by an ill-conceived Tyler-solo "country" album in 2016), but no new music came to fruition, and perhaps it never will, as Aerosmith doesn't seem overly motivated at this junction of their career to put out a fresh record. And at this point, I'm not sure the band has enough creative juices or the correct direction to pull it off properly should they even try.

Aerosmith still puts on a great live show, though, and as of this writing, had concert dates booked through the full back half of 2019. A farewell tour of some kind would seemingly be not far off as the band members age into their '70s, but it also wouldn't be surprising to see them carry on in some form or fashion for another five to seven years or so.

Bang Tango

After Beautiful Creatures were unceremoniously dropped by Warner Bros. in 2002, singer Joe Lesté went about reforming Bang Tango with an entirely new lineup, leaving himself as the only original member. The band then issued the excellent *Ready to Go* album in 2004, which was a little more laid-back than traditional Bang Tango records but a great set of songs just the same, including the terrific "Ready to Go," "The Other Side," and "Tell Me."

Lesté continued to work with a revised Beautiful Creatures lineup as well, and the band initially issued its super-heavy, hard rock sophomore album *Deuce* via Spitfire records, in Japan, in 2005; make sure to pick up the much-superior remixed and remastered 2017 version, however.

All Bang Tango's original members got back together for a special one-off show in 2006, but a sustained reunion wasn't in the cards and Lesté continued to tour Bang Tango thereafter with various lineups while releasing the albums *From the Hip* in 2006 and *Pistol Whipped in the Bible Belt* in 2011. Regrettably, both records failed to live up to the band's past output, containing only a couple of gems such as "Mother Mary" and "Suck It Up."

An attempt to relaunch Beautiful Creatures in 2017 (mostly inactive for the ten years prior) unfortunately fizzled, although the band did gather in the studio to place the new track "Get You High" on the *Deuce* reissue, which was one of the better songs I had heard in the past ten years from *any* band (the song admittedly borrowed its chorus-structure from *Ready To Go*'s "The Other Side").

In late 2019, it was surprisingly announced that the original five members of Bang Tango would magnificently be reuniting for select future live performances—count me in, with bells on. Dare I hope for a new album, as well? One can certainly dream.

Kix

In 2012, the '80s hair metal, life-saving label Frontiers Records miraculously signed Kix to a new record contract. The band courageously reformed minus bassist and primary songwriter Donnie Purnell, who the other band members always found difficult with whom to work.

The reunion shows were an enormous success, and the group released a live album in 2013 followed by Kix's first new studio album in almost two decades, 2014's delightful *Rock Your Face Off.* Amazingly (especially given Purnell's absence), the record sounded *exactly* like a Kix album from the '80s! While it may not have been in quite the same league as *Blow My Fuse* or *Hot Wire*, just the fact that the band could issue such an unabashed set of pleasure-seeking, '80s party-rock tunes after a twenty-year absence was quite impressive. Fans *loved* the album, and it impressively hit No. 49 on the Billboard Albums chart while ranking No. 1 on Amazon Hard Rock for three consecutive weeks.

In 2018 Kix issued a much-appreciated, remixed, superior-sounding version of *Blow My Fuse* to celebrate the album's thirtieth anniversary. Kix continues to tour to enthusiastic audiences, treating them to fantastic performances as Steve Whiteman has seemingly not aged a day or lost a single step in the past thirty years. Kix remains one of the absolute best live bands of the hair metal era, hands down.

Trixter

Fourteen years after they broke up in 1994, all four original members of Trixter unexpectedly reunited for a few sporadic live performances in 2008 and released a live album, *Alive in Japan*, featuring two new studio tracks. Then, in 2012, the band issued their fantastic comeback album, *New Audio Machine*, via Frontiers Records, representing perhaps the absolute best record of Trixter's career. The quality was stunning with the band appearing tighter than ever, and the majority of songs rocking with all the '80s hair metal splendor one could muster. "Drag Me Down," "Get on It," "Dirty Love," "Machine," "Ride," and "Save Your Soul" were as good as it gets, with singer Peter Loran sounding terrific and talented guitarist Steve Brown churning out a set of impressive riffs and blazing solos.

A run of successful live shows commenced followed by the band's follow-up album *Human Era* in 2015, also an excellent record in classic hair metal style if perhaps not as impressive as *New Audio Machine.* Standout tracks included "Rockin' to the Edge of the Night," "Midnight in Your Eyes," and "All Night Long." Trixter can be found continuing to work the touring circuit in 2019.

FireHouse

FireHouse released their seventh studio album, *Prime Time*, in 2003, which wasn't overly notable aside from the riffing rocker "Crash" and the soulful ballad "Let Go." Other than an album of re-recorded hits in 2011 (*Full Circle*), though, there hasn't been any new music from FireHouse in the past sixteen years, although the band has remained active with terrific live performances and concert tours almost every year.

Guitarist Bill Leverty, meanwhile, has released a few bluesy solo albums, while singer CJ Snare paired up with Furyon/Pride guitarist to form Rubicon Cross, who released their self-titled debut album in 2014. *Rubicon Cross* is more than worth checking out, with a sound akin to a much heavier, more modern version of FireHouse, particularly the excellent tracks "Locked and Loaded" and "Moving On."

Slaughter

Slaughter performed on multiple occasions from 2000 through 2004 prior to taking an extended hiatus and re-emerging in 2011, after which the band conducted annual tours up through the present. All shows between 2011 and 2019 featured the entertaining Zoltan Chaney on drums, as original drummer Blas Elias left the band in the mid-'00s to perform with the Las Vegas act Blue Man Group and other various bands. Elias pleasingly made his return to the group in 2019, however. The other members of Slaughter (minus singer Mark Slaughter) have also served as

Vince Neil's backing band during his solo tours for the past ten years.

Disappointingly, there hasn't been a new Slaughter album since 1999's *Back to Reality.* Mark Slaughter, however, recently issued two solo albums, 2015's *Reflections in a Rear View Mirror* and 2017's *Halfway There,* on which Slaughter impressively handled all writing, production, and instrumentation (other than drums) as a one-man show.

The style of the records is generally hard rock and hair metal, and while the albums may be a notch below Slaughter's full-band efforts overall, they do contain several great songs such as "Away I Go," "Never Givin' Up," 'Carry Me Back Home," "Hey You," and "Supernatural." Slaughter's voice may be a little rougher versus his younger days, but he still carries quite a tune and has also evolved into an accomplished guitarist. Slaughter also keeps busy as a voice-over actor and composer of music for both movies and television.

Unfortunately, it's unlikely we see another full-band Slaughter album, but certainly, stranger things have happened.

Danger Danger

Danger Danger reunited with original singer Ted Poley in 2004, and five years later issued their first album back together in almost two decades, titled *Revolve.* The songs were styled as classic Danger Danger melodic pop-metal, but for me, the new material lacked the spark and edge of their earlier work and failed to impress, overall. There has been no new music from the band in the ten years since that time, although the group still actively tours.

Outside of Danger Danger, Poley has been one of the hardest working artists in the business, releasing eleven other albums as a solo artist or with side-project bands over the past two decades. The very best of these records (easily, as many were just average, at best) is the 2017 self-titled *Tokyo Motor Fist,* issued by the band of the same name Poley formed with Trixter guitarist Steve Brown. The album features first-class production, several top-notch hair metal anthems courtesy of the brilliant songwriting of Brown, and Poley in top form as a vocalist. *Tokyo Motor*

Fist in many ways represents what *Revolve* should have sounded like, with classic pop-metal songs such as "Pickin' up the Pieces," "Love Me Insane," and the beautiful ballad "Love," alongside harder-edged, Def Leppard-sounding tracks like "Done to Me" and "Put Me to Shame."

Poley and Brown are currently preparing Tokyo Motor Fist's sophomore record for 2020, which is certainly something for hair metal fans to look forward to, but if we can be greedy, how about also a great new Danger Danger album to perhaps redeem the band's legacy?

Steelheart

Miljenko Matijevic reformed Steelheart in 2006 as the only remaining original member and, in 2008, released *Good 2B Alive*, the first album to carry the Steelheart name since 1996's *Wait*. The new songs weren't exactly in the hair metal vein, with the music leaning more toward a heavy, modern/alternative rock sound, but still, it was good to hear Matijevic's voice again, even if his vocals were curiously too often unnecessarily layered with distortion effects in many places.

Steelheart toured sporadically during the years that followed while also releasing *Through the Worlds of Stardust* in 2017, which was much in the same modern style as *Good 2B Alive* but did feature the cool tracks "Stream Line Savings" and "My Dirty Girl." (Check out one of Matijevic's classic "screams" at the beginning of the latter track.)

As of late 2019, Steelheart was in the process of re-recording several of their favorite songs for a thirtieth-anniversary celebration album to be released in 2020.

The Quireboys

The Quireboys were a model of consistency after reforming in 2001, frequently touring and releasing ten albums over the next eighteen years, all mostly of equal quality and well-representative of the classic Quireboys sound. *Homewreckers & Heartbreakers*, issued in 2008, was among the best of the bunch, although there were plenty of great songs across all the records, including "Mona Lisa Smiled," "Talk of the Town," "Beautiful

Curse," "Stubborn Kinda Heart," "Gracie B," and the title track from 2019's *Amazing Disgrace.*

Faster Pussycat

Lead singer Taime Downe continued pushing his version of Faster Pussycat toward a more industrial sound on the 2006 album *The Power & The Glory Hole*, and while it was undeniably a shift away from classic hair metal, the new style worked quite well, in my view, shaping a unique mix of hard rock guitars, driving beats, and industrial backing effects. Songs like "Number 1 With a Bullet," "Sex, Drugs & Rock-n-Roll," "Hey You," and the album's title track flat-out rocked, no question about it.

Not all Faster Pussycat fans adapted so well to the new sound, however, and three of the band's former members took a higher level of exception, choosing to create their own version of Faster Pussycat while promising to perform the group's classic songs, as they stated, "the way they were meant to be heard," opposed to Downe's more recent industrial interpretations.

The "alternate" version of Faster Pussycat disbanded within a year, however, while Downe and his crew continued to march forward, slowly getting back to more hair metal versions of the band's early material while performing live in more recent years.

It would be awesome to someday hear a new album from Faster Pussycat, but regrettably, the odds don't seem to favor it.

Other '80s hair metal Heroes

Many other '80s hair bands also continued to tour and record new music over the past two decades, at various times with assorted different lineups; if you are a fan, be sure to keep up with the latest offerings from Quiet Riot, Dokken, Great White/Jack Russel, Black N' Blue, Tigertailz, Tora Tora, Lillian Axe, and Babylon A.D., just to name a few.

<u>Best Albums 2002-2019</u> ('80s Legacy Artists)

1. Nelson – *Lightning Strikes Twice (2010) (Top 25 in Genre!)*

2. Trixter – *New Audio Machine (2012)*
3. Whitesnake – *Flesh & Blood (2019)*
4. Pretty Boy Floyd – *Public Enemies (2017)*
5. Sebastian Bach – *Angel Down (2007)*
6. Sammy Hagar – *Livin' It Up! (2006)*
7. Electric Boys – *And Them Boys Done Swang (2011)*
8. Donnie Vie – *Beautiful Things (2018)*
9. Mötley Crüe – *Saints of Los Angeles (2008)*
10. Mr. Big – *What If... (2011)*
11. Whitesnake – *Good to Be Bad (2008)*
12. Bon Jovi – *100,000,000 Bon Jovi Fans Can't Be Wrong... (2004)*
13. Donnie Vie – *Just Enough (2003)*
14. Def Leppard – *Def Leppard (2015)*
15. Scorpions – *Return to Forever (2015)*
16. Winger – *Karma (2009)*
17. Jack Russel – *For You (2002)*
18. Bang Tango – *Ready to Go (2004)*
19. L.A. Guns – *Waking the Dead (2002)*
20. Paul Gilbert – *United States (2009)*
21. Def Leppard – *X (2002)*
22. Trixter – *Human Era (2015)*
23. Tesla – *Shock (2019)*
24. Mike Tramp – *More to Life Than This (2003)*

Chapter 24
Youth Gone Wild
(2002-2019)
New Hair Metal Artists

In addition to the longevity and active continuance of many '80s legacy artists, the emergence of countless *new* hair metal bands in the new millennium has been particularly enjoyable and notably encouraging for the health of the genre overall. These fresh artists built upon the foundations laid down by their heroes and influences from the '80s, and in many instances, succeeded at generating a sound and style consistent with the sacred echoes of hair metal past. In other cases, recent acts have managed to merge hair metal's traditional roots with more modern techniques and flavors attempting to combine the best of both worlds, many with great success.

These new bands have become commonly known and referred to as "The New Wave of Hair Metal," with "hair metal" often interchangeable with the phrasings "sleaze" or "glam" metal. Of particular note is the geographic location from which these latest artists originate; of the roughly fifty most prominent new hair metal bands, a staggering 80 percent come from outside the US (hair metal's birthplace), and astoundingly, more than *half* hail from the Nordic region, specifically Sweden and Finland. There must be something in the water up there, as the prevalent music scene on-site in these counties bears a remarkable resemblance to Los Angeles' Sunset Strip, circa 1988. Why exactly this is,

I can't be sure, but God bless them. (Let's not also forget that one of the genre's earliest forerunners hailed from Finland—a little band called Hanoi Rocks.)

In the US, however, despite the resilient nostalgia for legacy hair metal acts, thriving new artists in the genre are harder to find, as the dominant domestic music formats of the past two decades have clearly been hip-hop, pop, and country. That said, the US has indeed managed to produce perhaps the singular most popular new hair metal act, Steel Panther, who, along with fantastic overseas bands Hardcore Superstar and Reckless Love, represent my three favorite new bands of the twenty-first century.

Steel Panther, for all their ability and popularity, are a polarizing enigma. They're a band that brazenly and unabashedly embraces all things '80s hair metal, from music and fashion to even lifestyle (allegedly). But sometimes it's hard to tell: does the band truly love hair metal, or are they simply a novelty act, poking fun at and satirizing the era? No one can really know for sure, it would seem, but all bets are on the former (as the band would claim), with perhaps a little of the latter mixed in for good measure. One thing's for certain—Steel Panther are unquestionably the genre's new-generation torchbearers and are largely responsible for cultivating a younger legion of both converts and cohorts.

All outward appearances to perhaps the contrary, Steel Panther are, legitimately, an extremely talented group of musicians, consisting of singer Ralph Saenz (Michael Starr), guitarist Russ Parrish (Satchel), bassist Travis Haley (Lexxi Foxx), and drummer Darren Leader (Stix Zadinia). Saenz is a gifted vocalist and dazzling showman who previously fronted the Van Halen tribute band Atomic Punks and even spent a brief stint as the lead singer for L.A. Guns in the late '90s. Parrish, meanwhile, graduated from The Guitar Institute of Technology, and prior to Steel Panther worked extensively as an instructor while also playing in several different bands, including Saenz's Atomic Punks and Rob Halford's Fight in the early '90s.

Steel Panther's music is unequivocally pure, unadulterated '80s hair metal, but the outlandish lyrics instantly pop out as a rather eccentric anomaly. While primary songwriter Satchel's unparalleled choice of words indeed focuses on the most popular hair metal topics of sex, drugs and partying, it does so in the absolute most juvenile, profane way imaginable—entirely in jest, however. This is possibly the integral part of the Steel Panther shtick, which is somewhat ironic, as the band members appear to be of reasonably high savvy and intellect (behind the scenes and off camera, of course), with a carefully calculated business strategy.

And while their over-the-top live show includes every '80s rock cliché they can conjure, while also containing a good deal of comedy-based spontaneity and improvisation, the band always puts on a super-tight, professional performance. When Steel Panther plays cover versions of classic hair metal tracks, the irony is they often perform them *better* than the originals (or at least better than many legacy acts are able to deliver them today).

Steel Panther's origins trace back to the early/mid-'00s when the band was known as Metal Shop, and then later Metal Skool. The group mainly indulged in cover songs but did release the original independent record, *Hole Patrol*, in 2003. In 2008 the band officially adopted the Steel Panther moniker and issued their debut album, *Feel the Steel*, on June 8, 2009. The record hit No. 98 on the Billboard Albums chart and surprisingly went all the way to No. 1 on the Billboard Comedy chart! Standout tracks included "Death to All But Metal," "Asian Hooker," and the "Livin' on a Prayer"-inspired "Party All Day (Fuck All Night)."

The similarly styled *Balls Out* was released in 2011, achieving even greater success with a No. 40 rank on the Billboard Albums chart and another No.1 placement on the Comedy chart. Three additional albums were then subsequently put out: 2014's fantastic *All You Can Eat* (No. 24 on Billboard), 2017's *Lower The Bar*, and 2019's appropriately-titled *Heavy Metal Rules*, each one sticking to Steel Panther's tried and true formula, while the band's audience continued to swell and their live shows became legendary parties. Among the best songs from these recent albums are "Party Like Tomorrow Is the End of the World," "The Burden of Being Wonderful," "Gloryhole," "Poontang Boomerang," and "All I Wanna Do Is Fuck (Myself Tonight)."

People tend to either "get" Steel Panther or they don't, and they either love them or hate them, it would seem. Personally, count me firmly in with the former camp, and although I could probably do without the juvenile vulgarity, I supposed that ingredient is an essential part of what makes them Steel Panther. Either way, it would be impossible to refuse the incredible music and amazing performances. One thing is for certain—if you are a fan of hair metal and haven't yet made it to a Steel Panther concert, you are definitely doing yourself a disservice. The band's shows are much more than a concert, often spilling over into an extravagant, celebratory, and crowd-participating '80s metal party. There's simply nothing else like it on the market today. Nothing.

What's particularly intriguing (and impressive) is the considerable number of young people (aged twenty through thirty) who show up in Steel Panther's audience, specifically the large volume of adoring young ladies. How the band is pulling this off I will never understand, but hats off to them.

I'm not sure how long Steel Panther can keep the lyrical joke fresh (if it hasn't possibly started to sour already), and I would more than welcome a more "serious-minded" album from the band at some point in the future (although I suspect I should be careful what I wish for), but in the interim, I'll be plenty happy just to see the group continuing to carry the hair metal flag so proficiently and proudly. All hail Steel Panther.

Originating from Sweden, **Hardcore Superstar** is my singular favorite "new" hair metal act. Ironically, the band's first three albums, released between 1998 and 2003, were more punk and pop-rock than hair metal, but Hardcore Superstar somewhat reinvented themselves on their breakthrough self-titled 2005 album, which was much heavier hard rock but still contained wildly catchy and accessible melodies—sound familiar?

The album was a huge success in the band's home country, spawning several hit singles while also being nominated for a local Grammy award.

Hardcore Superstar's 2007 release, *Dreamin' in a Casket*, was even more powerful, with a significant focus on heavy guitar riffs and pounding drums alongside the strength of lead singer Jocke Berg's distinct vocals. Stylistically, the album was in the sleaze metal category similar to L.A. Guns, but possessed a higher level of intensity comparable to early Guns N' Roses, or perhaps even Beautiful Creatures' debut album in 2000. The combination of these potent styles spawned the popular new label, "street metal."

Original guitarist Thomas Silver left the group in 2008 and was replaced with ex-Crazy Lixx axe-slinger Vic Zino, but the band's 2009 release, *Beg for It*, showed Hardcore Superstar hadn't lost a step, continuing their onslaught of hard and heavy riffs combined with distinct melodic phrasings and crushing choruses.

Hardcore Superstar rarely issues the exact same album twice, and the group's next three releases (2010's *Split Your Lip*, 2013's *C'mon Take on Me* and 2015's *HCSS*) were a relatively eclectic and diverse set of hard rock music, although all were rooted in the band's post-2004 style. While I, personally, prefer the overall sleaze metal consistency of *Dreamin' in a Casket* and *Beg for It*, each new album featured a slew of terrific songs, most notably "Sadistic Girls," "Touch the Sky," and the magnificent "One More Minute."

Despite being one of the biggest and most popular rock artists in Sweden, Hardcore Superstar has yet to fully "break" in the US, although after a ten-year absence, the band did make its first appearance back in America in January 2015, gloriously headlining a wild set to a frenzied, sold-out crowd at the famous Whisky a Go Go in West Hollywood, California.

Three years later, in 2018, the band released what was perhaps their masterpiece album, appropriately titled *You Can't Kill My Rock 'n Roll.* An incredible record from start to finish, Hardcore Superstar finally managed to hit on the perfect combination of aggressive hard rock combined with the more melodic pop-elements that have always been sprinkled throughout their catalog. The amazing set of songs was supported by a crystal clear, powerful production and the album was universally praised, landing at the top of many hair metal website year-end "best of" lists.

I regret not yet having had the privilege of seeing Hardcore Superstar live in concert, but it is definitely up there on my bucket list. "You can't kill my rock 'n roll," indeed.

Reckless Love was founded in Finland in the early '00s, first starting out as Reckless Life and operating as a Guns N' Roses cover band. Shifting to craft their own music, the band released their self-titled debut album in 2009, a tributary ode to the classic glam metal of the mid-to-late '80s. Reckless Love were more pop-metal versus the harder edge of Hardcore Superstar, closer akin to Poison as opposed to early Guns N' Roses. The album reached No. 13 on Finland's local charts and spawned three Top 10 hit singles. Critics such as William Clark of Guitar International praised the album and perhaps put it best, stating, "Reckless Love are just what glam metal fans across the globe have been waiting for: a band with a fresh sound, a standout lead vocalist, and some vivid retro '80s influences."

The group's sophomore album, *Animal Attraction*, was released in 2011 and included the two hit singles "Hot" and "Animal Attraction." The band continued to build up a strong local and global following and released their third album, *Spirit*, in 2013, which featured their best set of hair metal and glam rock tunes yet, including "Night on Fire," "Bad Lovin'," "So Happy I Could Die," the melodic ballad "Edge of Our Dreams," and "I Love Heavy Metal," a tribute song to all things '80s rock that saw the band drop numerous names and lyrics from the genre's classic artists and albums.

We last heard from Reckless Love on their 2016 album, *In Vader*, on which the group ventured further into pure pop territory on some tracks, a move that disagreed with a particular segment of their fanbase but was personally welcomed, as songs like "Child of the Sun" and "Scandinavian Girls" were flat out fantastic, no matter the genre. Further, the album still featured some of the band's greatest hard rock songs to date, including the party-anthem "We Are the Weekend," the monstrous "Hands," and the cocksure combination of "Rock It" and "Pretty Boy Swagger."

Put together a "best of" compilation with the top songs from all four Reckless Love albums and you'd have one of the finest hair metal records around. Similar to Hardcore Superstar, the band has yet to "hit" in the US, but that doesn't stop devoted hair metal fans all over the world from seeking out and hunting down their music, as Reckless Love represents the genre with flying colors.

One additional quick nod should perhaps be given to the band **Halestorm**. The trick is, Halestorm doesn't fit very cleanly into the hair metal category (if they do at all), but there are undeniably touchpoints worthy of mention, particularly as the band has released a couple of fantastic hard rock albums. Granted, their 2009 self-titled debut and third album, *Into the Wild Life*, venture pretty far into modern/alternative stylings in the eyes of some, but I would think any fan of '80s rock would find much to enjoy on the band's hair metal-influenced sophomore album *The Strange Case Of...*, or even their Black Sabbath-ish heavy metal fourth album, *Vicious*.

I suspect many will question (and possibly deride) Halestorm's inclusion in this book (however brief), but there are definitely hair metal breadcrumbs to follow, starting with the band's blistering Grammy award-winning 2012 track "Love Bites (So Do I)," which Halestorm wrote solely because, as they stated, "the band needed a song that was similar to Skid Row's 'Slave to the Grind.'" Another nugget can be found on Halestorm's album cover for *Into the Wild Life*, where the dynamic and amazing singer/guitarist Lzzy Hale made it a point to wear the same pin Tom Keifer donned on Cinderella's *Night Songs*, a precious gift he proudly endowed to her as a friend and admirer or her talents. (Also, make sure to check out videos of Hale duetting with Keifer live on their rendition of Cinderella's "Nobody's Fool"—killer stuff.)

Halestorm may not fit perfectly into the hair metal lexicon, but they wear their '80s rock roots proudly and have several songs that are sure to please quite a few discerning hair metal fans (Make sure not to miss the pounding "I Like It Heavy," where Hale sings of "headbanging in the pit" and "throwing (her) horns" while expressing her fondness for "cranking up" "Sabbath, Zeppelin, and Lemmy.")

There have been many additional terrific new hair metal artists to emerge in the past two decades as well. A dozen other quick standouts:

Bombay Black (US): fantastic meat-and-potatoes hair metal and melodic hard rock. Each of their six albums is worth picking up. Key songs: "Without You," "Out of Your Mind," "Love Like This," "You For Me," "The Ride," and "Bye Bye Juliet."

Crazy Lixx (Sweden): classic melodic pop-metal. Key albums: 2010's *New Religion* and 2019's *Forever Wild.*

Diemonds (Canada): female-fronted hard rock, heavy metal, and even pop on later work. Key songs: "Never Wanna Die," "Hell Is Full," "Ain't That Kinda Girl," "Breathe," "Waiting for Something."

Kissin' Dynamite (Germany): edgy hard rock and '80s melodic pop-metal. The band really came into their own on their fantastic sixth album, 2018's *Ecstasy*, featuring the spark-filled, "I've Got the Fire," "Ecstasy," "Wild Wind," and rousing "No Time to Wonder."

Gemini Five (Sweden): heavy sleaze metal. Out of the game since 2008, their final album *Sex, Drugs, Anarchy*, was a formidable statement.

Wig Wam (Norway): popular glam and pop-metal band from 2001 through 2014. Their 2012 album, *Wall Street*, was one of their best. Be sure also to not miss lead singer Åge Sten Nilsen's post-Wig Wam band, Ammunition, particularly the excellent 2014 record, *Shanghaied.*

Marcus Allen Christopher (US): talented hair metal singer/guitarist with vocals akin to Tom Keifer. Check out his work with the band M!ss Crazy, in addition to the impressive 2009 *Freakshow* album recorded with Cinderella's Jeff LaBar and Quiet Riot's Frankie Banali.

Tango Down (US): straightforward hard rock and hair metal. Key albums: *Charming Devil* (2014), *Bulletproof* (2016).

Distorted Wonderland (Sweden): Aggressive sleaze metal. Their 2010 self-titled album featured the great songs "Losing It," "Never Had Nothing," and "Raised on Rock 'n' Roll."

Robin Black & The Intergalactic Rock Stars (Canada): Glam metal and occasional punk rock. The title of their 2005 album, *Instant Classic*, says it all.

Johnny Diva & The Rockets of Love (US): Their 2019 release, *Mama Said Rock Is Dead*, is fabulously about as close to 1989-hair metal as you can possibly get these days.

Platinum Overdose (US): Essential late '80s-based glam rock. With their 2019 release *Murder In High Heels*, their website perhaps says it all: "On the 8th day, the devil created '80s metal, and with that spawned the sin forever known as Platinum Overdose."

There are literally masses of other new hair metal bands worth checking out as well; among them:

Sweden: Crashdïet, Fatal Smile, Confess, Bulletrain, 44 Caliber, Laney's Legion, ToxicRose, HEAT, Vains Of Jenna, The Poodles, Dynazty.

Finland: Santa Cruz, Shiraz Lane, Baby Snakes, The Cruel Intentions, While Flame

UK: The Darkness, Knock Out Kaine, Midnite City

Germany: Julian Angel's Beautiful Beast

USA: Kickin' Valentina, Station, Brand New Machine

Italy: Hell in the Club

France: BlackRain

Canada: Löve Razër

Brazil: Lipztick, Tales from the Porn

So much new, young hair metal is emerging that there is literally *at least* one new album to check out almost every week. Granted, most of these releases don't perfectly live up to heightened expectations, but several do, and I suspect many young bands will continue to hone and refine their craft, just as Bon Jovi did long ago on their first two albums before hitting it big with *Slippery When Wet.*

The sheer volume of new bands and music alone is proof positive that hair metal still lives strong in the hearts of many, both old and young, and the genre is thankfully well-poised to continue kicking ass far into the future.

Best Albums 2002-2019 (New hair metal Artists)

1. Hardcore Superstar – *Dreamin' in a Casket (2007) (Top 25 in Genre!)*
2. Hardcore Superstar – *You Can't Kill My Rock 'n Roll (2018) (Top 25 in Genre!)*
3. Steel Panther – *All You Can Eat (2014)*
4. Reckless Love – *InVader (2016)*
5. Hardcore Superstar – *Hardcore Superstar (2005)*
6. Halestorm – *The Strange Case Of. . . (2012)*
7. Freakshow – *Freakshow (2009)*
8. Halestorm – *Vicious (2018)*
9. Hardcore Superstar – *Beg for It (2009)*
10. Steel Panther – *Feel the Steel (2009)*
11. Kissin' Dynamite – *Ecstasy (2018)*
12. Murderdolls – *Women and Children Last (2010)*
13. Bombay Black – *Anger Management (2006)*
14. Robin Black (& The Intergalactic Rock Stars) – *Instant Classic (2005)*
15. Ammunition – *Shanghaied (2015)*
16. Kickin' Valentina – *Imaginary Creatures (2017)*
17. Gemini Five – *Sex Drugs Anarchy (2008)*
18. Wig Wam – *Wall Street (2012)*

Epilogue

Hair metal's story played out as quite the exciting and wild ride—originating with its dramatic and auspicious beginnings in the early '80s, to its sensational rise to success and extravagance at its peak later that decade, on through the turbulent dark days of the '90s, and up to the genre's remarkable rebirth and sustained perseverance throughout the twenty-first century.

As a genre, hair metal perhaps stands alone in the uniqueness of both its spectacular historical journey and its immense impact on both music and popular culture alike. The artists, songs, albums, styles, and personalities that comprised the era have influenced and touched countless lives—the music has simply meant so much to so many, myself included.

Hair metal has come a long way over the last forty years, and what was once at the top of the world and then subsequently left for dead is back alive and well again in 2019, as of this writing. It is hard to believe. In many aspects, the music, times and styles of the '80s are gone forever; all things inevitably change and come to pass. But in many other ways, the era continues to live on—in the artists from that time who continue to make music and delivery spirited performances, in new bands who model their sound on influences from hair metal's golden age, and perhaps most importantly, in the hearts and minds of the true fans whose allegiance to the genre is without fail and forever resolute.

Hair metal clearly still has immense drawing power and the ability to operate at a high level, as evidenced by recent events such as the staggering popularity of Guns N' Roses record-setting Not in This Lifetime Tour, Mötley Crüe's successful movie-adaptation of their New York Times best-selling autobiography, and the global popularity of the emerging "New Wave of Hair Metal."

Granted, at some point, the majority of the "'80s bands" will no longer exist, and fans who grew up in that era will age onward, but there is still so much more to come before any of that happens. Plus, as long as new artists like Steel Panther continue to keep the flame alive while cultivating entirely new generations of younger fans, the future couldn't be brighter in many aspects. Hair metal's story is far from over.

And at the end of the day, hair metal isn't necessarily all about prominence and commercial success anyway, and it never really was. Warrant guitarist Joey Allen reminds us:

> *"The music wasn't meant to be groundbreaking. We were just out to have a good time and try to translate that to the people who worked 9-to-5. We wanted to say 'Hey, for now, you don't have to worry about work or your bills; just come out and party with us. That's what we were all about. It's something the current generation of rockers seems to have forgotten. I meet a lot of these guys on the road, and they always say, 'God, you were in a band when it was fun.' If I can say anything, it's don't forget to have a good time; don't take it so seriously. We're not trying to save the world or whatever; we're musicians. People enjoy the music because it takes them to another place. Don't forget to have fun!"*

At its core, hair metal is about dreams, expression, and escapism. Music exists to make us feel emotions, and the one sentiment we could all use a bit more of in today's often challenging environment is a little fun and happiness. So, don't forget to occasionally crank the tunes, throw your horns in the air, and in the immortal words of hair metal glam-kings Poison—treat yourself to *Nothing But a Good Time!*

Made in the USA
Las Vegas, NV
05 May 2022